Children of the Sun

Children of the Sun

A Narrative of "Decadence"
in England after 1918

Martin Green

Axios Press
P.O. Box 118
Mount Jackson, VA 22842
888.542.9467   info@axiospress.com

Distributed by NATIONAL BOOK NETWORK.

Library of Congress Cataloging-in-Publication Data

Green, Martin Burgess, 1927–
    Children of the sun : a narrative of decadence in England after 1918 / Martin Green.
        p.   cm.
    Includes bibliographical references and index.
    ISBN-13: 978-1-60419-001-4 (pbk.)
    ISBN-10: 0-09-461430-X (cloth)

    1. English literature—20th century—History and criticism. 2. Decadence (Literary movement)—Great Britain. 3. Acton, Harold Mario Mitchell, 1904- 4. Howard, Brian, 1905-1958. 5. Authors, English—20th century—Biography. 6. Dandies—Great Britain—Biography. 7. England—Intellectual life—20th century. I. Title.

PR478.D43G7 2008
820.9'0091—dc22

                                                   2008024306

This book is dedicated to
Nicholas Temperley
and
Mark Roskill
the two Old Etonians among my friends

Contents

Chapter Eight

Chapter Nine

Chapter Ten

Chapter Eleven

Acknowledgments

OF THE MANY people who have helped me with this book, it is Sir Harold Acton who of course deserves my main salute of acknowledgment. He was courtesy and hospitality itself to me; a model of all a biographer could hope for from his subject. And next Marie-Jacqueline Lancaster, who opened up to my use the papers and pictures she had collected for her own book on Brian Howard, and who was ready, again and again, to discuss and suggest and share her much greater knowledge of the social milieu I was exploring. I was also helped by Mrs. Carley Dawson, Brian Howard's cousin, who saw me more than once in her home; and by Jimmy Stern, a good friend to many of the men I was writing about and by now a good friend to me too.

To list everyone who contributed anything would I think be pointless, but I must say that Sonia Orwell and Philip Toynbee and Alec Waugh all gave me helpful hints and a generous response to my ideas. Arthur Byron wrote to me at length and sent me pictures; Peter Quennell and Christopher Sykes and Lord Kinross gave me interviews.

And, as with *The Von Richthofen Sisters,* my editor Erwin Glikes, and his assistant Carol Vance, both forwarded the project by their enthusiastic appreciation and their practical help.

Illustrations

Located in the center of the book, and listed in the order in which they appear:

Brian Howard	*Lenare Ltd. and James Stern*
Randolph Churchill	*Lenare Ltd.*
Rupert Brooke	*Radio Times Hulton Picture Library*
The Prince of Wales	*Radio Times Hulton Picture Library*
Sir Oswald Mosley	*The Illustrated London News*
Rudyard Kipling and King George V	*Radio Times Hulton Picture Library*
Lord Beaverbrook	*First Beaverbrook Foundation*

Winston Churchill and
David Lloyd-George

*Sport and General Press
Agency*

Edith and Osbert Sitwell

*Radio Times Hulton
Picture Library*

Virginia Woolf and
Lytton Strachey

The Granger Collection

Jean Cocteau and
Sergei Diaghilev

*Radio Times Hulton
Picture Library*

Vaslav Nijinsky

The Bettman Archive

William Acton

Sir Harold Acton

Osbert Sitwell

*Macmillan London, and
Basingstoke*

Brian Howard

*The executors of the late
Mrs. Francis Howard*

Harold Acton

Sir Harold Acton

Brian Howard

*The executors of the late
Mrs. Francis Howard*

Cartoons of Brian Howard
and Harold Acton

*The Cherwell;
A.D. Peters and Co. Ltd.*

Evelyn Waugh

Transworld

Harold Acton

Sir Harold Acton

Children of the Sun
at an Oxford Party

*The executors of the late
Mrs. Francis Howard*

Nancy Cunard

*London News Agency
Photos Ltd.*

Lady Diana Cooper

*Radio Times Hulton
Picture Library*

A Mozart Party of Bright
Young Things in London

Transworld

Stephen Spender

Humanities Research Center, The University of Texas at Austin

W. H. Auden and Christopher Isherwood

Radio Times Hulton Picture Library

Evelyn Waugh and Randolph Churchill

Transworld

J. Robert Oppenheimer and Major General Leslie R. Groves

UPI Photo

Guy Burgess

Beaverbrook Newspapers Ltd., London

Donald Maclean

Keystone Press Agency

Kim Philby

Beaverbrook Newspapers Ltd., London

F. R. Leavis

The Guardian

George Orwell

The Granger Collection

Kingsley Amis

Beaverbrook Newspapers Ltd., London

Prologue
A Visit to La Pietra

WHEN I RANG the bell at La Pietra and asked for Signor Acton, I had no chance to explain who I was or that he was expecting me, because the young servant in a white jacket ushered me in with eager smiles and nods and bows, opening doors for me, moving furniture out of my way; and before we got through the vestibule he was joined by an older man, the butler, who was just as eager and smiling and voluble; not that they spoke to me, and only secondarily to each other; primarily they just spoke.

The vestibule had soared up to nearly the height of two London storeys. The central circular court I now entered soared up to the sky, though the roof had been glassed in, and a curving stairway ran around the curving wall, ending exactly above the point where it began. There was a fountain in the center, gilded columns, dim towering doorways, a life-sized Venus with mirror, huge Negro busts in lunettes. Everything was so large. When the stairway finally reached what was evidently the bedroom floor, it seemed about at the level of a London roof.

The butler bustled forward to knock at one of the doors and waved me after him, while the other man hovered behind, quivering with sympathetic excitement. Then I was in the *gran' salone,* a huge room, its furniture making several different cities within it, and Harold Acton rose from a tall wing chair and came across to greet me. He was a big man and carried himself with just enough style to create a faintly comic presence. Not that the stylization was excessive—on the contrary, it was discreet; but that the style was one I associated with comedy. He carried one shoulder slightly lower than the other, and glided slightly, like the actor Alastair Sim; he spoke in the somewhat hushed, rich, precise tones of Sim in that sort of role; or perhaps of Gilly Potter, the tones of P. G. Wodehouse's prose; but *not* Robert Morley—Morley's is much too gross to be compared.

He inquired solicitously after my journey, and the butler and footman bustled in again with an elegant Italian variation on afternoon tea. The tray and all its accoutrements were very splendid, but there was nothing to make one feel oppressed, and I was soon to realize how fine my host's hospitality was. Although his manners were elaborate, and punctilious, and generally not democratic, I felt no pressure on me to do likewise, no pressure of scrutiny.

When he went back to his chair and made conversation, I noticed that he was wearing a very English tweed suit, and that on a table by his side was a large photograph of Princess Margaret. He seemed in every way very English; there was no hint, to my ear, of that Italianate accent which his contemporaries at Oxford in the 1920s had spoken of. But then there wasn't much hint of that Oxford dandy at all, the hero of a hundred semi-scandalous anecdotes, and of quite a few novels, the partial model for Anthony Blanche in Evelyn Waugh's *Brideshead Revisited* and Ambrose Silk in Waugh's *Put Out More Flags.* That brilliant and flamboyant figure, who had affronted a thousand British prejudices and shibboleths, was now transformed into a bulwark of Britishness.

Of course I could remember some words of Evelyn Waugh about him which might still apply—"vividly alive to every literary and artistic fashion, exuberantly appreciative, light and funny and energetic." My host was vivacious, and always potentially funny, by virtue of his style. But there was a paradox in finding that idea a connection to the old Acton, since our conversation had already made it clear that he was not alive to every *current* fashion and certainly not appreciative of some he was alive to. *His* fashions, those expressive of his temperament and of that Oxford world of the 1920s on which he had imposed a similar temperament, had been very unlike, say Norman Mailer, R. D. Laing, and *Last Tango in Paris*. Edith Sitwell's "Façade" and T. S. Eliot's "Love Song of J. Alfred Prufrock," exquisitely precise art, both gaily and sadly withdrawn from "normality"—these had marked the taste of those twenties Children of the Sun.

He took me to the window and showed me the famous gardens of La Pietra (created by his father), the vistas punctuated with elegant baroque statues, each curving at the hips as if in a dance. I reminded myself that as the master of La Pietra Harold Acton had a third role to play, a third persona to live out, beside the dandy-aesthete he had been and the scholarly historian he had become. He was also still involved in his father's world of art collectors and garden designers, a society of Florentine expatriates, exchanging personal and aesthetic gossip over marble tea tables—the world of Henry James.

There was indeed a touch of Henry James in my host's bland and balding face, though without those terrible eyes—that demonic gaze burning through the wax mask. James was the literary master of ceremonies of that world, and though Acton associates his boyhood rather with Bernard Berenson, since he saw more of him, James's elaborately discriminating manner was what he started from. But at Oxford Acton had devised a new modernist style for himself, and in a sense imposed it on all his contemporaries there, including at least a dozen of the liveliest writers. Those who refused to accept his style ceased to be contemporary, whatever their birth date. Men like F. R. Leavis and George Orwell had to become post-Victorians, reactionaries, for a long time. Harold and his friends had planted the banner of Pierrot on the ramparts of Oxford and London. For a time he seemed to have captured all England for his flamboyant Sunchildren. Pierrot—that was the identity I was trying to detect beneath my host's donnish manner; I was looking to see that baggy white silk emerge from his neat tweed sleeve.

But soon he indicated that no doubt I would like to retire for a while to my room, to rest before dinner, and he led me up that musically curving stairway, which rang in my ears with the heels of a dozen June Allysons tripping down it in confections of silk and lace. My room was more like a house. As far as I could calculate, it was forty-eight feet long, thirty-eight feet broad, and sixteen feet high, with two windows, each twelve feet high. The bed was four-poster with gilded columns, spiraled and rising to culminate in pineapples. There were six tapestried armchairs; eighteen paintings, one a triptych of the Madonna; and two tapestries, one twelve feet by twelve, the other a bit smaller. Then the room had a bathroom attached, itself about twenty-four feet by eighteen, and of course sixteen feet high, elaborately furnished with, for instance, twenty-eight panels of embroidery on the walls. And there was an entrance hall to my room, which was itself twenty-four feet by twelve, and which held a sofa and four armchairs, a chandelier of blue and white crystals in drooping chains, two Buddhas, two Negro heads, two mirrors with marble and painted panels above.

I found the effect quite stupefying. That was why I tried to master it by counting and measuring. As I looked out of the windows I saw the tree-bordered avenue that ran arrow-straight between olive and vine fields from the front door to the gate house on the Via Bolognese, the latter running down into Florence in one direction and up over the Futra Pass to Bologna in the other. That geometrically straight avenue confused itself in my mind with the road I had driven from Pisa, where I had got off the plane earlier that afternoon. That morning I had been in London, which had been gray and damp. Here everything was bright and hard and dry and colored. The sky was a dome, a heaven, of lapis lazuli; the farm houses along the road had handsome proportions and surfaces of ochre and lemon; the poplars and cypresses had such bold and elegant shapes, such close firm textures. And the villa below me, for instance the *salone,* was a crystallization and intensification of that beauty, in the dim, old, various, brown-and-gold harmoniousness that the aesthetes favored—one touched the whole of that Italy on that painted wall, one grasped it all like a lump of amber. That was the idea that Harold Acton had taken to Oxford with him in 1922, the idea of form. And in 1922 it seemed that at last the idea he took down that road was really going to strike the English imagination.

In my mind, however, that road overlaid another one, quite different in character: a northern English industrial-town street, bordered with mean little houses that nevertheless sheltered warm and vivid lives—the road to Wigan Pier. Orwell's road had always been my road. I had always preferred to find the things I loved hidden under those exteriors. Because that was my England. The world of four-poster beds and marble floors and gilded chandeliers had always seemed to me comic if correctly handled, distasteful if brought close, immoral if taken seriously.

But here I was, and not on false pretenses. I had told my host that I belonged to the opposite camp from him, that I had been a student of Leavis, an enthusiast for Orwell, but now I wanted to write about him—and he had invited me to come to see him. I'd mentioned my book *Mirror for Anglo-Saxons* to him, so he could see, if he wanted to, how hostile I'd been about people like him. Of course I'd promised, in effect, that I didn't intend to take that tone about him, but still he knew, or could have known, who I was. I was not so much uneasy about him as about myself. What was I doing in a golden bed?

And then, of course, there were going to be so many questions I would hesitate to ask him, even though that was what I had come for. It was his life, and I didn't want to know anything more about it than he wanted to tell me. Or rather, I didn't want to ask him anything which he didn't want me to know, nor to find out anything behind his back; but, on the other hand, I wanted to reinterpret his facts in my own terms—I wanted to find out a good deal from the side. It seemed I should have to talk about just what he wanted to talk about and keep my own thinking to myself, which was itself not entirely frank, not entirely honorable, socially speaking. I couldn't ask, for instance, anything pointed about Brian Howard, his close friend and co-leader of dandy-aestheticism, who had committed suicide.

That death was on my mind, immediately, at La Pietra. It was the general tragedy of the English dandies made local in one violent action, and this villa held its own powerful resonances of that tragedy. I knew that Harold Acton had been oppressed by his father, the man who had created this house and its collection, just as Brian Howard had been oppressed by his father—in both cases *because* the sons were dandies. In the Actons' story there had been no violence, but the process by which Harold had remained his father's heir had been a long tense struggle which had taken up much of his energy. La Pietra was in its way a sinister house, which had cost a lot. But I could not ask about Arthur Acton, or about Brian Howard—or rather I could not press for an answer that would tell me anything new. It was clear that Harold had said what he had to say on such matters, in his books. He now only remembered such events and people in the public terms he had used from them in writing. Or at least he had a public memory of them—if he had also a private memory, that was something I could not ask him to unlock for me because my use of it could not promise to be purely reverent. I should have to reinterpret and use whatever I was told, so I must not ask for anything more than the public memory.

When I went downstairs again—tripping down all fifty marble steps—I gave him the two presents I had brought from London. One was the elaborate, pretentious, and, to my mind, preposterous study of Ronald Firbank by Brigid Brophy. It was at least a proof that the dandy tradition in literature, to which Harold had affiliated himself at Oxford, was still alive in England. And I think he enjoyed reading it, without necessarily dissenting from my judgment of it. (Judgment, in such matters, was not particularly his concern; his interest, even when quite intense, was essentially playful.) The other gift was a catalog of a recent sale at the Chenil Galleries of the last of the Diaghilev ballet costumes. I ought to have taken him one of the costumes, but they looked a bit shabby close up, and it would have been a big anticlimax to risk, my unwrapping a bundle of tinseled rags before his puzzled eyes. But the subject of Diaghilev was a happy one to introduce, for that had been a real enthusiasm of his; more than playfulness was evident when he talked of the ballet. After all, the Ballets Russes de Serge Diaghilev had been on the public plane what his own taste and personality and poetry had been on the private plane; they were both first performances in the England of the 1920s of the dandy-aesthete cult. About such topics I could question him without embarrassment.

However, when he rose to greet me—always so polite—he said something which quite drove those thoughts out of my mind, and evoked the doubts I had felt in my room. As he addressed himself to making me a gin and tonic—with some suggestion by gesture that this was an esoteric rite he'd only heard about, he asked me, over his shoulder, "I trust you do not object to royalty?" The tone was gracious, the gesture this time graceful, a benevolent glance around, but just for that reason the effect was disconcerting. It was clear that he was leading up to something roguish, something that made him smile to himself. My eyes flew to the Princess's photograph and then circled the room, while my mind canvassed a number of agitating possibilities. Was Princess Margaret in person going to emerge from a door? Or would any answer lead to either the right or the left hook; either, "Well, if you don't why do you use that peevish and underbred tone about them?" or, "Well, if you do, why are you making up to one of the few friends they have left?" Or, more likely, was he leading up to "I have, you see, been glancing at one or two of your little efforts before you arrived."

In fact my answer, whatever it was, led only to the proposal that I accompany him to lunch the next day with two old friends, ex-Queen Helen of Rumania and ex-Princess Olga of Yugoslavia, who lived nearby. And that, though a facer of a different kind, was manageable enough for the moment. "Charmed, I'm sure," I murmured, sipping my drink with as much of an air as I could command. The road to Wigan Pier could run on without me all right for a few days.

But as we went on to talk of Firbank and Diaghilev, of the *commedia dell'arte* and the Ballets Russes, I felt that I had found what I had been looking for. He had not, I thought, been totally unaware of the disconcerting effect he had produced—it had not been *totally* unintended. And indeed the phrasing and delivery of that line had been worthy of Ambrose Silk and Anthony Blanche in their more playful moments. I had seen the flash of Pierrot's baggy costume, the derisive grace of his gestures, and I could conjure up for myself the skullcap and the white makeup and the alienated eyes sitting opposite me. And with that I knew what I was doing there. I was on one of those twenties treasure hunts, in which people drove across London, across all England, in search of some otherwise unprocurable item, something unique and unimaginable, to complete the treasure prescribed to them to collect. What I was after here was Pierrot, and I needed him precisely in order to put him beside Wigan Pier, because he too was a part, an important part, of my treasure, my England.

Chapter One
Children of the Sun

Definitions and Perspectives

I WANT TO DESCRIBE the imaginative life of English culture after 1918 and to trace the prominence within it, the partial dominance over it, established by men of one intellectual temperament, the men I call England's Children of the Sun. I am concerned primarily with the high culture of the country, and within that primarily with the intellectual and imaginative literature, though I want to use that as a focus, a lens, and to look through it at the imaginative life of the whole society. If I am granted that point of view, I think I can show that a certain type of experience, appropriate to a certain mode of being, was cultivated by the young men who felt that they were *the* generation of English writers growing up after the War; who convinced most of their contemporaries who cared about books that they were right; and who, therefore, established a new identity for "England," a new meaning to "being English," in the world at large and in the privacy of individual minds.

The hegemony of this temperament was always challenged by many who disliked this idea of "Englishness," who stood for an older or a different idea of England. At the end of the period I shall describe—that is, by 1957—these other men seemed to have won the cultural battle, although now it is not so clear that that hegemony was ever completely deposed. In any case, the occurrence of such challenges and contradictions is a necessary part of any cultural dialectic, and so of any temperamental hegemony. The imaginative history of any period can be, should be, described in terms of the clashes between a dominant temperament, the culture's "thesis," and its opponents, the "antithesis." The thesis itself always begins as a contradiction of something previously established—in this case the consensus humanism of Victorian and Edwardian culture, against which the 20th-century Children of the Sun rebelled. But their dandyism provoked rebellion too. Thus we shall expect to find men of other intellectual temperaments who claimed to be "England" in this period. But we shall also expect to find that their books (their ideologies, their narratives, their images) present themselves as being *in opposition*.

And this is surely what we *do* find in the writings of George Orwell and F. R. Leavis, and of their allies and disciples, in *Scrutiny* and *Tribune* and Julian Symons' magazine, *Twentieth Century Verse*. These are the men of the antithesis, and a characteristic note in their writings is a bitter protest against "the gang," or gangs, that had taken over English literary life in the 20th century, had usurped the great heritage of 19th-century England. One of these gangs they identify with the names of Cyril Connolly, Peter Quennell, Evelyn Waugh, John Betjeman; another with those of W. H. Auden, Christopher Isherwood, Stephen Spender, John Lehmann.

These are the men of the thesis, and they themselves acknowledged the existence and the functioning of their "gangs." The two sub-sets thought of themselves, in the early 1930s, as mutually opposed, because the first were frankly aesthetes, the second aggressively not so. But it will be my contention that both were varieties of the same imaginative temperament. And allied to one or other of these groups—usually to both—were other figures, some not primarily of the world of the arts, like Randolph Churchill, Guy Burgess, and Brian Howard. The life of

Brian Howard, together with that of his close friend, Harold Acton, will provide the narrative nexus of this study, because between them they tried nearly all the major options of self-realization which the period offered to men of that temperament.

These two were respectively thirteen and fourteen when the war ended, both schoolboys at Eton. They had been to good prep schools, and were to go on to Christ Church College, Oxford. They were central, socially, to the first group of writers I mentioned, and ahead of it intellectually and aesthetically until about 1930. At the same time they had always been outside the main stream of English culture because they were born into families that were Roman Catholic, American, and "aesthetic." Both their fathers had been painters and art dealers, and lived in the world of cosmopolitan connoisseurs. This heritage put at the disposal of Brian and Harold ideas, styles of expression, worlds of experience, unknown to their schoolfellows, with which to lead the latter in rebellion against British philistinism. But above all it was by means of their own personalities that they took that lead—by making those personalities such vivid manifestations of the dandy temperament and by defying the disapprobation of more mature and responsible and "English" types.

Both were themselves poets and fiction writers to begin with, but more importantly they were impresarios of others' talents and of the international modernist movement. They were friends of the Sitwells, and Gertrude Stein, and Jean Cocteau, and others. After they came down from Oxford in 1925 they were members of those groups of Bright Young People who figured so often in the gossip columns. But as the initial impetus of their dandy revolt wore off, they realized that some hitherto more obscure members of their group—for instance Evelyn Waugh—were making more of that revolt in literary terms, and that they themselves must find new ideas.

In the 1930s their paths diverged. Harold Acton spent the years 1932 to 1939 in China, cultivating a "Chinese" kind of pacific serenity and aesthetic scholarship; he wanted to make himself an ambassador of hedonistic wisdom between East and West. Brian Howard's equivalent adventure was in Germany, where he encountered first a religion of life-values, of living according to the rhythms of the earth, and then the anti-Nazi and, more generally, the anti-Fascist movement. He became a leading spokesman against Nazism in the literary world, and a friend of Auden, Isherwood, and Spender.

During the second war, both were in England most of the time, in fairly ignominious positions. After the war, both went to live abroad again, Harold Acton in Italy, Brian Howard mostly in France, where he committed suicide in the first weeks of 1958. With his death I shall close the narrative, because it coincided with the eclipse of dandyism in England and the rise of the Angry Young Men. That coincidence was appropriate, for Brian's life, and Harold Acton's, was an adventure of ideas, and those adventures were interwoven with the main fabric of the imaginative life in England in those years. Many readers will have already met the two men without knowing their names, for they were the men from whom Evelyn Waugh drew Anthony Blanche in *Brideshead Revisited* and Ambrose Silk in *Put Out More Flags;* and Brian was, as much as anyone else, the fashionable left-wing intellectual whom Orwell and Leavis often denounced. Above all, throughout this period the major currents of English life can be seen through their individual lives, because they knew everybody, including non-literary figures like Guy Burgess and Randolph Churchill. They moved with all the people who, in their various ways, seem to me to have belonged by temperament to the cultural "thesis."

What I mean by their temperament is most briefly to be explained by calling it *dandyism,* although the dandy is only one type, one crystallization, of the temperament, and its other types are quite different. But we are concentrating on writers, and they were very often dandies; they were preoccupied with style, worshipped Adonis or Narcissus, were rebellious against both their fathers' and their mothers' modes of seriousness, were in love with ornament, splendor, high manners, and so on—all that is commonly meant by dandyism. In order to really understand the idea of the Children of the Sun, however, we need to both broaden and deepen our definition. We need to associate the dandy with two other types, seemingly unrelated, the *rogue* and the *naïf,* and to see that temperamentally the three types are all first cousins. All three go in defiance of the "mature" modes of seriousness that our culture sponsors; all are "young men's" styles of being. And we need to give a longer evolutionary perspective to these terms by calling all these types—on occasion—*Sonnenkinder*—Children of the Sun. This extra dignity is appropriate when these young-men types are made the objects of an imaginative cult, when a group of people significant in numbers, talent, or power idolizes the young man as the supreme form of life. To some degree, such a cult *always* exists. It can be traced back throughout the history of Western culture; but it has taken very different forms and very varying degrees of importance in different phases of that culture.

The simplest psychological fact at the root of this cult is that worship of the male adolescent by older men that is expressed in the myths of Narcissus, Adonis, and such. This phenomenon occurs, and recurs, even in cultural contexts that make nothing of it. But certain phases of Western culture have made particular use of it, have developed activities and institutions that have—often secretly—that worship at their core.

One manifestation of this we call dandyism. In its simplest form, the young man loves his own beauty and makes that love insolently manifest in his clothes, posture, manners, conversation, judgments, imposing on everything a style that defies the "mature" values of his father and mother. But there are many more complex forms: some men, neither young nor beautiful themselves, adore those who are, wear similar clothes, and cultivate the same insolent or defiant style; other men, past the age for personal dandyism, transfer to art and style in art the feeling they formerly devoted to their bodies' beauty; yet other men, never interested in young men's beauty themselves, become passionate connoisseurs of the luxury consumed by that insolent style, the *objets d'art* and *objets de luxe* created for it.

Related to but separable from dandyism is aestheticism, the worship of art seen as fantasy triumphant over reality, the worship of fantasy and beauty in art in opposition to maturity and responsibility. This can be found in men who do not themselves worship adolescent male beauty. But it is very often found, habitually found, in alliance with dandyism, and as part of the cult of the *Sonnenkind.* Moreover, the study of certain genres of art and certain periods of civilization is an intellectual branch of the cult, comparable in function to the study of church history or ecclesiastical art in Christianity. In the case of the *Sonnenkinder* of 20th-century England, the rococo, the baroque, the *commedia dell'arte,* Byzantine painting, and ballet have been the intellectual foci for the cult.

In some ways closer than dandyism to what I called "the simplest psychological fact" is the cult of the *naïf* at the core of thirties Marxism—the image of the sun-bronzed young man with his shirt open, bringing the radiant candor of his gaze to bear on the mess the fathers have made of the world. This is harder to study in book form, because the intellectual and political activities of Marxism were temperamentally in the style of the fathers. (It is easy to study the equivalent cult of the naïf within the Fascist and Nazi movements—e.g., in the banners and posters of the *Hitlerjugend*—but those movements were repudiated by most of the people we are concerned with.) But one need only consult the photographs of the thirties Marxist writers to see the cult of the *Sonnenkind* in its naïf form.

Least ideological of all was the cult of the *rogue,* who is likely to scorn the intellectual actions of both naïf and dandy, being probably a Tory radical in politics, and yet is their effective ally against the fathers and the mothers. Perhaps the most familiar type of rogue is the hoaxer—the young man who dresses up as a professor, a prime minister, an admiral, a millionaire, who can talk and act just like the real thing, and who often becomes the real thing thirty years later with very little change in general attitudes or in what is called maturity. He often seems better (brighter, cleaner, gayer, truer) as a mock adult than as the real thing, better to himself and to other people— especially to those who enjoyed their own lives most before they took on the responsibilities of manhood, who are therefore ready to make a cult (unselfconsciously, nine times out of ten) of the young rogue figure.

A brutal and bloodthirsty specimen of this type, who makes a perhaps typical rogue's career in the army, is Evelyn Waugh's character, Brigadier Ritchie-Hook, based on a real-life soldier. Ritchie-Hook appears in the trilogy of novels about the second war;[1] he engages in elaborate practical jokes—lavatory jokes—in persecution of one of the other officers, but he also comes back from a foolhardy beach raid carrying a still-dripping human head, and he dies in a single-handed assault on a German blockhouse with all its guns blazing. It is typical of Waugh's insight into these matters that he makes Ritchie-Hook a member, an important member, of that very conservative and traditional regiment, the Halberdiers. The Halberdiers and Ritchie-Hook belong together, Waugh shows us, and together they renew Guy Crouchback's faith in England, in manliness, in life. Crouchback is a modern Englishman, melancholic, mature, ultra-responsible—all too much the servant of the Reality Principle; yet Ritchie-Hook, who is notably immature, a gigantic little-boy, is the authority figure Guy has been looking for all his life.*

The one organized movement in our period clearly intended to mobilize these three types was Sir Oswald Mosley's New Party, that short-lived precursor to the British Union of Fascists. Mosley briefly held together dandy-aesthetes like Osbert and Sacheverell Sitwell, and Oliver Messel and Cecil Beaton, with political naïfs like Oliver Baldwin and Christopher Isherwood and Alan Pryce-Jones, and rogues like the young Esmond Romilly and Mosley himself and those he took with him into the British Union of Fascists. Other famous members of the New Party were Harold Nicolson and John Strachey, both deeply—though indirectly—devoted to the cult of the young man. But Mosley was not the leader (too impatient and irritable) and

---

* We might note also that Waugh declares Ritchie-Hook's main motive to be not domination or destruction but surprise—the need to startle, baffle, dazzle his victims; it is notable because Waugh declares this to be the essence of his dandies' motives also. The desire to affront everything settled and conventional is the motive that unites all these young-man types.

politics was not the area (too heavily patrolled by father-figures) to win success in England then. The ideas suddenly crystallized in the New Party, the individuals suddenly conjoined, found their real fruition in much more scattered and delayed and various ways. The historical connection between them seems paradoxical until they are studied from this point of view of temperament.

At the root of all these phenomena is that worship of the young male adolescent, not yet entangled in the world or in marriage, that we defined before. But we must expect to find no more direct connection between "Adonis" and these various cults than between "Christ on the Cross" and Gregorian chant or theological controversy, the Trappists, or the Crusades—or than between Christ himself and Luther or Prince Myshkin or Baron von Hügel or St. Catherine of Siena.

First, then, I will define the three types as they appear in Western culture in recent centuries; that is, in the forms most familiar to us and most similar to those life-stories that we are going to study in detail. For dandyism, we may start with Ellen Moers' definition in her fine study of the phenomenon in the 19th century, *The Dandy*:[2]

> A man dedicated solely to his own perfection through a ritual of taste . . . free of all human commitments that conflict with taste: passions, moralities, ambitions, politics or occupations.

One might amplify the first part of that by saying that the dandy may cultivate goodness, beauty, and truth, but it will be by the means of acquiring them, appropriating them, as parts of his own style. At his most intense and interesting, he may be said to worship those traditional values as much as the mature man does, but it will be by incarnating them, by realizing in his own clothes and manners, epigrams and anecdotes, all the beauty, wit, taste, and strength potential in the world. And one might add to the second part of her definition by saying that the dandy must be very negative. He disbelieves, insofar as he is a dandy, in both the world of men and the world of woman. He is a rebel, or more often a cynic, about many things in which most men and women find the good, the true, and the beautiful. Marriage and the home are values as dubious to him as are responsibility and business success. As Baudelaire put it, dandies are interested in neither money nor love. They are interested in style, in refinement, and in fantasy. Beau Brummell complained that he had caught a cold from sitting in a room with a damp stranger. Reality, including the reality of the physical world, and even that of one's own instinctual life, is something to be dominated. To be oneself, as Ellen Moers puts it, is to tighten, to control, to resist. The self is not animal, but ideal. And the self is all important.

The dandy is always "immature," always "selfish," because the criteria of maturity and unselfishness are crucial parts of the official value schemes of our culture, against which the dandy rebels. He rebels against both the fathers and the mothers of his culture, both of the great forces whose internecine conflict J. J. Bachofen studied in his *Das Mutterrecht*. This pioneer study of matriarchy, published in 1861, speculated about the cultural values that had centered around the great goddess Demeter, the great mother of all life, before society began to worship male gods. But both Demeter and Apollo teach maturity, and although their values can conflict (the opposing ideologies of D. H. Lawrence and Max Weber exemplify that conflict), they also can cooperate in an idea of maturity. The *Sonnenkinder* break away from that in a way that parallels the adolescent's break away from home. Bachofen proposed a scheme of religious history that showed men as worshiping first female powers, then a *Sonnenkind* god, then Dionysus, and then the Olympian pantheon that includes Apollo. If the individual adolescent's "regression" to self-absorption and selfishness is typically followed by a Dionysian worship of sensual power and then by an Apollonian assumption of responsibilities, then Bachofen's scheme shows our culture's development to be parallel with that of the individual.

However that may be, we can certainly see dandyism as rooted sexually in narcissism. We can see it in some varied forms of relationship enacted by dandy life and art; besides Narcissus' love of himself, the relationship of Dorian Gray and Lord Henry (in Wilde's *The Picture of Dorian Gray)*, that of Lucien de Rubempré and Vautrín (in Balzac's *La Père Goriot)*, that of Nijinsky and Diaghilev, that of the Narrator and Albertine (in Proust's *À la recherche du temps perdu)*, that of Edith Sitwell and Tchelitchew, that of Lolita and Humbert Humbert (in Nabokov's *Lolita)*. These relationships are various, but they share certain characteristics. Among them we might note aestheticism—both partners share powerful aesthetic interests and/or one of them sees the other as a work of art or shapes their affair the way an artist shapes his work; and sexual obsession—the sexual appetite is fixed on its object in opposition to the lover's imaginative-moral interests, the god of his eroticism is Priapus. We can see dandyism also expressing itself in the worship of art; in the fellowship of other dandies; in making a cult of clothes and manners; and in making a cult of luxury and aristocracy. The dandy is likely always to be a snob, because he wants to crystallize life into perfect form, into a style—often a somewhat fantastic style—chosen and achieved deliberately, and for that purpose money and private traditions are an advantage. (Of course snobbery can and does reverse its tastes, and its loyalties to class and money, without ceasing to be snobbery.)

Ellen Moers sharply distinguishes the dandy from the aesthete. The transition in Oscar Wilde's costume in the mid-1880s from knee breeches, velvet, and long hair to faultless and severe evening dress—the transition from aesthete to dandy—is for her a crucial change. And for the purposes of her argument, she is right. The aesthete *is* crucially different from the dandy in being much more concerned with something outside himself—art, beauty, the cultural heritage; he need not be so hard and "heroically" negative. His energies go into receiving impressions and sensations rather than into making them, and although he must be indifferent to the ordinary man's major concerns, he need not be aggressive about them. He worships Apollo as well as Adonis. But the example of Wilde will remind us that—since he remained Wilde after the transition—the aesthete and the dandy are very closely related, and frequently the same person is both. Very often the two phases are alternative ways of embodying the same idea, the same temperamental drive. In this study we shall regard the two types most of the time as twin aspects of one identity—the dandy-aesthete. Of our two principal figures, Harold Acton was perceptibly more the aesthete, Brian Howard perceptibly more the dandy, but both were both.

The rogue-rebel is a type one often finds in conjunction with the dandy-aesthete, even though he is the latter's opposite by ordinary criteria. The rogue is often coarse, rough, brutal, and careless. He is like the dandy, however, in his conscious enjoyment of his own style and in his rebellion against mature and responsible morality. Sexually he is as much the narcissist as the dandy is, but "typically" the rogue is heterosexual, the dandy homosexual. Wilde said, "What the paradox was to me in the sphere of thought, perversity became to me in the sphere of passion." (Paradox is more the mode of the dandy than of the rogue, but we are going to see in the diplomat-spy Guy Burgess how many overlaps there are between these types.) Despite this and other important differences, one finds the two types linked together in the world of the arts—in the real-life relationships of Verlaine and Rimbaud and of Cocteau and Radiguet, in the character-types of Restoration comedy, and in those of the novels of Evelyn Waugh, the keenest observer and commentator on our subject in our period. In Waugh's novel *Put Out More Flags,* the dandy-aesthete character, Ambrose Silk, is linked indissolubly to the rogue-rebel, Basil Seal. Waugh drew Seal partly from Peter Rodd, a rogue he knew at Oxford who married Nancy Mitford, one of the dandy-writers, so that marriage exemplified the link between the two types.* And Waugh himself, the most gifted aesthete of the group I will be discussing, was a

---

* Women can be dandies—besides Nancy Mitford, we shall meet Virginia Woolf and Edith Sitwell and the young Nancy Cunard. The older Nancy Cunard seems to have behaved more like a rogue—and that category fits Eleanor Smith. As for the naïf, that has always been a common intellectual type among women; in our period, Rosamund Lehmann, Katherine Mansfield, and Jean Rhys all wrote naively. On the whole, men were more prominent among Children of the Sun writers and artists, but women were to be found in the movement, and socially they were less outshone.

great friend of Randolph Churchill, one of its principal rogues. Up to a point, each of these men combined the aesthete and the rogue in himself, and Brian Howard's biographer applied to Howard, an aesthete, an epitaph originally devised for the rogue Churchill—"born to success but doomed to failure." The same epitaphs suit both types because both fit equally badly into the "real" world, rebel against its categories with equally irritable impatience. But the two types are not to be seen as the same, nor—or at least, only rarely—as allied characteristics of the same man. More typically, there is an alliance between the dandy-aesthete and the rogue-rebel in a common cause, the cause of defying their fathers' mode of seriousness.

Such an alliance is not a matter of ordinary affection or ordinary loyalty, as we see in Basil's cruel betrayal of Ambrose; Waugh describes their relationship as always "shadowy and mutually derisive." But they are nonetheless allies, and each accords the other a sardonic freedom to perform his own style, a freedom from all ordinary judgmental criteria but those of style. More important, they share a sense of humor, a humor directed against "mature and responsible" values and developed to abnormal intensity, so that it takes over psychic and social functions usually performed by the erotic or idealistic components of personality. When two men have laughed together *orgiastically,* Waugh tells us, they seal their friendship on a plane rarer and loftier than normal human intercourse. Speaking now of Guy Crouchback and Tommy Blackhouse (in the war trilogy), he says that these two men were caught up by "that sacred wind which once blew freely over the young world." They hear cymbals and flutes, feel scented breezes, and see Aegean stars above them—all because they have just spent an evening with a family of crazy old-fashioned recluses.[3] In some sense, as Auberon Waugh says, all England was in this period held together by this hypertrophied sense of humor, of which P. G. Wodehouse was the great master.

The naïf is a form of *Sonnenkind* less prominent in the literature of the '20s, although there were specimens in real life in the Oxford of Waugh, Acton, and Cyril Connolly. There were young men who offered themselves as essentially responsive to others and open to every invitation, who established their identity in indeterminacy and sheer attractiveness. The most obvious example in fiction is Sebastian of *Brideshead Revisited*. But such a figure is not far from being a mere object of other men's passions, a mere Dorian Gray, while the naïf as a cultural image is more than that. It was in the '30s that naïfs like Stephen Spender and Philip Toynbee and Christopher Isherwood and John Strachey began (in different ways) to offer their minds and hearts as being all limpid sensitiveness and generous responsiveness, as being things as attractive and beautiful as a face or body. They too rebelled against patriarchal and matriarchal values, offering themselves as an alternative source of value, but they differed from the dandy and the rogue in that theirs was essentially a potential self. The naïf (novel heroes from *Tom Jones* on exemplify this) offers himself as being in process of formation, in search of values and models by which to form himself, and thus as having no final form in himself, or only the form of ardent and generous responsiveness. He seems always about to adopt some traditional "mature" temperament. Typically, the naïfs of the 1930s seemed about to join the Communist party, and to become comrades, fighters, members. But most of them didn't, or did so in impermanent ways, because, as naïfs, they would have betrayed their identities by becoming "members."

These, then, are the three types who may become *Sonnenkinder,* Children of the Sun. They assume this identity if a whole generation loves them above all other types, if a whole movement focuses passionate values and aspirations on them—as opposed to focusing them on the wise old man, the babe in arms, or a figure of maturity. *Sonnenkind* is a term used by certain anthropologists of culture, notably Bachofen and T. J. Perry, and to get a full sense of all its implies, with all its ideological perspectives, we must consult them. (I have given a sketch of their ideas in Appendix B.)

What this book offers to discuss is only the imaginative life of English high culture between 1918 and 1957, seen in terms of cultural psychology; that is, in terms of the temperamental styles cultivated among intellectuals and artists and their work. Those styles "belonged to" the dandy, the rogue, and the naïf types, and those types can be grouped together and to some extent "understood," just by calling them Children of the Sun, and setting them in the perspectives referred to. They were, and saw themselves as, originators of a new "aesthetic" phase in English high culture, to be characterized by ornament and brilliancy, playfulness and youthfulness, and by a turning of the back on the old forms of seriousness and power. They denied the comfortable features in the traditional image of the young man, and accentuated others— made themselves into sharp-edged fragments of the full *Sonnenkind*.

I have, of course, transformed these anthropological perspectives as I appropriated them. Bachofen and T. J. Perry were concerned with a huge chronological scheme, in which the *Sonnenkind* phase of culture followed an earlier and preceded a later, while I treat it as one cult among many practiced in a narrowly limited time and place— one that was in some sense dominant in the forty years I take but was always in conflict and combination with others. My interest could be called "psychological" rather than anthropological, in that I look at individuals or small groups. On the other hand, my material is not the inner lives of those individuals, not at least as a depth-psychologist would understand them, for I take account only of what those individuals report of that inner life. My material might best be called the *cultic* life of those individuals and groups, the value-bearing images they cultivated in their imaginative life. That cultivation took the form of actual behavior and, of course, of ideological commitments, but it was centrally a matter of the artistic genres they loved and their imaginative response to them, of the heroes, the narratives, the tunes, the pictures they contemplated. I pay most attention to books, films, plays, poems, letters; and to their writers and readers, in their clubs, schools, homes, and marriages. I see all these artefacts and affiliations as parts of a cult worship, as acts—and the results of acts—of contemplation, consecration, self-design, and self-formation. My method is, therefore, closer to that cultural, or cultic, literary criticism that we might associate with Orwell, even though it borrows its set of terms from Bachofen.

Let me take a couple of examples of this cultic self-formation from the main subject. The iconography of the *commedia dell'arte,* in paintings and in literary forms as well as in all kinds of stage performances, seems to have been importantly charged with *Sonnenkind* cultic significance for many people in the 1920s. One can see this in America, for instance in the work of Edna Millay, Edmund Wilson, John Peale Bishop, and F. Scott Fitzgerald. The figure, the costume, the fate, of Pierrot, and those of Harlequin and of Columbine, turn up time and time again in conjunction with the cult of youth and grace and with the protest against the mature and responsible world of the fathers and mothers. Books and paintings in which they figured could be sacred objects—the sacredness varied from case to case naturally—and reading or looking at them could be acts of devotion.

And the life of social groups, as well as the memory of other such groups in the past, also had a cultic significance. For instance, the dandies of the 1920s looked back to those of the 1890s. In many cases they made a conscious cult of their predecessors, and can be seen to have formed themselves by that cult. They exchanged anecdotes about them, recited remarks they had made, collected objects associated with them, sought out acquaintances who had known them, designed clothes and rooms and houses like theirs, and simply and literally imitated them. Things as concrete and intimate as certain tones of voice and gestures of the hand were passed on from one to the other, as well as certain words, certain tastes, certain enthusiasms and disgusts, certain subjects and objects of interest. Ronald Firbank, for instance, cultivated the memory of Wilde this way, and the Sitwells cultivated Firbank. Harold Acton listened devotedly to Reggie Turner's talk of Oscar Wilde, and noted how his voice "descended to the depth of an imaginary corpulence, his gestures became sculptured and hieratic, and his fingers sprouted scarab rings, when he repeated Oscar's sayings."[4]

Similarly the dandies of the 1890s had looked back to those of the Regency. Max Beerbohm wrote a book about Beau Brummell, and Disraeli's early Regency-style novels were popular reading in Wilde's circle. And the dandies of the Regency looked back to those of the Restoration, or were at least aware of that heritage. Captain Gronow, who wrote the first biography of Brummell, soon after his death, lists the succession of beaus that linked Beau Hewitt, the original of Sir Fopling Flutter in Etherege's play, with Brummell. And of course among Brummell's contemporaries, literal imitation of him was a major manifestation of dandyism. While, to turn to literary form, both those who read and those who wrote the fashionable novels about dandies in the 1840s were conscious of continuing the tradition of Restoration comedy. Going further back, we need hardly demonstrate that dandies, and dandified literary genres, played a prominent part in the imaginative life of the Elizabethan period. There too, incidentally, the dandy, the rogue, and the naïf are linked types, as they are in Restoration comedy.

To summarize this section, let me propose the unchallenging generalization that there have been dandies, sartorial and artistic, in every phase of Western culture, and that in many phases they were prominent and in some dominant. The particular proposition of this book is that England after 1918 was in such a phase, and to study this cultically is to watch certain intellectuals forming themselves as dandies by a version of the religious life—by imitation, legend, saints' lives, contemplation, reliquaries, and so on.

Of the three *Sonnenkind* types, the rogue and the naïf ally themselves much more easily than the dandy to traditional structures of feeling. Boys are in some sense supposed to be rogues, and girls to be naïfs, as a phase of their development; and when it becomes clear that certain individuals have realized themselves permanently in those forms, the discrepancy is easily enough dismissed as "they just never grew up." The dandy represents more of a challenge, and the rogue and the naïf become more recalcitrant figures in periods under his influence. That is why we take the dandy as the central figure here, and also why the history of the dandy is more full of significant clashes with other figures of manhood and morality—why the dandy *has* more of a history.

However, individuals *can* be seen forming themselves cultically into the rogue and the naïf types, although usually that seems to be a less self-conscious process with them than with dandies. And the cult of all three types can be studied as something found in certain areas of research, courses of action, genres of art, even in certain careers and institutions that carry the cult within them. In this book I shall follow all of these lines of study over the forty years after 1918 in England, shifting from one to the other to find the one most appropriate to the changing facts that the chronological sequence brings into view. The psychology of dandyism remains no doubt a predominant interest, but it is only *primus inter pares*.

Some preliminary glances at English and French literature in the 19th century will throw light on this. These two countries were in this period dominant over the rest of Europe and, therefore, over the world. Their history, including that imaginative history of temperamental types and their hegemony over the culture, was paradigmatic for other countries at the time, and in the later period we are concerned with, when they were no longer dominant, for France and England themselves.

Dandyism in the 19th Century

Beau Brummell and "Caliph" Beckford (the author of *Vathek*) represent, in the early 19th century, the archetypal dandy and aesthete, rebelling against the emphatically masculine style of manhood that ranged from Squire Western (in Fielding's *Tom Jones*) to George III and even to Dr. Johnson. They led a rebellion against a long-established English consensus manliness, which might be compared with the rebellion led by our two principals in the early 20th century. But if it was in England that the dandy and the aesthete most dramatically defied the criteria of manhood, it was in France, during the rest of the century, that that defiance was developed and semi-institutionalized in art to the point of becoming a kind of counterculture. France in the heyday of Brummell and Beckford provided no setting for dandies or aesthetes, occupied as it was with the heroic excitements first of the Revolution and then of Napoleon. But after 1815 a series of regimes were set up there that notably lacked such excitements and failed in imaginative authority. The world of men in France then seemed to France's intensest imaginations palpably inauthentic, and the best work in the arts was done in a spirit of defying the established culture, using the style and temperament of Brummell and Beckford but going further in developing an aesthetic from them. Thus Barbey d'Aurevilly's *Du dandysme et de George Brummell* (1845) was followed by Baudelaire's *Le peintre de la vie moderne* (1863). In England, meanwhile, that style and temperament had been exiled to the fringe of eccentricity, because Victorian society worked out a consensus culture that had enough imaginative authority to command the cooperation of major artistic talents.

One of the most fascinating chapters in Ellen Moers' book deals with Victorian literature and its relationship to dandyism—a relationship so important that much Victorian literature can be defined as an attack on dandyism. 1830 saw the death of George IV, who, as the wicked Prince Regent, was so long the leader of the dandies and a rebel against his bourgeois-virtuous father, George III. In the same year *Fraser's Magazine* was born and set itself to oppose everything associated with George IV and with his ex-friend Brummell. It was exorcizing the dandy bewitchment of British culture during the Regency and, in effect, preparing the way for Victorianism. Its first editor, William Maginn, led a war of the men of talent, industry, and reading against the exclusives, the elegant, the idle. His writers were often Scottish or Irish, and his victims usually Londoners. The most famous of his writers was Thomas Carlyle, the most famous of his victims Edward Bulwer-Lytton, a dandy in life and an author of dandy novels. *Fraser's* set itself against the fashion for French literature and brought in the taste for German. In 1833-34 it published Carlyle's *Sartor Resartus,* the first uplifting of the serious voice of Victorianism. The famous chapter in that book on "The Dandiacal Body" had been inspired by an earlier *Fraser's* attack on Lytton's *Pelham;* from this is derived the whole metaphor of clothes, which is so central to Carlyle's rhetoric.

Maginn gave voice quite consciously to a middle-class indignation against irresponsibility—immaturity, selfishness, dandyism—in high places. He differed from the great Victorians only in that he used heartier and coarser tones than they were to do. His persona "Oliver Yorke" was a high-handed, heavy-drinking blusterer, and in real life Maginn led his writers in heavy drinking and loud singing of Irish songs. But this too was an anti-dandiacal gesture, and so was recognized as morally serious by the great Victorians. Thackeray, for instance, who particularly pursued Lytton with ridicule in the pages of *Fraser's*, exhorted him to leave off his scents and hair oil, to become a *man*, and in order to do so to drink more—"to swell his slim waist and redden his fair face." This was in 1858, and in 1841 he urged Lytton to get out of his dressing gown and into a jacket. In *Pendennis* Thackeray offered us as moral hero George Warrington, who smoked a pipe and wiped beer from his bristly beard, sat astride a table, and wore a ragged shooting jacket—"He was drinking beer like a coal-heaver and yet you couldn't but perceive that he was a gentleman." *Gentleman* was a key Victorian word, and it was promoted as defining a manly alternative to the dandy. Warrington was the true and manly friend to the unworthy Pendennis, himself a dandy, just as Dobbin was to George Osborne in *Vanity Fair*, and the contrast repeated itself in many other Victorian novels.

Charles Dickens habitually used dandies to play the villains' parts in his melodramas. For instance, Harthouse in *Hard Times*, Gowan in *Little Dorrit*, old Turveydrop and Harold Skimpole in *Bleak House*, the young and selfish Pip in *Great Expectations*. In *David Copperfield* there is a Thackeray-like exposure of the dandy Steerforth. But like Thackeray, Dickens betrays something of a bad conscience about his treatment of dandies and redeems Eugene Wrayburn in *Our Mutual Friend* and Sidney Carton in *A Tale of Two Cities*. He clearly connected the dandy with the artist. Like Thackeray again, Dickens was himself quite a dandy in real life, and the scandals of his later career seem to indicate that he found bourgeois virtuousness a strain to keep up.

Then Tennyson, who himself conducted a feud with Bulwer-Lytton in 1845, also used dandy figures as villains, as in *Maud;* and in *The Mill on the Floss,* George Eliot made Stephen, the unworthy lover and seducer of Maggie, a dandy. One may say that all the major Victorian writers took over from Carlyle and *Fraser's* the anti-dandy cult, and derived from it by antithesis the major moral affirmations—of work, of home, of duty, of responsibility, of struggle—that made up the Victorian frame of mind. Thus the rebellion against Victorianism by the dandies of the 1890s, and then again of the 1920s, may legitimately be called revenge or reaction, another episode in a long serial conflict, which itself has no clear-cut beginning or end. Victorianism was a deliberate assertion of patriarchal and matriarchal "maturity," imposed against opposition as much as the dandyism of the '90s and the '20s was to be. We may see cultural history as an alternation of such hegemonies, as first one and then another temperament established dominance over the others amongst the most articulate members of a generation.

In France there was no real equivalent to Victorianism, because there the major talents of the 19th century did not all cooperate in the service of the "mature" values. The voice of the *Sonnenkind* was heard much more loudly there because in France young people in rebellion implicitly adored the Adonis, the young-man, and so made the dandy a significant figure, a hero. Besides the explicit dandyism of Baudelaire, Barbey d'Aurevilly, and Villiers de l'Isle Adam, there was a powerful *Sonnenkind* ferment in the work of the great novelists, notably Stendhal, Honoré de Balzac, and Théophile Gautier, which made them a valuable resource to the English artists in revolt against Victorianism. The tradition of dandyism, Cyril Connolly noted in 1938, is purer in France. It was writers like Stendhal, Balzac, and Gautier who made George Moore say that in France the 19th century had been the century of the young man, while in England it had belonged to the girl—"The young girl may evoke no ideal but that of home . . . [and].

. . . that most odious word, papa."[5] Moore made it his lifework to win the English novel for the young man (that is, for the dandy), and he was a powerful influence on the '20s in England.

Moving somewhat outside the world of letters, it was in 19th-century France that the clown became a prominent imaginative symbol and *commedia dell'arte* performances became a cult of the *Sonnenkind* sensibility. At the Théâtre des Funambules an acrobat-mime called Jean-Gaspard Deburau played Pierrot in a series of farces, and Jules Janin, the critic, wrote *Deburau—Histoire du Théâtre à 4 sous* about him in 1832. Janin described this Pierrot as representing the people and therefore as resisting the authority of established bourgeois culture. Théophile Gautier, the poet, took up the same idea. He said, "Pierrot, pallid and slender, dressed in sad colors, always hungry and always beaten, is the ancient slave, the modern proletarian, the pariah, the passive and disinherited being, who, glum and sly, witnesses the orgies and follies of his masters."[6] Janin wrote about the way Deburau's life outside the theater, and inside the family troupe, also followed the lines of Pierrot's story. Deburau grew very melancholy as he became famous, suffered disappointment in love, and nearly committed suicide. As a result of Janin's book, he became a popular, or fashionable, figure of hopeless love, a haggard Hamlet, silently offering roses to his beloved Columbine, who scorns or at least betrays him. Gautier wrote pantomimes with ambitious themes for Deburau to perform, and even better ones were written by Jules Champfleury.[7] Both these men had a wide circle of friends among the French intelligentsia—including, for instance, Baudelaire; and all that circle became very interested in the *commedia dell'arte* styles and myths, and particularly in the figure of Pierrot, who came to represent to them the artist in modern society. In Baudelaire's years of personal dandyism, 1842–1844, he wore black all the time and shaved off his beard and moustaches. The pale and naked face, on Pierrots accentuated by the skullcap they wore, the subjugation of all animal and even physical exuberance, was the mark of Pierrot dandyism.

This was, of course, a very poetic and pathetic kind of dandyism. In *The History of Harlequin,* Cyril Beaumont describes Pierrot thus:

"The butt of fools, the sport of bullies, the vanquished in love—he has aroused sympathy from his first birthday. His pale, woebegone countenance, his listless air, the long drooping sleeves of his jacket, everything about him incites pity." Harlequin, on the other hand, is to be associated with the rogue figure. Beaumont quotes Riccoboni, an authority on the subject: "Down to the 17th century Harlequin's performance consisted of a series of extravagant capers, of violent movements and outrageous blackguardisms. He was at once insolent, mocking, clownish, and above all, obscene." Of course the character of these figures when played varies with the actor—one man's Pierrot may be quite Harlequin-like, compared with another's; but one constant difference is suggested by the fact that Harlequin always carries a stick. Within the history of French literature, Arthur Rimbaud and Raymond Radiguet, the tough boys, have been nearly as much Harlequin-figures as Jules Laforgue and Paul Verlaine have been Pierrot-figures.

The Columbine figure also has a history in French culture parallel to those of the two men. We recognize a Columbine, for instance, in the heroine of Dumas fils' very popular play *Camille.* The whore-with-the-heart-of-gold emerged in the 1830s and has been popular ever since, although its most brilliant manifestations have perhaps been the work of actresses rather than of writers. Sarah Bernhardt is the most famous of 19th-century Camilles, but most of the great actresses seem to have played the part, and many off the stage as well as on it.

The three figures are mutually dependent. Pierrot is romantically in love with Columbine, she is realistically resigned to Harlequin, he cheats on both but relies on both. It is a self-completing pattern, a comic-melancholic cycle, objective-correlative to the same mood as is the merry-go-round and the circus ring, also images dear to dandy writers (see the merry-go-round image at the end of Evelyn Waugh's *Decline and Fall).* And the three separate figures, insofar as talented people used them as mirrors in which to contemplate their own fates, were icons of the *Sonnenkind* cult. Of course these figures—especially in their more popular manifestations—did not incite their audiences to any serious rebellion against bourgeois values. But they did tend to evoke—and the more intensely they were felt the more they had this effect—a private world of beauty and emotion that was hostile to the worlds of work and marriage. Those parents who uneasily disliked their children's absorption in such stories were not mistaken.

Painting too played an important part in the cult of the *commedia*. Emile Deroy, Baudelaire's friend, first suggested that Watteau's paintings were melancholy in the 1840s, and this line of thought was taken up by Gérard Nerval and Théodore de Banville, men who were also interested in the Théâtre des Funambules. It seems to have been Jules Michelet in the 1860s who first discussed the melancholy in particular of *Gilles,* the painting of Pierrot that particularly inspired Jules Laforgue. It had, of course, always been known that Watteau was painting *commedia* actors, but the idea that the paintings expressed such profound and spiritual melancholy was left for these mid-19th-century Frenchmen to discover. Modern research has confirmed their intuition by identifying elements of Christ-iconography incorporated into the figures. The artists saw themselves as performers, and saw performers as the prisoners and victims of their audiences; they thus saw themselves in an image that paradoxically, and protestingly, combined elements of both the most elevated and the most degraded self-esteem. Modern research has also revealed that the *commedia* actors are usually depicted by Watteau on "parade" outside their show-booths, being shown off to their prospective audiences before performance, a context that modern painters and choreographers have seized on. Watteau remained a figure of special interest to French intellectuals, because of his iconography, up to the end of the century. Then many modernist painters, notably Picasso and Rouault, began painting Pierrots, Harlequins, clowns, and so on. Guillaume Apollinaire, the great impresario of modernist painting, wrote *Le théâtre italien* in 1910.

Thus in the second half of the 19th century it seems that the *commedia* provided a whole set of stories and icons for French artists, an alternative to those of the classical and Christian myths. Victor Hugo, Théophile Gautier, Alfred de Musset, George Sand, all wrote about

Deburau, and in 1883 Sarah Bernhardt played him on the stage. Most important for poetry, in the 1880s Jules Laforgue worked out a poetic persona for himself based on Pierrot, which concentrated the techniques of modernism into the form that proved most fruitful for the postwar generation.[8] And it was because French artistic culture had worked these images and techniques out so fully that English artists apprenticed themselves to France in particular at the beginning of the 20th century. Paris was a magic city for Englishmen because it was the home of Pierrot.

Pierrot was a figure of fantasy, the *commedia* was a world of fantasy, and Englishmen found in them—in addition to all the things already mentioned—a triumph for the fantastic elements within the creative processes of literature and art in general. This was an important aspect of the cultural development we are going to study, the enthusiasm for fantasy and its assault on realism. Thus we shall find the Sitwells often declaring themselves the representatives and champions of fantasy, and the Leavises, in resistance, speaking for realism, in terms of a stress on artistic "maturity" and "responsibility." The close relation of modern fantasy and aestheticism to the *commedia* is implied in Harold Acton's 1962 introduction to Carlo Gozzi's *Useless Memoirs.* Gozzi was a Venetian of the decadence, who wrote fairy dramas, *fiabe,* for Sacchi's *commedia* troupe in the 1760s. He identified himself with that troupe, made his emotional and intellectual life with those actors. He was the bitter enemy of Carlo Goldoni, who stood for that realism and moral responsibility in the theater that eventually drove Gozzi and the *commedia* together out of favor. Acton, who often speaks for fantasy himself, and means fantasy often when he speaks of beauty or poetry, takes a very sympathetic interest in Gozzi. Moreover, he points out that in his own lifetime Jean Cocteau and Samuel Beckett had led fantasy to triumph in our theater. It is a triumph for Acton that French writers have done this—his "prejudice in favour of things French" was one of the things he preached to his contemporaries at Oxford—and we can link France and fantasy and the *commedia* all together.

At the beginning of this century French Literature gave the English dandies their great novel—Proust's *À la recherche du temps perdu*.[9] It turns the experience of young men, young men who refuse the adult commitments of politics, government, power, and marriage, who occupy themselves with questions of social and sexual and aesthetic taste, into the material of great art. We shall see that the English dandies of the '20s, typically during their years at Oxford, were profoundly influenced by Proust—more than by any other writer. Proust had been reproached by his literary rivals at the Lycée and later—by André Gide, for instance—for betraying literature in his pursuit of social success of the most snobbish and dandified kind, and this novel was, among other things, a self-justification. Its triumphant success redeemed dandy behavior for the English literary dandies too, and their cult of him represented a significant step for them in the aestheticization of culture—his novel came to *represent* novels for them, displacing other representatives with more George Eliot-like affiliations. Thus Cyril Connolly tells us that Proust replaced Henry James for him, that he could no longer read James after discovering Proust at Oxford, because the latter then did for him all that James had done. Connolly adds that for him as an undergraduate *À la recherche du temps perdu* was the greatest literary achievement of the century, and he tried then to talk like Proust, think like Proust, and write like Proust.[10]*

Then twentieth-century French literature also provided a writer much more like our two principals, Jean Cocteau, who was in fact something of a model for them.[11] He inherited the various dandyisms of 19th-century French art, and concentrated, purified, intensified them in his own person. He sometimes signed himself Narcisse and dressed in *commedia* costume. His combination of roles—his combination of the serious poet, painter, and so on with the impresario of modernism, with the society-page celebrity, with the admitted narcissistic *poseur*—constituted the model Brian Howard and Harold

---

* Most portraits of Proust reveal his Pierrot-identity—as do those of Kafka, another writer particularly appreciated by 20th century *Sonnenkinder*.

Acton followed. From 1912 on, says Acton, Cocteau felt the pulse of each Muse in turn and prescribed the exact regime she had to follow. The effect of those regimes was to make French high culture lighter, brighter, more playful, more skillful, more dandified. And thus the pattern of Cocteau's relationships, his passionate self-apprenticeship to more serious artists, his intrigues and flirtations with the factions of the art world, his dependence on powerful ladies of society, his dependence on his mother, his much publicized attempts at committing himself to some religious or political affiliation, such patterns are to be detected in their lives too, particularly in Brian Howard's.

But the great intellectual and imaginative experience of his life had occurred earlier. Cocteau was present at Sergei Diaghilev's debut in Paris in 1909, and he immediately attached himself to the Russian ballet in every way he could. Diaghilev gave him an artistic directive—"Jean étonne-moi"—that was to become famous and was to bear much fruit in Cocteau's subsequent career. Cocteau also attached himself to Igor Stravinsky, whom he met in 1913. He dedicated to him his first modernist book, *Le Potomak* (its literary techniques inspired by Rimbaud and Gertrude Stein), and began to cooperate with Stravinsky on a ballet almost immediately. And he attached himself to Picasso, whom he met in 1916; on his second visit to the painter, he wore a Harlequin costume under his raincoat, in invocation of the *commedia dell'arte* characters who fascinated them both. In 1917 Cocteau succeeded in creating a *commedia* ballet, *Parade,* which employed the talents of Picasso and Erik Satie as well as those of Diaghilev and himself. This was indeed quite an important achievement, a step in the history of the ballet, because it introduced the use of acrobatics, sports, and jazz. It set Diaghilev upon his second phase, which was much more French and modernist than the first; it established Satie as a composer; and it brought Picasso out of the Bohemian milieu in which he had until then been mostly known. It was in his review of that ballet that Apollinaire invented the word *surréalisme.*

Thus already in 1918, when our story begins, Cocteau's dandy-modernist style was established, and he was known; known, for instance to the two boys whose careers we shall follow. They were never to have a success comparable to his, by whatever criteria one employs, but they got from him a clear idea of the kind of success they wanted. It was from France that the English dandies took their tips in 1918, once the cultural field opened up before them, and Cocteau was the major tipster.

The Commedia Dell'arte and the Ballet

Perhaps the most important figure to both English and French dandies in 1918—and perhaps the most important figure in all 20th-century art, at least from our point of view—was the Russian Diaghilev.[12] He had taken the seedling of the 1890s and cultivated it to exotic and rampant growth in the soil and climate of Russian culture, where power and privilege, education and taste, were distributed so unequally, in such strange combinations, that the moderating and maturing and rationalizing influences of the West failed to work. In that setting aestheticism, like other Western ideas, grew to monstrous and wonderful proportions. Diaghilev then brought back to the West the imaginative cult that partly changed its temperament. And it was clearly a *Sonnenkind* cult, a cult of the young man and the artist in revolt against the world of men in all its forms, political, religious, moral, sexual.

Diaghilev was himself an aesthete—who brought aestheticism to European triumph—and himself a dandy, in every sense. Arnold Haskell says that that was the first thing one saw about him— "someone intensely interested in his person, the actual physical rather than the adornment . . . [sic] . . . the careful toilette . . . the sense of poise—the whole stance shows his knowledge of his absolute superiority." Haskell speaks also of the feeling of *weight* he gave, and of the sensuous fleshy mouth in a face without lines, in a head too large for its body, under a shining opera hat. The whole image is Oscar Wilde again, of course, and Diaghilev *was* another embodiment of the '90s, in talents, taste, face, body, clothes, personality, and sexuality.

It is of some importance to his work even that Diaghilev was a homosexual. For his creative life as impresario ran parallel to his sexual life, in an apparent sterility as far as creative art went (unlike, say, Proust) which he turned into fecundity by a sexual paradox. He made the dancer Nijinsky first his lover and then his choreographer, slyly displacing Michel Fokine and inspiring Nijinsky to become the company's chief ballet-creator. Diaghilev's superb taste and knowledge-ableness, also his massive personal authority and conviction, were made manifest in this new Nijinsky, the choreographer, and in the ballets he created. These works of art were the children of Diaghilev's sexual passion. The same thing happened later with Léonide Massine and Serge Lifar. (It did not occur with Fokine and with George Balanchine, who seem to have been creatively independent of Diaghilev.) These men created ballets under the spell of Diaghilev's passion, and he created through them.

Diaghilev's homosexuality was also important in a more general cultural sense. He was one of a group of brilliant homosexual artists who played a big part in the modernist art that rebelled against the 19th-century consensus. French high culture was early dominated by almost overt homosexuals. In England the equivalent groups—Bloomsbury and the people we are studying—were paralyzingly discreet about their sexual heresy. But in France the styles of artistic behavior were more flamboyant, and the individual artists supported and encouraged each other in that flamboyance. Thus Proust and his admirer, Cocteau (for Cocteau, Lucien Daudet, and Maurice Rostand were the three early promoters of Proust's reputation), were also enthusiastic members of Diaghilev's audience and entourage. Proust was there for the opening night of Diaghilev's 1910 season—the performance was *Scheherazade,* of which he said to Reynaldo Hahn, "I never saw anything so beautiful"—and attached himself socially to the company. Hahn, who was perhaps Proust's closest friend, went back to St. Petersburg with the Diaghilev company. He composed the music for their *Le train bleu,* a ballet whose story was written by Cocteau. It is the *cooperation* of all these people in these enterprises that is so significant. Cyril Connolly has spoken of the great homosexual trailblazers in the arts in the early 20th century who avenged on the bourgeoisie the latter's killing of Oscar Wilde. He calls the persecution of Wilde England's Dreyfus case and names as the avengers Diaghilev, Proust, Cocteau, and Gide.[13] Diaghilev was the leader, or impresario, of them all. This role of impresario was as important as that of homosexual in the model he provided to other men of sensibility.

Diaghilev's career in the arts began in 1893, when he inherited his mother's money and started to buy pictures. He had wanted to make a career in music, but Rimsky-Korsakov discouraged his composing, and his singing also failed. He knew he had no creative talents in painting or in literature. By 1895 he had decided that he wanted to become an impresario. He wrote to his stepmother that year:

> I am firstly a great charlatan, though *con brio;* secondly, a great *charmeur;* thirdly, I have any amount of cheek; fourthly, I am a man with a great quantity of logic, but with very few principles; fifthly, I think I have no real gifts. All the same, I think I have just found my true vocation—being a Maecenas. I have all that is necessary save the money—*mais ça viendra.*

This is a classic piece of dandy prose in the best sense.

In 1897 he organized his first exhibition of paintings, which was international in scope and without social message, and thereby declared war against the leading group of Russian artists outside the academies, the Ambulants, or Wanderers or Peripatetics—so named because they wanted to take Russian art to the provinces in a series of traveling exhibitions. These artists were trying to create a Russian art that would serve a healthy Russian culture, and they followed as best they could the prescriptions of Nikolai Chernyshevsky, the author of *What Then Must We Do?,* who was a hero and martyr of the radical movement of the 1860s. In 1865 thirteen such rebels against the Academy had founded an Artel des Artistes, a communist association of painters, and they proposed to create a Russian art concerned with Russian social problems, according to Chernyshevsky's precepts. Unlike Diaghilev, they wanted to fight the established world of men in Russia with its own weapons, of political and social ideas, and manly and womanly images.

The Ambulants were typically, and by intention, of lower social origin and made no grand tours of European metropolises, such as Diaghilev and his friends made. And when Diaghilev called his magazine *The World of Art,* it was in deliberate defiance of their "union of artists"—so named to sound as if they were artisans—and in exaltation of the spiritual freedom of art. He wanted to save art in Russia from serving a social or political function. His first editorial said:

> The artist is confined in a mysterious way. . . . The creator must love only beauty. He must only commune with beauty, where his divine nature is manifest. . . . The reactions of art to earthly difficulty are not worthy of the soul of the Divinity. . . . The sole function of art is pleasure, its only instrument beauty. . . .

His magazine was a very beautiful thing in itself, printed on special paper, and with blocks specially made in Germany. He took immense pains to see that it was perfect in every detail, and used every kind of coaxing, pleading, and bullying to get his friends to cooperate with him. Besides his close friends, Alexander Bevois and Walter Nouvelar, Valentin Serov and Léon Bakst were the most prominent contributors, and through Bakst the influence of Aubrey Beardsley was noticeable. Thus, through this magazine, and later through the Ballets Russes, the influence of the '90s returned in triumph to Western Europe just after England had seemed to have defeated it. Literature and music were also discussed in the pages of *The World of Art,* but painting continued to be Diaghilev's main interest.

The World of Art was a living antithesis to the world of men in Russia. All the men associated with the magazine treated the revolution of 1905 aesthetically rather than politically. Indeed, for them 1905 was the year not of the revolution but of Diaghilev's great exhibition of 18th-century Russian art. (Just so Cocteau could say seriously that the greatest battle of 1917 was that over his ballet *Parade.*) Soon Diaghilev sought an international scope and freedom for his creativity. In 1906 he organized the Russian exhibit for the Salon d'Automne in Paris; in 1907, the concerts, that presented Feodor Chaliapin to the West; in 1908, a production of Moussorgsky's "Boris Godunov." And in 1909, the Ballets Russes de Diaghilev made its debut, presenting Benois' and Fokine's *Le Pavilion d'Armide,* danced by Anna Pavlova and Nijinsky, Ida Rubinstein's *Cleopatra,* Fokine's *Polovtsian Dances,* and *Les Sylphides,* with Nijinsky, Karsavina, and Pavlova. This season was one of the great events of the artistic history of the 20th century, and it was the work of the dandy impresario as much as of any of the artistes or artists who contributed.

From 1909 on, Diaghilev lived in hotels out of half-unpacked suitcases, with bills that had to be paid at the last minute—usually by rich patrons. He spent immense energy on getting the right people to come to his exhibitions and performances and to meet the performers, and he often rebuilt parts of a theater and hall to get the perfect setting. He was now doing for all Europe, and beyond, what other dandy-aesthetes had done for their own countries—dominating all the arts to make them the vehicle for that temperament.

In 1911, the coronation year of George V, he came to London, where his ballets made as immense an impression as they had in Paris. Osbert Sitwell says that the company's performance of *The Firebird* changed his life: "Now I knew where I stood. I would be, for so long as I lived, on the side of the arts." Harold Acton says that for many an artist then young, *Scheherazade* was an inspiration equivalent to that of Gothic architecture for the Romantics, or Quattrocento frescoes for the Pre-Raphaelites. But it was not only aesthetes who so reacted. *The Times* in its very first reviews was both enthusiastic and perceptive, seeing, for instance, the superiority of what Diaghilev was doing to what Pavlova did as an impresario of ballet. It said of *Carnaval:* "It is immensely serious as Art, but never for a moment serious as Life." This was a distinction that it took much longer to make prevail in literature. In some sense all British artistic life seems to have capitulated to the Ballets Russes immediately. Rupert Brooke said: "They, if anything can, justify our civilization. I'd give anything to be a ballet designer."[14]

1911 was also the year Diaghilev began to build a year-long ballet program around Nijinsky, who had been dismissed from the Imperial Theaters in Moscow for dancing before the Empress Dowager without wearing trunks over his tights. The element of sexual display and sexual provocation was always a part of the ballet; there was a scandal at the first night of *L'Après-midi d'un faune* in Paris because of Nijinsky's simulated orgasm at the end. And there was also the scandal of hysteria and madness—there had been Serge Legat, who cut his throat; there was Nijinsky, who went mad; and there was to be Felix, the Spanish gypsy brought to London to instruct Léonide Massine in Spanish steps, who was found crazily dancing on a church altar on the first night of the ballet he had been used for. These scandals only extended the exotic intimations of ballets like *The Rite of Spring* into more comprehensible terms. They surrounded the pure and precise art of the classical ballet, and the pure and lyric pathos of Pavlova's kind of dancing, with something more lurid. Diaghilev's taste after all expressed a flamboyant temperament, largely in revolt against the world of maturity and responsibility.

1911 was also the year of Stravinsky's *Petrouchka,* about the unhappy fairground figure. This is particularly important to us because Petrouchka is another name for Pierrot, and from this time on the Ballets Russes were also major transmitters of the iconography of the *commedia dell'arte.* The Russian dancers had in St. Petersburg been taught acrobatic and mimetic tricks by the Italian dancers Cecchetti, Brianza, and Legnani, who had brought them something of the heritage of the *commedia* directly. Cecchetti traveled with the Diaghilev company for many years as an instructor. Beside *Petrouchka* and *Parade,* Picasso's curtain for which Sacheverell Sitwell described as the greatest modern painting of Harlequin, there were many other ballets that were essentially *commedia* performances, like *The Good-Natured Ladies, Polichinelle,* and *Carnaval,* which in 1910 introduced Lydia Lopokova, then fresh from school, later to marry John Maynard Keynes. She played Columbine, and always excelled in parts of that kind.

It will be clear from what has already been said that the *commedia* and the ballet were preordained allies, if not manifestations of the same principle. While the ballet could give the *commedia* figures the prestige of the highest and purest art, the *commedia* figures could give the ballet a set of meanings that was widespread and vigorous at many levels of culture in the years 1910–1930. Diaghilev became the general of an army of cultural images. The *commedia* figures had become prominent in the art of the 1890s, in both England and France. They had always been seen in the music halls, where for instance Dan Leno's clowning was much admired by dandy-aesthetes like Max Beerbohm. They became a great popular success in the early movies, in the work of Charlie Chaplin, Buster Keaton, Laurel and Hardy, and the Marx Brothers. They inspired modern poetry, as we shall see, through Jules Laforgue and T. S. Eliot. And in the 1920s they entered fiction.

Thus it may be helpful to see Evelyn Waugh's comic fantasies as a kind of *commedia dell'arte*. They differ from ordinary novels in the way that *commedia* differs from ordinary drama. We might say, for instance, that in *Put Out More Flags* Ambrose, Basil, and Susie are versions of Pierrot, Harlequin, and Columbine. And in American fiction it is surely undeniable that Fitzgerald's Gatsby, Tom, and Daisy are Pierrot, Harlequin, and Columbine, and Hemingway's Brett (in *The Sun Also Rises*) is another, different, Columbine. Waugh admitted that his Virginia Troy—in his war trilogy—was the last of a line of heroines that included Brett and others. (He also admitted that *The Sun Also Rises* had influenced him at the beginning of his career, and that he had enjoyed Fitzgerald—significant admissions because he was chary of such attributions.) Other fictional heroines Waugh mentions in that tradition—Michael Arlen's Iris Storm and Aldous Huxley's Myra Viveash—were in fact derived from Nancy Cunard, an Englishwoman who in real life enacted the Columbine femme fatale.

I want to suggest that the postwar sensibility as a whole was in some sense dominated by the *commedia*. The femme fatale, the dandy, the rogue, and the naïf are after all *commedia dell'arte* kinds of categories. The rogue and the naïf might be compared with Harlequin and Pierrot directly, but the similarity is rather that they are both products of the same way of conceiving human types and life's conditions. Also the fantasy, naïveté, and formalism of the genre seem particularly suited to the *Sonnenkind* temperament. This becomes clear as soon as you contrast it with "realism," the artistic mode or modes appropriate to a mature and responsible temperament. The elegance and artificiality and unseriousness of the *commedia* figures, their power to excite lyric velleities of melancholy, gaiety, and nostalgia, even while including the coarsest farce and the most brutal sadism, madness, and murder in their action—these traits set them in opposition to all moralistic "realism."

Moreover, modernism entered English poetry under the clear aegis of Pierrot. T. S. Eliot's poetry in his Prufrock volume of 1917, and to some extent in *The Waste Land,* was heavily influenced and inspired by that of Jules Laforgue, who was himself inspired, and indeed obsessed, by the figure of Pierrot. The latter's 1886 volume, *L'Imitation de Notre Dame de la Lune,* includes forty-one poems, of which twenty-three deal with Pierrot and his ideas. Laforgue transformed his other major objective correlatives, Hamlet and Lohengrin, into versions of Pierrot, pale, ineffectual, ironic, yearning figures. It has been pointed out that Laforgue did better than either Stéphane Mallarmé or Villiers at creating a modernist drama, and that his "Hamlet" is a foreshadowing of Samuel Beckett's *Endgame*—indeed, all Beckett's work uses the iconography of the *commedia,* modified. Columbine/Woman is to this Pierrot a ruthless life-mechanism whose impulses derive directly from the Unconscious, a force that the poet/Pierrot ineffectually tries to control or resist with the forces of sensibility and reflection. Laforgue was devoted to Watteau's painting of *Gilles,* but he made his Pierrot essentially a modern figure and gave him the background of the modern Waste Land.

This vision of the Waste Land of modern civilization, with or without the artist portrayed standing against it as Pierrot, was the crux of the first, twenties, phase of modernism. Eliot said that his discipleship to Laforgue had been a "sort of possession by a stronger personality," and for poems like "Portrait of a Lady" this does not seem extravagant. Later Ezra Pound came to know Laforgue too, through Eliot. Pound wrote an essay on him in 1918, and shows his influence in "Hugh Selwyn Mauberley." Malcolm Cowley says that Laforgue was *the* poet for his generation of American poets, and that Hart Crane, Allen Tate, Maxwell Bodenheim, Walter Arensberg, and Wallace Stevens, among American poets, seem all to have learned from him. Whether or not a Pierrot figure is recognizable in their verse, the Waste Land townscape, the fragmentation of the composed sentence, the mutterings and chantings of madness, lyricism, philosophy, science, these are always to be found.[15]

Of course Laforgue had not been the only Pierrot poet. Verlaine wrote Pierrot poems, J. K. Huysmans wrote a "Pierrot sceptique," and Adolphe Willette drew Pierrots (and contrastive Moors) quite obsessively. Willette founded a literary review called *Pierrot* and entitled his memoirs *Feu pierrot.* Twenty-one Pierrot poems by the Belgian Albert Giraud, entitled *Pierrot lunaire,* were set to modernist music by Arnold Schoenberg in 1912. The *Sprechgesang* he devised for them later became familiar to all Europe as the appropriate music for modern urban melancholy, because it was used by Kurt Weill for Bertolt Brecht's operas. Giraud's poems are full of the familiar Pierrot motifs— moons, madness, murder, squalor. These motifs surface in such poems as "Mondestrunken," "Columbine," "Le Dandy," "Valse de Chopin," "Madonna," "Der Mond," "Gebet an Pierrot," "Galgenlied"—song of the gallows, and "Enthauptung"—beheading. Thus Pierrot was a figurehead and a banner in many of the attacks launched by the modernist arts against philistia. And for at least the first decade after 1918, the *commedia,* in the form of the ballet mostly, brought to England a tremendous liberation of temperament. The magic of its images set free the *Sonnenkinder,* released them from their social servitude to old social forms like cricket.

C. P. Snow's protagonist in *The Search* observes, apropos of an afternoon at Lord's cricket ground, that the game of cricket was the supreme expression of Edwardian England, just as the Russian ballet was the supreme expression of Edwardian Europe. This is a very suggestive conjunction, for it seems undeniable that the two did serve similar functions in comparable countries—each was a sumptuous ritual celebrating beauty and style and grace and youth—but they did so to very different ends. The ballet was much more aesthetic, much more sexual, much more of a media-happening. While all the secondary phenomena of cricket—the team spirit, the village green, the school-training, the afternoon outdoors—led one back from connoisseurship to social responsibility, the ballet lured one on into a closed world of fantasy, where exquisite swans and princes leaped and died for passion and wizards in jewelled masks wove spells to weird and thunderous music. The ritual of cricket was completely subdued to, subordinate to, the large rituals of "life"—the serious things like government and marriage. The ritual of the ballet was insubordinate, implicitly in revolt against such seriousness.

In 1918, moreover, the two can be seen as historical alternatives. Alec Waugh loved cricket, to his father's delight, but his attempt to teach it to his younger brother Evelyn only made the latter hate it. Evelyn, on the other hand, loved Diaghilev and the ballet. This difference, more clearly than anything else, marked the way in which the older brother belonged to a whole older generation, even though only five years lay between them. Of course there were dandies in that older England also, but they gloried in the game of cricket, and so were manly heroes too. The public school and university novels of the period make a cult of the frail figure in white, whose tirelessly elegant strokes, all through a long, golden afternoon, save the team—and who later, though in scarlet now, saves the regiment out in the desert, still crying "Play up and play the game." (See, for instance, Sir Henry Newbolt's novel of 1911, *The Twymans,* with its celebration of the national and imperial values made manifest in "the mere beauty of the white young figures shining so coolly in the slant evening sunlight.") Men as acute as Ronald Knox and John Buchan found in such images satisfaction for quite passionate feelings. But there came a time, and it was 1918, when such images would no longer satisfy those feelings, and Diaghilev's images drove those of cricket out of imaginative circulation. In *Greenmantle,* John Buchan's novel of 1916, some British heroes in Turkey are assaulted by the spirit of madness and evil made manifest in a performance of dionysiac dancing that is compared to the Ballets Russes. To fight off this spirit takes all their public school training, for it is the spirit of the times. This moment when the images changed—naturally a time of peril for the public schools and for all the old England—was the epoch of the *Sonnenkinder's* bid for independence.

Chapter Two

England in 1918

The Men of Action

Fathers and Sons

OF COURSE AN event purely in the aesthetic dimension of English culture, such as the performances of the Ballets Russes, could not by itself create a profound change in the value and image structure of that culture as a whole. It was the Great War of 1914–1918 that gave such a profound shock to Britain's national life that the cultural implications of the ballet could take effect in so many young imaginations, enabling the cult of the *Sonnenkind* to break free from its traditional subordination. The war had the effect that the sons of England no longer wanted to grow up to become fathers themselves. Instinctively but also consciously, they wanted to achieve themselves as sons, as Children of the Sun, and that marked a profound change from prewar England.*

---

* What I say of England was true of all the countries of the West. In varying measure the Germans, the French, the Russians, the Americans, all felt a similar reaction against the

But the war delivered its shock to a culture that was already in some ways uncertain of its imaginative values. England in 1914 was far far from being the vigorously expansive country of mid-Victorian times, and its imaginative life was no longer organized around strong images of responsibility and maturity. That life was already more in thrall to the beauty of the matriarchal mystery, in the novels of Thomas Hardy and D. H. Lawrence, and—less seriously—to young-man images. To understand the impact the war had, we must take account of that Edwardian relaxation, which was often unseriousness, self-indulgent hedonism.

For there had certainly been dandies in England before 1918, and powerful images of them. The 1890s had left their mark on even popular heroes, like Raffles, the gentleman cracksman, and Sherlock Holmes, the brilliant detective, and Anthony Hope's charmingly bored young men. There had been rogues, and celebrated as such, in Rudyard Kipling's immensely popular work. There had been naïfs; what else are Conrad's Lord Jim, Pater's Emerald Uthwart, and the pathetic heroes of A. E. Housman's poems? In such books, and popular romances like A. E. W. Mason's *The Four Feathers,* there is a concentration of feeling about and upon these handsome young men in uniform, who so often don't know quite what they are doing or what is happening to them, whose soul is in their pink cheeks and ready smile and puzzled stubborn frown. The plot usually separates the naïf from his natural social context, so that he is morally bewildered, makes blunders, and eventually dies in consequence—a fish out of water. A classic example is American, Herman Melville's Billy Budd, but the English cases gain extra significance from the emphasis on their Englishness, extra poignancy from their lushly English settings. The pathetic or tragic naïf

---

fathers. I limit myself to England not to imply a contrast but to give myself a chance of delineating these complexities accurately. However, it seems to me likely that the English phenomenon was in some ways larger than the equivalent in France and Germany—and certainly than in Russia and America. England had seemed respectable still in 1914, and it became in some ways notably naughty. The manifestations of "decadence" in other countries were sometimes more flamboyant, but their establishment values seem to have been less completely pervaded and changed by the *Sonnenkind* influence.

was an English theme. "To my generation," says Auden (and Orwell said much the same), "no other English poet seemed so perfectly to express the sensibility of the male adolescent" as A. E. Housman.[1]

The theme was acted out in real life, moreover. Rupert Brooke's death in the war and Housman's poetry about it express a similar range of feelings—express an adolescent death-wish, as T. C. Worsley says in his pages on Brooke in *Barbarians and Philistines.* Worsley quotes one of Brooke's last letters on the apathy of some Englishmen in the war: "And I really think that large numbers of people don't want to die . . . which is odd . . . I've never been quite so happy in my life." Worsley points out that this is the source of the exultation in Brooke's war poems that made him a national hero—as when he told his contemporaries to thank God for "matching them with this hour," so that they could turn away from the dreariness of *life,* "turn like swimmers into cleanness leaping." This source is what Winston Churchill explicitly saluted in his eulogy of Brooke in *The Times,* saying that Brooke had expressed better than anyone else Youth's "thoughts of self-*surrender.*" Moreover, Worsley traces this death-wish back to Brooke's consciousness of having been the perfect public schoolboy, having been fulfilled in adolescence.

> I had been happier at Rugby than I can find words to say. As I looked back at those five years I seemed to see almost every hour as golden and radiant, and always increasing in beauty as I grew more conscious; and I could not and cannot hope for or even imagine such happiness elsewhere. . . .

When the war gave him a certainty of what God wanted of him—to kill Germans—he admitted that in peacetime and maturity he had been miserably uncertain. In Brooke's letters and poetry we can see the Adonis myth of prewar England being acted out, and in his contemporary legend we can see how everyone else understood that myth.

In 1914, then, English culture was no longer Victorian. Its dominant images were no longer those of maturity and responsibility; some of the liveliest ones were already young-men images. But they were still in a "safe" relation to the paternal and maternal values the country ostensibly lived by. The moral defiance characteristic of French high culture, the amoralism of Diaghilev's aestheticism, still felt un-English.

Thus, the naïf was very much a felt presence in English culture before and around 1914, but, together with the dandy and the rogue, he enjoyed only a limited scope, a diminished pathos, a reduced fate, because larger values from the world of men entered his story to over-shadow him—the army he enlisted in, the war he was fighting, the England he was serving. These young men, once they had been loved, had to die, because there was no place for feelings that seriously idol-ized them in that England. (The stories about them reproached the adult world, but only implicitly; after 1918 those reproaches became explicit.) Just so, the pre-1914 dandies had to be punished, like Dorian Gray, or had to die, like Flavian, the dandy-poet in Pater's *Marius the Epicurean*—a young man who "as with the privilege of a natural aris-tocracy, believed only in himself, in the brilliant, and mainly sensuous gifts, he had, or meant to acquire"; for such young men, to die of fever was the only acceptable end.

The rogues, interestingly, did not have to die. Kipling—this was his genius—brought his heroes into a more viable relationship with the dominant values and their cultural images than dandy or naïf could achieve. His rogues usually had—like Kipling himself—useful trades at their fingertips. They were respectable citizens of the world of work. More important, they lived by a private code that rebelled against the official values but also harmonized with them. They were rogues but also men. So it was appropriate to show them to us at the stories' ends fruitfully serving England, although typically they were doing so at some far-flung frontier of the empire. Kipling still had to exile his rogues.

But after 1918 *Sonnenkinder* needed neither to be killed off nor exiled, because the ideals of patriarchal virtue no longer commanded the general imagination. Young men no longer wanted to grow up to be men—that is, they did not want to be fathers-husbands-masters.

For what the Great War had meant to England, from our point of view, was *public* disillusionment with the ideals of maturity cherished there before. On July 1, 1916, an attack began on the Somme front in which 100,000 men were lost, on the Allied side alone, on the first day. It took the Allied armies three months to advance three miles, and England alone lost 500,000 men in those months. The disaster was of such a magnitude that it was recognized as such immediately, and a change in national leadership and national direction began forthwith. David Lloyd George took over from Lord Kitchener at the War Office, and by the end of the year was prime minister; and he refused to send General Haig any more reserves to have slaughtered. But on the men of keen sensibility among the young, the effect of the Somme was something much too profound to be satisfied by a substitution of one man for another as prime minister. They felt they had been betrayed, and by their fathers—by England's fathers.

Among the dead were most of the starry spirits of the generation born between 1890 and 1900, the leaders and elder brothers of those who survived. The men we are concerned with here, who were born between 1900 and 1910, nearly all lost an older brother or a father— they lost them at very least by four years absence from home, but often too by death. Among Old Etonians, for instance, of the 5,600 who served in the war, 1,150 died. Eton's College Election of 1908, Aldous Huxley's Election, consisted of sixteen boys, of whom six were killed in the war. They were remembered. We hear, for instance, of Henry Dundas, cousin, in effect elder brother, and hero to Robert (later Lord) Boothby, one of Churchill's political lieutenants in the Second World War. Dundas was captain of Oppidans at Eton, captain of the rugby team, later scholar of Christ Church, Oxford. Boothby began his autobiography of 1947 by describing Dundas and saying, "I still cannot write about him with restraint." And of course, Eton was only typical of the public schools. Alec Waugh says that of the forty-four boys who went to Sherborne with him, eighteen were killed in the war.[2]

The most famous group of white hopes who died included Patrick Shaw Stewart, Charles Lister, Edward Hornby, Raymond Asquith,

Aubrey Herbert, and the Grenfell brothers. These were friends and heroes to quite a large circle, who survived to tell of them in post-war England, including Ronald Knox and John Buchan, Hilaire Belloc and Compton MacKenzie, Duff Cooper and Lady Diana Cooper (née Manners); these friends still mourned them, both as friends and as England's lost hope, forty years later. They were commemorated more than once by Evelyn Waugh, who never himself knew them. These were England's last true *Sonnenkinder,* whole images of glamour, of which the postwar dandies were only the sharp-edged fragments.*

These golden lads had been sacrificed, it was felt, by "the old men," "the generals," and "the hard-faced men who did well out of the war." Siegfried Sassoon's book of poems, *Counter-Attack,* published while the war was still being fought, demanded a crushing of England's rulers, to follow on the crushing of Germany's. Nevertheless, Lloyd George's Coalition party, which had been in power the last two years of the War, won 516 seats in the 1919 Election, while Asquith's Liberals won only 27, and Labour 62. The memory of the war was sentimentally institutionalized: a war memorial was built in every village in the country; there were tours organized to see the war cemeteries, and to see the trenches; there was a Soldiers' Dog Fund, and even a fund to bring home in honor the troops' transport horses and mules. Thus the war was made a source of feelings that energized the most conservative kinds of patriotism. There were small-scale strikes among the soldiers, it is true, and even a Soviet of 2,000 British infantry in Calais

---

* I am sorry this is confusing, but the truth is that the Sunchild image was both more and less present in England after the war. I use the image of sharp-edged fragments to suggest the paradox that the dandy, rogue, and naïf were less completely *Sonnenkinder* than the golden lads who died in the war; but they were more radically *Sonnenkinder* in their hostility to other values and their determination to remain young-men and not to become men. The golden lads of England in 1914 promised to go on to become mild and magnificent men. They implicitly promised the world that one could combine Adonis with Apollo (and Ares and Zeus), radiant youth with magnificent manhood. (America has gone on producing such *Sonnenkinder*—for instance, the Kennedys.) The types who became dominant in post-1918 England were narrower, sharper—both more and less Sonnenkinder, therefore. I must ask the reader to be ready for the difficulties this ambiguity brings.

in January 1919, which Lord Byng was sent to deal with. But it soon became clear that there would be no spontaneous or national movement against war and the policies that led to war. The dandies felt it had been left to them to keep that memory alive. Cyril Connolly remembers his father-figure at Oxford, the don Maurice Bowra, saying to him often while he was an undergraduate: "Whatever you hear about the War, remember it was far far worse: inconceivably bloody. . . ."[3] It had been a determining experience for Bowra, and he meant it to be one for Connolly too.

The War was Mosley's great experience, and one he constantly invoked in his politics. As late as 1930, in *The Sunday Express,* he described modern man as "a hard, realistic type, hammered into existence on the anvil of great ordeal. . . . For this age is dynamic, and the pre-war age was static." His Fascism was a soldier's socialism, designed for "the War generation." In his autobiography, *My Life* (1968), he described the experience of Armistice Day, 1918.

> Smooth, smug people, who had never fought or suffered, seemed to the eyes of youth—at that moment age-old with sadness, weariness, and bitterness—to be eating, drinking, laughing on the graves of our companions. I stood aside from the delirious throng; silent and alone, ravaged by memory. Driving purpose had begun; there must be no more war. I dedicated myself to politics.

As Robert Skidelsky shows, in his *Oswald Mosley* (1975) his frequent changes of party (which did much to discredit Mosley politically) derived not from lack of party loyalty so much as from his belief in having a trans-party constituency, the war-generation youth.

W. H. Auden remarks, in *A Certain World,* on the enormous change brought by the war in the cultural value of "soldier" and "fighting." He says that from then on even the *Iliad* became uncomfortable reading for men of Western culture, who henceforth found the Chinese poets more congenial on such subjects, because they were pacific and hedonistic. But the reaction was not simply pacifist. Philip Toynbee tells of reciting the word Passchendaele to himself as a boy "in an ecstasy of excitement and regret,"[4] and both George Orwell and Christopher Isherwood felt deprived by not having fought.[5] Orwell told Richard Rees that his "generation must be marked for ever by the humiliation of not having taken part"; while Isherwood felt the war to have been the great test of his manhood, which he had somehow failed even though he had had no chance to take it. (Presumably because he had failed all the smaller tests of "manhood" of which that was the great archetype.) For these men the war meant not so much the great mistake as the great failure—it meant the political diminishment of England and the moral enfeeblement of the new postwar Englishman. But both interpretations aroused the same feeling of the horror of the war, and of the official patriotism that had energized it. The men of letters remembered that, and since the nation as a whole was not going to change, they in some sense withdrew from the nation.

There was also a feeling that England's old hierarchical order had been injured irreparably, in various ways. One was the breaking up of old landed estates, a process that had, in fact, begun before but that felt like a postwar phenomenon. Another, less tangible, was the decline in sports. Sports had been a national enthusiasm that had linked the aristocracy in particular with the working class—Lord Lonsdale, the sporting peer, was said to be the most popular man in England; but after the war England's prestige in sports passed to America, and its pride and enthusiasm in sports generally failed. And along with the decline in the aristocracy's privileges and inhibitions went a decline in its responsibilities. The arduous habits of charity amongst aristocratic ladies, and of justice amongst aristocratic men, did not survive the War.[6] The old order of society, the fathers' order, was morally diminished.

Economically speaking, England ended the war hopelessly in debt to America, and although it was owed even more by other nations, it felt itself humiliated. Moreover, major industries were crippled. The Indian market for cotton goods was lost for good to Indian and Japanese industry; and in June 1921 there were two million unemployed.

This bore out and gave force to J. M. Keynes's remark, in *The Economic Consequences of the Peace* (1919), about the "great capitalist class in England," that "the terror and personal timidity of the individuals of this class is now so great, their confidence in their place in society and in their necessity to the social organism so diminished, that they are the easy victims of intimidation. This was not so in England twenty-five years ago, any more than it is now in the United States." This marks the economic defeat of the fathers of England, of which the sons were quick to take imaginative advantage.

As for politics, Lloyd George, "the Man Who Won the War" (his campaign slogan), was forced to resign his premiership in 1922, when Horatio Bottomley was sent to jail—a man who had earned large sums during the war by making recruiting speeches and drumming up the crudest war fever. (It is worth noting the coincidence of these events with the publication of *The Waste Land* and *Ulysses*—modernism in literature sailed on the tide of revulsion from war and politics.) Lloyd George was succeeded by the Conservative, Andrew Bonar Law, who campaigned on the slogan of "Tranquillity"; the modern age was felt to be an age of noise—jazz and cocktail parties, among other things— and Law promised a return from all that to old dignities and order. He was succeeded, in 1923, by Stanley Baldwin, whose campaign slogan was "Honesty" and who promised a return to the old decencies and severities of the world of men. In terms of politics, England may be said to have put back the clock—at the cost of exiling the most able politicians from power.

In terms of the arts and entertainment, England yielded, gradually and grudgingly, to the contemporary mood. For instance, Kipling had in 1918 eighteen more years of literary productiveness ahead of him; but T. S. Eliot, reviewing a new volume of his verse in 1919, remarked that it would not cause the least ripple of response amongst literary readers. And he was right. The rest of Kipling's work was, as far as literary readers went, unreadable. Kipling stood in 1918 for the last imaginative attempt to revitalize the country and save it from becoming over civilized; and so to young men of "feeling" he was odious and ridiculous. They looked for young-men images that would be frankly hostile to "England"; they looked for decadence and for the flag of rebellion against the fathers.

Stanley Baldwin, the Conservative leader, stood for the political reaction against that decadence, a reaction that could succeed much better than Kipling's after 1918 because Baldwin operated outside the realm of the arts, where the *Sonnenkinder* were strong. The first twenty years after the war have been called politically the Baldwin Age, and he was indeed a dominant and representative figure; his Conservative successor, Neville Chamberlain, and his Socialist rival, Ramsay Mac-Donald, were equally men of the past. And Baldwin had clear cultural affiliations, too, with the old England. He was first cousin to Kipling, his aunt married Edward Burne-Jones, the Pre-Raphaelite painter, and he himself had literary tastes, epitomized in his liking for Mary Webb. He was an honest and honorable man, so shocked by the debts that Britain had acquired during the war and could not pay, that in 1919 he anonymously gave £120,000 (20 percent of his fortune) to the Treasury, and hoped that other people would follow his example. He was a country squire, a cultivator of his inheritance, a pious traditionalist, a father. He felt uncomfortable in postwar Britain, even in that very unmodernist section of it to be met among Conservative politicians. He was shocked by the members of the inner circle of Lloyd George's government in 1921—the premier himself, Winston Churchill, F. E. Smith, Austen Chamberlain, men of intellectual vivacity and considerable cynicism, to some extent rogues. Baldwin led the revolt against them on moral grounds, and when in power he did much cleaning up of British public life—and was both valued and hated for what he did. Among his more honorable enemies were the newspaper magnates Lord Beaverbrook and Lord Rothermere, who had acquired such power in the previous twenty years that even Lloyd George had avoided quarrelling with them.

Baldwin is a representative figure also because he was identified with "the fathers," "the old men," those who had "betrayed the young," even within his own family. His son, Oliver Baldwin, accused him of that in so many words. Oliver had gone to Eton but hated it, and after the war he rebelled against England in many ways. He became a member of Parliament, but as a Socialist, and refused to go home or speak to his father during most of the '20s. There was great bitterness of feeling between them, as there was between many other fathers and sons.[7] Soon he fell under Mosley's influence, and became one of the founder-members of the New Party in 1931. Skidelsky, in *Oswald Mosley,* describes him as "The fair-haired Oliver Baldwin . . . spoilt, unstable, homosexual, and naive." But this syndrome of traits, here so cavalierly dismissed, belonged to a type of great importance in England then. Another example of father-son bitterness was to be found in the royal family itself.

King George V was England's Hindenburg; he stood for the "old England," in politics, personal appearance, family life, the arts, everything. He was valued as a symbol of the old times by his older and more conservative subjects, and was treated as a joke by many of the younger generation. Brian Howard named his book of poems, mockingly, *God Save the King;* Harold Acton proposed similarly mocking toasts to "Our dear, good King"; John Betjeman's poem on the king's death (in 1936) is all about his love of shooting and stamp-collecting and his concern for "correct" clothes.[8]

Whereas the Prince of Wales, who was always in conflict with his father, was the most public image of the *Sonnenkind* of the period—so youthful, slender, blond, ingenuous, pleasure-seeking. He was young England, so fair-haired, clean-skinned, straight-backed, quite at home in his various uniforms; but at the same time he was Pierrot, in his fragility, his transparency, his smallness, in the immobility of his hangdog eyes and long melancholy mouth. To translate the Pierrot figure into English upperclass terms at that moment of history took a touch of genius, and the grace of his pathos on a hundred photographs convinces one that, in his own terms, the Prince knew what he was doing. Harold Acton, according to Cyril Connolly, adored the prince. Whether he was seen sympathizing with the out-of-work miners in South Wales or dancing the Charleston in Mayfair, he was the symbol of the "new England," of the forces that would change the old England. After he succeeded to the throne (as Edward VIII), the "King's Friends," those who supported him in the abdication crisis of 1936, were led by the rogue figures, Lloyd George and Churchill, Beaverbrook and Rothermere, Mosley and the Fascists; his enemies were led by the father figures, Baldwin and the archbishop of Canterbury. And in the world of society hostesses, both Emerald Cunard (Nancy's mother) and Diana Cooper were the prince's friends and had promised themselves a cultural renaissance when he became king. The former was publicly blamed for his match with Wallis Simpson, which caused the crisis.

Thus in the families of both major Establishment symbols, the king and the prime minister, the sons rebelled. The enormous success of Warwick Deeping's novel, *Sorrell and Son* (1925), surely owed something to its theme, which was the close relationship that a postwar father, an unemployed and divorced ex-officer, gradually builds up with his young son. This was a theme that meant a lot to the readers of 1925.

A lot of hopes had been invested in the prince. And roughly at the same time as Edward VIII abdicated, T. E. Lawrence died in a road accident. Lawrence of Arabia was the other great figure of the *Sonnenkind* in public life. He had, of course, a much more substantial achievement behind him in leading the desert tribes in rebellion against Turkey during the war. When he came back to England in 1919 he was believed to have refused the crown of Arabia, and he was certainly the prince of Mecca. But his glamour was due to his style as well as to his achievement. He was portrayed everywhere in his long robes and long hair, looking the reverse of the military type, with his virginal and narcissist beauty. He appeared the reverse of, say, Haig or Kitchener on the recruiting posters; yet while they had failed as soldiers, he had brilliantly succeeded.* He was the "new England" as

---

* Basil Liddell Hart, his admirer and biographer, was the man who had exposed Douglas Haig. Hart, another of the young voices ignored by the fathers, kept pressing for a mechanization of Britain's army, but in vain. Only at the level of creating a cultural image did he succeed; his biography of Lawrence, which came out while the latter was alive, went into many printings immediately.

much as the prince. It is noteworthy that the Fascist movement in England both supported Edward VIII in the abdication crisis and sought to attach Colonel Lawrence to its cause; moreover, Winston Churchill, the leader of the "King's Friends," wanted Lawrence made minister of defense; the two figureheads meant much the same thing. It is also significant that neither of these two potential leaders, nor any of the other *Sonnenkinder* in politics, came close to power.

The one who came closest was of course Oswald Mosley. He was born in 1896, into a very wealthy country-squire family, and brought up by an adoring mother and grandfather—his father had early repudiated all family and social responsibilities. It is worth noting that Rolleston, the Mosley estate, employed thirty men as gardeners alone, before 1914; and that the men of the family were traditionally keen boxers who staged matches in the ballroom and took part in them themselves, like Regency rakes. Mosley described Rolleston as "a classless society" because of things like that, but they rather suggest that social hierarchy was so deeply accepted there that it needed no props. From this heritage he brought with him into politics the older, ranker masculinity of the rogue-rebel.

He was an expert swordsman as well as boxer, enjoyed military college, where he got into trouble for rough practical jokes, and served during the War in first the Royal Flying Corps and then the trenches. In 1918 he entered Parliament, and was soon known to be its most brilliant young member. This was the judgment of Beatrice Webb, for instance, and it was endorsed by Winston Churchill and Lord Rothermere. He was a brilliant speaker, debater, and election winner, a very hard worker, and a man of ideas. Skidelsky demonstrates how often Mosley's solutions to the problems of the day were more original and practicable than those actually adopted. He was also a figure in the society life of the times, and in the intellectual-artistic world—several novels of the 1920s depict him. He was a film-starishly handsome man, nicknamed "The Sheikh," with highly polished manner. Skidelsky titles one chapter "The Dandy of the Revolution," and cites a newspaper article about him in 1927, which says that Mosley

is the one member of Parliament who has "made an art of himself."
He apparently modeled himself on Ferdinand Lassalle, the brilliant
dandy who long challenged Marx for the leadership of the German
socialist movement. But there was always a suggestion of violence
about Mosley, in his practical jokes as well as his politics, which made
him a Harlequin rather than a Pierrot.

Of course there were many minor public figures of both father
and son. Among the emblems of boyish beauty, there were Rupert
Brooke (posthumously), Charles Lindbergh, George Mallory (a
climber of Mount Everest), and the actors John Gielgud and Ivor
Novello. And among the public fathers there were many of a cruder
conservatism than Baldwin or George V. The most official figure to
interfere in the arts and entertainment was "Jix," Sir William Joynson-Hicks, who became home secretary in 1924. He was the man
responsible for the closing of D. H. Lawrence's exhibition of paintings in 1929, and the closing of the mails against *Lady Chatterley's
Lover*. He also conducted a vendetta against the night clubs that
were such a feature of the period and tried to prevent immorality in
the public parks of London. Other literary victims of official puritanism, beside Lawrence, were Radclyffe Hall, the Lesbian writer,
and Aldous Huxley, whose novel *Antic Hay* was denounced as blas-
phemous by James Douglas (a well-established book reviewer and
critic). "Jix" was born in 1865, the year Lord Palmerston died, and
he said that he prayed he might inherit "Pam's" spirit; indeed he was
much more Victorian in his morals than Palmerston himself. He was
the father as policeman. He had signed the pledge to abstain from
alcohol when he was fourteen, became a solicitor, married money,
and made a political career out of representing society's suspicions
of everything new and different. He was, for instance, anti-Semitic
and hostile to all aliens.

To balance "Jix" we should take note of John Buchan, who was
a more respectable carrier of the styles of the fathers' England, the
England of Arthur Balfour and Herbert Asquith, into the new age—
where he employed them in both the imaginative arts and adminis-

trative politics. He was born in 1875, the son of a Scottish minister, and was brought up in austere surroundings and traditions. But the austerity was modified by a very genial and humanist historical imagination derived from Walter Scott, which Buchan also inherited; and after Glasgow University he went to Oxford, where he won the Stanhope Essay Prize, the Newdigate Poetry Prize, the presidency of the Oxford Union, and a first-class degree. It was in some sense typical of Edwardian England that such a strenuous pursuit of the official prizes should be found in someone who came from outside England.

At Edwardian Oxford, Buchan knew that very glittering group that combined the young men Raymond Asquith, Aubrey Herbert, the Grenfells, and others who were to die in the war and also the older men who admired them, Hilaire Belloc, Maurice Baring, and Ronald Knox. In Buchan's account of Raymond Asquith (the son of the prime minister) one hears a note of that prewar dandyism, that over-ripeness and weary elegance, that only the Scotsman in the group could quite escape:

> He had come up from Winchester with a great reputation, and also, I think, a little tired. His scholarship was almost too ripe for his years . . . his whole-hearted delight in Oxford and his lack of reverence for the standards that ruled outside it . . . delicate ribaldry . . . easily the most finished debater of our time.[9]

(Similar phrases can be found in Dorothy Sayers's descriptions of Lord Peter Wimsey, and the serious half of her conception of him is, indeed, rooted in John Buchan's Oxford, although the other half belongs to P. G. Wodehouse and the Aldwych farces.) Lord Milner tried to get Asquith to come to South Africa to join the "school" of brilliant young men whom he trained there to become administrators of England's colonies. But Asquith was too much the dandy to go-too fastidious, too whimsical, too hard to please, and too unwilling to commit himself. Buchan did go, and made a success of that as of everything else. The difference between prewar and postwar England is that in the former there were still Buchans to balance the Asquiths.

In 1927, Buchan became a member of Parliament, in 1933 lord high commissioner to the Church of Scotland, and in 1935 governor-general of Canada. All the time he was writing books that were enormously successful; the first had been published in 1898. His books were of two main types: biographies of great historical figures like Montrose, Cromwell, and Caesar; and popular romances, about adventure in the service of England.

He wrote eleven romances in the *Greenmantle* series (of which *The Thirty-nine Steps* is the first) and three in the *Huntingtower* series; together they cover the period from 1908 to 1938, describing the exploits of one or several of Buchan's band of adventurer heroes, who have to defend civilization against the plots of brilliant but ruthless idealists, modern intellectuals with twisted natures and no traditions, mad fanatics. Buchan's heroes are men outside society and are even described as rogues, or toughs, but they are not really like Kipling's rogues. Buchan was romantically refined, and he did not really imagine his heroes as rogues, but as aristocrats, heroes of romance. They do not really rebel against the values of their fathers, they know they will soon become fathers themselves. And the interesting thing is that he based them on the young men he knew at Oxford before 1914. His romances made available to the general English public that romantic hero-worship (pre-1914 *Sonnenkind* worship) that had been the cult of an inner social circle. In the first months of the war, Buchan invented "Richard Hannay" from Sir Edmund Ironside, who had served, disguised as a German, with the German staff in the war in South-West Africa; "Sandy Arbuthnot" from Aubrey Herbert, with touches of T. E. Lawrence; "Vernon Milburne" from Raymond Asquith; and "Lord Lamancha" from Basil Blackwood. Buchan was creating a saga of heroes for modern England, quite consciously; Sandy Arbuthnot tells Richard Hannay that one of the latter's tales has the "grave good sense of the Nordic or Greek sagas."

An interesting comparable case is provided by Compton Mackenzie. He had published a very successful novel about Oxford, *Sinister Street* and was, before 1914, taken quite seriously as a writer. After 1918 he published four volumes of reminiscences about the war, of which the first was *Gallipoli Memories* (1929). The tone of the narrative is dandified (in a pre-1914 dandy style); he tells us a lot about the cut of his uniform, and his silk pajamas and the comments they caused, and describes other people often as "fat" or "oafish." Moreover, his friends are all, in his descriptions of them, unmistakably dandies. Eddie Keeling, with whom he shares "fits of laughter" at everything, has an "exquisite Foreign Office drawl"; Cecil Aspinall has a monocle and "exquisite clothes"; Guy Dawnay is "a fragile figure with something of exquisitely fashioned porcelain in the finely chiseled features of his small face." And Mackenzie gives us a sharp sense of how these Englishmen were forced into a further dandyism by their contact with the Australian troops in Gallipoli. (Australia stood in the same relation to England as America did, as usurping younger brother or new heir.) These troops apparently oppressed the English officers by staring them in the eye and challenging them to force a salute. They sneered openly at the "breeding" that they thought the Englishmen were priding themselves on. Mackenzie describes the Australians as "rough" and "tough," and implicitly acknowledges a superior virility in them. Seeing them bathing, he describes them as "naked heroes," so many Ajaxes and Achilles (and there is much invocation of Homer in his book, so this phrasing makes them primitive and mythical) and speaks of their jungle litheness and powerful grace. The English working-class troops, on the other hand, he presents as small and comic and nearly always as loyal and deferential.*

In postwar England, Buchan was still a great popular success, both as a public servant and as a writer. But he was also completely outdated imaginatively, because the hegemony of temperament had passed to the rogue and the dandy. His sister, Anna, who wrote under the name of "O. Douglas," published a series of thirteen novels between 1912 and 1940, which are a successful feminine equivalent of her broth-

---

* In the 19th century, the English had looked huge to Americans as well as to themselves—see Emerson's *English Traits*—had looked harder, heartier, more patriarchal than other men.

er's. The Buchans show how England came to depend on the children of the manse and of the Border, on Scotland and the Presbyterian Church, to create Establishment images of men of action and their womenfolk. The Buchans served the fathers and mothers of England in the battle for their sons' souls.

But they contended not only with foreigners and aesthetes, like Diaghilev, but with English rogues, who more heartily and cheerily denied official values. Such men had always been there, but their cynicism and antinomianism had a different effect and a different significance after 1918.

Uncles for Rogues

John Buchan lived in the Cotswolds, not far from Oxford, in the 1920s, and he made his house there a link between the university and the great world of affairs by bringing together visitors from both Oxford and London. Another great success in the styles of the old England, who also kept close connections with both Oxford and London and who dispensed lavish hospitality at a house in the Cotswolds, was F. E. Smith.[10] His house, Charlton, was panelled inside to look like his Oxford college, Wadham, and there were always lots of undergraduates there, playing golf, tennis, or bridge or riding. But Smith's influence on those undergraduates was, from our point of view, significantly unlike Buchan's influence.

Smith was a brilliant lawyer, politician, and orator, who was Attorney General from 1915 to 1919, Lord High Chancellor from 1919 to 1922, and Secretary for India from 1924 to 1928. He was of comparatively humble origin, but rose from being plain Mr. Smith to become a knight in 1915, a baronet in 1918, a baron in 1919, Viscount Furneaux in 1921, and earl of Birkenhead in 1930.[10] It is typical of his career that one of its great moments should have been the prosecution of Sir Roger Casement in 1916. Casement was on trial officially as a traitor (having sought German aid for an uprising in Ireland) and unofficially as a homosexual; and both charges took on extra luridness from his prewar career as a moral reformer, a crusader against colonialism.

He was the enemy of the fathers in all these ways. Smith secured his condemnation, and execution, by a remorseless and vindictive prosecution. In the postwar years Casement became a hero, or at least a martyr, to young English intellectuals and artists, and to them Smith seemed a typically brutal philistine of the Establishment. He was said to have threatened to resign if Casement were reprieved; he was said to have forged the homosexual diaries. But officially Smith was a legend of success, and he spoke often of the "glittering prizes" that life still had to award, to spur on other men to compete. He loved Oxford and attended Union debates, and intervened in them, all through the 1920s. He made himself a mentor to all the young men he thought might "succeed"—for instance, to Robert Boothby, who went up in 1919 and who became secretary of the Conservative party's Canning Club there. In his autobiography, Boothby remembers Smith fondly as still an undergraduate at heart, although lord chancellor of England and the most worldly wise man he had ever known. It is part of the same pattern that Boothby should describe himself as a Tory radical, who could politically follow only such leaders as Lord Randolph Churchill, or Lloyd George, or—his actual leader—Winston Churchill. Smith was a great friend of Winston Churchill, and shared the latter's fondness for cigars and whisky, gambling, and high-living—Smith was said to smoke cigars even while bathing. His wife, moreover, was a great friend of Brian Howard's mother. Thus his example and his maxims acted with peculiar immediacy on both Randolph Churchill and Brian Howard, two of our principal *Sonnenkinder.*

Smith was a kind of uncle to such young men, and in a larger ideological sense than may at first appear. Like Buchan, he incited them to compete for what he called the "glittering prizes which life still has to offer," but unlike Buchan, he at the same time conveyed an attitude of unscrupulous roguery about the "rules of life." He was in most ways anti-idealistic, and very scornful of, for instance, Woodrow Wilson. The famous phrase of his just quoted occurred in an attack on idealism in politics, made in a speech to the students of Glasgow in 1923. When he ran for election to the post of chancellor of the University of Oxford, the dons there found him "too worldly." To them, Smith stood for champagne, titles, and success—success achieved by force of personality and force of intellect, and also by bending the rules. Beaverbrook called Smith "the cleverest man in the kingdom," and the phrasing implies the competitive worldliness of both men. They were wicked bachelor uncles to the *Sonnenkinder* of the 1920s, not pious father-figures like Baldwin and Buchan.

Winston Churchill himself was another such figure. He was, of course, a *Sonnenkind* in the old style—the kind who never dreamed of rebelling against manhood himself, because in his day (in his country and class) a young man could confidently blend the brilliant impudence of youth into the solid power of manhood without any break or halt, much less any change of direction. He had been a rogue-rebel, idle at school, an instinctive breaker of all the rules, a breakaway from party and class, who yet believed in "tradition"—who believed in nothing *but* tradition. He could rebel against all the father-sponsored values in his own life, and yet present himself as a father-figure to England. He could do this with authority (as his son Randolph could not) because he was born in 1874, when England and Queen and Parliament were massive presences that no amount of high-spirited impudence could shake. Randolph came of age in 1932, in the middle of the Depression; Winston in 1895, when England was still the greatest country in the world, governed by the greatest men. Winston could afford to take every short cut to greatness himself, to break the social contract and climb on the dullards' backs, because he and they all believed instinctively in the greatness they were part of. As long as a rogue can do this, he may make a great patriot too. But when he no longer has that instinctive belief, he may become a menace or nuisance to his society. This is part of the difference between the rogue-uncles of 1918 and their rogue-nephews.

There were other such uncles, particularly to be found in the circle round Churchill—for instance, F. A. Lindemann, later Lord Cherwell, and Max Aitken, Lord Beaverbrook. (To some degree the famous hostesses, Diana Cooper, Emerald Cunard, Sybil Colefax, and oth-

ers, provided a feminine equivalent for *Sonnenkinder* all the way from
Robert Boothby to Harold Acton.) Lindemann as an intellectual and
a scientist we shall discuss later, but it is worth spending a moment
here on his function as uncle.[11]

Lindemann was an exotic figure in English society. His father was
of a rich Franco-German family, his mother an American, and his
temperament dramatized that alienness his fellows felt in him. His
mother had been handsome, dominating, full of vitality, and he had
loved her very much early, resented her very much later. His emotional life as he developed was characterized first by a series of close
emotional ties with other men, whether heroes like Churchill or followers like a favorite student, Bolton King, or his valet, Harvey; and
second by a division of the world into a few such friends and many
small fry whom he ignored as long as they didn't get in his way. He
was a fiercely competitive man, at work and play (he was an almost
professional tennis player), a great intriguer, a passionate resenter of
slights, a passionately loyal adherent. He loved power for himself, but
even more he worshiped it in others. He cultivated the friendship
of the great landed families, the leading politicians, and the richest
industrialists—the men of power. He spent nearly every weekend at
the greatest country houses. He was a dandy and a snob for serious
as well as trivial reasons, a lover of luxury and aristocracy, of brilliant
men and beautiful women, and of the high style.

Lindemann was himself a brilliant scientist, who had studied physics in Germany and had from 1908 until the war worked under Walther
Nernst in Berlin, where he knew Albert Einstein and Max Planck.
In 1919 he became professor of physics at Oxford, where he built the
Clarendon Laboratory up from more or less nothing into a position
of scientific eminence. Oxford became his home and sphere of influence, although he was very unpopular with most of his colleagues.

His two greatest friends were F. E. Smith, whom he met in 1919,
and Winston Churchill, whom he met in 1921 and with whom he
first collaborated on the anti-strike newspaper that Churchill brought
out during the General Strike of 1926. Churchill and his lieutenant,

Brendan Bracken, and Smith, campaigned for Lindemann when he sought political office at Oxford; and he put all his skills at Churchill's disposal in national and international politics. Churchill would often say, "Prof has a beautiful mind," and it was in fact an instrument that he made great use of; during the Second World War Lindemann was his closest and most constant adviser, on far more than scientific matters. Lindemann had, his biographer tells us, a "canine devotion" to Churchill. Politically, of course, the two men were natural allies. Both wanted the country governed by brilliant men who would make use of traditional methods and beliefs; neither had any interest in the average man or full democracy, equality, or liberty; both had a keen interest in *Realpolitik* and war. Lindemann favored hanging and flogging as civil measures, worked on weaponry in time of peace, and admired the Roman Catholic Church for the severity of both its discipline and its theology. Fairly clearly, this is not just a matter of politics, but of intellectual temperament. Einstein, for instance, was an emblematic figure of naïveté to Lindemann, a criminally naïve simpleton who should never have been allowed outside his laboratory. The electricity of Lindemann's life flowed away from Einstein and toward Churchill.

In sum, Lindemann was not a *Sonnenkind* himself—he was too much the counselor for that, and perhaps too Faustian and tormented also—but he was a lover of *Sonnenkinder,* an uncle to young men like, for instance, Randolph Churchill and Frederick Furneaux, Smith's son. He gave them a great deal of attention, singled them out from their contemporaries, treated them as his intellectual equals, flatteringly expected them to win "life's glittering prizes," and conspired with them against institutions and their petty laws and their petty pedagogues, such as those of Oxford itself.

This was the mode of operation of all the uncles, dispensing lifewisdom over the dinner table, or in their study, surrounded by the monuments of their success. The culminating occasion, the apotheosis of such avuncular tutorials, was Randolph Churchill's twenty-first birthday party, at which a number of famous fathers with brilliant sons had dinner together and made brilliant after-dinner speeches in competition with each other. And it is significant that few of the sons there *did* succeed in the same measure as their fathers. The rogue model their uncles offered them was not now really helpful; it stood in too scornful a relation to the institutions and their rules.

It was Lord Beaverbrook, apart from Churchill himself, who was the most substantial and long-lasting of these uncles.[12] He is also the one whose career reminds us most vividly of Kipling and the image of the rogue that we know in literature. Someone said once that Beaverbrook was not a bad man, he was a bad boy; and in many of his photographs that is what one sees, the cheeky grin of irrepressible mischievousness that was the signature of Mark Twain's bad boys and the sign of the most innocent kind of rogue. He was, moreover, like Kipling himself, a son of the empire, both by birth and by conviction. Born in 1879, Max Aitken was at first literally a bad boy, who did badly at school and afterwards up to the age of twenty-one, playing at a series of enterprises, none of which he took seriously. Then he started selling bonds and took part in Canada's boom-prosperity of those years; he was a millionaire by the time he was twenty-eight, and among his early friends, James Dunn, R. B. Bennett, and I. W. Killam all became multi-millionaires, richer than Aitken himself. Aitken's essential loyalties went to his men friends, above all to father-leader figures like Bonar Law and later Churchill, and to son-protégé figures like Michael Foot and Captain Wardell. His wife, although the marriage was not unsuccessful, played a very small part in his life.

Aitken came to England in 1910, a Canadian millionaire, and immediately ran for Parliament, with the help of F. E. Smith and Kipling. He was always a Conservative democrat in politics, with a special interest in the empire—he ran the "Empire Crusade" in 1930–31. Behind the political scenes he was a powerful figure; he organized the resignation of Asquith, and the succession of Lloyd George as prime minister in 1916. That was also the year in which he acquired the *Daily Express,* and began his career as a press lord. Like the other uncle-figures, he went in for champagne and cigars and beautiful women—he sent every year on his birthday and for Christmas £100 each to a number of society beauties. Prominent among these was Lady Diana Cooper, Evelyn Waugh's friend, who was also given, for instance, a car by Beaverbrook when she got married. He was an uncle to her, and to Daphne Weymouth, and Venetia Montagu, and Edwina Mountbatten, and other beauties of the day. He was naturally a long-standing enemy of Baldwin, and of the orthodox and pious Conservatives of the fathers' type. He seems to have been one of the most successful of the uncles at winning over young men to his influence. The books about him include some by nephews who had a strong political or moral prejudice against him at the beginning of their acquaintance, but were seduced. The same was true, of course, of many other young men taken up by Churchill and by Smith. In England after 1918 a whole generation of young men was, in a sense, seduced by such uncles.

The Men of Feeling

The Undermining of the Fathers

But the young men we are most concerned with, the men of acute sensibility born between 1900 and 1910, looked to other sponsors. They had a different sense of England, and were unconsciously content—though consciously many of them denied this—to leave to America the Puritan passions and the roles of "responsible manhood." England was very much aware that America had emerged from the war much stronger than it had, that America now definitely surpassed it as a world power—and this seems to have reinforced the seductions the *Sonnenkind* image already had for it. The major masculine roles were, among Anglo-Saxons, obviously preempted by America. After the war American teams won the world championships in tennis, boxing, golf, yachting, and athletics away from England. Their sportsmen were supposed to be less scrupulous than the English— their speedboat champion was supposed to have sunk his English rival in his backwash—but this redounded to the credit of their virility. Like the Australians, they seemed rougher and tougher, bolder and solider—more male. There was a literary equivalent in figures like

Hemingway and Pound, who seemed much tougher than their English equivalents.

Most obviously, the Americans were richer than the English. They despoiled England, as by right. They bought famous English paintings, like Gainsborough's *Blue Boy* for £175,000; they bought the Christie-Miller Library, for £500,000; they bought Great Lodge in Essex and Agecroft Hall in Lancashire, and rebuilt them in America; they rented grouse moors in Scotland, paying as much as £7000 for three months—in 1927, Americans spent £750,000 in moor rents; and they referred to England as a mangy old lion, licking her sores, and as a future Denmark. This produced various and complicated reactions in England, including some slavish admiration and some bulldog determination to beat America at its own game. But the largest consequence seems to have been the defiant readiness to adopt effete or dandy gestures—and a distrust of the major masculine roles and the heartier moral tones about both cultural and political matters.[13]

Our principals could not listen to John Buchan or to anyone else who brought such pious and orthodox messages. They felt they knew from the inside how such messages got written. They were, many of them, the sons of literary families who had seen their fathers and uncles living out those values in ignoble domesticity. For instance, Stephen Spender was the son of an editor of the *Westminster Review,* John Strachey, son of the editor of *The Spectator,* Evelyn Waugh, son of an editor at Chapman and Hall; Aldous Huxley, son of an editor of the *Cornhill;* Virginia Woolf, daughter of another editor of the *Cornhill;* John Lehmann, son of an editor of *Punch.* The fathers of these men were articulate, humorous, kindly men of culture, but there was a gap, and a hostility, between them and their sons. It is notable that in all these cases there was an older child, who in significant ways stood between father and son; in Waugh's case, for instance, that brother fulfilled the father's hopes and absorbed his love. But the materials we have to work on cannot justify us in basing much on early experience. At best, we know only what these men made of that experience much later. We are on safer ground in discussing the cultural image of manhood against which they reacted, and to which each adapted his individual experience. Bertrand Russell is said to have asked John Strachey whether it was his father, his childhood, or his school that he had hated, to make him a socialist. Strachey answered, "a bit of all three"; and we too shall assume that persons and institutions merged into a single "cultural" experience for these men.

One shaping influence in the experience was, of course, literature. The typical authors of the older generation were Rudyard Kipling, H. G. Wells, Arnold Bennett, John Galsworthy, Robert Bridges, Joseph Conrad, John Masefield, John Buchan, names out of which an image of Edwardian manhood arises naturally enough. Lord Berners, one of the dandies' mentors, describes his sports master (who also had a heavy military moustache, like Kitchener) as always smoking a pipe; and says that his face "like the faces of so many of our modern English novelists, looked as though the pipe had been there first and the face grew around it afterwards."[14] This pipe-smoking line was to be continued by J. B. Priestly, C. P. Snow, Neville Shute, and others, but it had been broken by D. H. Lawrence, James Joyce, T. S. Eliot, William Butler Yeats, and the dandy and aesthete authors we shall study.

One of the striking things about the work of this latter group is the explicit rebellion against the father to be found in so much of it. For instance, Osbert Sitwell's immense autobiography is quite dominated by the figure of his father, and by the humor he wrings out of his father's oddity. Moreover, after reading that autobiography, one realizes how much of Osbert's other work, how much of his and his sister's and brother's sensibility and their careers as writers derive directly from their reaction and rebellion against that father. Another example is the work of Nancy and Jessica Mitford, in which their father too is quite a dominating presence; he appears as General Murgatroyd in *Highland Fling* and as Uncle Matthew in the *Love in a Cold Climate* series of novels. Another example is the Sitwells' friend and portraitist, Nina Hamnett; her father was an army officer, and her two volumes of autobiography are full of anger at him and glee in the exploits by which she has defied him. But what is so striking in both the Sitwells' and the Mitfords' work is the familiarity and the freedom, the purely humorous character, of their mockery of their fathers; it lacks the tension felt in, for instance, Franz Kafka's "Letter to My Father." Father is essentially an old joke to them, and the point of the individual anecdotes is just *how* crazy he is. There is no tension in the humor, no sense of sacrilege or impiety in laughing at one's father, and indeed the humor suffers from the lack of that tension. They feel sure that their audience will sympathize, will have had the same experience. And if you put these portraits together with Virginia Woolf's portrait of her father in *To the Lighthouse* and Evelyn Waugh's versions of a father, in *Brideshead Revisited* and *Work Suspended,* you get a clear cultural image of bumbling and outdated and preposterous paternity.

The atmosphere of all this writing is summed up in the title of one of Osbert Sitwell's volumes of autobiography, *Laughter in the Next Room.* The story behind that phrase is that the Sitwell family, when they entertained at Montegufoni, would set dinner tables in two rooms, one headed by the father, Sir George, and the other by Osbert; and that Osbert's table, surrounded by Osbert's friends, would be in an uproar of laughter half the time, while Sir George sat listening, baffled and infuriated, unable to participate or to prevent. Thus did the younger Sitwells revenge themselves upon their father, and thus did all England after 1918.

There are, of course, more lurid and tragic stories to be read about the father-son relations of the writers of the period. Thus Beverley Nichols begins his book *Father-Figure* (1972): "The first time I remember my father he was lying dead drunk on the dining-room floor." He goes on to detail how his father bullied his mother, swore at her, and insulted her—syphilis was a major theme of his abuse— while she suffered it all uncomplainingly. By 1929, when his literary and social career was at its height, Beverley had three times tried to kill his father—by putting aspirins in his broth, by setting a roller in motion to crush him as he lay drunk on the lawn, and by locking him out in the snow when drunk. Allied to this story, and obviously related to it, is the story of his own homosexuality—seduction by a neighbor with a gift of *Dorian Gray,* and persecution and bullying by his father. Beverley was very precocious, and wrote a novel while still at public school that was published in his second term at Oxford. He became president of the Union there, a very highly paid journalist thereafter, and published his autobiography, called *25,* in 1930. His was the classic success story of the young man of letters in those years, and behind it stood this classic tragedy of father-son conflict.

J. R. Ackerley's *My Father and I,* although it avoids melodrama and has, in fact, a less melodramatic story to tell, makes equally clear the antithetical connection between the coarsely heterosexual, Edwardian style of the father and the sensitive, literary, homosexual son. So too does T. C. Worsley's autobiography, *Flannelled Fool,* although Worsley finally found a spiritual father and family for himself at *The New Statesman,* where he became literary editor and was the employer and admirer of Brian Howard. This alienation is the tragic paradigm of the father-son relationship in this period.

There are comparatively few literary portraits of powerful mothers or powerful female presences. It was only the women who *felt* their mothers as powerful; for instance, Virginia Woolf, Vita Sackville-West, and Nancy Cunard. Of course the mothers had a powerful influence over, notably, Brian Howard and Harold Acton, but it was an influence too close, too insidious, to be objectified, depicted, and repudiated, like that of the fathers. Their mothers were figures of affection and reassurance to nearly all of these people; however they may have undermined their children's confidence in their bolder gestures, they offered no significant challenge or inspiration. Beside the fathers, they counted for nothing. This is striking when one looks back to the then so-recent work of D. H. Lawrence, E. M. Forster, and Thomas Hardy, in which the figure of the mother, or of woman, and of the earth, nature, and life itself identified with woman, is so overwhelmingly important. That erotic movement, which had seemed in the years just before the war about to release the English imagination from its enchainment to the world of men, to redeem it from its slavish slothfulness, was completely defeated.

Of course, there were continuers of that line, like the Powys brothers and Mary Webb, but they were no more the voice of the English imagination in those years than were J. B. Priestley and C. P. Snow. It was the fathers who counted—as enemies.

The world of men was undermined not only in the persons of fathers (and families), but also in the schools (and other institutions). The attitude toward school was ambivalent, because the school years are particularly important and enjoyable to *Sonnenkinder*. However, schools themselves are institutions *in loco parentis,* and so to be defied; moreover, they were the only institutions these men had to fight. By the time the first of these boys left school, in 1922, the cultural battle seemed to be won, and even Oxford and Cambridge could be ignored or used—many of these young men, for instance, came down from their universities without bothering to take degrees. But school meant a great deal to all of them—as an institution; it was the old England, against which they had to rebel. Much is suggested by a remark of Auden's, in *A Certain World,* about cold baths. He says that from perhaps 1840 until 1918 not only all boarding-school boys but all ex-boarding-school males in England had taken a cold bath every day; *his* was the first generation of ruling-class schoolboys who determined that from the moment they got away from school discipline to university freedom they would never take a cold bath again. In this symbol a dozen rebellions against the old England are concentrated.

The average "intellectual's" attitude to public school values in the 1920s is probably represented by the ambivalence of Harold Nicolson in *Some People* (1927). In one story, "J. D. Marstock," he describes his subjugation, while at Wellington, to the school hero, and his later triumph over him when they meet again and measure each other by adult and "civilized" standards. On the other hand, in "Lambert Orme," he describes meeting Ronald Firbank and being deeply alienated by him. Nicolson could not renounce the public school ethos for fear that meant allying himself to Firbank and the '90s. In his essay in *The Old School* he says, "People who have not endured the restrictive shaping of an English school are apt in after life to be ego-centric, formless, and inconsiderate."

One document of the intellectuals' experience is this volume of essays, *The Old School,* which was edited by Graham Greene in 1934. The guiding idea is set out in the preface: "Whatever the political changes in this country during the next few years, one thing surely is almost certain; the class distinctions will not remain unaltered and the public school, as it exists today, will disappear." But that tone of stern exultance expresses only half the book's attitude to the old school. Most of the contributors (who, in addition to Nicolson, included W. H. Auden, Stephen Spender, Anthony Powell, William Plomer, and L. P. Hartley) were more ambivalent than that suggests, and admitted taking much delight in their schoolboy experience. As disciplinary and even as educational institutions, the schools are sharply reproved, but as social institutions—as, in effect, the centers of dandyism—they are quite lovingly analyzed.

Hartley, for instance, wrote an essay on Harrow that deserves to partner Cyril Connolly's classic piece on Eton. "Success" was the key value at Harrow and was a very intense experience. It could be achieved "by being beautiful, by being wicked, by being a wit" and/or "by being foul-mouthed, by being daring, by being always in trouble." Here we see adumbrations of two of our categories, the dandy and the rogue, and of their modes of interaction.

> Public opinion was extraordinarily sensitive to whose star was rising and whose setting.. . . . It was this very insecurity which made school life so exciting. Every week some valley was exalted, some mountain or hill laid low.... Almost to the last it seemed glorious, the worthy goal of a life's endeavour, to wear a bow-tie and a braided waistcoat and write letters on the notepaper of the Philathletic Club. . . .

Surely it is clear that the writer remembers all this so vividly because the rest of life has not been so different in character. School was his definitive experience of institutional life, of society in its organized and purposive aspect, and he looks back on it with recognition. "In all my life I can remember no sensations more deliriously exciting than seeing Blount and Wilson make their centuries at Lords."

Anthony Powell, in his essay on Eton, tells us that the day after he arrived at school he saw a boy whistling a popular song, with his hat on the back of his head, his hand in his pocket, and "an almost perfect specimen of the world-famous Eton slouch"—one shoulder high, both knees sagging.

> This was the most sophisticated thing that I had ever seen. . . . All this elegance gave me at an early stage in my career a conception of the school of which I was never able to divest myself entirely. . . . There was a certainty about the standards of the people I found myself among which was to make the assurance even of undergraduates seem vapid and self-conscious.

Like many of the other contributors, Powell had hated his preparatory school, and he claimed he would remember Oxford only in terms of "querulous phantoms." Eton, however, was a romantic experience.

> It was assumed, or so it seemed to me, that every boy would at one time or another be in some such position as viceroy of India. Masters who failed there left to become cabinet ministers or political bosses in truculent Balkan kingdoms.

He lists the privileges that went with belonging to "Pop," the Eton Society, and says, "These may seem small things now but they did not at the time. . . . Its membership was considered life's highest ambition." His irony of tone here, as throughout his essay, does not inhibit imaginative participation in the experience, but rather facilitates it- the irony is there mostly to allow us to enter into these dangerous sentiments, this *Sonnenkind* cult.

Of course, the contributors to *The Old School* had all been members of intellectual elites within their schools, and the contemporaries they had been surrounded by were much more acquiescent in the traditions of "England," and "typically English" manliness. For an example of what the dandies called "typically English," we might look at the Borton family of Cheveney, Kent, some of whose documents have been published in *My Warrior Sons: The Borton Family Diary of 1914.** The family includes the father, who was a colonel and justice of the peace, and two sons, who both went to Eton and who both became war heroes, one in the army, the other in the Royal Flying Corps. Arthur (known as Bosky), who had been a failure in civilian life, won a Distinguished Service Order and Victoria Cross, while Amyas (known as Biffy) also won a D.S.O., was recommended for a V.C., and became an air vice-marshal. Their virtues were, as the editor says, those of discipline, courage, courtesy, kindness, modesty—the virtues Evelyn Waugh ascribes to Lady Circumference in *Vile Bodies.* Their limitations, which were hers too, derived from an inflexibility of imagination that forbade them any emotions except "official" ones, to which they could only embarrassedly allude within quotation marks. The Borton brothers describe the war and all their other experiences in the vocabulary of *Boys' Own Paper,* that decadent British ruling-class dialect against which the dandies reacted so strongly. Thus they talk of the "plucky fight" put up by "the men" in a "devil of a scrap," when they themselves have been strikingly bloodthirsty, brutal, and brave. They are proudly loyal to Kitchener, uneasily contemptuous of Asquith (a "long-haired" politician), and gruffly disapproving of their sister when she engages in war work. The women of England, they say, should stay at home; they should stay women, and leave struggle to their menfolk. Perhaps most striking in the diary is the eager competition for medals and for official approval. They treat the authorities in the War Office, and in Downing Street, as if they were the schoolmasters, who award the sports prizes without themselves being athletes—authorities about whom one grumbles but whom one never judges. They accepted the school of English society and abided by its rules and by its punishments when they broke the rules. They accepted their fathers, literal and symbolic. *They* were no rogues. They were *hearties.* But after the war, the men of imagination could easily laugh at them.

---

* Edited by Guy Slater, London, 1973.

Most of our writers came from families much more literary and cultured than the Bortons, but James Stern, who was at preparatory and public school with Harold Acton, knew this England at close quarters. In his autobiographical writings, he presents his father as "the Major," a man interested in only two things, the trees of Britain and British regimental uniforms, and a man who disciplined his sons as if they were men in his regiment. He inspected his sons' cleanliness, clothes, and hair so severely, so regimentally, that all these things took on nightmarish importance; Stern says, in an essay of 1970,[15] that he still cannot bear to have anyone touch his hair. He describes his father as "a man incapable of expressing his feelings, of little humour and few words, who saw all things in terms of right and wrong, black and white, the world through the eyes of an old-fashioned professional soldier." He addressed his son in a bark.

The bark was frightening because it would be accompanied by what we were too young to realize was an effort to smile: the massed brown needles of moustache would rise to reveal teeth normally invisible . . . like a fox at the moment of sniffing prey . . . only once did I allow myself to be trapped alone with him in the same room.

It is clear why the son of this man would find liberation at school in the company and example of Harold Acton, already a young David against the pedagogic Goliath, a brave defier of the British philistines.

Uncles for Dandies

There were still a few representatives of the nineties dandyism and aestheticism to be found, a few inheritors of its rebellion against English dullness. And there were other, less risky, semirebellions that offered some encouragement and support to the dandies of the '20s. Because these rebellions were in some sense established, incorporated into the established culture, even while decidedly hostile to the values of the fathers, we may perhaps call the rebels involved uncles to the twenties dandies, just as we have described Beaverbrook, Birkenhead, Lloyd George, Churchill, and others as uncles to the rogues. Among the dandies' uncles, we can distinguish three groups. The first we might call the contemplatives, because their dissent from the England around them was expressed by a withdrawal from it, sometimes a literal withdrawal to Italy, more often a withdrawal into the walled garden of their own group's society. To these belonged the Bloomsbury group and a similar group around Bernard Berenson and Logan Pearsall Smith. These people were all profoundly hostile to the England of the fathers, and were even dandies themselves in important ways, but they were also, in the loose sense, Neoplatonists—cultivators of ideal values. This marks the difference between them and the postwar dandies, who did not "live toward" ideal values, nor think of their group in a semicloistral way. Because of these differences, these uncles offered little direct inspiration or encouragement to the dandies.

Some members of Bloomsbury were certainly dandies—in their theories, like Clive Bell, or in their persons, like Virginia Woolf, or in both, like Lytton Strachey. But the word *dandy* is not one to sum up the essence of Bloomsbury. There was a prevailing high-mindedness about the group. Their neoplatonism linked them to a world of ideals. A true dandy, Osbert Sitwell, discussing the modern novel, said that Virginia Woolf and E. M. Forster could both be the children of George Eliot by John Ruskin.[16] He praised Gertrude Stein rather than them. Also the members of Bloomsbury were hard workers, often submerging their personal style—always so precious to a true dandy—in work that demands other terms of description. Not even Virginia Woolf's novels can be called "dandy novels"—as some of Waugh's can; much less J. M. Keynes' economics. Woolf's novels *can* perhaps be called "aesthetic"; Forster did call her an aesthete. And in her *Mr. Bennett and Mrs. Brown* of 1924 she mocked the hearty, old-fashioned novels of Arnold Bennett and his ilk, which we might fairly associate with the old familial England. But still her own novels pay elaborate tribute to the old forms of family and class and the old values.

It is only the less interesting members of the group, like Strachey, who can be circumscribed by the term *dandy*. (Incidentally, he saw more of the twenties dandies socially than any of his Bloomsbury friends did.) And it is probably significant that the Bloomsbury people were all slightly earlier in date than the people who concern us. Bloomsbury had grown up and formed itself before the war occurred. For that and other reasons it did not afford much support and encouragement to the dandies.

Another group very similar to Bloomsbury, that centering on Berenson and Smith, did support at least some of the dandies, those who gathered round Berenson at Fiesole about the year 1900. Berenson and Smith did act as "masters," quite explicitly, to individual members of the latter group—Berenson to Kenneth Clark and later to Harold Acton, Smith to Connolly and later to Robert Gathorne-Hardy—but they tutored them in the scholar and aesthete phases of their careers, rather than as dandies. Berenson and his wife and Logan Pearsall Smith put out a publication called *The Golden Urn* in 1897, which described itself thus:

> The Golden Urn is published by certain people of leisure and curiosity, who have thought it worth while to print for their entertainment some impressions of art and life, some experiments in letters. Appreciation, untrammelled thought, scholarship, its editors will welcome, but above all the loving or ironic study of the human soul, treasuring the expression of an exquisite mood far more than any excitement of drama or action. . . . Contemporary literature will of course hardly be mentioned.

The quietism is what reminds us of Bloomsbury, and the fact that it is to be achieved by semireligious means. These "certain people" are said to live in Altamura, in the monastery of St. Dion, which has a year-long ritual—worshiping, for instance, in April Youth and Dawn, Keats and Marlowe, Giorgione and Mozart; in May Love, including David and Jonathan, Orestes and Pylades; in July Rank and Pomp, Riches, and Great Ladies; and so on. "Thus freed from the feverish grind of passions and activities called 'Life,' they get a richer sense of self-conscious existence, and the burden of the world's joylessness is abated."

There were, of course, other figures whose influence went in the same direction. There was, for instance, Henry James. We find Leonard Woolf writing to Strachey in 1905, "I have just finished *The Golden Bowl* and am astounded. Did he invent us or did we invent him? He uses *all* our words in their most technical sense and we can't have got them all from him." There was also Walter Pater, whose *Marius the Epicurean* (1885) was a manifesto of a comparable withdrawal from the world; and whose "Denys l'Auxerrois" (1887) is a myth of Dionysus' return to medieval France, and his reintroduction of the gay reign of young men, after so much sad piety. Pater was the man to whom Moore dedicated his *Confessions of a Young Man,* and it was an appropriate dedication.

The second group of uncles for the dandies contained the humorists. Beside the Bloomsbury/Altamura tradition of quietism, there was a tradition of satiric humor in England that mocked the world of the fathers from an Adonis point of view—and so offered some protection to the dandies—without the dangerous overtness of the '90s. A major representative of this tradition was Max Beerbohm, whose *Zuleika Dobson* of 1911 is an Oxford novel that all the twenties dandies read with great relish, and took seriously. When Harold Acton came down from Oxford in 1925, publishers suggested to him that he write an Oxford novel, but he refused, he tells us, because he knew that Beerbohm had already written a minor masterpiece in that genre. Beerbohm's book presents us with the ideal Oxford undergraduate, the duke of Dorset (sometimes pronounced *d'Orsay),* an elegant aristocrat who gets a First without trying, is adored by all the other young men, and never falls in love. He is triumphantly contrasted with the dowdy Noaks, a middle-class type who scrapes a Second by hard work, and with the Rhodes Scholars, who display eagerness about life and use rhetoric. But he meets his doom in Zuleika, who is a greater dandy than he. She does not want men to fall in love with her, so when at first she finds the duke indifferent, she is delighted and falls in love with him. But then he softens, and she reacts against him because he has lost his virtue. I would suggest that this plot, as much as the setting, *is* Oxford.

There was also "Saki," the pen name of Hector Hugh Munro, whose best known book was *The Unbearable Bassington* of 1912. The name "Saki" was taken from the *Rubaiyat,* and the fiction written above it was full of both insolent scorn for the mature figures of English civilization and a romantic-ironical fondness for its young and beautiful boys. "There is one thing I care for, and that is youth," Munro said. Evelyn Waugh wrote an introduction to *The Unbearable Bassington* in 1947, in which he recommends it as brilliant and shows a strong feeling for its serious core of meaning. He takes Comus (the unbearable boy of the title) to represent all the boys of England in 1912. He says that since we now know that Comus was to be killed two years later—that is, in 1914—it is impossible not to hate his mother, Francesca. That is, we feel *for* the young man and *against* his mother. The book itself is more ambivalent. It presents Comus as "impossible"—a rogue-rebel—and Francesca as a charming English lady of great taste, whose prize possession, a painting by van der Meulen, turns out to be a forgery. Waugh says that it is impossible now not to see Francesca as a type of that English civilization that sends its sons to death in defense of a home whose chief ornament turns out, too late, to be spurious. (Waugh was writing just after the Second World War, remember.) He brings out the serious implications of this sense of humor.

Above all, there was P. G. Wodehouse, who took the dangerous insolence out of dandy humor and gave it a self-enclosing, self-sustaining movement of its own, built a world of fantasy remarkably indirect and playful in its contacts with real experience. This was done too by the children's books of the period, and writers like Edward Lear, Lewis Carroll, Kenneth Grahame, and Beatrix Potter were much appreciated and employed by the writers of the '20s. It was also done by some of the detective-story writers, notably G. K. Chesterton, Ronald Knox, and Dorothy Sayers. But it is still fair to say that Wodehouse's position is unique, because of the fervent protestations of devotion to him from so many of the writers we are concerned with. Evelyn Waugh described him as one of the age's masters of literary technique; Anthony Powell called him "a kind of genius"; John Betjeman said, "I have loved every word he has written, I think I have read every one from the days he appeared in *The Captain*"; Malcolm Muggeridge and Claud Cockburn, although political and religious radicals, are equally enthusiastic. And it is not merely a matter of style and technique. They love reading Wodehouse because they love the fantasy he created, which is a fantasy of prolonged adolescence. As Waugh says, "for Mr. Wodehouse there has been no Fall of Man. . . . The Gardens of Blandings Castle are that original garden from which we are all exiled." This is the same point as F. R. Leavis makes *against* Wodehouse when he says that the whole point of his humor is the refusal of maturity. (It was appropriate, from every point of view, that Leavis should have been the one critic to protest against Oxford's conferring an honorary doctorate upon Wodehouse in 1939.)

Wodehouse wrote about cricket more or less seriously for cricket magazines, and in novels too, until 1909, when he hit upon his own line of mocking and self-mocking fantasy; this appears half way through the novel *Mike,* with the introduction of the character Psmith. Evelyn Waugh says that the sacred flame touched Wodehouse at that point. And it is perhaps worth noting that Waugh's conservative father and elder brother loved Wodehouse just as much as Waugh himself and his satirist son, Auberon. Wodehouse unites the generations, across the divide of temperament we are studying. This is so because he was an enthusiast for cricket and other aspects of the old England, but he saw that that enthusiasm could no longer be conveyed directly, that it must be expressed in fantastically humorous form. However, his humor is so innocuous that it appeals directly to both father and son, to both pre-1914 and post-1914 Englishmen, and there is a strong note of gratitude—gratitude for pleasures shared with others whom one found it hard to reach in other ways—in the appreciations of his work.

Psmith, then, was the first achieved Wodehouse character, but he had elements of Raffles in him and was too nearly related to themes of Edwardian romance. In 1917, at the very beginning of our period, Wodehouse created Bertie Wooster, the perfect Wodehouse hero, and Jeeves his valet. Bertie went to Eton and Oxford, and joined the

Drones Club in London when he came down. He is tall, willowy, blond, burbling, monocled, and innocent. He is always about to be forced into adult responsibilities by ferocious aunts or predatory girls, and always restored at the last to his delayed and infinitely delayable boyhood. The authority figures, who are typically aunts—"aunt calling to aunt, like mastodons bellowing across primeval swamps"—are always discomfited, and the authority mocked in them is reinvested, mockingly, in Jeeves, the servant. The same process is observable in the handling of language, which mockingly mixes clichés—"I do adore evening service in the summer. All that stilly hush and what not. . . . " The virtuoso play with cliché has been, as I have pointed out elsewhere, a major feature of English culture in this century. And Wodehouse seems to have been popular reading, in the semi-highbrow way typical of his cult, at Eton especially early. The Eton provost of the 1920s, M. R. James, used to tell the boys that Wodehouse's command of English was unrivaled. Wodehouse, then, has been an important influence on English dandyism, creating—with his enormous sales over sixty years—an audience ready to appreciate the bolder flights of writers like Waugh and Powell.* His sales increased even during the Second World War, when the scandal was raised about his broadcasting for the Germans, and his cult expresses some significant rebellion against all seriousness on the part of the intellectuals. Auberon Waugh calls him the Father of the Great English Joke.

And then, in addition to the quietists who withdrew from English heartiness and the humorists who mocked it, there were various representatives of "Art," who also represented an alternative to the domi-

---

* Waugh seems to have reworked Jeeves and Wooster in making one of his most serious fictional statements about modern England. In *Officers and Gentlemen* the aristocratic young dandy Ivor Claire and his plummy-voiced plebeian corporal Ludovic are surely a reworking of Wodehouse's comedy duo in the terms of national tragedy—Ivor turns traitor under pressure, and Ludovic, a sinister intellectual Jeeves (or Bunter, as Dorothy Sayers calls her equivalent), is ready even to murder his commanders. Waugh is showing what will happen when military commissions are given to real-life Bertie Woosters and Peter Wimseys, with their attendant Jeeveses and Burners. There are many examples of this kind, showing how the semimythical *Sonnenkind* material first current at the lower levels of England's cultural life gradually was taken up for serious artistic uses.

nant ethos. This was the third group of uncles to the dandies of 1918 England. One of these, already mentioned, was Henry James, another was Arnold Bennett; but the two with most personal contact with our two principals were George Moore and Norman Douglas, two Grand Old Men of letters.

Moore had lived in Paris from 1870 to 1880, and he came back to England determined to win for English fiction the same freedom of subject matter and perfection of form as French fiction had achieved. He made a great deal out of being an Artist—spoke of "composing" his works and of the hard discipline of the Muse—and out of opposing the British philistine. He rewrote his own books even after they were in print; beside making extensive changes in proof, and adding or omitting chapters in new editions, he would substantially rewrite a story when it was reprinted.

Art was his escape from his native society and the religion he was brought up in—from democracy, from Jesus, "the pale socialist of Galilee," and from pity, "that vilest of the virtues, unknown to the great pagan world." His *Confessions of a Young Man* gave a defiantly assertive ring to the phrase "young man"; the book was a manifesto of the *Sonnenkind,* and a directive to young Englishmen on how to become one by going to live in France.

Moore was devoted to France, the land of Art and of Love. He instructed his biographers (he had appointed more than one before he died) in how he had won freedom for English fiction and how he had loved with a grand passion. (He spoke roguishly of "passages d'amour," but respectfully of the great love tragedies.) The object of his grand passion, which began in 1894, was Emerald, Lady Cunard, the great patron of opera in England and later the protectress of many of the dandy writers. Lady Cunard, an American by birth, played an important part in the dandy artistic life of England in this period. Harold Acton says she civilized its aristocracy—the Barbarians, as Arnold called them—but did it so lightly that they never knew. For instance, she would buy a dozen copies of a book by an unknown author and give one each to "ambassadors and statesmen and others beyond his ken." She persuaded the Prince of Wales to visit Moore (his only official honor) and secured the King's Bounty for James Joyce. She arranged official employment for painters as war-artists during the war. Above all, she was a patron of music. She is said to have secured an opera season for London in 1921, she gave £1,000 to the Imperial League of Opera in 1928, and she was one of the founders of the New Opera Syndicate in 1933. For her opera took the place of religion, says Sacheverell Sitwell. She allied the arts to luxury and aristocracy and was a great friend to many of the dandy aesthetes, especially Harold Acton. She presented him to George Moore, with the introduction that Acton was the Beardsley of modern English prose.

Moore had an equally interesting relationship—but as great artist not as great lover—with Emerald's daughter Nancy Cunard, one of the brilliant dandy figures of the next generation. As the artist Moore was the "master" to her, and she treated him just like an eccentric but respected schoolmaster. She and her friends imitated his manner of speech to each other, and she describes him always in terms of visual caricature—as an oval white balloon or a fine white oval. But the disrespect just took the strain out of her respect for him. She sent her poems to him, and in fact he wrote a long review in *The Observer* of her first volume, *Outlaws,* in 1921.[17]

There were several strands to the connection between the twenties literary dandies and their nineties uncles. Moore was a family friend of the Howards, and prophesied Brian's literary future during his boyhood. The Howards were an artistic family, and Moore was an incarnation of Art. Harold Acton only got to know Moore when he came down from Oxford, but he then became devoted to him, admired him more than any other English novelist. On the other hand, Acton had known Norman Douglas from early on, because the Actons were an artistic family in Florence, where Douglas often stayed. He was giving Harold important advice as early as 1922. Their first lunch together the latter remembers as a significant moment of consecration to literature.[18] Douglas did not get to know Brian Howard until much later, perhaps until the second war broke out, but when he did, the connection was close. Howard took on the commission of becoming Douglas's biographer, although he never fulfilled it. It was in fact Nancy Cunard who wrote a book about Douglas, which she called *Grand Man*. Douglas may be said to have taken over the role of schoolmaster to her after Moore died. Thus the Artist uncles were very close to their various dandy nephews and nieces.

Douglas was an exile, as Moore had been briefly, but he lived in Italy, not France. And he was homosexual, which Moore was not. He was more Bohemian and penurious, more modern in style generally. And his one famous novel, *South Wind,* had much more influence on the twenties' writers than anything of Moore's. Cyril Connolly said that that book stated the predicament of the Petrouchka hero of twenties' fiction—the clever young man who is cut out in love by a coarser rival, Harlequin the Moor.[19]* Michael Swan has said that out of that seminal work came Aldous Huxley's *Barren Leaves,* Compton Mackenzie's *Vestal Fires,* and Connolly's *Rock Pool.* Douglas's hero, Dennis, is said to have established for these other writers the viability and profitability of the Petrouchka hero, who stumbles his innocent way through exotic adventure. The figure is detectable in early Waugh and Powell novels too. Douglas's books were more typically essays and travel narratives, but these too were something of a model for the younger writers. Moreover, both he and Moore were "wickeder" than Bloomsbury, and together they incited the young dandies—above all because they encouraged them personally—to defy the conventions of their society.

Neither Douglas nor Moore were dandies themselves, however. All these uncles had come to an accommodation with the fathers at points of behavior and career where the dandies wished to be provocative. Like the other uncles, they were ostensibly in alliance with the fathers. The temperamental forces they represented, in their own lives and in what they wrote, were only half-heartedly rebellious. They both were

---

* In fact, fiction seems to have been better served by making Harlequin the hero, not Pierrot. At least this seems to be true of Waugh and Nabokov, as I have tried to show elsewhere.

and were not saints of the *Sonnenkind* religion, their books were, and were not, icons for the dandies to contemplate. As scholars, or artists, or humorists, these uncles all offered something that the fathers could take with good-humored appreciation, and thus with a reinforcement of their own personas. The sons were looking for heroes and models who with every gesture and every word made the fathers uneasy. And they found this in the heritage of the 1890s.

The Defiance of the Fathers

The '90s had been the great period of defiance of patriarchal maturity and responsibility. From James Whistler's triumph over John Ruskin in the famous libel suit of 1878 until the catastrophe of Oscar Wilde's condemnation in 1895, a dandified "spirit of the '90s" was prominent, and in some sense dominant, in art in England. Ruskin had accused Whistler of being (as a painter) a "coxcomb," one of the Regency words for a dandy, and indeed Whistler, a great hero of Harold Acton's, was aesthetically as well as sartorially a dandy. This period reenacted the Regency's defiance of 18th-century respectability, but with more concentration on the arts and ideas. The Marlborough House set, around the Prince of Wales, was the equivalent of the Carlton House set around the prince regent; John Lane was the publisher equivalent of Henry Colburn, the promoter of the fashionable Regency novels; and popular novelists, from Anthony Hope to Marie Corelli, again wrote about fashionable life and clothes and tastes. Artists themselves were as a group fashionable. There were fierce quarrels between them in the correspondence columns, suits for libel, lecture tours, and so on. John Lane was able to sell nearly everything he published as a "first edition."

The style of the nineties was transmitted to the later dandies through various survivors, like Reggie Turner and Reggie Temple and the painter Charles Ricketts, also a friend and involuntary imitator of Wilde. Ricketts was a devotee of Watteau and El Greco, a theater designer like Léon Bakst and Edward Gordon Craig, a book illustrator like Aubrey Beardsley. He became a friend of, among others, the young Harold Acton. But the '90s came to the '20s above all through Ronald Firbank and the Sitwells.

Born in 1886, Firbank was homosexual and maladjusted to normal society from very early on. He withdrew from his public school, and from every similar institutionalization of the ethos he was born into. He dabbled in magic and entered the Roman Catholic Church, being prepared by Monsignor Robert Hugh Benson, who was a ritualist and occultist figure on the fringe of nineties' dandyism, a friend to Lord Alfred Douglas and a literary collaborator with "Baron Corvo." Firbank himself cultivated a number of similar occultist and "decadent" tastes, holding at arm's length the hearty philistine healthiness that oppressed him. Some were as harmless as his enthusiasm for star actresses, for black singers and dancers, and for the memory of Oscar Wilde. For instance, he was one of those present at the twenty-first birthday party for Vyvyan Holland, Wilde's son—together with Henry James, Ricketts and Charles Shannon, Robbie Ross and Reggie Turner; it was a feast of commemoration of Wilde and the '90s.

However, Firbank was also in touch with more modern and exotic developments. He went to Cuba and wrote a novel about black life there, lived in Rome and tried to join the Papal Guard. Like Cocteau, he admired Anna de Noailles, and others of that Paris circle. He himself was described as the Cocteau of England by his admirer Carl van Vechten. His own self-nomination was as the "ballerina" of literature; he told Siegfried Sassoon that the latter was a Tolstoy, digging for worms, while he, Firbank, was a Pavlova, pursuing butterflies. And indeed he appeared to live on champagne, fruit, and flowers—he was not observed to consume anything else. As a writer, Firbank was completely unsuccessful with the general public, and with the orthodox critics. During the roughly dozen years of his publishing career, which began in 1916, all his publications were paid for by himself. But he became a writer of considerable importance to both Waugh and Powell, as well as to figures more limited to the '20s. Alan Pryce-Jones says that in his time at Oxford the test of whether a man was really an aesthete was whether he owned any Firbank books.

It was Osbert and Sacheverell Sitwell who did most to promote Firbank's career while he was alive, and they did so in characteristic ways and for characteristic motives. Osbert tells us that it was in 1912, when he was aching to escape the company of his fellow officers with their "monosyllabic discussions of horses and dogs" (his father had consigned him to the army against his will), that he first began to notice a very odd-looking man at the ballet and at concerts and exhibitions, who giggled and hid his painted face behind his hand, talked in a high-pitched voice, and tripped along as if hoping to disappear. Sitwell was immediately possessed with a devouring desire to know him—Firbank seemed an entry into a world of eccentricity that would deliver him from his father's world of asserted normality. We might say that what Sitwell saw was an incarnation of Pierrot in Edwardian London. Then the war broke out and "smashed the diminutive spiritual paradise (of books and music) into which I had made my way. . . ."

After the war Sitwell rediscovered Firbank at Oxford. Having now read something by him, he persuaded him to read some new work aloud to a small audience of literary people and published it in *Life and Letters,* the magazine Sitwell was then editing. He tells an anecdote that helps one understand his enthusiasm. Firbank apparently had a local gardener come in once a day to water his palm tree when he lived in Sloane Square; when he moved to Piccadilly, he retained his services, on the condition that the man walk all the way to his new quarters, wearing a green baize apron and carrying the watering can. "We can still recall the joy it used to give us, as we sailed down the ugly desert of Sloane Street on the top of a then open motor omnibus, to see this solemn rather self-conscious procession of one, and to realize that a familiar, fantastic sense of humour was once more at play amongst us." It was Pierrot's sense of humor.[20]

The Sitwells are of great importance to our story. They were the major preceptors of the postwar generation. As D. H. Lawrence said, they taught young England how to be young. Edith Sitwell was born in 1887, Osbert in 1892, Sacheverell in 1897, and they grew up on the family estate of Renishaw, feeling very alien to all its traditions. Edith first fell in love with the Renishaw peacock, she tells us,[21] and walked round the garden with her arms around its lovely neck. She was hurt when it turned its affections to the peahen, "a most uninteresting creature in my eyes." Osbert at prep school was given an orchid every Sunday ("I was already a lover of exotics"), and Sacheverell had a fat pet lamb. These were their emblems.

They suffered a great deal, especially Edith, from early parental oppression, because their father, although himself very eccentric, was determined to form his children into perfectly normal specimens of the British ruling class. When Osbert gave him Samuel Butler's *The Way of All Flesh* to read, Sir George identified with Mr. Pontifex (most dissimilar to him in everything but his "principles" as a father) and got so angry with the book that he had to spend three days in bed. The oppression and injustice were real enough. Between 1912 and 1915 their mother was involved in a series of scandalous law suits over large debts (as much as £30,000) that she had unwittingly incurred. Sir George, although a rich man, refused to help her, and she pleaded (without truth) that she had been paying Osbert's debts—so the children felt themselves betrayed by both parents and the objects of general and public reprobation. But it was above all their father who made use of patriarchal institutions to interfere in their lives—sending Osbert into the army against his will at the age of thirty, for instance—because they refused to grow up as he understood growing up.

The Sitwells saw their escape from their sense of being inferior (as measured by their father's standards) in nominating themselves as artists, above all, poets. This they did publicly and provocatively, so that the claim always trembled on the edge of being a joke; but it was also serious, and even solemn. Edith's lines from "Colonel Fantock" identify their style as well as anything else:

> But Dagobert and Peregrine and I
> Were children then; we walked like shy gazelles
> Among the music of the thin flower bells
> And life still held some promise—never ask
> Of what—but life seemed less a stranger then

Then ever after in this cold existence.
I always was a little outside life—
And so the things we touch could comfort me;
I loved the shy dreams we could hear and see—
For I was like one dead, with a small ghost,
A little cold air wandering and lost.
All day within the straw-roof arabesque
Of the tower castle and the sleepy gardens wandered
We; those delicate paladins the waves
Told us fantastic legends that we pondered.[22]

"Delicate," "fantastic," "arabesques"—the words sufficiently suggest the whole self-stylization.

The war, with all the shocks it delivered to the established system, came just in time to give them a sense of winning their battle. Edith had been lucky enough, in 1903, to acquire a companion who understood her—a woman called Helen Rootham, who translated Rimbaud, and with whom she traveled or lived abroad between 1907 and 1914. In 1916 Edith brought out the first issue of her yearly anthology, *Wheels,* in which she published herself and her brothers, and, among others, Aldous Huxley and Nancy Cunard. In 1917 she published, with Osbert, *20th Century Harlequinade* and in 1919, *Clowns' Houses.* The culmination to this period of her work was *Façade* in 1923, which made an immense *succès de scandale* and became the public's idea of modern poetry. This work was all full of *commedia* figures and nursery rhymes.

The war brought the three siblings close together and gave them courage against the common enemy, the fathers. Osbert's poem "Corpse-Day" was early and powerful antiwar propaganda. And they led the country's rebels against all the pieties of the time. Thus Osbert, "In early youth I took a dislike to simplicity, morris-dancing, a sense of humour, and all sports." One of the best stories about him describes a fellow officer (while Osbert was in the Grenadier Guards) asking him, "Do you like horses?", a question that one can only imagine aris-ing—in that context—as a crucial test of his loyalties and as the climax to a series of suspicions against him. Osbert is supposed to have replied, "No, but I adore giraffes," and this catches many aspects of his and his siblings' rebellion against county pieties—not least because the giraffe is such a "Douanier" Rousseau animal. The Sitwells may be said to have *been* three elegantly spotted and elongated giraffes, confronting the horses of England in the latter's home paddock. They were great impresarios, party-givers, concert- and exhibition-arrangers, introducers of artists to publicists, and publicists themselves. And they early attracted attention, not unfavorably, from the literary establishment. Osbert met Arnold Bennett at the Reform Club in 1918, and when he complained that the young had no magazine in which their material could be published, Bennett offered to back one financially on condition that Osbert edited it. This was the magazine, *Life and Letters,* in which he published Firbank. The Sitwells were the leaders of Youth.

From our point of view, the symbolic date in 1918 is November 11. This is not merely because of the signing of the Armistice on that day, but also because of a party held to celebrate the signing in Montague Shearman's rooms in the Albany. A lot of people in the arts gathered there in the course of the evening. Osbert and Sacheverell Sitwell were there, and they brought Diaghilev and Massine, who had dined with them that evening. (The Sitwells rather than Bloomsbury were the patrons of the ballet. As Osbert says in his autobiography, Roger Fry was suspicious of any art that was sumptuous, while he, Osbert, was at home on the "wrong" side of the theater, the expensive side.) Clive and Vanessa Bell were there, and several other members of Bloomsbury, D. H. Lawrence and Frieda, David Garnett and Francis Birrell, Nina Hamnett, Sir Henry Mond, and others. Most people were delighted to see the end of the war and in the mood for enjoyment, but Lawrence denounced the peace as well as the war and forecast disaster. Among those who listened to him with growing alienation was David Garnett, who had been among those young people (he was twenty-six in 1918) who before the war had looked up to Lawrence and welcomed his message. The two had drawn apart during the war, and Lawrence had denounced Bloomsbury and Francis Birrell as corrupt, no doubt, as Keynes said, with a view particularly to their influence on Garnett. At this party, Garnett tells us,[23] he listened to Lawrence for a while and then finally turned away from him. He subsequently joined Birrell in running a bookshop and made his friends henceforth in Bloomsbury and Bohemia.

This incident can be said to reflect in miniature the turning away from Lawrence of many young and uncommitted Englishmen, people uncommitted in the sense that they were deeply distrustful of the Establishment, and the patriarchal society they were born into, and were looking for an alternative. Lawrence had offered them one, but it involved serious commitment to another kind of maturity, to the matriarchal world of Woman, of love and life, of the earth and the seasons. Birrell and Bloomsbury offered a rebellion that felt less committed to maturity, a playing under the sign of Adonis, Orpheus, Narcissus.

And the other people at the party help to define the significance of that choice. Massine and Diaghilev represented the ballet, the *commedia,* and the whole cult of the dandy-aesthete. They stood in alliance with the Bloomsbury figures, only having gone even further in the same direction. And the Sitwell brothers may be said to have been extensions of Diaghilev—to have modeled themselves on him and to have been carrying his message into especially English realms of literature and art. Among the regular audiences at the ballet, always faultlessly and splendidly dressed for the occasion, wearing the dandy's uniform, we should have seen nearly all the people who concern us. That is where they went, that is what they turned to, when they turned away from D. H. Lawrence in 1918. And even as schoolboys, Harold Acton and Brian Howard made notable entrances into those theaters, made a notably exquisite pair who aroused wide speculation and high expectation—as being apter apprentices than the rest to the dandyism and aestheticism they were all studying.

Chatpter Three
The New Dandies
Arrive

IN 1918 OUR two principal figures were only schoolboys beginning at Eton. Harold Acton was fourteen, Brian Howard thirteen. They were, however, remarkably precocious—an avant-garde of the sons of England—in their attack upon its fathers. They were already dandies and aesthetes, and were to show themselves, while still at Eton, as miniature Diaghilevs. Like the great impresario himself, they were general aesthetes, connoisseurs of all the arts, but it is significant that they took their keenest artistic pleasure in the same genre as he did, in his creation, the Ballets Russes de Sergei Diaghilev.

It is in camp-religious language that Harold Acton, in his *Memoirs of an Aesthete,* describes going to see these ballets in London in 1918: "Through the traffic jams of thoroughfares decorated in honor of President Wilson's arrival, I made my way to this extraordinary temple." To him, of course, President Wilson was nothing, Diaghilev everything. By "this extraordinary temple" he meant the Coliseum Theatre, a music hall where the ballet company was then performing

Prince Igor as one of the acts. He goes on to describe the ballet itself as
". . . like a perfect lotus springing from a swamp. As each petal of the
lotus opened, as Massine and Karsavina danced in their splendour, no
mortal eye was sharp enough to seize every detail of the vision, every
fleeting finesse of pose and gesture and expression. . . . I gazed in a
fever, with fevered breath and beating pulse, adrift in time and space."
He went again and again, and cut out of the magazines every picture
he could find of Massine, Tchernicheva, Nijinsky, and other ballet figures. He listened to all the gossip about them, followed their tastes in
music, painting, and so on, and imagined himself in Russia, Monte
Carlo, South America, all the places associated with them.

Moreover, he and Brian made a performance of their own out of
attending the ballet performances. This too was analogous—in its
miniature way—to Diaghilev's own performance as connoisseur-
dandy. His whole enterprise carried with it authoritative suggestions
about the right way for ballet lovers to behave, to dress, to feel, to
speak. Thus when one of their Eton contemporaries described seeing
the two boys at the ballet, the stylishness he noted so enviously was
more than a personal idiosyncrasy.

One time I happened to be at the Alhambra when Brian and Harold walked into the stalls, in full evening dress, with long white gloves
draped over one arm, and carrying silver-topped canes and top-hats,
looking perhaps like a couple of Oscar Wildes. My step-mother was
astonished at the sight of them, and thought they must be foreigners.
I was much too nervous, at about fifteen, to say that they were two
of my great friends from Eton. I was very relieved that we were safely
installed out of sight in the dress circle![1]

This anecdote shows us in dramatic form the kind of leadership
the pair established over their more imaginative contemporaries at
school, and how essentially it was a matter of appreciating Diaghilev
and the ballet.

But they also apprenticed themselves to the ballet temperament
in other ways. Most notably, the two of them danced together to
records of Russian ballet music, in literal imitation of Massine and

Nijinsky, Karsavina and Tchernicheva. They did so, for instance, in a room they hired at the back of Dyson's, the jeweller's at Eton, and we can take their terpsichorean sessions there as a single cell of what was to become a giant growth. "Without having seen Massine's performance of the miller's dance in *The Three-Cornered Hat*" Acton says, "Brian could stamp his heels and snap his fingers to de Falla's rhythm, and produce a creditable equivalent." We hear of Brian dancing in many other places, notably in an Arab café in Tangier, where he startled the Americans he was accompanying by taking over from the dancing girls. Harold's brother, William, and Brian's cousin, Carley Robinson, also made themselves amateur ballet dancers. Indeed, at Lady Ottoline Morrell's parties, and even in Bloomsbury, it seems that half the intelligentsia of England were dressing up in exotic costumes and leaping, twirling, pirouetting. The Diaghilev virus was at work, weakening the sober rhythms of manliness, fevering the pulse to dandy pitch. It is no accident that Maria Huxley and Zelda Fitzgerald wanted to become ballerinas, or that Gerald Murphy's Paris (the Dick Diver of *Tender Is the Night*) was centered on the Diaghilev company.

But Brian and Harold were also equipped to emulate Diaghilev in other ways. Both were well acquainted with modernist painting, writing, and composing at a time when most Eton boys, and even masters, were not. They read Pound and Cocteau, they knew Bakst and Augustus John personally, they were themselves poets published in national magazines, and their work had been praised by Edith Sitwell. Before they left Eton they had founded the Eton Society of the Arts, which brought together Anthony Powell, Henry Green, Robert Byron, and Cyril Connolly, and above all they had produced a magazine, *The Eton Candle*, which announced the modernist revolution in the arts. This magazine was largely written by the two of them, in both its critical and its creative aspects, and it was an achievement comparable with those of Cocteau and Diaghilev, granted the difference in scale made inevitable by the difference in age. In the eyes of their Eton contemporaries they quite properly bulked large, both for these achievements and for their personalities, which defied the pressures of English society in so many ways.

Those personalities were not, of course, identical, and since we shall by and large assimilate the one to the other, it may be as well first to mark the differences. In appearance Brian was tall and lean and boldly, if rather cadaverously, handsome; he had large bold eyes, noticeable eyelashes, and a prominent nose. James Stern, a close friend, speaks of Brian's "El Greco" looks, and the phrase gives us a clue, paradoxically, to something specifically modern in his face—the pallor, the fleshlessness, the nervous haggardness. El Greco was the fashionable painter then, and Brian was fashionably of the '20s—a pale and tragic Pierrot, the antithesis of Anglo-Saxon rosy plumpness. He was often compared to Max Beerbohm, and to Disraeli, in looks, and his face seems to have been the main evidence behind the theory that he was really Jewish. This theory, which Brian himself believed, spread while he was at Eton; and it must have caused him much anguish, because it gave such pleasure to his enemies. It was connected with the "discovery" that his father's name was properly Gassaway, not Howard. It was widely supposed that there was something shady about Brian's father, and Brian himself was on very bad terms with him. But now it seemed that Brian himself was an involuntary social fraud, his grand name—Brian Christian de Clavering Howard—a facade for some German-Jewish upstart. In fact Brian came by his names quite honestly; even Howard, if invented, and no one yet knows, was invented by his grandmother. But the legend of his Jewishness suited Brian—and in a different sense suited his enemies at Eton—so well that it formed henceforth a part of his identity. Roger Hinks, one of his Eton contemporaries, used to refer to him as "*die geborene* Gassaway."

As this hints, he was vulnerable also because of his homosexuality—and because of the aggressive pretentiousness of his style, which won him many enemies, and because of his malice and malevolence, which left many victims seeking revenge. He was intensely ambitious and full of talents, both artistic and social, but he was apparently incapable of application or hard work. And he was unhappy and self-destructive, and cruelly destructive to others.

Harold Acton had a rather large head and was always rather plump and "Chinese" in face—not categorically handsome; and there was a good deal more vulnerability and timidity in his personality, although in his prime this was concealed by a very exotic facade. Both boys cultivated exaggerated mannerisms of speech and gesture, but Harold made use of his Italian and American affiliations to suggest that he was barely acclimatized in England. He too had plenty of panache, at Eton and at Oxford, but it was not malevolent. He was essentially teasing, often protectively kind, typically "amusing." There was even something preposterous about his panache; as one laughed with him (at British philistinism) one could also laugh at him, and without fearing, as one did with Brian, some brutal retribution. Both were, of course, great social performers, both quite aggressively seductive, and both brought with them intimations of great plans—particular plans for parties or trips to the theater, or new poets to be appreciated, or new magazines to be launched, but also a general plan for subverting or supplanting the Establishment.

Because they played such similar roles vis-à-vis their contemporaries, they were rivals and only uneasy allies. But in the context of British social institutions, they seemed, from a distance, almost twins. Brian, however, was to be described by W. H. Auden as "the most desperately unhappy person I have ever known," and was to describe his own disabling sense of guilt as "life's gift to those who are selfish, know it, and hate it."[2] We are told of no comparable dialectic and drama in Harold Acton's life; and what he hints at as its equivalent—a sense of unhappiness and a series of unstable moods, at the end of the 1920s, when his poetic career foundered—seems to have been "cured" by the measures that he took for that purpose, that is, his self-exile to China and his self-immersion in Chinese culture. It is hard to imagine Brian Howard removing himself from the London scene, or in any other way really alleviating the stresses of his temperament. *His* conversion in those years was a purely ideological conversion to left-wing politics, which did nothing to check the ravages of his alternately destructive and self-destructive life-style. There was then a prudence and humility in Harold, beneath the dandy's panache, where in Brian there was a desperation and destructiveness.

Both were well equipped by family heritage to introduce modernism and dandyism to the England of 1918. Their family histories were remarkably similar, in some ways. Both had American mothers who were artistic and the friends of artists; and both had painter-art-dealer fathers, who were themselves not completely English. Harold Acton's father, Arthur, was born into a branch of the Acton family that was long settled in Italy and accepted as part of Italian society. Arthur himself lived in an old villa in Florence, to which he had in some sense devoted his life, collecting furniture and paintings for it and reconstructing its neglected gardens, until he had built up a shrine of art and taste comparable to Bernard Berenson's villa, I Tatti. In his early years, Acton had been assistant to the American architect, Stanford White, and had collected on his behalf the furniture, paintings, tapestries, statues, and such that White used to furnish the plutocratic mansions and clubs he built along the East Coast of America.

Arthur Acton's wife, born Hortense Mitchell, came from a wealthy Chicago family that took an interest in the arts. She belonged to the milieu of Mrs. Potter Palmer and was a close friend of Mrs. Richard Crane. Thus the Actons' marriage bore some resemblance to that of Isabel Archer and Gilbert Osmond in James's *Portrait of a Lady*—in the couple's joint retreat from the vulgar materialism of business in America, where their money was made, into the refined connoisseurship of art collecting in Italy, where their money was spent. It was with Mrs. Acton's money that La Pietra was bought and restored. There were, moreover, extramarital scandals about Arthur Acton and other women and their children, as there were about Gilbert Osmond. The resemblance is perhaps rather external, in that there seems no reason to suppose an inner conflict similar to Isabel Archer's in Hortense Acton. But the Actons did belong, in inner ways too, to the world about which Henry James wrote. They knew the Berensons, Vernon

Lee, and Edith Wharton and lived the life James described. They also knew, through Mabel Dodge, the world of Gertrude Stein. Arthur Acton was not himself in sympathy with modernism, but his son was in a position to meet some of its leading figures, and to identify himself with it in opposition to his father—and in opposition, later, to Eton and England. Diaghilev came to La Pietra in 1917 and brought Bakst with him. Bakst praised young William Acton's paintings and invited both brothers to visit his studio in Paris. As a boy, Harold discussed poetry with Reggie Turner, Oscar Wilde's friend and disciple, and he read *Dorian Gray* when he was twelve. He met Max Beerbohm, who had already prophesied, "The future belongs to the dandy. It is the exquisites who are going to rule."[3]

Brian Howard's father, Francis, lived in London, but he was an American by birth. Like Arthur Acton, he went to Roman Catholic schools in England, then to colleges on the Continent, and then to art school in Paris. Thus both were excluded from the normal patterns of English upper-class training from the very beginning. By coincidence, Francis Howard's and Arthur Acton's parents were friends of Cardinal Manning's, who was consulted about both boys' education. It was not so much a coincidence that both men, when they grew up, came to know J. E. Blanche, the French portrait painter, writer, dandy, and social figure, the friend of Proust, Cocteau, and Robert de Montesquiou. Blanche painted portraits of both Arthur Acton and Harold. He was a vigorous center to the international social life of aesthetes, and so naturally came in contact with both Francis Howard and Arthur Acton (although those two men themselves never met each other), for they were figures in that society. In and through them, we glimpse that prewar seedbed of postwar dandyism.

As a young man, Francis Howard tried his hand at various artistic and journalistic enterprises and then settled down to become an art dealer and later a gallery manager. He managed the Grosvenor Gallery in London from 1912 to 1921, and thereafter the Grafton. He was known as a portrait painter at the time of his marriage, in 1903. So was Arthur Acton, although he was even more of an amateur. Howard also had a career in the world of artists' professional associations. He was a friend of Whistler's, with whom he founded the International Society of Engravers and Artists. Howard became its secretary, while first Whistler and then Rodin were presidents, and he apparently did valuable work for the profession of artist, particularly of the portrait painter, in England. Sir Gerald Kelly says that he helped, specifically, Charles Ricketts and Charles Shannon, William Orpen, Augustus John, and others. He arranged exhibitions of contemporary French paintings in London, but Whistler, Rodin, and Sargent represented his own, only moderately contemporary, taste. He was above all a *figure* in the world of art, a friend to Sir Gerald Kelly, later president of the Royal Academy, and to Sir Hugh Lane, the famous collector of paintings. Like Arthur Acton, he was not himself modernist in his taste, but he and his family knew everyone; so his son met, for instance, Augustus John at a time when the latter was only a name, if that, to most of his contemporaries at Eton and Oxford.

Such men were very unlike the average father of an Eton boy at that time, whom we can picture, I gather, as belonging to some landowning family and practicing some profession, or even more likely serving in the army or the church. This average Englishman (average upper-class man, of course) had by comparison a very limited purview of both art and society—a very English and very philistine view. Mr. Howard gave his son, as godfathers, George Meredith and Prince Christian of Schleswig-Holstein. He was also an art adviser and a friend to King George of Greece, and Mr. Acton was the same to Prince Paul of Yugoslavia. They advised these royal friends on their purchase of paintings, and received private and even official recognition in return. Both were ambitious socially, and Mr. Howard at least could be described as a great snob. The occasion of his final break with his wife involved the king of Greece. He found in a blotter a love letter that Brian had written to a man, and had left there. Mr. Howard pictured to himself his shame if his royal friend had found that letter, and told his wife that she must choose between him and their son. She replied that the choice was easily made—in Brian's favor. Her marriage had been a bitter disappointment and defeat, while her motherhood, if also bitter, was a great love affair.

Mrs. Howard was, like Hortense Acton, an American heiress with aesthetic interests. Born Lura Chess, in a Louisville family that had made money in oil and in whisky barrels, she had perhaps more intellectual pretensions and social ambitions than Mrs. Acton. As girls, she and her sister had spent their summers in Chautauqua, where their home was regarded as something of a "cultural" center. Her culture seems to have been a matter of Browning's poetry, Wagner's operas, the arranging of flowers and furniture, and some "spiritual" religion. Both Mrs. Howard and Mrs. Acton were quiet, refined, artistic women, quite beautiful and beautifully dressed; in some ways defeated in their own lives, they possessed their sons' emotional lives in unconscious revenge, according to a familiar "feminine" pattern.

Both marriages were highly traditional in their allotment of the sexual roles. Arthur Acton and Francis Howard, although aesthetes, were Don Juans and as "masculine" as their wives were "feminine." They were notorious for their affairs with other women, and both their sons encountered, in one form or another, the claim of strangers to be their siblings and coheirs. The sons suffered outrage at their fathers' treatment of their mothers, and humiliation at their fathers' treatment of themselves. The case of the Howards was the more lurid (which is perhaps reflected in the more tragic strain in Brian's temperament and fate) in that Francis Howard met another woman during his three-year engagement to Lura Chess, who engaged his heart more than Lura did and kept it all his life long, insofar as it could be kept. Howard was fairly clearly a fortune hunter, who had pursued other American heiresses before Lura, and who had decided he could not afford to marry for love. But he left the other woman, "Dolly" Peache, half his fortune when he died, although he had been the lover of many brilliant women along the way. "Dolly" (her real names were Rose Elsie—equally Edwardian) bore him a child just before he married Lura. Lura discovered her husband and his mistress together soon after her marriage and attempted suicide; and the illegitimate son, who strikingly resembled Brian, killed himself at the age of 20, after quarrels that originated in a resentment at his half-brother's handsomer fate. The two boys never met, and Brian knew nothing of Clement Peache until later, but his parents always feared a chance meeting, because the brothers looked so alike that Brian must have then asked questions. Lura bestowed all her love, hope, and indulgence on her child, and Francis, perhaps in jealousy for his other son, was hostile to him from the beginning.

Mr. Howard lived on his wife's, and her father's, money, and exploited his own charm and talent quite unscrupulously; these were facts fairly publicly acknowledged. He was a handsome man, and he had liaisons with famous beauties, including, perhaps, Lily Langtry, who was for a time King Edward VII's mistress. He was a brilliant tennis player. And he was a bravura anecdotalist; on one occasion he held his son and two of the latter's friends spellbound with a ghost story that he afterward admitted getting out of a book—and this when they were grown up. Such negligently masterful manipulation of a potentially hostile audience was an achievement Brian must have envied him, since he himself aimed at something similar so often.[4]

If the Actons' marriage can remind us of the Osmonds' in *The Portrait of a Lady,* the Howards' suggests a pair in another James novel, the Faranges in *What Maisie Knew.* The similarity lies in the ugly truths of sexual and financial exploitation and in the fate of the child torn between warring parents, all of it taking place in a smart London house. Brian's home in Bryanston Square seemed to his Eton friends strikingly opulent. But Francis Howard seems to have conducted his marriage as ruthlessly as Mr. Farange, and Lura Howard's resentment and passion for intrigue and quarreling seem as great as Mrs. Farange's. And if we compare Pansy Osmond with Harold Acton and Maisie Farange with Brian Howard, we may decide that the two boys are the more likely, in some sense the "truer," products and heirs of the marriages James described. The old-fashioned innocence James ascribes to the girls seems a sentimental flourish when you look at the boys. *They,* the postwar dandies, were to be the next generation of James's world—

were in a parodic way to bring that world to triumph over Philistia. In both cases, the son recoiled away from the male role exemplified by his hostile father and found "normal" sexuality impossible. However, because they had the courage to flaunt this fact, at least by the time they got to Oxford, they were able to add the most flagrant sexual provocation to their aesthetic defiance of "Englishness."

Both stressed their Americanness from time to time, claiming that this gave them an extra lien on modernism and the modern, a freedom from the fuss and fusty restraints they saw around them in England. They came more easily to the repudiation of "dull frowsy England—awful men in bowler hats and bad tempers trotting up and down the wet pavements." That is Brian's phrase—characteristic of him in its note of falsetto irritability—but some such repudiation was made sooner or later by *all* the English dandies. Probably an even more important service done Brian and Harold by being American was their heritage of the American dandy-or-aesthete-in-exile tradition. The Florentine society in which Harold Acton grew up included a number of brilliant figures of that kind—Bernard Berenson and his wife, Mabel Dodge and her husband Edwin, an architect, Lily Braggiotti, and Bayard Cutting—while Edith Wharton, Gertrude Stein, Alice B. Toklas, Muriel Draper, and others often visited. Berenson is one of the four men to whom Harold Acton acknowledges a large personal debt, and it is striking how many men of Berenson's group and generation were "masters" to the men we shall study. In addition to Berenson's "tutorship" of Acton, there was George Santayana's of Wallace Stevens, and Logan Pearsall Smith's of Cyril Connolly; while in more purely literary ways T. S. Eliot and Pound were, of course, great influences on them all. American culture has been unkinder to dandies and aesthetes than almost any other, but just for that reason there has always been a highly self-conscious colony of American dandies in exile. In some sense both the Acton and the Howard families belonged in that colony.

How that American heritage acted on the two boys, how their two fates were predisposed by it, we can see by tracing the family histories back a few decades. Mrs. Acton's family, the Mitchells, were bankers, whose fortunes were very much identified with Chicago, rising and falling with those of the city. Her father, William Hamilton Mitchell, founded the Illinois Trust and Savings Bank. He seems to have started with nothing, and to have acquired enough to make a considerable contribution to La Pietra (his name is inscribed on its walls) even though Mrs. Acton was one of many siblings. Her father had children by three wives, and some of them and their children lived as far from Chicago as Honolulu, Florence, and Spain, and in styles as un-Chicagoan as their locations. Not all, of course. One son, John J. Mitchell, went into the family bank, was one of the first agents of the Chicago Stock Exchange (opened in 1882), and, together with Cyrus McCormick, Marshall Field, and other Chicago financiers, formed syndicates in 1888 to acquire control of railroads in the West and Midwest. He is said to have made a great deal of money out of the rebuilding of the city after the great fire, and his sister married a Blair, one of the great commercial families of Chicago. However, even John J. Mitchell became director of the Art Institute of Chicago (founded 1882), and there are many such signs that the Mitchell family developed aesthetic tastes quite early and participated in the city's cultural renaissance, after 1890. For instance, the third Mrs. William Hamilton Mitchell named her children Hortense, Marguerite, and Guy (Mrs. Potter Palmer named her son Honoré), and Guy became an amateur painter. It can be viewed as a kind of climax to this aestheticism that Hortense should leave Chicago to live in Florence and—apparently with some participation by her father—build up around her there a private world of beauty and taste.

There was much in the circumstances of her marriage to connect—in our minds—that private event with the public history of the arts and the imagination in America. Let us start with the arrival of Arthur Acton in Chicago, as assistant to Stanford White, for the World's Columbian Exposition of 1893. The Columbian Exposition, which covered 686 acres, was recognized as Chicago's great chance to show the world what it stood for aesthetically.

Before 1893 what it had stood for, in architecture, was a kind of functionalism. Between 1880 and 1893, Siegfried Giedion says, the Loop area of Chicago was the world's center of architectural development. The fire of 1871 had destroyed 2,000 acres of buildings and so created enormous opportunities, artistic as well as financial, in the rebuilding. The Chicago architects were Louis H. Sullivan, John W. Root, Frank Lloyd Wright, and Charles Burnham, and between 1875 and 1915 they used the steel cage, which had been invented by William le Baron Jenney, a military engineer, to build the stockyards, the commercial buildings in the Loop, and the whole industrial town of Pullman, in a new style. This gave Chicago a position unique among American cities. Boston too had had a fire, and had a fine architect, H. H. Richardson, but it created no new and modern architectural style; and New York, until 1910, imported Chicagoans to build its skyscrapers.

The rich patrons of taste in Chicago, however, had never wanted functional architecture. People like the Mitchells had a much more ornamental and sumptuous image of "Art." Mrs. Potter Palmer's "Rhine Castle" on Lake Shore Drive, full of Gobelin tapestries, Louis XVI beds, Impressionist paintings, and Moorish and Japanese furniture (and described by Thorstein Veblen to his students at the University of Chicago as a glaring example of conspicuous consumption)— that was more what Hortense Acton and her friend Mrs. Crane had in mind as beautiful building. And what happened in 1893 was that in the committee planning the Exposition buildings Burnham and Root persuaded the others to adopt a predominantly classical style, and to give the contracts for the new buildings to five firms, none of which belonged to Chicago, that habitually designed classical forms. The modernist Chicago style was described as being a triumph of engineering, but not of architecture. Later Sullivan and other Chicagoans were brought in to cooperate with the other (New York and Boston) firms, but Sullivan still thought the scheme an appalling calamity for architecture in Chicago. (In the 1930s the Bauhaus group under László Moholy-Nagy founded the Chicago Institute of Design, and

Mies van der Rohe became director of the Illinois Institute of Technology, and modernist functionalism was restored to Chicago.)[5]

One of the three New York firms thus given an exposition contract was McKim, Mead, and White, and to fulfill that contract Stanford White came to Chicago, and with him his assistant, Arthur Acton. Acton traveled quite regularly between Chicago, New York, and Florence from 1893 to 1903, the year he married Hortense Mitchell. The classicism of the Exposition architecture charmed Charles Eliot Norton, the Harvard professor of fine arts, Henry Adams, Henry James, and others. The men of taste from the East, who had been so nervous of the Midwest, "came round to" Chicago when they saw those graceful tributes to the styles of the past. It was a big triumph for "culture" in the American imagination. And the marriage of Hortense Mitchell—the assumption into La Pietra of the Chicago millionaire's daughter—must have seemed a picturesque moment in the triumph.

Stanford White, who half-adopted the fatherless Arthur Acton, had studied architecture with H. H. Richardson and had emulated the latter's big, bibulous, magniloquent "Renaissance" persona. He had married money himself, and built a home on Long Island that contained gilded Spanish columns, Renaissance fireplaces, Persian rugs, Roman fragments, Delft tiles—the spoils of every style of artistic magnificence. He was said to be the Cellini of his firm, in contrast to McKim's Bramante. He gradually developed an Italianate style of building, which was very popular with the wealthy citizens of New York, Newport, and the Berkshires. He built the Century, the Players, and the Metropolitan clubs in New York, and in 1889 he built Madison Square Garden, where he kept an apartment and gave dinners whose lavishness made them the talk of the town—and where he tragically died. For White's personal life too was Renaissance in its exuberance. At one of his dinners it is alleged that a fifteen-year-old girl in a gauze dress emerged from a pie when it was sliced. It is also alleged that this girl later died in want. Whether or not the latter was an apocryphal detail, added to satisfy the audience's sense of sinful luxury, it seems established that White, although a devoted husband

and father, was also a determined seducer of young girls. His style of architecture found its counterpart in his sexual life.

This exuberance led to his murder, in 1906, and because of his close relationship to Arthur Acton, who seems to have modeled himself to some degree on his older friend, the story of that murder is worth our noting.

In 1901, White met a showgirl called Evelyn Nesbitt, from Ziegfeld's Floradora chorus. She was, then sixteen, and looked even younger, but White seduced her. The millionaire Harry Thaw, who was jealous of White on various other grounds, also admired her. Thaw eventually married her, in 1905, suffered great jealousy, and shot White dead fourteen months later in Madison Square Garden's restaurant.[6]

Thaw, too, saw himself as a great lover and bravura personality. When he came into his fortune on his twenty-first birthday, he gave a dinner for a hundred actresses, each of whom found a gift of jewellery beside her plate. He fought policemen, rode a horse up the steps of a Fifth Avenue club, and so on. In other words, he apprenticed himself—he was much younger than White—to the latter's style of virility. On the other hand, he was defended in court as a chivalrous knight, protecting American womanhood and the American home against the ravages of this seducer; and there is some evidence that he was genuinely shocked by and indignant at White. For instance, he had already left money in a trust fund to support paternity suits against White by his victims; and on a visit to Joan of Arc's birthplace in Domrémy he wrote surreptitiously in the visitors' book, "Jean d'Arc would not have been a virgin long if Stanford White had been around."

The contradiction in Thaw is, after all, a contradiction in patriarchal morality, which makes a man try to be both an insatiable animal and a husband and father toward the delicate, passive victim, woman. That contradiction is also apparent, if in less psychically lurid form, in Stanford White. And the interest of the story for us is that we see there the "manliness" to which Arthur Acton corresponded (he is said to have been involved in duels about amorous affairs as late as the period when his son was at Oxford) and against which Harold Acton, half-helplessly, reacted. Harold's *Sonnenkind* panache was a parody of that manly immoralism.

Although less typical of the larger social context than the Mitchells, the Actons also had an interesting and significant history. The branch of the family that concerns us had long been exiles from England and had developed a very un-English style. Commodore John Acton, who became prime minister of Naples under Queen Maria Carolina, married his niece by papal dispensation in 1800, when he was sixty-three and she was fourteen. Among his grandchildren were Lord Acton, the famous Roman Catholic historian, who belonged to the various aristocracies of England, France, Germany, Austria, and Naples; and Laura Acton, who married first Prince Camporeale and then Mario Minghetti (a distinguished writer who was also prime minister of Italy from 1873 to 1876), and who ran the most intellectual salon of her day in Rome. Laura Minghetti was a great figure in Berlin as well as Rome, and her daughter married Prince von Bülow, later chancellor of Germany. In other words, it was a brilliant international family. There was a cardinal and two of Laura's brothers were admirals in the Italian navy, in the tradition of the commodore, and there have been others since. The Actons have also kept up their connection with Naples and Sicily, and their loyalty to the Bourbon kings of Sicily. Ferdinando Acton, the prince of Leporano, who served in the Italian army against Abyssinia, and his brother Francesco, who made his career in the navy, recently compiled a genealogy of the family. On the other hand, not all the Actons have been distinguished, or even respectable, and there even seems to have been something shady about the commodore himself. The kingdom of Naples, and the court of the Bourbons there, was a gathering ground for the adventurers, the impostors, and the disgraced men of Europe; and the cause of the Bourbons since Garibaldi has been a classically (not to say preposterously) reactionary one. However, Harold Acton's sub-branch of the family was somewhat separate. Two more of Laura Acton's brothers, Harold and Roger, returned to England in the 1850s, to claim British citizenship. Roger, who went to work for the khedive of Egypt, was the father of Arthur and grandfather of Harold. However, as Arthur was born out of wedlock and brought up under the guardianship of his uncle Harold, he never really knew either his father or his mother.

The Acton family story is made up, then, of splendors and shadows, princedoms, cardinalates, and bastardies, like those "Barry Lyndon" figures of unrespectability conjured up by Thackeray to shock and amuse Victorian readers. David Mathew, in his biography of Lord Acton, speaks of "the elegant and dubious northern gentlemen who haunted the purlieus of the Court of Naples in the period of Alfred d'Orsay," and something in Harold Acton's alienation from "English" Puritanism may have found encouragement in his heritage. This heritage has minor counterparts in the story of the Howards. There are no princes there, but poets and governors of Florida, and a justice of the supreme court of Arkansas; no bastards, but a deliberate concealment of the facts of Francis Howard's parentage and his mother's marriages. Thus in the Howard family there was perhaps an even stronger intimation of something shaky and shady in the background of brilliant social performances. This part of their heritages, as distinct from their fathers' manliness, the two boys appropriated. Their triumph over the intellectual, aesthetic, and moral stodginess of their English contemporaries was a revenge for all those "Barry Lyndon" exiles from Victorian respectability.

The Acton villa, La Pietra, was built in part in the 15th century, but mostly in the 16th. Arthur Acton made for it extremely valuable collections of paintings, furniture, statuary, and so on, in a grand and luxurious style. In the main hall there were gilded columns in Temple-of-Solomon-style, a gilded Venus with mirror, a black and gold slave boy offering real flowers, and two huge Negro busts in lunettes. In the main salon there were two Negro slave boys on round marble plinths, wearing soft boots and Turkish costumes and cockades of gilded feathers, who bore coffers out of which spilled strings of jewels. But the villa's great triumph was the gardens. These were large and elaborate, with over a hundred statues, and beautiful vistas so planned that whichever way one turned one found things falling into groups

and patterns. He bought the property at the time when several people were reconstructing such houses and gardens. Mabel Dodge had
just moved into the Villa Curonia (and Edwin Dodge was one of the
architects consulted in the reconstruction of La Pietra); Edith Wharton's book on Italian gardens came out in 1904, the year after the
Acton-Mitchell marriage; Janet Ross published her *Florentine Palaces* and *Florentine Villas* in the same decade; and Princess Ghika and
Miss Blood began, with Arthur Acton's help, restoring the gardens of
La Ghirlandaio. Among the other great villas around Florence were
Berenson's I Tatti, Myron Taylor's La Schiffanoia, Franchetti's Bello-
sguardo, Loeser's La Gattaia, and Lina Waterfield's Poggio Gherardo.
Their occupants formed an aesthetic aristocracy.

Among these people, one has left us with a vivid portrait of Arthur
Acton and a sketch of Hortense. In *European Experiences,* published
in 1935, Mabel Dodge describes Arthur as tall and plump, with a
small prim mouth, unexpressive-looking as if made of wax, but in
fact hard, imperious, and "interesting." (Both his sons, Harold and
William, looked very like him, as Brian looked very like his father
and grandfather—facts that made the rebellion of temperament the
harder to bear.) Mrs. Acton is described by Mabel Dodge as petite,
pretty, self-conscious, and repressed—exquisitely dressed, and with a
slight but perfect charm. She sat in Mabel's presence without moving
or speaking, apparently. Edwin Dodge, to Mabel's fury, flirted with
Mrs. Acton at first, but Hortense soon withdrew from the friendship,
while Mabel and Arthur continued to see a lot of each other and to
influence each other's lives. It was Arthur, for instance, who arranged
for Eleanora Duse to come to the Villa Curonia: "In his quiet stealthy
way, marked by his waxen countenance, full of good will and collector's curiosity, he brought people together," says Mabel. She speaks of
his shy gauche gestures, smoothing his impeccably symmetrical moustache with two long, blind white fingers, of his round pink cheeks,
and of his blurred smile from behind his glasses; he looked noncom-
mittal, with his large, bland white hands, but he was nervous inside,
like an ill-regulated waxwork, and brusque little movements betrayed

that. Mrs. Acton, who disliked and disapproved of Mrs. Dodge, had a "perfect, Dresden china charm." Mabel says that the two sons were not much in evidence at La Pietra, that instead there were thousands of *putti*—and Harold Acton agrees that his father had no patience with family life. He preferred large social occasions, although he came away from those exhausted and irritable. He was both an aesthete and a socialite, a conventionally manly man.

As a manly man, as the husband-father-master, he represented all his son had to rebel against. In those roles he represented—and the same was true of Francis Howard—the world of men of prewar England, against which Harold Acton and Brian Howard led the attack of the new *Sonnenkinder.* But as an aesthete, as an artist, as a cosmopolitan, as a connoisseur of art and a lover of beauty rather than a businessman or an administrator, he was himself a rebel against philistine "Englishness," and his sons were his followers in every sense. They were much advanced in their lifework by all that he had been and done before them.

For instance, the Acton boys were given a highly aesthetic education. The only modern furniture in the villa was in the nurseries, and that was expelled as the boys grew older. They had elegant and distinguished toys, to which Harold enjoyed playing impresario when visitors came. Their English nurses, who for instance disapproved of the naked statues in the gardens, appear in Harold's *Memoirs* as grotesque philistines. At six, Harold tells us, his favorite painter was Botticelli, and he collected postcard reproductions. He loved Edgar Allan Poe's stories and fairy tales about mermaids and nightingales—so much so that his parents took alarm and gave him a volume of the *Boys' Own Paper* to win him back to normality. But Harold could never bring himself to read it:

> It loomed from my bookcase like an ugly threat . . . a memento mori. I would have to meet such creatures one of these days, and enter into their games and learn their jargon, but not yet, I prayed, not yet. . . .

Other writers tell us of similar forebodings, derived from the *Boys' Own Paper,* or from Kipling, or from the idea of school—forebodings of all that they, as dandies and aesthetes, were destined to suffer from a community dominated by *hearties*. (Let us use that term for the thoroughly boyish boys and men, wholly assimilated to the old England, and keep *rogues* for those rebels against the conventions in whom, however "hearty" they might be in some ways, the dandies often found their allies.) Thus Osbert Sitwell tells us how his heart sank when he was given a pigskin collar box with his initials stamped on it, a foretaste of school "from which could be deduced the boredom, the bullying, the lack of all save sadistic imagination." And in fact, he says, school spoiled his health, his temper, his looks, his faith in life, his imagination, and his curiosity. Alan Pryce-Jones tells us that at the age of ten he read a Kiplingesque boys' book that made a big distinction between "real boys" and "muffs"; he took alarm and put some effort into becoming a real boy himself, but found that he just could not enjoy playing cricket, making toffee, collecting birds' eggs, or torturing cats.[7] And John Betjeman and Cecil Beaton have vivid stories about their actual sufferings in prep school.

But only Acton had a full-fledged aesthetic alternative to boyhood at hand, in his own home and in the lavish internationalism of his family's style. In the summers they went to his grandfather's home in Chicago, and to his estate on Lake Geneva, Wisconsin, where the Norwegian lodge from the Columbian Exposition had been reerected as a summer house. They also traveled in Europe, going in 1910 to Paris; in 1911 to Etretat; and in 1912 to Berlin, Scandinavia, and Binz on the German island of Rügen, where Harold acquired a lump of amber that accompanied him as a talisman all through his Oxford days and beyond.

The Actons were an artistically gifted family. Harold's father painted, Harold painted, and his brother William, two years his junior, painted the best of all. William was the general favorite, being handsome, strong, and outgoing, but he was just as much the aesthete as Harold. Both boys loved Beardsley and Bakst the best of all painters after the great masters, and they found England, when they went there to school, much inferior to Florence in its gardens, houses, and ladies. Harold liked the Brighton Pavilion, but not the grey Gothicism, nor the Ruskiny ruins. He had identified himself with Florence and with exotic figures like the Marchesa Casati. Harold took with him to school a postcard reproduction of one of Giovanni Boldini's portraits of the Marchesa. Painted also by Bakst, she was a great female dandy, who kept albino blackbirds, mauve monkeys, a leopard, a snake, a black boy whom she painted gold, and such. She was to society what Ida Rubinstein was to the stage, Acton tells us; both acted the legends they had created. At school Harold felt himself reduced to being a child among children. He had never liked children, and least of all English boys at play. " 'Games' was anathema to me. From now on I would have to indulge in them day after day. My spirit rebelled and remained perverse until Oxford set me free."

Mabel Dodge's book gives one an admirably full account of how Florentine villas like the Actons' were furnished and maintained. Edwin Dodge bought the Villa Curonia, but her mother gave them $40,000–50,000 to do it over, and the couple spent their combined incomes on it for several years. For instance, they bought six cinquecento tapestry chairs for $200 each. The *gran' salone,* much admired by Berenson, was ninety feet long and opened onto a loggia. It was decorated in ruby-red damask, its doorway came from a church in Pisa, and its hangings included an old silver brocade curtain, embroidered with green and purple grapes, and Flemish tapestries. The fireplace was 14th-century and more than four feet wide. Over it hung a life-sized Gothic madonna, and nearby stood a carved wooden Kali-Shiva-Vishnu, much admired by Roger Fry. Mabel's first "at home" took the form of a Medicean feast, at which the guests strolled among the peacocks on the garlanded terrace, listening in the twilight to the Evening Star song from *Tannhäuser.* Later she planned with Gordon Craig a cinquecento pageant for all Florence, which would so engulf the city, so lift it away from ordinary concerns, that one would, for example, be able to buy only 16th-century food in the restaurants. Her judgment on the villa is implied in a moment of narrative:

> . . . the Villa Curonia loomed above me, heavy, golden—carried so far towards perfection, it seemed important to me—a

career in itself. I had given so much thought to it—so much time. I was a part of every room in it, of every strip of velvet and silk.

and, as an effective corollary to those sentiments:

The only people who counted, who were visible to the trained eyes of the Florentine world, were those who resembled works of art of a bygone day, so that everyone did his best, often unconsciously, to revert.

Mabel Dodge later rebelled against this, and found in D. H. Lawrence an ideology that centered all values in life and love, in the world of Woman. But Harold and Brian Howard, although both certainly felt the strains of the art collector's life, and rebelled against it, could not take Lawrence's way out. They were committed to an opposite temperament.

Francis Howard's family line was full of mysteries, and some of those mysteries oppressed Brian's imagination and added importantly to his sense of insecurity. As late as the Second World War his letters to his mother are full of references to their not knowing who his father *was,* in the sense that they did not know who Francis's father had been. They assumed—and so did everyone else—that the unknown grandfather had been Jewish, and that the ducal name of Howard was a vulgar fraud. If Mr. Howard knew any details, he apparently refused to tell his wife and son, refused to discuss the matter with them—and it seems likely that they made of their shared grievance and anger a bond to hold them together against him. It seems now that the assumption of Jewishness was unwarranted, but the mystery is still unsolved.

Francis Howard (if that was his name) was the son of a woman born Elizabeth Paschal in Texas. She was the daughter of a divorce lawyer called George Washington Paschal, who was a supreme court justice of the state of Arkansas before the Civil War and who was also a law reporter, political journalist, and lecturer. Elizabeth, known as Bessie, became a belle of Washington society at the age of sixteen, about 1872. She seems to have married a man called Frank Harrison

Gassaway, who became a minor poet, and to have borne her child in 1874, or perhaps 1875. He seems to have disappeared soon after that, and she claims that she then married a man called Howard, who went mad and shot himself within the year.

This is the tale told by Bessie herself, and it is unsupported by documentary evidence and full of internal inconsistencies. But she certainly called herself Elizabeth Howard, and her son Francis Howard, in the 1880s. And it seems definite that Francis Howard's full name was Francis Aloysius Harrison Gassaway Howard, and that he believed his father to be Frank Harrison Gassaway. It is also quite definite that there was such a person as Frank Harrison Gassaway and that he resembled Francis and Brian physically. Some of the details of his life and work are vividly representative of his times and deserve to be recorded, even though they were probably unknown to his son and grandson. Like the story of Stanford White and Harry Thaw, they represent as well as anything else cultural forces that were certainly known to Brian, and to which he reacted.

Gassaway arrived in Oakland, California, from Washington, D.C., in 1880, and wrote for *The San Francisco Examiner* and *The San Francisco Chronicle.* He contributed first a humorous column, in Mark Twain style, over the name of Derrick Dodd—some of them later published in a volume called *Summer Saunterings*—and then a number of sentimental and narrative Civil War poems, which became great favorites with reciters. "The Pride of Battery B," for instance, about a little orphan girl who is adopted by the rough soldiers of that battery and who spreads a reconciling influence around her, was copied in over 2,000 newspapers and included in over fifty anthologies. It was a centerpiece of several Gilded Age "literary" occasions in the 1890s. An actress, Clara Morris, who particularly liked it, was invited to a "High Jinks" (400 gentlemen and one lone woman) at the Bohemian Club when she visited San Francisco. While the men awaited her arrival a Shanghai Committee constrained various members to make impromptu speeches, and three evaded the duty by reciting "The Pride of Battery B" instead; then, when the guest of honor arrived, *she* recited it in place of a speech of thanks. After her return to New York, Morris was invited to a similar function at the Lotus Club. On that occasion she recited the poem to deafening applause, encored it to not a dry eye in the place, and retired into a private room with thirty notables and did it for them alone; and then, when Henry Ward Beecher arrived late and heard what he had missed, she did it all over again. The assembly then appointed a committee of one to write a letter thanking the poet; the appointee was Oliver Wendell Holmes, who wrote a witty and sentimental message on the back of a menu, and the letter was signed by Generals Grant, Sherman, and Porter, Senators Conkling, Lamar, and Gorman, Commodore Vanderbilt, Henry Ward Beecher, Charles A. Dana, Bayard Taylor, and Edwin Booth—the whole of the Gilded Age.[8] Gassaway was a central Gilded Age poet, a poor man's Mark Twain.

It is appropriate that the other moment of Gassaway's life that appears in the history books is his signature, in 1892, of a contract that has become infamous in the history of American journalism. He was then business manager of William Randolph Hearst's paper, *The Examiner,* and he signed on behalf of Hearst the contract that brought Hearst $30,000-worth of advertising from the Southern Pacific Railroad, in return for a promise that the railroad would not be criticized or investigated by the paper. Gassaway seems to have remained one of Hearst's court, and when his book, *Poems,* was finally published, in 1920, it was dedicated to Hearst as "the greatest publisher, the greatest American, and the greatest-hearted gentleman its author has ever known."

In 1920, Brian Howard was reading T. S. Eliot and Ezra Pound, and Frank Gassaway's poems would have seemed to him, in subject, form, and diction, ridiculous in their relation to the poetry he loved and odious in their relation to the social forces they served. They were typical of all that he was rebelling against. Let us quote the last stanzas of "The Marines," inspired by a reception given by British troops for American marines at the end of the First World War, and imagined to be spoken there by Kipling.

And they came as at Dover the breakers
    boil over
The cliffs, and they smothered the Hun
Then—we dropped asleep—kneeling—and standing—all
    feeling
The job out in front was well done.
They are round us tonight in the ballroom's bright light
'Mid the waltzes' soft surges and foam.
Though the hands are now hid in
    immaculate kid
That once drove the bayonet home.
But we know 'till are furled the war flags of the world
What the cult of blood-brotherhood means—
That their Liberty's light will e'er flash through the night
"Sit tight—till I send my Marines."

Gassaway was apparently referred to by the London *Times* as "the American Kipling," and his is exactly the sort of poetry from which Eliot, Pound, and Edith Sitwell provided an escape. For boys like Brian, the militarism, the chauvinism, the public cliché sentiment, were fused with the mechanical rhythms and the vulgar diction into an emblem of all they hated in the society they were born into.

And here are a few lines of "The Knights of Gutenberg," a poem more clearly related to Gassaway's own position and experiences because it is about the saving function of newspapers in democratic culture.

Till at length—oh that great day of mercy
When lo! at the high God's command,
His Arch-angel passed down from Heaven
The weapon that naught might withstand.
And that day was born the great order
The Gutenberg knights of the Press
Whose far-ranging missiles forever
Bade tyrants no longer oppress. . . .
And behold, the device on the standard

> Of today's Knight Commander, the first
> In the van of humanity's soldiers,
> Is the "Monarch"—the banner of HEARST.

If Brian had got hold of his grandfather's poems, this one might have made one of his best recitations, but it seems—from his references to "the Civil War poet"—that he never actually read him.

Meanwhile, Elizabeth Paschal became a journalist in New York in the 1880s and on a trip to England met the Irish member of Parliament, T. P. O'Connor, whom she married in 1885—signing the register inexplicably as Elizabeth Paschal *Wright*. T. P. O'Connor was one of Charles Parnell's lieutenants in the House of Commons, the first Irishman to represent an English constituency; he remained in Parliament long enough to become known as the Father of the House. He was a professional Irishman culturally too—known as "Tay Pay" in allusion to his picturesque brogue—and a prolific journalist, lecturer, and biographer. He ran a series of radical newspapers, for which his wife and her son wrote, one of which was called *T. P.'s Weekly*. As time went by he became less the serious radical and more the picturesque personality. In other words, he was not unlike George Washington Paschal, Frank Harrison Gassaway, and indeed Elizabeth Paschal herself, all "personalities," on the fringe of public and artistic life. T. P. and Bessie soon quarreled and parted.

Bessie was a brilliant social personality, with literary ambitions, and a great egotist. She was quite a beautiful woman, with a lot of Southern charm, and an amateur actress. She was a great friend of the Southern writer Thomas Nelson Page and a minor collaborator with him in constructing the nostalgic myth of the aristocratic South. She wrote a book called *My Beloved South*. She used to recite Joel Chandler Harris stories. She also wrote a play called *The Lady from Texas,* in which she acted. (Gassaway, in San Francisco, also wrote some plays.) She also wrote a volume of autobiography, called *I Myself.*[9] Bessie was president of the League of Women Journalists for a time. And, according to family legend, she hired a series of young men as secretaries, to whom she dictated her books while in bed or in her bath.

Her marriage to T. P. did not last very long, because she objected to being left out of, or subordinate in, so many of his activities. She and he both thought of her as a "typical American woman," who demanded more deference from her husband than an English, or Irish, man was prepared to give. In consequence she spent a lot of time with her son and his wife—she lived with Francis and Lura during the war years, for instance—and she often writes in her books about her beautiful grandson, Brian, her "Boysey," her "little Thank-you," with his beautiful eyes. And although much is confused or dubious in her account of herself, the main thing—for her impact on Brian—is clear; she was a genteel Southern lady, full of genteel feminism, resentment, and cynicism beneath her warmth and charm. The atmosphere of her books is one made familiar by the plays of Tennessee Williams. She is Amanda from *The Glass Menagerie*. In fact, her autobiography reads very like the book about Williams by his mother. And it is, of course, no accident that the dandy writers of America have typically come from Southern families; the South is the locus of American dandyism in part because of that Southern style of feminine feminism. That is another link between our two principals and America.

It seems clear that Brian's mother acted on him in much the same way as his grandmother did, although more powerfully; he was very close to them both and very much at odds with his father from the beginning. Lura Howard was, like her mother-in-law, a woman of social ambitions and intellectual pretensions, betrayed by her husband, and of the genteel Southern culture. By her flattery, indulgence, reproach, self-pity, self-dramatization, and flirtatiousness, she fostered the same tendencies in the boy as did Bessie. Lura too was a defeated woman, and defeated not only by her husband; she was outmatched, for instance, by her younger sister. Grace Chess had married Avery Robinson, a composer (he composed "Waterboy," among other spirituals) who became a stockbroker when their original fortune was lost in the Depression. Mrs. Robinson herself developed remarkable and profitable artistic talents. For a time she was a maker of artificial flowers—botanically exact in every detail, some miniaturized, made first in parchment and then in metal—that were exhibited and sold at enormous prices to, for instance, Queen Mary, decorators like Syrie Maugham, and rich people like Hugh Walpole and Lady Beaverbrook. Later she turned her skills to the creation of perfumes, bath oils, creams, and such, which she sold commercially as Mary Chess Ltd. She had a shop on 57th Street in New York, and then one in Mayfair, and other shops and department stores sold her products. It was not a firm on the scale of Elizabeth Arden or Helena Rubinstein, or with the same image of high society glamor. Mary Chess offered the snobbish appeal of Southern gentlewoman restraint, delicacy, and refinement—and traditional recipes allegedly handed down in the Chess family.

Lura Howard managed the London shop during the war years, 1939–1945, and Brian pilfered large quantities of its stock for use by himself and his friends. When in danger of losing an argument, Brian would dab some Mary Chess perfume on his opponent and say, "Now that you smell like a tart, my dear, your arguments carry very little weight." So in a sense Mary Chess represented to him what La Pietra did to Harold Acton. (Of course his father's gallery and private collection did so too, but Mary Chess represented something more specific to Brian.) These were the achievements of their parents against which the boys had to react—toward modernism in the arts and radicalism in politics. But those achievements were always there, all through their lives, setting a limit to their reaction because more substantial than their own achievement, and finally, fatally, setting a stamp *on* their own achievement; the antiquarian scholarship of art, on the one hand, the luxury trade of it on the other, these were limits they could not escape. Harold Acton says, in the very last sentence of *Memoirs of an Aesthete,* that his vision has been enhanced, but also circumscribed, by La Pietra.

In 1913, just before the First World War, Harold Acton was sent to a preparatory school in England, where he was contemporary with Kenneth Clark, James Stern, Billy Clonmore, Mark Ogilvie-Grant, and other people who continued to figure in his story. This was Wixenford, a leading prep school. When Harold arrived at Eton, he found forty Wixenford boys already there. But Wixenford was for him a

poor exchange for La Pietra and the Uffizi Gallery in Florence. In the
school library he searched the back volumes of the *Illustrated London News* for Constantin Guy's drawings, and ignored the stacks of
G. H. Henty, R. M. Ballantyne, and Captain Marryat boys' stories on
the shelves. Since his Italianate English provoked laughter, he exaggerated his accent, sang Italian songs to mollify bullies, and developed
a style of self-mocking buffoonery. He had brought with him a vial of
attar of roses and his talismanic lump of amber, and when the other
boys showed him photographs of their mothers, he got out his Boldini portrait of Casati, flamboyantly dressed and extravagantly posed.
He represented himself to the other boys as of great erotic experience,
claiming to have been seduced by an American Negress with a velvet
skin and a watermelon mouth, and led them in feats of extravagance
and impudence. James Stern tells anecdotes of Acton at Wixenford
that explain why he could look to the latter as one of the liberators
he has known. (Another liberator for Stern was D. H. Lawrence,
and that odd conjunction illustrates the point of this book—the two
routes of escape from Stern's situation were represented by Acton and
Lawrence.) With Billy Clonmore and Mark Ogilvie-Grant Acton
created a museum of natural and unnatural history (exhibits included
Medici poisons, a chastity belt, some thumbscrews) and a magazine of
art and fashion. Going home to La Pietra in the holidays, he appreciated all its beauties "feverishly." When war broke out, he shrank from
the mood of jingo jauntiness and the clichés—only Chaplin cheered
him in the general ugliness. He wrote an article for the school paper,
proposing that the British army should march in uniforms designed
by Bakst and to marches composed by Stravinsky—and what about
making a Don Cossack choir out of the Grenadier Guards? And why
was there no British d'Annunzio? (Gabriele d'Annunzio lived in a villa
quite near La Pietra for a time, and Harold grew up, he tells us, "under
d'Annunzio's spell.")

It was considered unsafe to send Harold back to Wixenford during
the war, so he went to a school in Geneva, and spent a lot of time at home.
He read *The Picture of Dorian Gray* and composed romantic-decadent

novelettes in the Italian manner. The influence of Diaghilev was at its zenith in 1914, in his parents' circle, and the fancy dress balls and *tableaux vivants* were sumptuous and spectacular to a degree unrealized since. The marchesa Casati, "the d'Annunzio muse incarnate," wore costumes quite fantastic in their extravagance. His parents attended a Persian/Venetian ball at the Villa Schiffanoia in costumes designed by Paul Poiret from Persian miniatures; and his mother and brother (the latter in a huge turban and puffed-out satin trousers) took part in an elegant revue-pageant staged in Florence called "Un Po' di Colore," designed by Brunelleschi, the designer of the Folies Bergères. In 1918 Harold went back to England to be coached and finally to enter Eton, where he met Brian Howard for the first time.

Brian arrived at Eton as the best turned-out new boy ever seen there, but also carrying copies of Ezra Pound's poetry, which he had bought at the "Bomb" bookshop on the Charing Cross Road. He painted a Bakst frontispiece on the cover of his fag-master's scrapbook, and in other ways "represented" aestheticism and defied schoolboy conventions. But he was protected by two powerful dandies of the hour, Edward Jessel and Maurice Bridgeman, and soon became known as "one of the most amusing boys in the school." Harold Acton also tried to be "amusing," as did Cyril Connolly and lots of the others we shall study at their schools. It was necessarily a defensive and self-disguising role, a way of placating a society that might otherwise oppress members so alien to it, and so the performance inevitably left them a legacy of shame. But Howard and Acton, by their impudence, transformed defensiveness into aggression. They set out to dominate those contemporaries whom they had had to begin by amusing. And by and large they succeeded, at Eton, at Oxford, and for several years afterward: they convinced their friends that they were further ahead along a route the rest were all following. But to understand how this could happen, we must first understand something about Eton.

Chapter Four

1918–1922:
Eton

Brian and Harold and Their School

ETON WAS A dandy, aesthete, and snob institution long before 1918, and for reasons that go back over centuries. The College received its charter in 1444 and has today the same number of Collegers—boys on scholarship and, nowadays, boys selected by examination—as it had then. But while that number has stayed at seventy, the number of Oppidans—boys who pay fees and, nowadays, usually boys with family connections with Eton—has risen enormously. In 1550 there were thirty of them, in 1835 there were 376, and in 1965, 1,132. And nearly all of this last number had been prepared at one or other of fifty fee-paying prep schools, of which there are some 300 trying to serve such a purpose.[1]

These figures give some idea of the selectivity—and of the criteria of selection, inevitably snobbish to some degree—that decide which boys go to Eton today—and in 1918. As a school in a democratic society it was already old-fashioned then. It had not changed in accordance with the country's social and political development; or at least the ways in which it had remained the same were more striking. The younger boys still served the older ones as fags. The Collegers still lived in Chamber and the Oppidans in Houses, which were each run ultimately by a housemaster but proximately by a largely self-elected group of boys called the Library, who had the power to cane others, and by another minor version of the same thing called the Debate. Within the school as a whole there were two groups comparable to Library and Debate in power: the Sixth Form Select, twenty-odd of the academically best boys, chosen by examination results; and Pop, the Eton Society, whose criteria of election were quite different. Members of these two groups had important privileges, and wore significantly different dress from the other boys: white stick-up collars and white bow ties. Members of Pop in addition wore black-ribbon braid on their tailcoats, black and white checked trousers, and waistcoats that were traditionally extravagant in color and design. For Pop was a dandy institution. Its members were self-elected for their beauty, elegance, and charm, for their power to amuse and dazzle, and as members of Pop they intensified and institutionalized those qualities in each other. Insofar as Etonians have been aware of Pop as one of the school's characterizing and culminating aspects—and by and large they have been *very* aware of it—their whole school has been a dandy institution. It has been the English aristocracy's "House of Life," to use Alfred Schuler's term, their *Sonnenkindergarten*.

However, Eton is in most ways a typical British public school—in the class origin of its boys, in its teaching methods and subjects, in its games and leisure occupations, in its ethos. Anthony Powell's account of it, in *The Old School,* does not differ that much from L. P. Hartley's account of Harrow, William Plomer's account of Rugby, or Harold Nicolson's of Wellington. At Eton, as at other such schools, the athletes have traditionally been the heroes of the community, and the intellectuals and aesthetes have been a minority. The Borton brothers described in Chapter II had gone to Eton, and their *Boys' Own Paper* idiom must be taken to have been that of the majority of Etonians—an idiom against which Harold and Brian reacted with extravagantly opposite styles of language. And behind and within that idiom lay, of course, its spirit—the public school spirit.

We might take as a typical expression of that ethos Shane Leslie's *The End of a Chapter,* published in 1916. He describes Dr. Warre, the famous headmaster who had just retired, as "a grand old man and worthy to flog future bishops and statesmen of England"; and continues, "I do not know how many hundreds of Eton boys slain in the battles of empire will not rise to do him reverence among the dead. The Headmaster of Eton has more to do with the soul of England than the primate of Canterbury." At the same time, Shane Leslie was something of an aesthete himself—he was to write Brian Howard an enthusiastic letter about *The Eton Candle*—and he saw Eton as a House of Life too. He describes the Eton-Harrow cricket match as an annual replay of the archetypal conflict of Cavaliers against Roundheads, and it is the Etonians he sees as Cavaliers, of course. They are the ones with the "effortless superiority."

And just because Eton was like other public schools in most ways, the features that distinguished it were important, because they gave it its particular character. It was certainly felt to be different by Etonians and by others. Harold Nicolson says that when he got to Oxford he found that Etonians were at least two years "ahead of" him. Nicolson had gone to Wellington, a more military school and had had to expend most of his energies, he tells us, on "being manly." Eton offered more escapes from that, more alternatives for aesthetes, than other schools. Brian Howard always remembered with gratitude that he was allowed to use the poetry he himself had written in the recitation class. John Betjeman, who went to Marlborough, has some funny lines in his verse autobiography, *Summoned by Bells,* in which he represents "one more solemn of our number" (a more solemn old Marlburian at Oxford, that is) as saying to him, "Spiritually, John, I was at Eton." In other words, he had been at Marlborough in the flesh only— his soul was meant for finer things. What he meant by Eton may be suggested by a note "William Cory" made in his diary for 1867, as a text for an essay: "Every school should make the most of that which is its characteristic; Eton should continue to cultivate taste."[2]

"William Cory" was the Eton master who wrote the Eton Boating Song, but he was also the quite distinguished poet of *Ionica.* Although entirely Victorian in its dates, his diary shows that cult of taste, which includes the cult of beauty and of the individual beautiful boy, that characterized the later Eton. Cory allowed himself very romantic friendships with certain boys, because he believed that personal affection alone gave value to life, and considered himself a pagan in religion as in taste. His protégé, Oscar Browning, continued the same tradition at Eton. On the other hand, Cory also inculcated patriotism and even militarism. Henry Newbolt's poem about him, "Ionicus," ends:

> His age from fame and power was far;
> But his heart was high to the end and dreamed
> Of the sound and splendour of England's war.

The combination of these values with homoerotic romanticism is what distinguishes all English prewar feeling about naïfs and dandies; we see this as much in Housman's poems and in Pater's "Emerald Uthwart" as in the public school novels. But at Eton the cult of ephebic beauty and style was even then dangerously pronounced, amost insubordinate to "mature" values like patriotism.

Cyril Connolly says that in his day at Eton a boy's status did not depend on his family's money, or on his own proficiency at lessons or even at games, but on "a curious blend of elegance and vitality, to which the addition was much appreciated of a certain mental alertness and the gift of being amusing." He says that the school's values were "social" in this sense, and highly sophisticated in this kind, so that the times when he is transported back there in imagination are when he reads the memoirs of the comte de Gramont, or *La Princesse de Clèves.* Eton was a small world, ordered by an exquisitely graduated, but intensely felt, code of manners; Connolly calls the atmosphere 18th-century, as in the days of Thomas Gray and Horace Walpole.

Connolly admits himself still (in 1935) the "victim" of the school, in that the habits of thought and feeling he learned there he still cannot discontinue.[3]

It is worth noting that Eton has always been a socially fashionable school, with a large number of titled parents, and has stood close to certain sorts of power—social and dynastic sorts rather than political and intellectual (the latter would be the province rather of Winchester). Cyril Connolly says that in his day at Eton it was assumed that most masters were dying to be asked to the boys' homes, and even to be spoken to by the "important" boys. It is significant that Windsor Castle lies at the other end of the street from Eton; members of the royal family have always had a close link with the school. And in 1970, 366 of the 1,000 members of the House of Lords (including nearly all the dukes) were Old Etonians. There is a link between Eton and the world of farming and land-owning, and—perhaps by extension—the worlds of racing and acting. In these ways too it has been less serious than some other schools. But on the other hand, there is a famous political tradition of Old Etonian prime ministers—since 1800 far more have come from Eton than from any other school—and, indeed, of Old Etonian members of Parliament. In 1960 there were seventy Old Etonian members of the House of Commons, and the Conservatives among them amounted to 20 percent of that party's strength. Thus we must see as Etonian a blend of social dandyism with social seriousness—a blend of social performance with social function.

We can get some insight into the Eton of Brian Howard's and Harold Acton's time just from the advertisements in *The Eton Candle,* which they edited in 1922. There are, of course, several by tailors, but the terms in which they describe themselves suggest not aesthetes' dandyism but that world of power and responsibility that the writers for the *Candle* were flouting. For instance, Adamson's of Oxford describe themselves as "university, court, and military tailors"; W. V. Brown of Eton offers a representative who is sent to Oxford and Cambridge during term; Tom Brown offers military, diplomatic, and other uniforms and liveries. Another connection is suggested by the advertisements of gunmakers, one of whom offers "Holiday Instruction for Young Shooters," and by a breeches-maker. The booksellers advertised many books about Eton and the glories of the past: John Murray had a memoir of Dr. Warre (the famous headmaster), *Eton in the 70's, Eton in the 80's, Memories of Eton 60 Years Ago,* and *The Prime Ministers of Britain 1721—1921;* Chatto and Windus offered *The Oppidan,* a novel of Eton, by Shane Leslie. The old duties were implicit in advertisements by The Missions to Seamen and by the London Orphan School. The most modern note was struck in the many pages of advertisements for motorcycles—Indian, Norton, Barker and Co., and Diederich-Wooler. But the motorcycles were only mechanized horses, and Eton boys were still being prepared to judge, to rule, to lead rural communities of dependents. The school was still what it had been in Brummell's day, a hothouse of leadership, producing administrators by intention but also dandies on the side; it was a commercially viable nursery of young oak trees, with a dangerously high proportion of orchids twining among them.

Going to Eton was an experience that was likely to increase a talented boy's, and particularly a talented dandy's, potential in later life. It certainly meant that to our two principals. And what their going there meant to the institution was that Eton dandyism became much more insolently hostile to majority values in consequence. In the days of William Cory, too, the school had been a center of adolescent dandyism; the figure of the ephebe, gilded with erotic feeling, "the dear form in light blue," was an ultimate in value for Cory. But Cory loved seeing a "dear form" in soldier's scarlet as much as in light blue, and he was ready to see death in battle as a natural end to this phase of splendor. In other words, he had a strong sense that the *Sonnenkind* could not last, and although, imaginatively, he preferred seeing him die to seeing his real fate, i.e., modulation into mere manhood, into being a mere patriarchal functionary, still he did not protest against that diminution. The new dandies did protest. The war had roused great anger against the fathers, as well as guilt among them, and great pathos and love for the fallen sons, and the new dandies were able to appeal to those feelings in support of their cult of youth. They refused to grow up into men of responsibility, fathers of families and of the state, soldiers.

Another interesting insight into Eton's values before the war can be gained from the case of Ronald Knox, one of the starry successes of its educational methods. When he fell ill, as a schoolboy there, in 1906, he was prayed for in chapel; there were wires of inquiry from Old Etonians at Oxford and Cambridge; a letter came to his nursing home from forty of his schoolmates; there was even distress in London itself, where Old Boys, some of whom had never known him, inquired anxiously about his health in their clubs. He said later, "If I had died then, it would have been at the apogee of my earthly glory."* He was known as the cleverest Etonian in living memory, and that gave him a national position already.

It is particularly interesting to read Evelyn Waugh's biography of Knox, because there we see a dandy's portrait framed and enhanced by someone of the next generation, one of the postwar dandies. Waugh points out the exquisite and dandified character of Knox's Etonian verse, and indeed all Etonian verse had something of that character. One sees it in, for instance, the work of J. K. Stephen, the most famous light-verse writer of the period. No doubt because the basis of Eton's literary studies was translation from the classics, the arts of imitation and parody were brought to a high pitch there. The boys learned how to sound like Sophocles or Aristophanes long before they had anything Aristophanic to say; they mastered complicated literary forms at any age when the only thing they could put into such forms had to be merely humorous. The tradition of parody at Eton was so refined that the clever boys became very subtle craftsmen in it, almost parodists of parody. This was the intellectual, or at least literary, equivalent of that cricket-and-rowing dandyism in which the school formed most of its boys.

Waugh's comments are shrewd partly because his interest in prewar dandyism was so ambivalent. On the one hand he admired its inno-

---

* Evelyn Waugh's *Monsignor Ronald Knox.*

cence, its ready submission to the imperatives of manliness; on the other hand he found it rather sad, rather dull and limited, in comparison with the dandyism he had known, in Brian Howard and Harold Acton. But Waugh understood the issues better than anyone else. He says, "Ronald had no desire to grow up. Adolescence, for him, was not a process of liberation or of adventure. Manhood threatened him with tedious duties and grave decisions." But a man he had to be, in those prewar days. After 1918 an Eton *Sonnenkind* could refuse to grow up; in *Brideshead Revisited* Waugh tells the tragedy of Sebastian, an exquisite ephebe who refused to become a man. But Knox acknowledged the rights of the adult world, even though he himself was so completely satisfied and realized in that pre-adult paradise.

Knox had apparently fallen in love with one of the other boys—the younger of two brothers who were at Eton with him, a pair who, Waugh says, "exercised a peculiar fascination over their seniors. . . . their cult was pure and romantic, but a cult it was, which spread beyond College to a heterogeneous and infatuated group." This sounds like the Grenfell brothers, who were among that group of "golden lads" who died in the war. Knox, according to Waugh, "established a primacy in this boy's little court of troubadours." But, of course, he accepted the call—in his case a religious call—to grow up and leave behind this world of innocent delight. He knew that the world of delight was only a curtain raiser to Reality. This is what Waugh admired in Knox, and this was a view of dandyism he could approve, although his keenest delight and appreciation went to the raucous and insolent rebellion of the 1920s.

Among Waugh's phrases listing Knox's good fortune in life, we find that he was "boon companion to a generation of legendary heroes," meaning the group mentioned before who died in the war. But they were legendary heroes at school too. From Kipling's time, if not earlier, the ideas of "legend" and "hero," like the ideas of "fame" and "success," were used to describe purely school experience, and semi-seriously. Christopher Hollis, in his book on Eton, describes the group narcissism of the "Ram" at chapel, the double file procession of seniors, largely Pop and the Select, into chapel after everyone else is seated for the service—"a spectacle that has been described as Eton worshipping itself." Hollis quotes from A. C. Benson, the Eton housemaster, describing his first sight of one boy in the Ram:

> His light curly hair, his sparkling smiling eyes, his under lip thrust out, all gave a look of intense animation and activity. Who could the hero be? I soon found out: it was Alfred Lyttelton, the unquestioned, undisputed king of the place, last of a long line of well-known brothers, and the most famous of all.

Lyttelton, says Hollis, was indeed probably the supreme example of the "king" type, the prewar, non-aesthetic dandy, although the name more often cited is that of J. K. Stephen, the writer for *Punch* and cousin to Virginia Woolf. (It is, incidentally, a theory popular among disgruntled Old Etonians that Stephen became Jack the Ripper in later life.) But it is the master's attitude toward him that is especially striking.

The change that gave the leadership to the aesthete-dandy instead of the king type was of course gradual and at best partial. The postwar debunking books like Lytton Strachey's *Eminent Victorians* seem to have had an especially immediate effect at Eton, but political cynicism did not necessarily result, much less bring aestheticism in its train. The pattern of most boys' thought on such matters changed not at all, or indeed in a nonaesthetic direction. There was, for instance, a serious *political* interest in the Election (a year's entry into College) of 1917, to which George Orwell belonged.[4] Its members protested against there being an Army Corps at Eton, instituted democratic changes in the system of self-government, and diminished the privileges of the dandy institutions like Pop. And one of the school's dandies of the next few years, according to Cyril Connolly, was Anthony Knebworth, who was a prewar type, a "king," not at all an aesthete.

Knebworth died young, and Connolly, who had been a friend of his, wrote a review of a commemorative book about him in 1935 called *Anthony,* compiled by the boy's father, the earl of Lytton.[5] Anthony was born in 1903, the same year as Evelyn Waugh, Harold Acton, and

George Orwell. His godfathers were Edward VII and Lord Salisbury, and he grew up to be a John Buchan hero in the style of those who had died in the war. He won prizes at school for racing, hurdling, boxing, skiing, and rugger, and he was adored by his contemporaries and his elders. The book about him assembles tributes by among others Duff Cooper, Sir James Barrie, who speaks of "the glamorous creature we knew him to be," Stanley Baldwin, and Arthur Bryant. The last says, "Had he lived he might have given to England in a new age gifts of leadership and imagination which she sorely needs, and a selfless service. . . . That quaint eager dark face—of a heroic boy poised for fighting—remains as I write clearly photographed in my memory." The image is significantly Kiplingesque.

But Connolly views Knebworth from a different perspective. He sees him as one of "a small group of powerful dandies, who were looked on with an awe that luckily in most of us atrophies, or we should be miserable still." Connolly was still rebelling against the domination of "heroic" values that Knebworth had represented to him so authoritatively. After Eton and Oxford, the latter had gone out to India when his father was viceroy, and had returned to become a Conservative member of Parliament. He had led a group of friends in a crusade against Noel Coward and the influence of the latter's cynicism; had resisted modernism in the arts; and at the end—he died in a flying accident at the age of twenty-nine—had been interested in Fascism and Roman Catholicism. In one of his letters he said that "civilized man has gradually been discarding discipline and obedience, reason and simplicity, in this mad search after freedom." He predicted, and wanted, a reaction on the part of the Right, to reestablish those old disciplines and simplicities. For Connolly, to review the book was clearly an occasion for self-justification, self-ratification in his status as a member of an Eton minority and opposition. Knebworth, the hero of the majority, had "gone bad" in his mind; and Connolly thought he could show that that happened because Knebworth, like other men of action, had never accepted the intelligence or the modern intelligentsia. Knebworth could not read contemporary literature. Connolly says, "The writers who were at Oxford with him, Evelyn Waugh and Peter Quennell, were impossible—they were aesthetes. . . ."; and Knebworth's letters mention only such Edwardian enthusiasms as Gilbert and Sullivan, G. K. Chesterton and Hilaire Belloc, and Maurice Baring and Philip Guedalla.

So we see that the dominant Eton dandies of these years were not aesthetes. But on the other hand, we will also see that the anti-aesthetes among them were soon in a rather difficult position.

Of our principals' early years at Eton we do not hear much that sounds significant. Harold Acton was beaten by Library for not knowing his house colors; Brian Howard took a toy engine to chapel and was nearly expelled. Both were notable leaders and inspirers of other boys' insolence against the system. James Stern tells anecdotes of Harold's impudent foolery with the Dames (like housemothers) and the masters—a foolery that had an edge of insolence and anarchic gaiety that made it exhilarating to the onlookers. William did no work, but since he was a good athlete, he fitted into the school life more easily than the other two. He took to riding, which he kept up at Oxford. One anecdote we hear describes him being taken to tea by Brian Howard with the latter's aunt. William arrived in a brown homburg and cut-velvet waistcoat, carrying a gold-knobbed cane, and made stately conversation of an aestheticism that, coming from a fifteen-year-old boy, seemed as startling as obscenity. "I think the velvets of the Cinquecento *are* to be preferred to those of *any* other period," is one sentence that family legend has preserved.

Brian acted girl parts in Eton plays with great success, and he told Harold Acton (and others) that he resembled Max Beerbohm in the days when the latter was beautiful as well as brilliant. Cyril Connolly describes him as having then a "distinguished impertinent face, a sensual mouth, and dark eyes with long eyelashes" and says that he became "the most fashionable boy in the school." And it may be of interest here to cite also some of Connolly's comments on Cecil Beaton's similar impact at prep school during wartime. Beaton sang "If you were the only boy in the world" at Saturday night concerts—in imitation of

Violet Lorraine—so charmingly that "the eighty odd boys in the audience felt there could be no other boy in the world for them." Connolly says that "for a moment the whole structure of character and duty tottered and even the principles of hanging on, muddling through, and building empires were called into question." That sounds exaggerated, but it is surely only probable that the mood Beaton and, later, Howard evoked in their schoolmates by these female impersonations were implicitly hostile to the moods of "duty" and "character."[6]

They evoked similar moods, more intellectually, by their taste in literature. Brian liked all "modern" writers except D. H. Lawrence, and he wrote to his mother, "I can't sit around reading Carlyle and James Russell Lowell. I *can't* do it. . . . let me smell green carnations while I am still of an appropriate age." He and his friends were very conscious of age, already. They worshiped youth while they were still adolescents.

Harold Acton hung a Whistler nocturne on the walls of his room— "an oasis in the desert of hunting prints"—and preached against Bloomsbury, and against the Omega Workshops where Roger Fry, Vanessa Bell, and Duncan Grant were designing new and startling fabrics and furnishings. Harold felt that the aesthetes at Eton had a mission, and he preached a taste for Berenson and scholarship about art, as opposed to Fry and the emphasis on uplift in art. (Echoes of his aesthetic creed are to be found in Waugh's *Brideshead Revisited.*) "At the Omega Workshops there was a painstaking revival of primitive forms," he says in his *Memoirs.* "The patterns a Polynesian produced intuitively in the calm of a coral atoll were refurbished in Bloomsbury amid much soul-stirring and high-flown discourse." But he accepted Bloomsbury as an ally against English obtuseness, even though he opposed it on purely aesthetic grounds: ". . . under the persuasive glow of his [Fry's] Bengal lights almost any amoeba could assume visionary shapes. Such fakirs have great virtues as missionaries among the Philistines."

In discussion of such matters, Brian and Harold walked from Eton to Slough every Sunday, feeling like "les frères Goncourt" after literary copy; for they were seeking out on the way suburban houses and human types that exemplified the "bourgeois macabre." Brian was particularly quick to detect hints of flagellation, black magic, murder, or cannibalism behind oppressively respectable facades. They agreed on most matters of taste, although in poetry Harold approved only T. S. Eliot and Edith Sitwell, while Brian was enthusiastic for Ezra Pound and Ford Madox Ford as well. The visual arts they gradually made so much the center of excitement at Eton that during their last two years there, 1920–1922, the numbers entering the painting competitions swelled, and one year Roger Fry himself came to judge the entries. (William Acton won one of the prizes.)

What they stood for at Eton was modernism in general, understood as the movement against the consensus culture of Victorian and Edwardian England. They stood for French poetry—Mallarmé, Rimbaud, Verlaine, and Laforgue—and for French fiction—Proust, Huysmans, and Cocteau—and for France in general—Paris and Poiret and Charvet (maker of the most exquisite ties) and just the sound of the French language. They stood for American poetry—Eliot, and Amy Lowell, and some Pound—and for cocktails and jazz. They stood for modern painting—Whistler and John, Picasso and Gauguin. Among English people and things they stood for the Sitwells, above all. And, of course, they stood for Diaghilev and everyone and everything associated with him, from Bakst and Stravinsky to Pierrot and Harlequin.

Perhaps their major ally in this battle of taste at Eton was one of the young teachers, Aldous Huxley. Acton describes him walking down Eton High Street like a juvenile giraffe escaped from a zoo, trailing an orange scarf or dangling over a dangling shoelace. He had made his own escape from Edwardian consensus culture by means of Laforgue, above all, and Proust, Verlaine, Rimbaud, and Mallarmé. Acton says Huxley was so saturated in Laforgue that he unconsciously paraphrased him in most of his prose poems. But he had found English masters too; it was he who spread the cult of John Donne and the Metaphysicals among the young Eton aesthetes, and so, says Acton, "freed us from the '90s." He was an avant-garde poet, who published his satirical novel, *Crome Yellow,* in 1921, and a figure of scandal to conventional littérateurs. Brian and Harold published his poems in the magazine with which they defied the school's conservatives. The modern movement was perceptibly, at Eton, launched.

And the importance, the effect, of that movement was cultural and personal as well as aesthetic. Cyril Connolly has pointed out the importance to his life of the fact that his personal adolescence, between 1918 and 1923, coincided with the flowering of that movement, because the movement itself was a kind of cultural adolescence. "I was, without knowing it, in search of a father—or father-replacement";* I think we can safely say that it was a father replacement and not a father he sought. For instance, in his twenties Connolly went to live in Sanary, in France, in order to be a neighbor of Aldous Huxley, whom he so much admired. Huxley was nobody's father; he was the kind of guru who guaranteed that fathers were out of date. The same is true of the other great modernists whom Connolly got to know in Paris, and who were part of "the explosion of my emotional life"—Joyce, Gide, and Hemingway. Modernism in the arts was the aesthetic aspect of the *Sonnenkind* movement.

But for Connolly, Paris and modernism were to come long *after* Eton. For Brian and Harold, these things were in their possession as schoolboys. This was especially true for Harold. Back in Florence on vacations, the Acton brothers saw a lot of notables of the English literary scene, always from the point of view of the dandies. With Norman Douglas, Harold met D. H. Lawrence; with Reggie Turner, he met Rebecca West and Ronald Firbank. Firbank embarrassed Reggie by his exaggerated voice and manners (which included rushing out of a flower shop laden with lilies to present to Reggie) and by their equivalent in literary manners, so that the latter declared that he preferred reading Wodehouse to Firbank. Later, to Florence, came Aldous Huxley and C. K. Scott-Moncrieff, Richard Aldington and Radclyffe Hall. And at Montegufoni the Sitwell brothers, unbeknown to their father, were having Gino Severini paint a whole room with *commedia* figures.

---

* "The Modern Movement," *Evening Colonnade*, 1973.

Other Etonians

Among Harold's and Brian's contemporaries at Eton and of some minor importance to our story were Oliver Messel, Robert Byron, Alan Clutton-Brock, Robert Gathorne-Hardy, and Ian Fleming. Messel was the son of a professional soldier, but he went into theater design, one of the most typical of aesthete's occupations. He chose the Slade School of Design in preference to Oxford. By 1926, when he was twenty-one, he was designing Charles Cochran revues, which usually included some ballet episodes, although his major ballet work seems to have begun in the 1930s. After the Second World War he also designed for the Glyndebourne and Covent Garden operas, and he has had probably the highest reputation of all British stage designers.

Robert Byron was born into a younger and impoverished branch of the poet's family. He was the most energetic and ambitious of all the group, and although he had no very specific vocation except to power and success, he showed ability in whatever he took up—from writing to politics and the appreciation of architecture. His was a violent and in some ways gross personality, always ready to quarrel and to hector, ready to fall asleep while someone else was speaking and even to rest his head on the speaker's arm. He was considered ugly and dressed eccentrically to heighten the effect. He was also shamelessly greedy and unscrupulous in pursuit of whatever he wanted. In short, he was a rogue, and it is a sign of the times that he was in such close alliance with such dandies as Harold Acton and Brian Howard.

Alan Clutton-Brock, son of Old Etonian Arthur Clutton-Brock, was a member of the group that produced *The Eton Candle,* but he afterward seems to have had little contact with them. After going to Cambridge he was art critic for *The Times,* and he later became a trustee of the National Gallery and Slade Professor of Fine Arts at Cambridge, in the '50s. He reappears in our story, however, as the squadron leader under whom Brian Howard served during the war.

Robert Gathorne-Hardy became a great friend of Lady Otto-line Morrell, and later secretary and companion to Logan Pearsall

Smith, in succession to Cyril Connolly. In those capacities he kept closer to the prewar style of socially subdued and "intellectual" dandyism. But his brother Edward, who went on from the bookshop in which they had shared to the Foreign Office, remained a lifelong friend of Brian Howard.

Ian Fleming, who was three years younger than Brian, was not a member of the dandies' group at Eton; nor did he go on to Oxford, but to Sandhurst and then to work as a journalist in Moscow. But after 1952, when he married a friend of Evelyn Waugh's, he saw a good deal of the latter, who took an interest in the James Bond stories. Above all, there is something Etonian about those stories. As Paul Johnson said in a *New Statesman* review of *Doctor No,* the main ingredients, "all thoroughly English," are schoolboy bullying, adolescent sex, and snobbery. Bond is the emblem of a new British dandyism, which we will discuss later, but it is worth noting now its Etonian connections.

It is also worth mentioning some Etonians who went into publishing: Roger Senhouse, who went to Secker and Warburg and was editor to both Cyril Connolly and George Orwell; Rupert Hart-Davis, who ran his own publishing house; and John Lehmann, about whom we will say more later. At Eton Lehmann seems to have accepted the public school ethos more completely than any of the other figures in our study. These names suggest the power of the school in the world of publishing.

But of all the boys who were at Eton with Brian and Harold, Cyril Connolly is the one who has written most and best about those experiences. His most famous essay on the subject is "A Georgian Boyhood" in *Enemies of Promise* (1938). Arriving at Eton he felt, he says, "no doubt that this was the place for me, for all of it was, from the St. Wulfric's point of view, utterly and absorbingly evil." "St. Wulfric's" (Connolly's name for his prep school, actually called St. Cyprian's) had insisted always on Character, while at Eton one could cultivate quite opposite values, which Connolly evokes with the phrase "the civilization of the lilies." A Colleger, he was bullied at first by Godfrey Meynell; but when the latter and his friend Highworth accepted

Connolly, the three became good friends. All three had fathers in the army; and Meynell followed that career himself, leading Ghurkas into Waziristan, getting killed, and being awarded a posthumous Victoria Cross. It was the fate of a Kipling hero. Connolly wrote,

> Such an end seems remote from the literary life, yet it was the end of one of my own age, with whom for four years I had been shaken about like stones in a tin. To a parent passing through College there must have seemed nothing to choose between Godfrey and myself. . . . Such was the reward of leadership, the destiny of character. . . .

Etonians have special occasions for reflecting on the paths they have taken, because their friends who took other paths are reported in the papers; and the dandy-aesthetes used those occasions more than most. They knew they had rejected "leadership" and "character," and they could never be entirely easy about their choice. Evelyn Waugh, for example, both ridiculed character/leadership and yearned for it; the contradiction made him a humorist.

Connolly says a good deal about the strongly erotic atmosphere at Eton, which derived he thinks from the classical literature they read, and about his intrigues to get to see a younger boy in whom he and a friend were "interested." In the dedicatory letter to his novel, *The Rock Pool,* he mentions the "moral weakness" and "unpleasantness" that English publishers had found in the manuscript (it was finally published in France) and explains them by his classical education. Despite their Sunday Christianity, the weekday god whom his Eton teachers struggled to cultivate was Horace, and when the Loeb editions appeared, the boys, too, discovered that youths *ought* to drink and make love, while men *ought* to talk and reflect. They then passed from Horace to Catullus and Petronius—of whom Connolly had bought two editions by the time he left school, two more by a year later, and two more thereafter, because he always thought the *Satyricon* so wonderful. "I was perfectly right. It is a very great book. Not great—magical is perhaps a better word, and, what is even rarer, it is a humane book." He describes Petronius enthusiastically as a dandy, a man who idled his way into fame, and as—like the Restoration rogue, Rochester, or some nobleman of Versailles—a poet and lover of low life. (Connolly clearly invites us to make some identification between Petronius and himself).[7]

Connolly described the set of Brian and Harold and their friends as

> a set of boys who were literary and artistic but too lazy to gargle quotations and become inoculated with the virus of good taste latent in Eton teaching, and too disorderly and bad at games to be overburdened with responsibility [that is, to 'succeed,' as Connolly himself had done], and who in fact gained most from Eton because of the little they gave. . . . They were the most vigorous group at Eton for they lived within their strength, yet my moral cowardice and academic outlook debarred me from making friends with them.

It is here one sees the moral primacy gradually established by the more dandified over the less. Connolly certainly knew, when he wrote that,[8] that he was more talented and knowledgeable than most of those he defers to, and that he had made more of his talents by most external standards. But he had not had the courage (then or later) to commit himself to their extreme and extravagant dandyism, the new-style dandyism that carried the new ideas and brought the new experiences. Connolly both won high academic honors at Eton and was elected to Pop, with an exultation that he describes. His withdrawal from the aesthete-dandies was related to Pop, in a way that was emblematic. Brian Howard had cultivated his acquaintance, but when Connolly arrived at Brian's rooms for tea, he found his own acceptance of the invitation, which he had written on Pop notepaper, displayed prominently on the mantlepiece—to let the world know that Brian was a friend of Connolly, a member of Pop. Connolly then felt, he says, "miserable," because he had been used, but also no doubt because he had betrayed Pop. Connolly always took such institutions more seriously emotionally than he could quite defend doing; he never risked finally offending any of them.

In "A Georgian Boyhood," Connolly advanced his "theory of permanent adolescence," the idea that experiences at great public schools are so intense as to dominate the lives and arrest the development of those who undergo them. "Those I know are haunted ruins in their early thirties. Some dream they are back in their old rooms while their wives and children hang about outside to disgrace them." This is the classic image for the dandy's sensibility, and it can be believed more readily if one remembers that Connolly's schooldays fell in the years when the adolescent boy believed in himself more intensely than usual—believed less intensely than usual in the adult manhood toward which he was told to move. It seems that at Eton then a new idea was being born that changed the idea of "Englishman."

In Connolly's own writing, and in that of other Old Etonians, images from schooldays have a remarkable vividness. In *The Rock Pool,* when the hero meets a Winchester boy whom he despises, someone who looks like a social liability, he feels like "the second most unpopular boy at a school receiving overtures from the first." And when he is attacked by the American woman with whom he has an affair, it is in these terms:

> All you English boys are brought up on marks. You say you got marks for learning the Collect, whatever that is, marks for taking out the best books from the library, marks for good conduct, for scholarships and examinations. Marks for every time you opened your mouth till you left Oxford, and now that they've stopped giving them, you don't know what to do.

Writing in *Horizon* during the war about what it felt like to be a civilian in such times, he said he was "the unpopular schoolboy in the keen, tough school;" and writing about Rimbaud, he said it was *the* English disease "to go through life looking always back to childhood." Why, he asks, do we tolerate a philosophy that envisages life as a paradise before puberty, a series of ecstatic moments in early youth, and a disastrous anticlimax, a gradation of decay, after the age of 26?[9]

Having won the Rosebery History Prize and the Brackenbury History Scholarship to Balliol, in 1922 Connolly left Eton for Oxford, the "third hot room of English education." He saw the transition as likely to be a diminution, a dimming of romance. He dreaded in advance "the uglification of life" that he foresaw at Oxford.

> Also we were attached to the past and used to a world of boys, boys with a certain grace who like the portraits in the Provost's Lodge wore their 18th century clothes with elegance. The world of matey young men with their pipes and grey bags and the blokeries to which we had been assigned, filled us with despair. . . .

In that passage, looking back on his Eton feelings, he identifies those feelings by using images appropriate to Harold Acton or Brian Howard. But it took him until 1938 to commit himself to those images in writing.[10]

Also among the boys at Eton then was "George Orwell," Eric Blair, who was a Colleger from 1917 to 1921. He too was to take up a position and to assimilate a temperament—one that was the opposite of Connolly's (although Orwell's idea too had, paradoxically, an Etonian source). This comes out clearly when you compare the two men's remarks about Eton. Orwell says, in a review of "A Georgian Boyhood," that it is almost incredible that Connolly's "theory of permanent adolescence" is meant seriously. He goes on to admit, however, that that theory tells the truth, "in an inverted fashion." When Orwell sets the truth the right way up, we find that "'cultured' middle class life has reached a depth of softness at which public-school education—'five years in a luke-warm bath of snobbery'—can actually be looked back upon as an eventful period." Nothing has happened to people like Connolly since Eton, to make them forget it: "Hunger, hardship, solitude, exile, war, prison, persecution, manual labour—hardly even words." Orwell is evoking a Reality in whose presence the whole world of Eton experiences will shrink to manageable proportions—so that the problem of the transition out of that enchanted garden will shrink with it. It was Evelyn Waugh's distinction that he refused to take this obvious way out of the problem. In

Brideshead Revisited he makes much of that enchanted garden—using just that image—and makes leaving it a tragedy. But some of Orwell's distinction shows itself in his admission that Connolly's account of Eton is "surprisingly accurate," and in his restriction of his weapons of attack to criteria acquired outside and after Eton. We must also realize that Orwell was able to condemn Connolly so confidently because the experience of their audience had changed. Orwell was writing in 1940,[11] when the voice of men of responsibility was again dominant over that of dandies and aesthetes.

Of course, Orwell did not rely inertly on his audience's prejudices. He had won his way back to a belief in responsibility and manhood, step by step, and before anybody else did. As early as 1936 he said, in reviewing Connolly's novel, *The Rock Pool,* that

> even to want to write about so-called artists who spend on sodomy what they have gained by sponging betrays a kind of spiritual inadequacy . . . a distaste for normal life and common decency . . . sluttish antinomianism—lying in bed till four in the afternoon, drinking Pernod. . . . The fact to which we have got to cling, as to a life-belt, is that it *is* possible to be a normal decent person and yet to be fully alive."[2]

Orwell's discovery of "normality" and "decency" was to be very important to England in the years ahead, and it is worth noting that he discovered them in reaction against Etonian aestheticism. Writing to Connolly during the years when he so astringently reviewed *The Rock Pool* and "A Georgian Childhood," he acknowledges that he wrote out of the same experience—even though he drew opposite conclusions from it. He says,

> Of course you were in every way much more of a success at school than I . . . but as far as essentials go we had very much the same experiences from 1912 to 1921. And our literary experiences impinged at certain points, too.

They had attended the same prep school, St. Cyprian's, where they had shared a copy of *Sinister Street,* Compton Mackenzie's romantic novel about Oxford, and had got into trouble for having such decadent tastes. Incidentally, it was Blair who lent Connolly *Sinister Street,* rather than the other way round—just as later, at Eton, he lent him *Dorian Gray,* a book he always liked but that Connolly found a bit childish.

In this letter to Connolly, written in 1938, Orwell says that while the latter is writing about Eton, *he* intends to write about St. Cyprian's; and he did so in "Such, Such Were the Joys," calling the school "Crossgates." In fact, Connolly also wrote about the school (in "Georgian Boyhood"), as "St. Wulfric's," and so did Cecil Beaton (in *The Wandering Years*) who was also there. What they have written about it agrees remarkably on all matters of substance—for instance, on the strong effect exerted upon all the boys by Mrs. Wilkes, the headmaster's wife, whom Connolly describes as "hotting up her favourites like so many little Alfa-Romeos for the Brooklands of life." Looking back, they all saw in her a personification of the public school ethos, of that England against which they all three, in such different ways, rebelled. And the most interesting point about which they agree is the *intensity* of the experience. Orwell says that it is at prep school that people's lives are ruined. (Apparently, he did not find that subsequent "hunger, hardship, solitude" and so on to put St. Cyprian's into perspective.) He says that Eton was for him one long period of relaxation from the rigors of St. Cyprian's; and that would explain the intellectual half of his rejection of "A Georgian Boyhood"—because to him Eton was *not* an intense experience.

About such matters, of course, one can only speculate, but there are reasons for supposing that Orwell's years at Eton were a dim experience to him even at the time. One of his contemporaries described him as having been the "dimmest" member of a brilliant Election, and he is practically unrecorded in all the diaries and minutes of club activities, in which he did, in some external sense, participate. He was known to everyone as Blair, not Eric. Anthony Powell says he cannot remember him there, even though they were both in the same company of the Army Corps; and Harold Acton could only remember a tall figure flapping somberly about the Yard in his black gown. His friends there, Gibson and King-Barlow, say that the stories he wrote for Hugh McNaghten's English club or for A. S. F. Gow's group of would-be writers were never praised. Indeed, his writing then does seem facile and uninteresting.

Surely all this suggests someone camouflaging himself, some sinking out of sight and under cover—a cover from which he was to emerge many years later as "George Orwell," having found in "manhood" and "citizenship" those usable stimuli to self-formation that he could not find in the Etonian *Sonnenkind*. In 1929 he was 117th out of 140 boys. Out of the fourteen boys of his Election, eleven went to Oxford or Cambridge, two went into family businesses, and Orwell left England for the Burma police. He had been a failure at Eton—all the more complete a failure for being a discreet one—and in every way. Intellectually, he was still a reader of Housman, not Eliot. His imagination was involuntarily fascinated by images of dandyism and aestheticism, but they were old-fashioned images. The Paris half of *Down and Out in Paris and London* is old-fashioned aestheticism, and only the social realism of the other half redeems the book. And the significance of this for our story lies in the contrast with Brian Howard and Harold Acton, who were successes—intellectually and imaginatively—at Eton. They were dandy-aesthetes in an age of the dandy-aesthete.

So public were they in their success that one can take it for granted that Orwell, since he aspired to write himself, was conscious of them. They were published, for instance, in national magazines. Moreover, Orwell's taste for *Sinister Street* and *Dorian Gray* put him on their wavelength in some ways. Anthony Powell speaks of P. G. Wodehouse mannerisms in Eric Blair and of a moustache (later) on George Orwell that was "a concession to the dandyism that undoubtedly existed below the surface" *(London Times Review, 1968)*. And it seems clear that Orwell, while he was at Eton, had no powerful defences against the stimulus to dandyism, and that a few pockmarks remained all his life in testimony to his inoculation. So he was almost certainly aware of our two principals, and almost certainly their challenge remained with him, however subcutaneously, as with other would-be writers among the boys.

Among the more "successful" boys (I use quotation marks because one of the kinds of success I mean is the Eton kind) was Anthony Powell. His father was, like Oliver Messel's, a lieutenant colonel. He had served in the Welsh Guards and then on the army general staff. Born in 1905, Anthony did not reach Eton until 1919, and so was a year behind our central pair. He differed also in that he became a sergeant in the Army Corps, admired the military adjutant there, and made a hobby out of military uniforms and regimental regalia. Thus he continued, with certain scholarly and aesthetic adjustments, his familial heritage. But he also became a novelist—something he explains, typically, by saying that at Eton, novel-writing was the ordinary thing to do, and he had always been taught to do the ordinary thing. His tone, and his tastes, have always been discreetly dandified. He was in those days, for instance, interested in Regency costume and book illustrations.

Powell has been the most dismissive of Brian Howard of all his contemporaries. "I never liked him, nor thought, even at Eton, that he had a vestige of real talent in any of the arts. All he seemed to be interested in was self-advertisement and forms of exhibitionism."[13] Nevertheless, Powell contributed to *The Eton Candle* and participated in the Eton Society of the Arts, both of which were organized by Brian Howard. I think we may assume that however dismissive his later opinions, and however negative his contemporary feelings, Powell was more *concerned* with Brian Howard and Harold Acton, at that point in his life, than he now admits.

He was certainly much concerned with Eton, as his contribution to *The Old School* shows, and his novels often seem to demonstrate Connolly's "theory of permanent adolescence." His most ambitious work, the novel sequence entitled *A Dance to the Music of Time,* takes its origins, in every sense, at Eton. The first scene in the first novel, *A Question of Upbringing,* presents the three main characters as schoolboys there; the school buffoon, Widmerpool, appears out of the autumn dusk from a solitary run, and Nick Jenkins goes into his study to discuss the phenomenon with Stringham. And the central story of the whole sequence is the decline of Stringham and the triumph of Widmerpool, as seen through the mildly startled eyes of Jenkins—startled because from the Etonian point of view that decline and that triumph are so unnatural and inexplicable. Stringham was one of the princes of Eton, one of its exquisite dandies, and Widmerpool was one of its butts and buffoons—he is a Billie Bunter, the fat boy of Frank Richard's schoolboy stories, gross, clumsy, anxious, indignant, alien, the schoolboy's nightmare. He is the opposite of a dandy. Stringham is described as looking like "one of those stiff sad young men in ruffs, whose long legs take up so much room in 18th century portraits; or perhaps a younger—and slighter—version of Veronese's Alexander." (There is a photograph of Brian Howard in El Greco fancy dress that would fit this description very well.) And Stringham's voice is the dandy voice. Thus, of the character Peter Templer: "'I'm devoted to Peter,' said Stringham, 'but really I'm not sure one could have him in the house, could one?'"

Widmerpool is Powell's most original creation, and in him he explores an aspect of dandyism that Waugh never successfully coped with. The negative pole of Etonian values, Widmerpool is a grownup Billie Bunter not only in his physique—the glasses, heavy breathing, clumsiness, heaviness, constant grievance of tone—but in the things that happen to him—the banana in the face from Budd, the sugar in the hair from Barbara Goring, the car that won't start and then runs out of control at Sir Magnus Donner's, and so on. *A Dance to the Music of Time* is in many ways a schoolboy saga.

In temperament, Widmerpool is a Caliban servant of the world of men, the world of the fathers, who refuses to acknowledge the standards of Adonis. Jenkins, on the other hand, can only live imaginatively by Adonis, although he sees very clearly—and with some satisfaction—that the world is run by those other principles that Widmerpool in his clumsy way represents. And the times and places of the novel are exactly those of this study. It seems to begin in 1919, for Nick Jenkins' father is at the Paris Peace Conference, and the first time he visits Stringham's family, they are going to the Russian ballet.

Stringham is said to be drawn from Henry Yorke (the future novelist "Henry Green"), who was at Eton with Powell. And although it seems likely that very few of the characters are "portraits," many must be composites, composed out of the people Powell knew at school, university, and afterwards—the people whose careers we are tracing. Connolly, Bowra, Waugh, all seem to be there, as reassembled parts.

Henry Yorke, or "Henry Green," has been more generous in his memories of Brian Howard.

> I think he was quite the most handsome boy I'd ever seen— and remained so as a man up till the war . . . [he was] a brilliant conversationalist, even as a boy, and was able to dominate people by his conversation. But he was also a terrible poseur and a wild snob, always making up to everyone in Pop. He became a great social success at Eton. Boys are easily ignored, but with Brian everything flowered there. . . . He had tremendous charm—and could put it on when he wanted to.[14]

Green had gone to a prep school in Kent, which he had hated, where most of the other boys were the sons of officers. The headmaster (the "tyrant," the "old devil," as Green calls him in his autobiography) was omnipotent. The boys all adored him and took over his chauvinist and philistine beliefs. In his autobiography, *Pack My Bag* (which was written just before the war and published in 1940) Green foresees that in the coming war England will be like school again and that it will again be criminal to be afraid. This school was a Fascist state (a comparison that Auden made also about his school), but Eton had at least phases of extraordinary romance. Green had an elder brother who was in Pop, and when the two of them walked together, "then indeed and only then, I have never afterwards known anything like it, one was the cynosure of all eyes. Success at school," he adds, "is more complete than any other kind at any other time." The climactic moment came when Green saw "another Son of Heaven coming towards us on our pavement. When G. stopped and they spoke naturally to each other my day was made." Green's whole vocabulary evokes the *Sonnenkind* myth.

Green was a friend of Brian Howard and Harold Acton. Indeed, he became the secretary of their Society of the Arts, although "characteristically," he says, he was too cautious to align himself entirely with the aesthetes. But he also says that knowing them was the experience that determined him to become a writer; and, in fact, his first novel, *Blindness,* published in 1926, was about Eton, even about the Eton Society of the Arts, and it mentions our principals in disguised form. The central figure, John Haye, is secretary to the Noat Art Society. He loves Lytton Strachey and hates public school, especially the O.T.C., because it makes intelligent men commonplace. He buys a horse's straw hat, paints it in concentric rings, and wears it—to everyone's anger. He admires the aesthetes who introduce Post-Impressionism to the school and affront maturity by playing with toy motors, and so on. Green insists that by comparison with the aesthetes, the masters were "a poor lot."

Finally, we can consult the testimony of Christopher Hollis, although since he left the school in 1919, he did not really know postwar Eton and was not really contemporary with our main group. His own tone, his whole persona, is much closer to those of pre-1914 manhood—he was, for instance, devoted to cricket as a boy—and it is perhaps not fanciful to explain this difference in part by the slight difference in time. He had gone to a famous prep school, Summer Fields, where Ronald Knox had gone earlier and where Anthony Asquith and Walter and Steven Runciman—dandies peripheral to our later story—were his contemporaries. Hollis, like Connolly later, won the Brackenbury History Scholarship to Balliol in 1918. He then had a last year at Eton, during which he professed, he says, to be an iconoclastic and satirical commentator on the place. But this profession was largely a device that allowed him to say sentimental things about Eton "ironically," and call his time there the happiest years of his life. Writing later, he says those *were* the happiest years of his life, the expression he then put within defensive quotation marks.[15]

It is significant that Hollis, like Knox and Waugh, was a Roman Catholic convert. Culturally speaking, Catholicism has often been a means whereby dandyism has been reconciled to reality; the repudiation of Protestantism has been a symbolic repudiation of philistinism and "squareness," and the acceptance of Rome and ritual has made dandyism seem a mode of paradoxical seriousness. But there have been two divergent strategies for Catholics to follow in developing a post-dandy ideology. One is the black romanticism of Huysmans; the other, the bright and cheerful clarity of Chesterton. Hollis and Knox followed the second, and on the whole Waugh did too, although he sometimes half-participated in the first option, which was more "modernist"—I am thinking of the *Waste Land* effects of *Vile Bodies* and so on.

Raising the Banner of Art

Our two main dandies were successful artists and ambitious amateurs of the arts while still at Eton. In 1920, Brian Howard had a poem and a satire accepted by A. R. Orage's magazine, *New Age*. He also exhibited a sketch at the International Exhibition in London and received the praises of Aldous Huxley, Gerald Kelly, Lady Lavery, and other notables. Harold Acton had poems printed in the *Spectator* and *The New Witness,* and William Acton got a painting prize from Roger Fry and sold pictures. But perhaps their most significant success came when Brian sent some Dadaist poems to Edith Sitwell, and she wrote back a long letter of enthusiasm. "There can be not the slightest doubt that your gifts and promise are exceedingly remarkable. You are undoubtedly what is known as 'a born writer'. . ." She assured him that he had more talent than anyone else under twenty, except her brother Sacheverell.[16]

She soon extended her patronage also to Harold Acton, who had been hearing about the Sitwells quite independently in Florence. A close friend of Oscar Wilde's, a novelist called Ada Leverson, lived in Florence and never stopped talking of "the fascinating trio," and what she had to say promised Harold—quite rightly—that they were going to be important friends and allies to him. Something he says about their poetry's appeal to him—"the intangible of fantasy, to which the Sitwells gave such musical form"—applies to everything about them, their personality, life style, and aesthetic. The primacy of fantasy was to become part of Harold's aesthetic creed too: "The conquest of poetic fact is more likely to come through fantasy than through other means."

The Sitwells were then the impresarios of the avant-garde in all the arts in England. 1919 was the year of the International Exhibition of Modern Art, arranged by Osbert and Sacheverell, which introduced Modigliani to England. As Connolly says in *The Evening Colonnade,*

> In the 20's they represented the rush towards pleasure and aesthetic enjoyment characteristic of the intelligent young who had come through the war; they were the natural allies of Cocteau and the Ecole de Paris, dandies, impeccably dressed and fed, who indicated to young men down from Oxford and even Cambridge that it was possible to reconcile art and fashion, as an alternative to Bloomsbury.*

We have mentioned the Sitwells' antipatriarchal stance and their humorists' stance, which we associate with Osbert in particular; and their propagation of a taste for the baroque and the rococo, which we associate with Sacheverell. A third aspect, which we might associate with Edith, was their work as publicists. Edith's taking up of Brian and Harold was of great immediate advantage to their reputations, for she knew how to win them notice, how to introduce their names to the public as members of her gang of young poets. She came to speak at Eton at Brian's invitation, and later to Oxford at Harold's, and she produced a formidable impression each time. She also wrote

---

* Connolly continues, "Dandyism is the prerogative of the youthful male in many bird and animal species. Why should this display be suspected only in the human? Even Dr. Leavis must have been young once and worn a tie." He, at least, has always been conscious of the cultural dialectic in England, of dandies versus anti-dandies.

humorous articles for the press about the occasions, and introduced extravagant praise for her protégés into them. She reviewed *The Eton Candle* at length for *The Sackbut*,[17] and so on. Her brothers gave William Walton, Constant Lambert, and Bernard van Dieren similar promotion in the musical world, and Pavel Tchelitchew was one of the painters who received the same treatment.

Edith Sitwell praised the *Candle* by noting that it escaped the nineties taint of affectation. These dandies knew that they were the children of the '90s, but they also knew that the '90s had been defeated, while they needed banners and emblems of defiance and triumph. So their remarks about the earlier period are often scornful and meant to dissociate themselves from it. But there is a clear enough acknowledgement of their debt in the manifesto of the Cremorne Club, which Brian devised for himself, the Actons, and Roger Spence, while they were at Eton:

> Life is an Art, and is to be encountered with a buttonhole of flowers. Members of the Cremorne Club must believe in the interpretation and appreciation of life as evolved in 1890, and must courageously oppose and denounce the modern tendency of hysterical revolution—speed and efficiency, in modern Art and Life.

The club's honorary members were Whistler, Beardsley, Swinburne, Mallarmé, Samain, Savage, Wilde, Symons, Verlaine, Gautier, Ricketts, Pryde, Housman, Tree, Beerbohm, and Meredith.

The Frenchmen were perhaps named more confidently, although the Englishmen more affectionately. The former were more useful in helping the Eton aesthetes escape the taint of the '90s. Brian read Arthur Symons's *The Symbolist Movement in Literature* (about the French) in 1922; and he wrote to Harold, "I HAVE JUST DISCOVERED OUR CATEGORY. I have just found out to what school we belong, whose work *we* are developing. We are the New Symbolists."[18] He and Harold were to take up, in the '20s, the work begun by the French writers of the '90s. This cry of self-discovery—reminding us of Leonard Woolf, discovering his friends foreshadowed in Henry

James's novels—is the best of Brian: his intense susceptibility to—inflammability by—ideas.

Brian had been reading Huysmans' *À rebours* when he composed the Cremorne Club manifesto. He had also been reading Cocteau, and it is worth remembering that these Eton years were for Cocteau the time of his greatest friendship with Proust (in the last months of 1922) and his passion for Radiguet. Both intellectually and emotionally, it was the intensest phase of dandyism in France.

This was Diaghilev's most Parisian period too. During his 1918 season at the London Coliseum, which Harold Acton attended, Diaghilev had become involved in a public controversy over music with the critic Ernest Newman, in which he attacked the dominance of the taste for German music in England. Diaghilev spoke for French music. "The War was nothing else but a struggle between two cultures," he said, meaning the German and French cultures, and German music was dead. "The music of Beethoven and Brahms is dangerous, not because it represents a corpse, but because flies feed upon it, and will infect the public with their poison."[19]

Everything was to be alive and new. In 1921, Diaghilev put on *Chout,* based on a Russian legend of buffoons, with music by Sergei Prokofiev and decor by Mikhail Larionov, a ballet so grotesque and violent that Newman again protested. (Larionov as a young man walked around Moscow with brightly colored pictures painted on his face, like a surrealist Firbank). The modern movement's natural locus was not London but Paris—and within Paris, the Diaghilev company. "In addition to being the focal point of the whole modern movement in the arts, the Diaghilev ballet was a kind of movement in itself," says Gerald Murphy. "Anybody who was interested in the company became a member automatically. You knew everybody, you knew all the dancers, and everybody asked your opinion on things."[20]

Gerald Murphy was the man Scott Fitzgerald drew as Dick Diver in *Tender Is the Night.* He was the symbol and center of the American movement of *Sonnenkinder* in exile. And he was rooted in Diaghilev's Paris. Gerald and Sara Murphy fled America and their families in 1922, came to Paris, and began to paint. Their teacher was Natalya Goncharova, Diaghilev's designer. And when some of the ballet scenery was destroyed in a fire that year, they eagerly volunteered to repaint it, and thus got to know the whole company, and its entourage—Picasso, Fernand Léger, and Stravinsky, in particular. One occasion that fixes all these figures for us in an appropriate grouping and action was the party the Murphys gave for Stravinsky's new ballet in 1923, *Les Noces*. This was a very "French" ballet; music for it was played on four pianos by Francis Poulenc, Georges Auric, Vittorio Rieti, and Marcelle Meyer; Goncharova did the decor; Balanchine came from Moscow to see it; the Murphys took e. e. cummings and John Dos Passos. At the Murphys' party, held on a barge on the Seine, Diaghilev, Stravinsky, Cocteau, Picasso, Darius Milhaud, Tristan Tzara, Blaise Cendrars, and other notables drank and danced and sang together. This was the life the Etonian aesthetes meant to live.

They meant to make their lives—lived in that style—central and exemplary for their whole generation, and at Oxford and for a few years afterwards in London, they may be said to have succeeded. They—in cooperation with the Sitwells and their ilk—aestheticized an Oxford generation. Art and power were radically linked. It is a constant theme of Brian's letters while at Eton that they will *rule* Oxford because of all they *know*. They saw Oxford as peopled by *amateurs*, weaklings, none of whom knew half as much as they did about art. It is this quasi-political scope to their aestheticism that makes it so interesting.

At Eton our two principals' main achievements were the Eton Society of the Arts, where Japanese art and puppet shows were introduced to Eton and Roger Fry's workshops were described (by Brian) as "a hive of criminal aesthetics"; and *The Eton Candle,* the single-issue magazine that they put out in 1922.

The *Candle's* debts to the 1890s were made clear. It was dedicated to Swinburne (an Old Etonian dandy-aesthete), and it was printed with extreme care for the look of the page. Harold Acton says that the print was chosen to emulate that used in Max Beerbohm's early books. There were enormous margins, one page contained only a

Maurice Baring clerihew in microscopic type, and the cover was in shocking pink.

Brian Howard wrote an essay, "The New Poetry," in defence of *vers libre* and the Sitwells. He attacked the Georgian poets and the group around Jack Squire at the London *Mercury*. He said that Swinburne had done all that could be done with conventional verse, and that what was needed now was a verse to correspond to the paintings of Gauguin, Whistler, John, and so on. He praised Aldous Huxley: "Huxley, already a leader in what will be known as one of the principal movements in the literature of the modern world (at the present moment this new spirit in creative work has outstripped that of 1890 in importance and influence) has a future that, by virtue of his accomplishments in the past, is by far the most interesting in English letters." And Edith Sitwell ("a genius") he described as "the greatest poet of the grotesquerie de cauchemar that ever lived." The essay is chiefly remarkable for the naïveté, in the good sense as well as the bad, of its praise and dispraise. He offers Ezra Pound, with his "amazing erudition and modernist irony," as a useful model for the average London *Mercury* poet, with his "Varsity naïveté." It all carries conviction as proceeding from some real enthusiasm for poetry, as well as from ambition and reckless exhibitionism.

Brian also included a poem of his own that was much praised at the time, on the War Dead.

> You were a great Young Generation . . .
> And then you went and got murdered—magnificently
> Went out and got murdered . . . because a parcel of damned
>   old men
> Wanted some fun or some power or something.

Insignificant as this is as poetry, it was significant—as the response at the time made clear—as expressing the general indignation against the "damned old men," and giving the dandy a larger social function than he could usually aspire to. As Cyril Connolly says in his comment on the *Candle,* in those days whenever you didn't get on with your father, you had all the glorious dead on your side.

Brian also printed a couple of his own stories in the *Candle*. "White and White" (dedicated to Harold) is about an Englishman who while young gets painted by Manet as one of the figures in *Déjeuner sur l'herbe,* and ten years later returns to Paris married to Edna, a "usual woman," who prefers Savernake Forest (the most English of beauty spots) to France. He rounds upon her with ". . . you made me fall in love with you—I . . . I, who have an appreciation of Life—Art—Culture—Literature. You've turned me into an egotist—you with your Birmingham Vicarage ways and ideas. . . ." And "Baroness Ada" is a fantasy about his calling in at one of those bourgeois macabre villas between Eton and Slough, and being smothered by decaying gentlewomen beneath piles of their old-fashioned clothes, in an elaborately but sordidly furnished bedroom.

As with his critical prose, there were crudities of style here that should not stop us seeing the force of these constant invocations of Art and France and Fantasy. These are the liturgical incantations and formulas of a young ritualist who is not so much an adept of his cult as a fanatic for it. This is the way such stories were felt by their readers at the time, and as such they had their effect.

The magazine also contained ten poems by Harold Acton. "La Belle au Bois Dormant," dedicated with permission to Bakst, has some nice lines.

> A frail princess of porcelain
> Is dancing with a mandarin
> Schéhérazade with fair disdain
> Steps from a jewelled palanquin.

There is also a good deal in the vein of "strange orchids with fantastic names" and of "puppet Pierrot death." But in "Coiffeur Choréographique" he hits upon a line of homely fantasy—a more *fantaisiste* version of John Betjeman's sensibility—that one can imagine him developing. When the barber shampoos his hair,

> Till down upon my head, Niagara Falls
> Descend with all the heat of music halls.

In "A Note on Jean Arthur Rimbaud and 3 of his Poems Done into English," Harold defended Rimbaud against the charge of decadence brought by English philistines. "Would such people kindly remember that no great art is *décadent* . . . or fang-de-seeaycle?" Rimbaud in his second period, he says, reminds us of Osbert Sitwell; in the Rimbaud of 1871 and the Sitwell of 1918 there is the same superbly managed contempt for the bourgeois. Here again we see the acolyte beating the gong and intoning the sacred names of his religion.

Harold also published there a chapter of a novel, dedicated to Brian, which is perhaps as good as anything he wrote after. It is called "Hansom Cab No. 213 bis," and it might be described as a Gilly Potter version of *À rebours*. Or one might compare it with *The Importance of Being Earnest,* the gestures of dandyism being prolonged and curved back upon themselves in pure silliness, but a silliness so exuberant and inventive as to give brilliant delight. Of course Acton's chapter is not to be compared with Wilde's play in discipline or formal control, but the strain of fantasy is one that could have been developed into comparable effects. The whole life of Athelstane, the hero, is a study—"a meticulous study of harmonies, cadences, blatancies, senses, discords." His sense is developed into an instrument "of such keen perceptions, of such shiveringly fine nerves, that the mere sounds of the outward world crushed him, the mere associations between himself and other human beings frightened him." We see him in a room that at night is Oriental—like some opiate apartment in Shiraz where orchids are cultivated in accompaniment to the music of mother-of-pearl zithers; but in early daylight, mid-Victorian boudoiriness is oozing everywhere—in each individual corner, little snuffboxes are chattering to their Dresden companions, roguish Corydons, and exquisite Amaryllises.

Athelstane wraps himself in a mandarin coat and sips some milk from a jade cup. "How fatuously the milk seemed to smile at him, how pathetically servile and domestic it glinted in its Morland Cottage healthiness." Then a deaf waitress called Jelly brings him a biscuit ornamented with a layer of startlingly pink sugar engraved with the word "Fairy": "Fairy—it reminded him of a certain prose poem of Rimbaud's." His bath is of blue marble, beneath a mauve glass dome, and in the approaching chamber he has an ancient cypress-wood organ.

> Daily an organist would come to play to him during his bath-ing hour—great purple canticles of Palestrina on some days, on others pale arias of Cimarosa; sometimes he would listen for hours to endless fugues of Bach. These were the hours Athelstane loved, to strip himself of his worldly garments and listen to some somnolent chord of a Gregorian chant.

He touches his hair and imagines it "some parasitic seaweed cling-ing to a putrescent limb at the bottom of the ocean. He could picture some great goggling fish swimming by. . . ." He goes to visit a friend and plays with his dog to avoid talking to the parson. "Borzois possess the divine gift of utter stupidity mingled with a refinement of nerves unusual in dogs of large size. This one had been christened Whis-tler, because he possessed all that gentleman's unadulterated vanity." Unfortunately, he is interrupted by a typical English girl, called Petu-nia. She is red-faced and tries to pose as La Belle Jardinière, in a big hat and watering can. "The sight of her made Athelstane physically ill: his intestines seemed to play odd tunes within him. . . ." Her jerky conver-sation is interlarded with "my dears," "rippings," and "pricelesses." "He could have slapped her, her face shone so with Carbolic Soap." Much characteristic English writing of the next twenty years—and some of the best, like Waugh's—was to develop along lines like these. It is a pity that the difficulties of Acton's career frustrated his talent.

The *Candle* had an Old Etonian supplement, with contributions from Aldous Huxley and Sacheverell Sitwell; the latter's poem was a "Portrait of a Harlequin," and there were several other traces of *com-media* iconography in the magazine. But the contents of the *Candle* are not so remarkable as the fact of the magazine itself. That these two boys could make it happen, that was their achievement—the orga-nizing energies and skills behind it. William Acton did the Russian-ballet-style posters advertising it, Roger Spence did the business managing, but it was mostly Brian's work. He was, of course, assisted by his family connections in the world of art. His father's friend, Gerald Kelly, had suggested he ask Sir Edmund Gosse if there were any unpublished poems by Swinburne in his custody, and Gosse gave him a sonnet; like Arnold Bennett, Gosse was disposed to make friends among the modernists.

Their achievement is also reflected in the fact that Robert Byron and Cyril Connolly both wrote *parody* modernist poems for the *Candle*. Connolly says he was too shy even to submit his; Byron's was rejected, once Brian discovered that it *was* parody. It was not easy for any of the boys to know if they were serious in their modernism, and it was no more easy for the adults who read it to recognize seriousness. Orage published a probably serious poem by Brian on his pastiche page in the *New Age*, taking it to be a satire on Joyce, while Peter Quennell had seriously meant a poem that, when published in *Public School Verse*, was commended in reviews for its satirical power. Neither the listeners' ears nor the speakers' voices could judge or control modernist effect. But it was Brian and Harold who risked seriousness. This is why Connolly retrospectively defers to them. As he says, ". . . the *Eton Candle* represented the only element in the school which was *avant-garde*, and most of us had not yet caught up with Brooke or Flecker."

The *Times Literary Supplement* reviewed the *Candle*; there was a second printing in London; Edith Sitwell, of course, praised it (and particularly Brian and Harold) highly; and Gosse and Shane Leslie also praised it in letters. Edith made Brian business manager of *Wheels*. And Harold received a letter from Thomas Balston, at Duckworth's, the publisher, that led to the publication of his first book of poems, *Aquarium*, while he was still an undergraduate. The *Candle* was a great success.

Let me conclude by quoting from a letter Brian Howard wrote to Harold Acton in 1922, telling him to go up to Oxford as a conqueror, as an exclusive.

> You see, Harold, if you start at Oxford on the definite plan of being *exclusive* you will (1) avoid being bored, (2) avoid being

patronized, (3) make a name for yourself. If you take up an attitude—not an offensive attitude—of calm conscious superiority and knowledge, you will get an enormous reputation as an intellectual. Do you realize, Harold,—please pay attention to this—that you and I are going to have rather a famous career at Oxford? Already we have got to a stage *way beyond* the Oxford intellectuals.... At present I am looking forward, Harold, to an Oxford which, on its artistic side, shall be ruled by you and I together—as we ruled Eton.[21]

This is worthy of Diaghilev or Brummell. And grandiose as the tone sounds, it was not out of touch with reality.

They *had* ruled Eton; Connolly, Green, Powell, even Orwell, in their different ways all looked back on their years at the school as a dandy-aesthete experience. At least in memory—the memory of hundreds of young Englishmen, as the years went by—Eton became an *institution* of dandy-aestheticism, diffusing that idea abroad. And Brian and Harold *did* go on to rule Oxford in a comparable sense—or indeed *more* completely; they made that too into an institutional center of the dandy-aesthete movement in England.

Chapter Five

1922–1925:
Oxford

Brian and Harold at Oxford

WHEN HAROLD ACTON came to Oxford in 1922, it was directly from Florence, and he says in *Memoirs of an Aesthete,* "On arriving at Oxford for matriculation in May, I felt I had left one capital of romance for another. The change of valley was the more exciting because here youth reigned instead of age." That excitement, that reign of youth, that island-of-romance feeling, sustained itself in him and in his friends throughout their three years there. Brian Howard wrote to William Acton that he had found nothing in the way of wit or art at Oxford, but that "one lives an extraordinarily marvellous life there—a sort of passionate party all the time—one rushes from one amusement to another."[1] And these parties were celebrations of the *Sonnenkind* supreme, a propagation of that cult among their contemporaries, making all Oxford a temple of that cult. Brian and Harold became prominent figures there, prominent enough to be visible from London and beyond.

During the war Oxford had been a much diminished thing. Only a few undergraduates were up, and the Union was actually closed. And the first year or two after the war was apparently dominated by serious and hard-working ex-servicemen. But a group of friends around Beverley Nichols, who became president of the Union in 1920 and who published a novel while still up, determined to restore the Edwardian style of elegant frivolity that had served the Edwardian *Sonnenkinder.* Nichols' novel *Patchwork* (1920) described such a restoration and was itself an attempt to recapture the style of Compton Mackenzie's *Sinister Street,* the very successful and daringly "modern" Oxford novel of 1914.* Nichols himself was a dandy—supposedly the first man to wear suede shoes (in Oxford); and his Oxford career made him a model for many other such.

Other forces, outside Oxford and even outside England, had a similar effect. In 1922 the Oxford Union for the first time sent a team of debaters on a tour of American universities, which they dazzled with their negligent brilliance and aristocratic frivolity. Bates College, Maine, had sent its team of highly trained debaters to Oxford the year before, and had been baffled by the Oxford style. The Bates men studied the subject of each debate thoroughly and jointly, coordinated their efforts completely (they referred to themselves corporately as "Bates"), and even carried a card file that grouped together all the counterarguments to any argument their opponents might advance. Their style was that of the efficiency expert, of the automated factory line. The Oxford debaters, so much more spontaneous, impudent, paradoxical, ingenious, and charming, enjoyed displaying their own style against such a contrast; it was, after all, a display of the sons' style against the fathers'. Their tour of America was extended and repeated, and such tours became a frequent and major manifestation of the Oxford style. America came to be the audience the dandies of debate had in mind; indeed, that was true of dandies outside debate; America

---

* Scott Fitzgerald's novel, *This Side of Paradise*, also 1920, was another attempt to recapture the magic of *Sinister Street*, as Edmund Wilson pointed out at the time. The dandy movements in England and America began in parallel.

became that audience of bigger, stronger, slower cousins before whom Englishmen paraded and peacocked, confident of an indulgent protection in time of trouble.[2]

Harold and Brian and William were, of course, great dandies in the most literal sense. They spent a lot of money on clothes, on the decoration of their rooms, on parties, on presents for each other, and so on. "Clothes were an intoxication," Cyril Connolly says about his Oxford years. "Waisted suits by Lesley and Roberts, white waistcoats from Hawes and Curtis with only a narrow white strap at the back, monogrammed silk shirts arrived in cardboard boxes...."[3] Many people have left descriptions of what they wore and how they wore it. We hear of Harold in a grey bowler, sidewhiskers and stock, "tittupping along the High" with tightly rolled umbrella, rolling his big head from side to side, as he led a band of aesthetes to some confrontation with a band of hearties. He often wore a long tubular black coat, below which his very broad pleated trousers opened out like a fan. These trousers—copied by more and more of his friends and then by others, till the style became known to the outside world as "Oxford bags"—were as much as twenty-six inches broad at the knee and twenty-four inches at the ankle, and spread to cover the shoes. They were often in light, bright shades, like silver, mauve, or pink, and sometimes had the effect of a pleated skirt. Other innovations in informal clothing that spread from Oxford to the rest of the country in those years were suede shoes and high-necked sweaters (often in bright colors—it caused a sensation in 1923 when the Prince of Wales wore a Fair Isle pattern), green velveteen trousers, and yellow hunting waistcoats. Contrasted with the three-piece broadcloth suits that had been standard for all young men of that class, the new clothes obviously flaunted frivolity. The dandies' suit jackets were cut in an early Victorian fashion, with high shoulders and big lapels, and their waistcoats were double-breasted and barely reached the waist. But there was an exaggeration even to their formal wear, a quality of fancy dress, which made that too a provocation to the outside world. And the outside world was there in Oxford, represented by most of their fellow undergraduates. We hear of William Acton, clad in a bottle-green Scholte suit and raspberry crêpe de chine shirt, knocking down a hearty who sneered at him.

On his arrival at Christ Church—the college to which all three went, although in different years—Harold painted his rooms lemon-yellow and filled them with Victorian bric-a-brac.

> Back to mahogany was my battle-cry. . . . The Early Victorian Era, trying to recover from the Napoleonic War, was closer to us than the 'nineties, that 'Twilight of the Gods' succeeded by the Age of Muddle. We wanted Dawns, not Twilights. We must blow the bugles and beat the drums and wake the Sleeping Beauty.

In this crusade he had a major ally in Robert Byron, who "believed that never had Britain been more resplendent than between 1846 and 1865. The vision of a 'large-limbed, high-coloured Victorian England, seated in honour and plenty' was constantly before him." This was the idea behind that fashion for wax fruit under bell jars, everlasting flowers, and so on. It was a way to save the new dandyism of the 1920s from that taint of affectation and defeat that had ruined the old nineties dandyism. They wanted to associate dandyism with the modern, the expansive, the new. Harold had met an Oxford aesthete on a preliminary visit there, and had been horrified by his drawl, his sickliness, his jaded mannerisms, his long hair, his ebony cane, and his timid prurience. "I made up my mind that if that eunuch represented Oxford aestheticism, something would have to be done about it soon." This note of virile aggression is something recurrent in Acton, and in its way something genuine. He believed in Oxford aestheticism, and was ready to crush such traitors to his cause with mockery, "and, if need be, with violence." He saw what had defeated dandyism in the past, and he saw how to avoid such defeats in the future. The cult of modern innovations—from jazz and cocktails to Picasso and T. S. Eliot, all of which were "on his side"—could replace in his friends' minds those old cults, ranging from Georgian poetry to Protestant pietism, that were on the fathers' side. "I was determined to clear the ground of linnet-infested thickets." In his *Memoirs* Acton describes Gershwin's

Rhapsody in Blue as translating into other terms the same emotions as Eliot's line, "April is the cruelest month."

> The total rhapsody, never so slickly performed as in the days of its pristine freshness, with each instrument enjoying its separate tinted spotlight, cast a twentieth century spell which dove-tailed into the divagations of Picasso, Mr. Prufrock, and Gertrude Stein. It seemed to contain all the intoxication of black and chromium cocktail bars. . . .

All these things worked together to advance his cause, or seemed to, as the *Rhapsody* "seeped through the gothic twilight of Oxford and gave us all the fidgets."

Acton and Byron planned an Early Victorian Exhibition, for which Lytton Strachey was to write a catalogue introduction; and when the Proctors of the university forbade it, they wrote letters of protest to the London press, describing their material as "the only really Christian art." They also planned a Victorian ballet, with Martin Harvey as the Queen and Harold Acton as Lytton Strachey—the latter wearing a red beard, and lying under a couch, taking notes. More seriously, Harold read papers to art societies about the Victorian painters, David Wilkie, Augustus Egg, William Frith, William Etty, and John Martin. He also read papers on El Greco and on Medicean villas.

Acton and Alfred Nicholson started a magazine called *Oxford Broom,* whose credo was the need for a new and *catholic* spirit in modern life and literature. "We believe in Platonic allegory, in the dream that haunts the slime." We need idealism incarnate—a modern Christ-like figure, singular, yet in passionate universal contact. (I think we may regard this idea as related to the Neoplatonism of Bernard Berenson's Altamura. Nicholson was in fact a nephew of Mrs. Berenson, and we know how impressed Acton was by Berenson himself.) Alfred Duggan wrote for the first number a praise of the England of 1850, with its limited franchise. "At the present moment we are ruled by the Prime Minister and Money. Personally I don't think that it is an improvement on government by the gentlemen and noblemen of Parliament." (Duggan later became a Communist, like John Strachey and several others of the reactionaries of that Oxford.)

An essay (almost certainly by Harold Acton) in the second number (April 1923) surveys recent verse anthologies and finds that only the Sitwells' *Wheels* escapes the heresy that poetry is a matter of suitable sentiments. In the Sitwells' poems, ". . . there were none of those nebulous, half-realized emotions that go down so well with the Mazzawattee tea at suburban 'at homes.'" The same number contains an account of the last summer's exhibition at the Pitti Palace, entitled "The Gruesome Apotheosis of the Seicentismo." Critics, the article says, are now claiming that Guido Reni, Caravaggio, Caracci, and so on are modern in feeling, analogous to Fascismo and Futurismo. But the one really impressive figure among these painters is Alessandro Magnasco, a follower of Salvator Rosa; he is like El Greco in the farouche technique with which he depicts monks suffering *crises de nerfs* in caverns. The Sitwell brothers founded the Magnasco Society about this time, to foster appreciation of Italian virtuoso painting of the 17th and 18th centuries—everything Ruskin had condemned—and in general to cultivate a baroque taste, in literature, music, everything. Thus, together with the Sitwells, Acton was providing new icons for English aesthetes to contemplate.

In the third number of *Oxford Broom* appeared Evelyn Waugh's first published story, "Anthony, Who Sought Things That Were Lost," written in a nineties style that he declared to have been influenced by James Branch Cabell. It is a very bad story, but there is some interest in noting that Anthony (who is tall, very beautiful, and of proud family, like many of Waugh's later and more contemporary heroes) is melodramatically betrayed by the beautiful girl he loves as soon as the latter is put under some stress of discomfort. Even before Waugh's divorce, then, his imaginative world was one in which men are always likely to be betrayed by the women they love. It is also of interest that Waugh first appeared in print under Harold Acton's aegis—in those days Acton was able to extend encouragement and protection to Waugh the artist. Like Peter Quennell, Desmond Harmsworth, and others, Waugh seemed intended to be one of Acton's discoveries.

But Harold Acton appeared at Oxford very much in the character of poet, as well as those of impresario, aesthete, and dandy. Both A. L. Rowse and Terence Greenidge refer to him as "the poet" in their Oxford memoirs. Like Waugh's Anthony Blanche, he declaimed poems by megaphone from the balcony of his rooms, to groups passing below in Christ Church meadow. He declaimed his own poems, T. S. Eliot's, Edith Sitwell's, and Robert Graves's. (Graves was then living in Oxford, and the two met—unsuccessfully. Acton found Graves to have a *masculine* style that belonged to the previous generation; he felt that Graves "needed a Mediterranean holiday.") Harold's first book of poems, *Aquarium,* came out in his second term there, which gave him great prestige.

Brian Howard did not appear as a poet. He became at Oxford the companion of peers, a cross between Proust and Brummell, as Peter Quennell implies. "The social arbiter of the Oxford *côté de Guermantes,*" says Quennell, was Brian Howard, "who played Beau Brummell to the good-natured grandees," instructing them in dandyism.[4] He did a lot of riding (which he said later had always terrified him), hung Surtees prints on his walls, and helped smash windows after Bullingdon dinners. (On one occasion the total bill for smashed windows—256 panes of glass—came to £60.) Brian never became a member of the Bullingdon—the most prestigious of Oxford clubs in terms of the great families belonging to it—but he rode and dined with its members constantly, lectured them on their clothes, furniture, tastes, and girl friends. He also tried to seduce many of them. It was his drama that he was for seven years unrequitedly in love with one of them, but he had affairs with and spent nights with other men all the time. His alliance with Harold Acton, and his vocation as a poet, were somewhat attenuated during these years, but they still represented the serious side of his life. He read *The Waste Land,* recognizing it as a great poem, and contributed to the *Oxford Poetry* of 1924, which Acton and Peter Quennell edited—some of those poems were recited on the radio in January 1925.

He also spoke occasionally at the Union and wrote for *The Cherwell,* but, as he wrote to his mother, "I'm not 'busy having a good time'— I'm busy LIVING, *for the first time in my life.* I have come into the popularity and companionship that I have always yearned after so, don't you see?"

Harold Acton's *Aquarium* was issued as part of a series that included Edith Sitwell's *Bucolic Comedies,* and the editor who encouraged Acton was Thomas Balston, later a patron of Evelyn Waugh and Anthony Powell as well as of the Sitwells. The title is significant. Imagery of fishes, aquariums, and baths is dominant in all Harold Acton's imaginative work. It is clearly enough appropriate to his highly relaxed and contemplative kind of narcissism; the central experience it returns to is the sensual pleasure of lying in a bath.

The poems in this collection show the influence of Eliot and Edith Sitwell, but their verbal felicity cannot really challenge that of those two masters. Perhaps the poem "Violoncello" in "Conversazione of Musical Instruments" is the best.

> I am the waxen fruit of instruments. . . .
> Voluptuously blatant in my greed, I am the woman garbed
>   in heliotrope,
> Whose bustle panics peacocks in the park.
> Some take my mellow notes for rosaries—
> So holy, steadfast, pure they seem to be.
> (Like dear Prince Albert on a promenade,
> Inspired apostle of the simple life,
> With all his homely virtues on parade.)
> And I am music's Edinburgh rock,
> A laxative caressing to the ear. . . .

The strength of that seems to lie in the frankness of the fear of large women, and the juxtaposition of the women with the peacocks. The weakness is the camp tone about Prince Albert, a tone so much less interesting than the kind of interest in Victorianism discussed before. Unfortunately the queen and the prince consort have been irresistible to all dandies since the Victorian period—they are, in historical as well as personal myth, the Father and Mother against which the *Sonnenkind* has to assert himself.

Aquarium had a certain success at the time (James Stephen, the Irish poet, wrote to tell Acton that *Aquarium* was "great verse"), and no doubt the talent displayed there *could* have developed into something considerable if the poet had had a secure sense of himself. But the strong influence of T. S. Eliot was a bad sign, even if to Acton's credit as a lover of poetry. Eliot's model was not one likely to be useful to him, because Eliot's dandyism was exquisitely modulated to a level of seriousness that was beyond Acton's scope or aim. Neither did Acton have—despite the success of his social performances—the secure sense of a comic self that John Betjeman had. His flamboyant pose was out of relation to the gentlemanly and scholarly self behind it. That is why one can rarely locate in his *Memoirs,* whose major statements were composed by that gentlemanly self, what it was that so shocked and delighted his contemporaries at Oxford.

There is, however, one teasing passage, apropos of *Aquarium* in the *Memoirs.*

How many copies of *Aquarium* did I autograph with tender dedications," he asks, and goes on to describe finding a copy in a secondhand bookshop many years later. "The fly-leaf was torn out. Had it compromised the owner? My thoughts returned to the bygone loves to whom I had given copies, to blue eyes, green eyes, eyes like black diamonds, to gentle struggles and showers of burning kisses. . . . Some of my inscriptions would have been embarrassing to explain. Nearly all my loves are married and parents of children I have no desire to meet. Why distress the gentle vegetation of middle-aged Darbies and Joans? No home-breaker I, no cuckoo in other nests. I culled the *prémices,* and it is a subtle satisfaction, even in retrospect, to have kindled flames in Elgin marble breasts. . . . Do they remember our ecstasies on the Thames and at Thame? Do they remember the poems they inspired? Let them blush as they read these words in their nuptial couches: I have not forgotten a single kiss. At the same time let them rest assured that with age I have learned discretion.

It is not surprising that such a passage should deal with the theme of sexuality, for that theme, with all its threats to conventional masculinity, was the most aggressive component in the dandyism of our two principals. The difference between them was that Harold Acton's insolence was only teasing and quite gentle, whereas Brian Howard's was much harsher and more stressful, both for his victim and for himself. We hear of one remark of Brian's from these years, addressed to a young man at a house party who was parading his hopeless love for one of the girls there. "My dear X," said Brian, "I feel that your fly buttons will burst open any minute and a large pink dirigible emerge, dripping ballast at intervals." There were almost Dostoevskian depths of malice to Brian's dandyism. Bryan Guinness, quite a close friend, said that although Brian was to them then the glass of fashion and the mold of form, they thought him—like Hamlet—haunted by some inward discontent. Evelyn Waugh described him as mad, bad, and dangerous to know.

Both Brian and Harold, and the other Oxford aesthetes, were subjected to rowdiness from the hearties there, who represented the traditional male styles. They did not triumph over the philistines without a battle. Alan Pryce-Jones says that the aesthetes at Oxford thought of themselves as one of the heroic minorities of history, like the Albigenses.[5] They had their rooms wrecked and their clothes torn off, particularly after rowing club Bump Suppers, when the athletic types were drunk. It was Harold Acton who was ducked, in his pyjamas, in the Mercury Fountain in Christ Church, an incident presented in *Brideshead Revisited*. He also had his rooms attacked in another scene that became a legend. He described the incident in a letter to Brian Howard. Thirty men had tried to break down the door to his room, and "I, tucked up in bed and contemplating the reflection of Luna on my walls, was immersed under showers of myriad particles of split glass, my head powdered with glass dust and my possessions vitrified." Brian replied that his mother had met a woman who told her that her son was one of the thirty: "If I'd been there I'd have unloosed her corsets on the spot."[6] After dark and after drink, the hearties still found the courage to persecute the aesthetes, but never with much wit or style.

William Acton, the most athletic of the dandies, was credited with inflicting severe physical damage on the hearties. He was also famous for his parties—in particular his lunches, at which he would serve, Brian says, a blood-like soup heavy with eggs and magical potions; Lobster Newburg was once served in a dustbin, and punch in a hip bath, and so on.[7] William was riding steeplechases and point-to-points with Brian, reenacting the vigor of rollicking old England in its early Victorian days. But his rooms Harold compares with the palaces of pre-Revolutionary St. Petersburg, with exotic shells and corals in glass tanks, goblets full of ivory beads, fruit made of brilliant porcelain, and a Negro mask by Oliver Messel with aquamarines set in its curls. It was a distinctly surrealist mise-en-scène, says Harold, at night a rainbow-colored grotto.

A favorite place to eat was the Spreadeagle at Thame, and Maurice Richardson tells a good anecdote about dining there in 1926.

> Suddenly a very tall young man with a pink face and a rather small head climbed over the window-sill into the room. "Er, I'm terribly sorry," he said, "but do you mind if I, er, go through . . . If a rather awful man called Howard asks if anybody went this way would you mind saying they didn't. I'm trying to escape. Thanks awfully." He rushed out. We heard from the garden outside a high authoritative voice calling, "Henry! Henry! Silly little creature, where are you, Henry? Come here at once!" Then Brian stepped into the room. "Has a rather tall peer with a head the size of a walnut passed this way? I see from your faces he has. Go on with your dinner. Don"t let me disturb you."[8]

This anecdote helps us to understand what is meant when Henry Green says that at Oxford Brian was absolutely commanding in looks and conversation, and when Evelyn Waugh says that Brian at nineteen had a kind of ferocity of elegance that belonged to the romantic era of a century before our own. Lord Birkenhead (son of the famous F. E. Smith, and a contemporary of Brian and Howard at Oxford) says more discreetly that he made a real contribution to Oxford life "in this most civilized period."

But Birkenhead thinks that Harold Acton's contribution was the more solid. "Harold, in particular, brought to it a Florentine culture which was previously unknown, and an authentic whiff of the great world beyond the University."⁹ Certainly Harold was working much the harder of the two, both at being a poet and at becoming a scholar. His second book of poems, *An Indian Ass,* appeared in 1925, while he was still up. He seemed to be way ahead of his contemporaries in his career. Roy Harrod, a don in economics and Harold's tutor, says, "To us it seemed obvious that he would be the literary leader of his generation, rather as Lytton Strachey had been in an earlier decade." The poems in *An Indian Ass* are more elaborately poetic than his earlier ones. "Lament for Adonis," for example, is very Keatsian; there are peacocks everywhere, and a great profusion of words like "orts," "hispid," and "gonfalons." At their best these poems can remind one of early Wallace Stevens ("The Comedian as the Letter C"), in lines like these:

> Orange-liveried marmosets
> Climb slender cypress minarets.

And there are hints of personal grief (very rare in his other verse) expressed with the imagery of the *commedia.*

> Our lives are cratered with great pocks and scabs . . .
> Then let us sing the world's hilarity. . . .
> Our clowns are turned into tragedians,
> And Pierrot's chalk-white face is crinkled up
> With bitter weeping; roguish Harlequin,
> His apple cheeks all wet and blobbed with tears,
> Wanders the streets of Bergamo alone.

But one has only to turn to the lines that Peter Quennell was writing at that same time (an example will be given later) to see that Harold

Acton lacked poetic individuality, that he did not in some sense care enough, did not push hard enough for absolute perfection or absolute authenticity. And the early silence of Peter Quennell as a poet reminds us of the striking fact that *all* the poetic efforts of the members of this group came to nothing. One might suppose that just by being dandies they were indisposed to the long steady effort of a lifework. But Wallace Stevens and Vladimir Nabokov made a literary success out of such material, out of being dandies, and although they had more serious elements in their psyches, so of course did the Englishmen. The explanation of the latter's failure—insofar as it is not merely a matter of differing original endowments—must be sought in the workings of this particular group in this particular national situation.

But during those years at Oxford, it seemed that Harold Acton and Brian Howard, and to a lesser degree their friends, were figures of brilliance. They left the imprint of that brilliance on hundreds of susceptible young minds. This was true even of men who followed a strikingly different ideological path from their own. Both W. H. Auden and Philip Toynbee say that while at Oxford they felt themselves unfortunate and inferior because they were not a part of that brilliant legendary generation. A. L. Rowse, in his autobiography, says of Harold Acton, "never was there such undergraduate réclame," and many people have said that Brian Howard influenced his whole group of titled friends toward an aestheticism they would otherwise never have known.

The relations of our two principals with each other, however, though often fervent, had never been easy, and by the time they left Oxford they were distinctly cool to each other. They were always somewhat jealous of each other, being necessarily in competition for the same applause. And Brian Howard, who was much more reckless in his use of drink and drugs, established an influence over William Acton, which led the latter into similar indulgences. Harold disapproved of this—and his parents held him somewhat responsible for his brother's welfare. A crisis was reached when William injured himself while intoxicated. Brian came to Harold's rooms to tell him that William had "done something wonderful," but what he meant was that William had jumped out of a third-floor window. Luckily he was so drunk that his body had been completely relaxed as he fell, and he was not badly injured, but he had to leave Oxford and go to recuperate at Hastings. Harold blamed Brian for this and for much of William's later misfortunes and unhappiness.[10]

Still, Brian's Oxford remained Harold's Oxford, and vice versa. They cooperated in that act of creation and in ignoring more official Oxfords; and other gifted undergraduates followed them. The dons—this is by universal agreement, and over a long period—counted for very little at Oxford. Louis MacNeice says they might as well have been in Cambridge for all they meant to him. He remembered them as lodged in upper rooms, hiding from each other behind cigarette smoke, and either catching facts in webs of hypothesis or reading detective stories.[11] Evelyn Waugh evokes a similar image in the first scene of *Decline and Fall.* Harold Acton tells us that Norman Douglas had advised him, before he set off for Oxford, not to let the dons get hold of him. In fact, Acton did make one don friend, who was among the most donnish—J. D. Beazley, a world-authority on Greek vases, and a prototypically eccentric and absent-minded scholar. Harold also speaks enthusiastically of F. A. Lindemann's high-table conversation. But nowhere, at least as far as these undergraduates were concerned, did anyone offer himself as a passionate *teacher,* as F. R. Leavis was beginning to do at Cambridge.

Oxford was not a place of study, but of exuberant, anarchic, fantasizing hedonism.

> For life was luncheons, luncheons all the way
> And evenings dining with the Georgeoisie. . . .

John Betjeman goes on to say that he and his friends put all their energies into social life, none into work:

> For while we ate Virginia hams
> Contemporaries passed exams.

Or as Louis MacNeice says, "I had not, however, gone to Oxford to study; that was what grammar school boys did." Betjeman was typical in finding such teaching as suited him not so much in the rooms of his own tutor (C. S. Lewis) as in Maurice Bowra's.

> Within those rooms I met my friends for life,
> True values there were handed on a plate
> As easily as sprouts and aubergines. . . .[12]

Bowra, classics tutor at Wadham College, seems to have been in some sense typical of those Oxford dons who *were* of some importance to our subjects. They exerted an influence that was social—indeed snobbish—in mode, although of course to some extent educational in effect. Others were Roy Harrod, economics tutor at Christ Church, and "Sligger" Urquhart, dean of Balliol. They all seem to have been flirtatious and deferential, although sometimes also malicious, in their relations with these brilliant undergraduates. Urquhart, who is supposed to have been used by Walter Pater as the model for Emerald Uthwart, took parties of chosen young men to Mont Blanc, and was apparently homoerotic. Bowra was famous above all for his tea parties and for the intrigues and gossip of which he was the center. It seems almost certain that these two were used as models for the figure of Sillery in Powell's *Music of Time* novel sequence. Cyril Connolly was close to both of these dons while he was an undergraduate, and so was Kenneth Clark, who went on from Oxford to work with Berenson at Settignano, where Bowra and John Sparrow went to visit him. (Sparrow was later to become Warden of All Souls and a powerful figure at Oxford.) Roy Harrod was a friend to the whole dandy set. It was he who had got Brian Howard into Christ Church, despite his being involved in cheating at his entrance exam. He says that Harold Acton then

> . . . seemed to know of everything of importance that was happening in Europe in contemporary writing, painting, and music. He had a very special voice with an undertone that was not perhaps quite English . . . he kept us laughing endlessly.

Harrod goes on to describe all the other in similarly gushing tones.[13] The undergraduates—those with the right style—got treated by the dons like avatars of Adonis or Orpheus.

The clubs that were most central to the dandies' Oxford seem to have been the Hypocrites and the Railway. The former was a kind of nightclub or standing party, where Robert Byron sang Victorian ballads, Mark Ogilvie-Grant Scottish Border songs, and David Plunket-Greene Harlem Blues. A Victorian party was given there, decorated by Oliver Messel, to which Robert Byron came dressed as Queen Victoria. The Railway Club was founded by John Sutro in 1923; its members went on railway trips in a specially reserved carriage, all dressed in the height of elegance, and eating and drinking luxuriously. Sutro's friends continued these jaunts until 1939.[14] Under such auspices a whole English generation, or those who felt themselves its leaders, joined in the cult of the *Sonnenkind.*

This Oxford dominated by Harold Acton and Brian Howard was not, of course, the only one. There were no doubt some undergraduates up in those years who were quite unaware that they existed. And others no doubt cast as cold an eye on our central pair as subsequent generations were to do. But it seems likely that they *were* central, that their Oxford was central to the other Oxfords. If one approaches the university life of those years from a tolerably objective point of view, one can still discern a geography in which they must have been one of the capital cities, a hub to which main roads led.

For instance, the already established novels of Oxford life—those that fixed its image in the general imagination—were *Sinister Street* and *Zuleika Dobson,* Beverley Nichols' *Patchwork* and Stephen McKenna's *Sonia,* all of which presented it as a place of "beautiful people" and brilliant parties. The ideas of learning, teaching, or studying, the idea of *work* of any kind, were already quite dissociated from Oxford. The oddity of this comes out in an anecdote about a visit by the great German university teacher, Professor Willemowitz-Moellendorf. He is said to have been taken up Magdalen Tower on a particularly beautiful May morning, to admire the blossoms and the river and the towers and so on, but to have turned away, murmuring "Nur eine Luststadt"—only a resort town.[15] And it was to be one of the most striking features of F. R. Leavis's career that he insisted that his work as a teacher, and his students' work as students, be taken seriously. This came as a radical challenge in the atmosphere of English university life. Before the war it was understood that the Oxford playfulness, like the Eton equivalent, was only an interlude. But the imagination even of for instance John Buchan, Hilaire Belloc, and F. E. Smith dwelt so much more lovingly on that period of play than on what it supposedly led on to that it required only a sharp jerk after the war (the jerk administered by Brian Howard and Harold Acton) to sever the connection.

Emotionally, moreover, the ambiance was quite generally homoerotic. One thing on which all observers agree is the marked subordination of women—their devaluation, almost their degradation—in the university's life. Women could become members of the university from 1919 on, but as late as 1938 John Betjeman felt free to say, in *An Oxford University Chest,* "State subsidized undergraduates are generally heterosexual. Probably they may have a fine romance with an undergraduate and will marry her when they go down. In that case the undergraduette has performed a better service than by getting her usual second after three years' unremitting work...." The brilliant men, the heroes of Oxford life, the men Betjeman cared about, would not have any such "fine romance." The romantic mood of the place—by almost universal testimony—was oriented toward young men.* For instance, Evelyn Waugh and Cyril Connolly, both notably heterosexual in later life, at Oxford competed for the favor of Richard Pares.[16] Since this was the case, figures like the dandy-aesthetes, who flaunted that affiliation, had an advantage in frankness and boldness and in freedom over the others who were more divided, more cautious, more discreet. The heterosexuals used to listen to the homosexuals' love complaints—about the

---

* Terence Greenidge, a friend of Evelyn Waugh's, discusses the question of homosexuality in a book of 1930, significantly entitled *Degenerate Oxford?*. He classified the feelings of the young men for each other as Romantic, and connects them with the romantic buildings and romantic charm of Oxford. "Conventional frivolling with conventional girls just would not do. Oxford is so different from Lyon's Corner House." His final declaration is against homosexuality, but his feeling is not, and this is typical.

hard-heartedness or infidelity or gold digging of their beloveds—and listened with at least some sense of being daring and compassionate in ways beyond the reach of their fathers and mothers. This was true even of tough and rakish types—of *rogues*.

It became clear during these Oxford years that the rogues could be quite sharply distinguished from the hearties, because the former were the allies of the dandies and aesthetes. Perhaps they sometimes joined in the persecution of the dandies, but they more often joined in their defense, and always joined in their defiance of the conventions and institutions of manhood. The hearties were out of date, imaginatively. Terence Greenidge says that their patron saint was Bulldog Drummond—the newly invented adventure-fiction hero. Robert Byron and Randolph Churchill, Peter Rodd, Basil Murray, and Evelyn Waugh, all rogues, were the friends of some of the most effeminate men there, and joined, for instance, in the camp jokes about Queen Victoria and so on. Thus the rogue-rebel and the dandy-aesthete made common cause—against the hearties and the fathers and the institutions and pieties of English society, and against the world of Woman and the idea of marriage and emotional maturity.

As moderate a commentator as Christopher Hollis remarks in his autobiography that most undergraduates in his day acted as if Oxford conditions would persist forever—as if they would never marry and have children, as if they would be young men living with their friends forever, and need not prepare for any other state of life. Indeed, there was a flaunting of effeminacy, even by people like Robert Byron, who were so tough and aggressive. Byron often dressed up as Queen Victoria, referred to her in *Cherwell* articles with capitalized pronouns ("with Her well-known generosity of mind"), and boasted of the feminine habits among Oxford men. The popular press was making much of the effeminacy of contemporary young men, and the boyishness of contemporary young girls, and the *Cherwell* accepted the charges and doubled the provocation. This is connected to the fact that Oxford then, this Oxford, was quite especially conscious of publicity, of its image in the eyes of the world, and the usefulness of being talked about. *Sonnenkinder* tend to devote more energy to publicity than other types, and these were all extremely ambitious men.

They quite outshone the traditional Oxford, which centered on institutions like the Union. Christopher Hollis, in his history of *The Oxford Union,* cites 1890 to 1895 as its golden age, when it was dominated by F. E. Smith, Hilaire Belloc, and John Simon. It was then still a fairly private institution, belonging exclusively to Oxford. In 1906, for the first time, *two* outside guests were invited to speak there—it is symptomatic that they were F. E. Smith and Winston Churchill—and from then on it became more of a national institution, with its eye on London audiences. It became a dandy institution, but with a prewar dandyism comparable to that we have discussed at Eton, wholly in the service of the world of men. Ronald Knox was president of the Union in 1909, Philip Guedalla in 1910, A. P. Herbert in 1913; and the line of frivolous epigram and fantasy those names suggest dominated the Union. That too was in some sense a brilliant period, but in the years after the war, when F. E. Smith often attended debates and intervened in them, the serious intellectuals and aesthetes avoided the place. They could do so because they were the university's center of life themselves. The one time Harold Acton did speak there, he drew an unexampled crowd.

It seems clear that he and Brian dominated the place imaginatively, turned the whole town into a backdrop for their performances. Of course, the very architecture of the colleges were already a stage set for dandyism. The quadrangles, the archways, the river, the punts, the bridges, the gardens, all differed from "ordinary" 20th-century buildings in such a way as to induce a sense of being on stage. The very rooms demanded epigrams and poses. The luxury of the setting—its luxury of historical and poetical suggestion, primarily—demanded a corresponding bravura of performance. When Brian and Harold provided the bravura, all the rest of Oxford clustered around them in ready submission, glad to become an appropriate decor.

The Larger Scene

All England in those years could be seen as an extension of Oxford, homogeneous with it in imaginative substance. Average earnings had risen 94 percent between 1914 and 1924, while the cost of living rose only 75 percent, so people had more to spend. Moreover, whereas in 1910, one percent of the population absorbed 30 percent of the national income, in 1929, 1.5 percent absorbed only 23 percent, so there was a tendency toward spreading the wealth out to more individuals, at least at the top. On the other hand, there was more unemployment than there had been in 1914.[17] These facts corresponded to, or caused, a certain feverishness and sense of instability in the national mood. Among the well-to-do young, for instance, there was a new sense of an "authority" who was repressing youthful gaiety—an authority identified most easily with Sir William Joynson-Hicks ("Jix") and DORA, the Defence of the Realm Act. The latter, passed during the war, was a measure giving the Home Secretary unusual powers of surveillance over public events and places; and "Jix" used these powers to fight immorality, in nightclubs and in the parks after dark. Thus the Chelsea Arts Ball of 1922 took as its motif "A Brighter London 100 Years Hence."

But it was already brighter. Before the war nice women had not used lipstick, only lip-salve, which was white, and *papier poudré,* not powder. After the war, cosmetic colors were brighter, and were applied much more publicly, even ostentatiously. The effect, significantly, was sometimes that of *commedia dell'arte* makeup. Round red cheeks were painted on stark white faces, and the line and color of the eyebrows was artificial to the point of fantasy. Cosmetics became a much bigger business. In 1917 in America, only two people had earned enough by "beauty-culture" to pay income tax on it; by 1927, 18,000 did. Wartime medical experience was also useful to plastic surgery, and this, of course, dramatized the popular sense of the face as a mask. Changes in clothing and hair styles express the change in sexual role-playing—away from the emphasis by women on their womanliness, and by man on their manliness, toward similarity and interchangeability. The jumper, for instance, was what the 1960s were to call a "unisex" garment. Men got rid of beards and moustaches and brushed their hair smoothly and shinily back into a Pierrot skullcap, leaving their faces as naked as possible. (The thick moustache was a key symbol of pre-1914 masculinity—Lord Berners mocks his sports master for his heavy military moustache—and Orwell's cultivation of one was a significant act of dissent from post-1918 styles). Women began to bob their hair immediately after the war, were shingling it by 1925, and by 1927 used the Eton crop, the most boyish style of all. In 1925 they also started wearing the cloche hat, which concealed all their hair. They now smoked, drank, drove, and made love, publicly. Michael Arlen's Iris Storm and Hemingway's Brett Ashley, two notable figures representing modern womanhood, both had boyishly short hair and were scandalously promiscuous.

Such women were castrators of their lovers, at least of the old-fashioned idealists among them. Brett's romantic admirer, Robert Cohen, is destroyed by her treatment of him. Iris Storm's first husband, a hero and idol of other men, called Boy Fenwick, committed suicide soon after their wedding because she had offended against his ideal of womanly purity. In real life we have the example of Violet Keppel's husband, Denys Trefusis, who was defeated in his marriage and in his pride in himself by her lesbianism—by her preference for the lesbian Vita Sackville-West, who was herself married to the homosexual Harold Nicolson. This famous, although secret, scandal of 1918 to 1921 is particularly representative, because Trefusis was a war hero of the most dashing style and beauty, and had also been one of the famous band that included Patrick Shaw-Stewart and the Grenfell brothers (in fact, Julian Grenfell himself had also been in love with Violet Keppel). That one of these legendary heroes should have been rejected—and reduced to tears, to ignominious pleading, to renunciation of his marital rights—in favor of sexual perversity, was the kind of story that sapped the strength of a whole range of orthodox sexual values. Social disciplines were being relaxed, new forces were being released, and old ones were suddenly crippled.

Even women's bodies changed. Corsets were discarded, and therewith waists and breasts disappeared; whereas legs became very apparent, as skirts were shortened drastically and high heels and silk stockings brought added glamour to nakedness. The sexual style of the *grandes cocottes* disappeared. Those erotic fantasies of the world of men before the war had been swellingly feminine in figure and elaborately frilly in attire, their heads a great blossoming of hair and hat; now youth, slenderness, and boyishness were what was wanted, and they were achieved by means like slimming, swimming, sunbathing, and sports.[18]

In London, nightclub life was lively, and it was symbolized by Kate Meyrick. Her clubs, and others like them, were the places persecuted by "Jix" and DORA. Their atmosphere was more illicit and daring than an ordinary nightclub today—perhaps more comparable to a gay bar today. Kate Meyrick began her underground club career in 1919, when she was divorced. In 1921 she opened her most famous club, the "43," where you could often find artists, like Jacob Epstein and Augustus John, and several writers, as well as socialites and millionaires out on the spree. In 1924, Mrs. Meyrick was finally caught out by the police and sent to jail for six months. But in 1925 she opened "The Manhattan," and in 1927 "The Glass Slipper," which had a dancing floor made of glass.[19]

Jazz dancing—like the Charleston, patronized by the Prince of Wales—can perhaps be said to have been *Sonnenkind* dancing; like jazz music, it was a choreographic defiance of older, statelier measures, and in itself bright, sharp, young. Folk dancing, on the other hand, went along with arts and crafts and cottages, under the sign of Demeter. Men who folk-danced, and went "back to the Land," were likely to wear beards—like D. H. Lawrence, whose beard, like Orwell's mustache, marked him off from the clean-shaven, wax-smooth masks of the dandies. (The eurhythmic Dalcroze movements, before the war an Aphroditean style of dance, also went out of fashion.)

The stars of the theater included two Americans, Tallulah Bankhead and Tom Douglas. She offered diabolical sophistication, he angelic innocence. Both were *commedia* figures, he a naïf, she a Columbine, and both were noted for their power to disturb sexual conventions, their power to attract people of their own sex. In the dramatization of Arlen's *The Green Hat,* Tallulah Bankhead played Iris Storm, the modern girl, so lacking in what had used to constitute femininity. Another celebration of the boyish girl, more "serious" in its historical setting and intellectual claims, was G. B. Shaw's *St. Joan,* produced in 1924, the same year as Arlen's novel. This ideal of womanhood had been seen socially as early as 1911, in Irene Castle, whose "healthy, boyish, long-striding sportiveness," as Cecil Beaton describes it, captivated London when she and Vernon Castle brought the modern style in ballroom dancing from America to London. But it was after the war that this style became dominant; Daisy Fellowes, Mrs. Dudley Ward, and Lady Mountbatten were much-photographed beauties of this kind, and Chanel was their chief Paris designer. The contrast they offered to the prewar charms of Gaby Deslys (all naughty dimples and diamonds) and Lina Cavalieri (all noble contours and regality) was immense. The new style was modern—which is to say hard, sharp, and aggressive.

This was the epoch of Noel Coward's debut, as a spokesman for modernity. He put on *The Young Idea* in 1923, *Vortex* (about drug-taking and homosexuals) in 1924, and *Fallen Angels* in 1925. Frederick Lonsdale's *Spring Cleaning* of 1924 presented a lesbian on stage. And cooperating with this fashion for "corruption" was a fashion for the purely childish. *The Young Visitors,* written twenty-five years before when its author, Daisy Ashford, was nine, was a great success when it was published—with an introduction by Sir James Barrie—in 1919. And Pamela Bianco's drawings, done when she also was nine, were described as Botticellian. Cecil Beaton wanted to decorate his rooms with them when he went up to Cambridge. The sophistication and the childishness were both to be seen in the newly popular party games, like "sardines," and in pyjama parties. Evelyn Waugh's early satires stress both elements in modernity; and the reason they cooperate is, of course, that both are rebellions against maturity. This was the "decadent" influence, whose center of emanation was Oxford. It did not go unchallenged, however. J. B. Priestley, who arrived in London to begin his literary career in 1922, brought with him the still-untainted manliness of Yorkshire. He and Aldous Huxley were both born in 1894, but Priestley determined to continue the prewar line, the prewar temperament. He first became a book reviewer and a publisher's reader for John Lane, and his social-literary life was passed with J. C. Squire of the London *Mercury*, Robert Lynd, Hilaire Belloc, J. B. Morton, and others of that healthy literary fellowship.

And a much more effectual resistance to the trends of the times was initiated by John Reith, who became general manager of the British Broadcasting Corporation in 1922. He was very unlike most of the men we are describing, in his relation to his father, who was a great preacher, as well as in other things. Although his father was forty-seven when John was born and the son could not as a child be intimate with him, yet he writes, "In magnificence of presence I have not met his equal. . . . I admired him tremendously: held him, as did most others, in considerable awe. . . ."[20] John Reith grew up greedy for admiration and awe himself. He was determined to *manage* the BBC and, by means of it, in some measure to manage the nation. He took a firm hand during the General Strike of 1926, assuring the prime minister, Stanley Baldwin, that the BBC stood with the government against the strikers and proposing that Baldwin should broadcast a speech to the nation—even writing some of that speech when the latter agreed. When the strike ended, he himself read the prime minister's new message to the nation and had himself played out with William Blake's "Jerusalem," rendered by a choir and orchestra. On the smaller scale, he insisted on strict uniform standards of "BBC English," (his committee on pronunciation could have been the germ of a literary Academy), on announcers wearing evening dress to read the news, and on Christianity and morality among all his employees. Thus when John Heygate was named as correspondent in the Evelyn Waugh divorce case, he lost his job at the BBC and was out of work for two years. Reith kept out of discussion topics like birth control and points of view like Communism, and maintained a strict sabbatarianism on the radio. Most of his employees were of a very different and more modern temperament than his, but they obeyed him as a strict headmaster. It was a joke of the times that every day the Prince of Wales got more democratic, and Sir John Reith more regal. In every way, Reith and the BBC represented old-fashioned paternalism and resistance to the trends of the times. But that resistance was quite ineffective as far as most young people of talent were concerned. Their trends—centrally, the Sitwell trends—were too powerful.

In 1924, Sacheverell Sitwell published *Southern Baroque Art,* which, as Osbert said, set a whole generation talking of baroque and rococo. He followed up this 1924 book with *German Baroque Art* in 1927, *Spanish Baroque Art* in 1931, *Country House Baroque* in 1940, and books on "baroque" subjects, like *Watteau, Mozart, Scarlatti, Beckford and Beckfordism,* and so on. His more elaborate productions, like *Southern Baroque Art,* are pieces of baroquerie in themselves, since both their structure and their texture are very elaborate, full of exotic people and places, sumptuous occasions and costumes, false perspectives in time and place, concealed transitions from fiction to historical fact, and transpositions of one art into terms of another.

One of Osbert's books in this period was *Discursions on Travel, Art, and Life* (1925), a book about Italy, which Cyril Connolly said had an important educational influence on him. It has indeed an interesting essay on "Fiume and d'Annunzio," which describes the Fascist movement as deriving from d'Annunzio, and says that together they offer us an escape from the Scylla and Charybdis of modern life, which are Russian Bolshevism and American capitalism. D'Annunzio attracted Sitwell (and others like him) as being a genius, poet, and aesthete who had actually founded a state—a state that honored the arts and genius and that attracted beautiful idealistic boys from all over Italy, and beyond, to fight in its undisciplined army. This essay crystallizes for us the political tendency of the *Sonnenkind* cult; Sitwell even included a partial translation of the constitution that d'Annunzio wrote for Fiume as an appendix to his book. He also discusses Charlie Chaplin, seeing him as a modern representative of the *commedia dell'arte,* and says that compulsory games for the boys at English public schools should be abolished in favor of compulsory Chaplin films for the teachers. And he also displays an interest in 19th-century Naples and particularly in King "Bomba," the fat cruel and pious tyrant who inherited the throne of Naples in 1830—an interest that is doubly relevant here because of Harold Acton's later interest in that figure and in comparable ones in 17th-century Florence. (Sacheverell also was fascinated by Naples.) "Bomba" of Naples and Gian Castone of Tuscany are grotesque Punchinellos of real life, and their courts, their countries, are domains of the *commedia* in history. That explains their fascination for Harold Acton and Osbert Sitwell as subjects.

The other remarkable literary achievement of the Sitwells in this period was Edith's *Facade,* which is dedicated to Sacheverell. It was performed first in the brothers' house in Carlyle Square in 1922, then at the Aeolian Hall, and then in the Chenil Galleries in King's Road. William Walton, a Sitwell protégé, composed music for it, and Edith declaimed the verses through a megaphone, wearing a mask. Later Frederick Ashton, another of their friends, made it into a ballet. Harold Acton took a party of his friends and protégés to the second performance, at the Aeolian Hall; Brian was at his crammer's, preparing for his entrance examinations to Oxford, so he could not come, but Evelyn Waugh, Desmond Harmsworth, and Francis Palmer were in the party, which Harold took on to the Sitwells' house afterwards. (As a result he got Edith to come to Oxford to speak, and through her persuaded Gertrude Stein to come also.) Cecil Beaton went to the Chenil Galleries Performance, with girls from the "bright young people" group.

On young men of talent at the time, like Cyril Connolly and Evelyn Waugh, the Sitwells were an important influence. They represented brilliant modernism, and surpassed even Bloomsbury in sophistication and dandyism. They met Connolly for the first time in Spain in 1925; and in 1957 we find him wondering whether, "if it had been my fate to have encountered High Bloomsbury in Almeria on their visit in 1923 rather than the Sitwells in 1925, I should have been purged of that trait of Oxford dandyism which brought down the epithet 'cocktail critic' on me in Virginia Woolf's journals many years later." And Waugh remarked about the same time that by 1939 the Sitwells had lightened and brightened English social life as a whole.[21] They were, for nearly everyone, the new England. Thus all *England* might be said to have clustered round the dandies like decor. All the new life seemed to point in their direction and reach a culmination in them. But Oxford remained their locus, the institution that of all institutions belonged to them and carried their influence.

New Friends

Among the people our principals got to know at Oxford, and who, therefore, now become parts of our story, the most important was Evelyn Waugh. He was the most important because of the close link of friendship that henceforth bound Harold Acton to him, because of the historical testimony he bore in various of his books to the dandies' achievement, but above all because he was the man of the greatest intelligence and force to get involved in the dandy enterprise. It was in his life and work that the dandy idea achieved its greatest moral and imaginative substance.

Waugh had gone to Lancing School—a far cry from Eton, being much more moralistic and puritan in ethos, much less brilliant socially and imaginatively. His favorite books there were *Sinister Street* and *Le Morte d'Arthur,* and he drew in the style of Aubrey Beardsley. But deeper down, he says, he stayed loyal to Ruskin—he never really liked the Paris school. He despised science, disrupted the school O.T.C., and founded a Corpse Club, for those weary of life, who should wear black and write on mourning paper. He was generally a force for anarchy, but not violently in rebellion.

He looked backed, nostalgically, to an England greater than the one he saw around him. In 1921 he read Rupert Brooke and decided that friendship and the beauty of living went out of the world in 1914, for a generation; he made a cult of the memory of those prewar "golden lads." In the same year he saw Lovat Fraser's production of *The Beggar's Opera,* and loved it. This was a moderated and anglicized version of Diaghilev's theater, and it was typical of Waugh that he inclined to the moderate and the melancholy, even though he also rebelled against those moods so violently.

From Lancing he went up to Hertford College, Oxford, an equally far cry, in social terms, from Christ Church. There he lived very quietly and economically for his first two terms, still pursuing a fairly orthodox post-Morris and post-Ruskin taste in art, literature, and ideas. Then, in 1923, he met Harold Acton and his friends, and was taken up into the fashionable and extravagant life, the exotic aesthetic tastes and the anarchic childish playfulness. And although he was to undergo several complex stages of reaction to that, it remained his greatest love and his determining experience.

The dandies' Oxford was such a liberating experience for him because Lancing had been so repressive and because he had been born into a middle-class literary home that had toyed lovingly with frivolity but remained essentially subdued to traditional values— the middle-class familial equivalent of institutions like prewar Eton and Oxford. His father, Arthur Waugh, was an editor in a publishing house, a minor writer, and an amateur actor. His literary career had been launched by Sir Edmund Gosse, the Edwardian man of letters, whose model in matters of taste and scholarship he followed; but his keener imaginative pleasures were associated with his son, Alec, an ardent cricketer and "zestful" schoolboy. (The word *zestful* is Evelyn's; *he* was not a zestful schoolboy nor an ardent cricketer, and Sir Edmund Gosse was *anathema* to him. Although only five years younger than Alec, there was a gulf fixed between them, and between Evelyn and his father, and he brought no pleasure to the latter.) As he grew up, Alec added a love of golf to that of cricket, and showed himself thoroughly "normal" in all his aspirations and gestures of manliness. Paradoxically, however, he was expelled from Sherborne School for homosexuality, and he wrote a "scandalous" novel, exposing public schools, that made him seem a "modern" writer in the 1920s. The relevance of such facts to our study is perhaps to make clear that the significant rebellion against the public schools was not expressed in literal homosexuality or in "exposure" novels about them. The significant, the dandy, rebellion was often much less direct in its attack.

Evelyn grew up, he says, a "normal, strong, brave, and clever little boy"; but he was attached to his mother exclusively, and had some marked, although masked, resentments against his father and brother. When Evelyn was six, his father welcomed Alec home from school by pasting a banner, "Welcome home to the heir of Underhill," over the clock in the hall (of their very suburban house). Evelyn is supposed to have said, "When Alec has Underhill and all that's in it, what will be left for me?" He says that up to the age of seven he saw his father very rarely and reacted to him as to someone who took his mother away from him.

> Many little boys look on their fathers as heroically strong and
> skillful; mighty hunters, the masters of machines; not so I.
> Nor did I ever fear him. He was restless rather than active. His
> sedentary and cerebral occupations appeared ignominious to
> me in my early childhood. I should have better respected a
> soldier or a sailor like my uncles . . . a man, even, who shaved
> with a cut-throat razor. . . . I never saw him as anything but
> old, indeed as decrepit.[22]

Evelyn's own manhood was to be marked by an alternation in styles between the aesthete and the man of action, and it seems likely that the latter ambition derived from a determination not to be like his father. He says that to him as a boy Gosse was "all that I found ignoble in the profession of letters," and he himself always hoped to avoid that profession. Of course he also deeply loved it, and often saw himself as an artist, but he did not really take to writing until all else failed.

His father was, of course, a very old-fashioned man of letters, who found T. S. Eliot absurd and D. H. Lawrence odious. He wrote about Eliot in *Quarterly Review* for October 1918, saying that in this new poetry everything English fathers had held wise and true was made false and foolish to their sons; and recalling how the fathers of Sparta had warned their sons away from unmanliness by the example of a drunken helot. But Arthur Waugh was no Spartan, being himself in reaction against his severe Victorian grandfather. More typically, he wrote about Tennyson and other standard authors, saying standard things. His enjoyment of them was no doubt sincere, but it was so unadventurous as to be in some sense inauthentic. One senses a keener delight in his references to cricket. He said, "With a thorough knowledge of the Bible, Shakespeare and Wisden [the cricket almanac] you cannot go far wrong," and that probably indicates fairly enough the relation of his passion for cricket to his respect for literature and religion. His interest in Sherborne's cricket team was so obsessive that he had the school's games' scores wired to him. Cricket was an important part of the national culture in its prewar dandy phases, and was often humorously linked with the Bible and Shakespeare as part of "the Englishman's religion." And it was particularly important to Arthur Waugh's type of the man of letters. It is typical that he thoroughly despised the technical manuals on which Chapman and Hall's fortunes were founded, and appropriate that he was first president of England's Publisher's Circle. Evelyn could not respond to anything in this image of manhood and culture. He rebelled deep down, at the sources of his temperament. When he first put on a tailcoat, at the age of sixteen, it was one that had been worn by his father and his brother before him, and he described it as having come down "from generation unto generation of them that hate me."[23]

In his autobiography and in semiautobiographical fiction like *Work Suspended* and *Brideshead Revisited,* his father (although really it is only a father-figure) is portrayed with a humor as elaborate and habitual as Osbert Sitwell's or Nancy Mitford's. It is a humor that, in all these cases, seems to derive from an extraordinary remoteness between father and child, from there never having been a normal bond that would at least give friction and electricity to this filial impiety, or perhaps from that bond's having been snapped by so complete a turning away.

At Lancing, Waugh had come under two powerful influences, from men who recognized in him remarkable talents and who symbolized to him the two models of manhood, the aesthete and the man of action, between which he oscillated and that governed his relations to the dandy idea as to everything else. One was J. F. Roxburgh, who became his housemaster after the war, and who later became a famous head-master at Stowe. He was a brilliant, commanding, virile figure, who gave the boys a strong sense of the world of action, and of the rewards that came from succeeding there. The other was Francis Crease, an eccentric, effeminate artist in script, who lodged near the school; he asked to be allowed to give Waugh private lessons, which developed into instruction in all kinds of aesthetic and Anglo-Catholic lore. The paradox to which Waugh draws our attention is that it was the first, and not the second, who was an active homosexual. But perhaps the deeper paradox was that Waugh should have been, as he says, for a year entirely captivated by Mr. Crease, whom he describes as a "neu-ter, evasive, hypochondriacal recluse." That is the paradox of Waugh's nature. For at the same time he was making himself a figure of power in the school, leading various kinds of rebellion, and dominating and bullying quite a few of his contemporaries. He was always much con-cerned with questions of power and precedence. He had a keen sense, for instance, of how low Lancing stood in the rank of public schools; and in a broadcast of 1953 he said that he had always wanted to be a man of action. On the other hand, when he got his taste of action, in the war, he started seeing himself as an artist and aesthete.

When he met the dandy idea among Etonians at Oxford, therefore, he responded with great enthusiasm to both sides of it—both to the bold defiance of the reality principle, the bold assertion of style and aristocracy and art, and to the frailty of the enterprise, its mere play-fulness, its being doomed to defeat. He says that to him Oxford "was a Kingdom of Cokayne, and I believe that I was especially fortunate in my generation. . . . I was reborn in full youth." He often refers to Oxford in those terms—as a rebirth into childhood after the "Sto-icism" of public school prefecthood.

None of the dons impressed him, predictably, and with one, Cruttwell, the dean of his college, Waugh waged a war that lasted long after he had left Oxford. He fell in love, in some sense, with a series of fellow undergraduates, Richard Pares, Alastair Graham, and Hugh Lygon. And he sat at the feet of Harold Acton, who he describes as bringing to Oxford the knowledge of the connoisseurs of Florence and the innovators of Paris; bringing, that is, the knowledge of Berenson and Stein, Magnasco and Cocteau and Eliot—bringing to Oxford what the Sitwells were bringing to the rest of England. "He led me away from Crease to the baroque, rococo, and *The Waste Land*." Personally he describes Acton as ". . . vividly alive to every literary and artistic fashion, exuberantly appreciative, punctilious, light and funny and energetic . . . the one quality he despised was languor . . . I was a little dazzled by his manifest superiorities of experience." What these two so different young men shared was gusto, which Waugh defines as zest for the variety and absurdity of life, a veneration for artists, a scorn for the bogus. "He was always the leader; I, not always, the follower." As for Brian Howard, he says, "Brian made himself more than the entertainer, the arbiter, almost the animator, of the easy-going aristocrats whom he set out to reform in his romantic model, like the youthful d'Israeli inspiring 'Young England.' " He was proud to know Brian, and Basil Murray and Peter Rodd, the two acknowledged models for Basil Seal, but he learned that they were all mad, bad, and dangerous to know.

He devotes some space in his autobiography to Robert Byron, who, he says, learned little at school and university and was later disposed to think that the dons had concealed information from him. Waugh's tone is often a little acid on the subject of Byron, whom he seems to have felt as more of a rival than any of the others in the early years. Thus he says that Byron never learned to write correct English (like Randolph Churchill, and other of the dandies, Waugh believed in a certain "Fowler" style as *the* correct form of English*); and that

---

* "Fowler" refers to H. W. Fowler's *Dictionary of Modern English Usage*, a manual of style much consulted by the British dandies in these years.

at Oxford Byron had been a pure clown, dressing to accentuate his ugliness and behaving similarly. He leered and scowled, screamed and snarled, simulated epileptic fits, and called from cars that he was being kidnapped. But beneath all this he was determined to force his way into the worlds of power and fashion. He was, Waugh says, much admired for this energy. Energy, violence, and hatred were qualities that both Waugh and Byron purveyed socially. (Christopher Hollis says that Waugh spoke at the Union in praise of hatred as a political passion—apropos the War—and quarreled with Hollis when the latter said he hoped that the country could avoid industrial violence.[24]) He and Byron were pursuing paths as parallel as Brian Howard's and Harold Acton's, and they were in similar competition.

Waugh's principal portrait of that Oxford is, of course, to be found in *Brideshead Revisited.* It is interesting how many of those who lived through the same experiences have praised this portrait as "accurate." This is interesting because the narrative does not give realistic portrait but a fantasy, of however brilliant a kind. It is not so much accurate as appropriate, because the experience, for all concerned, *was* fantasy, was a denial of the reality principle and an acting out of the pleasure principle. Their Oxford was a fairy tale come true, a hot spring of anarchy bubbling up out of the rocks, as Waugh says.

The major interest of that novel, however, is the statement it makes, in mythic form, about Waugh's failure as an artist. Charles Ryder, who represents Waugh, fails as an artist because he turns away from Anthony Blanche (the figure derived from Acton and Howard, an international dandy-aesthete) to make a friend of Sebastian Flyte (who stands for the prewar, purely English dandyism of the beautiful Etonian and Oxonian aristocrat). If Ryder had affiliated himself to Blanche (if Waugh had affiliated himself to Acton), he might have become a great artist. Instead he chose charm, playfulness, quaintness, and whimsy—and became the writer of *Brideshead Revisited.* Another Charles Ryder (John Betjeman) wrote *Summoned by Bells;* another, Cyril Connolly, wrote *The Unquiet Grave;* and so on. For Charles Ryder's wrong choice was the wrong choice of a whole generation of English writers, who preferred the purely playful dandyism of English aristocrats to the dangerously experimental dandyism of international aestheticism. Of course *Brideshead* implies that Waugh had won religious salvation in exchange for aesthetic, but that part of the novel is surely much less authentic; in any case the statement about the choice made at Oxford is independent of that.

It seems clear, if we correlate *Memoirs of an Aesthete* with *Brideshead Revisited,* that Waugh was fictionalizing a choice that Acton had really in some way presented him with. Thus Acton says of Waugh,

> The gentleness of his manner could not deceive me, nor could the neat black and white drawings, nor the taste for Eric Gill. Though his horns had been removed, he was capable of butting in other ways. So demure, and yet so wild.

This is very similar, in both tone and substance, to Blanche's teasing and coaxing exhortation of Ryder to become a real artist, to take the risk of decadence and unmanliness. And Acton's "prejudice in favour of things French," which he says irritated Waugh ("Doubtless my enthusiasm irritated those friends who looked to the Cotswolds for their inspiration. Evelyn Waugh winced at the sound of a French word. . . .")—this is the equivalent of Blanche's cosmopolitanism, which is set in opposition to Sebastian's exquisite Englishness.

Sebastian Flyte keeps a toy bear, "Aloysius," as an undergraduate—it is a sign of his rebellion against his fate of manhood. There were several equivalents to "Aloysius" in that Oxford, for instance Beverley Nichols' toy rabbit, "Cuthbert," which he took on his tour of America, as secretary to the British Universities Mission to the United States. Nichols took "Cuthbert" everywhere, even to the White House; in his account of the trip, "Cuthbert" is used as part of Nichols' impudence about patriarchal figures like President Butler of Columbia.[25] Another example was John Betjeman's toy bear, "Archibald."

John Betjeman is in many ways the figure most similar to Waugh, above all in the literary use he has made of his experience of escaping middle-class confines by joining the dandies at Oxford. He is also like Waugh in his obvious desire not to grow up and his use of childhood materials like the Grossmiths' *Diary of a Nobody* (Waugh used *The Wind in the Willows,* and Auden and Isherwood used *Alice in Wonderland* and Beatrix Potter). Apparently a psychiatrist once told Betjeman "You're a dear child of 12½," and there is much in Betjeman's work that suggests that he too made a "Sebastian-choice."

Betjeman's Sebastian was the Irish Marquis of Dufferin and Ava. The latter, however, although beautiful, extravagant, and improvident like Sebastian, was unlike him in having, apparently, "abominable manners" and in being very aggressive. He and Randolph Churchill and Freddie Furneaux (F. E. Smith's son, later the 2nd Lord Birkenhead) were friends, and we gather—from the last named's account— that Basil Ava and Randolph were of the same type. One of their exploits occurred at F. E. Smith's house, where, tiring of the exquisite tennis played by a group of professionals and near-professionals, Randolph and Basil insisted on taking a court themselves (although they knew nothing of the game) and played their grotesquely clumsy shots before that audience for a prize of £50. In other words, Basil Ava was a rogue rather than a dandy, and Betjeman's relation with him must have been more passively playful and admiring than Charles' was with Sebastian. But it was like the latter relation in being a middle-class boy's adoration of an aristocratic boy's style.[26]

In his autobiography, *Summoned by Bells,* Betjeman shows a very keen sense of class, apparently developed in childhood, and a strong sense of the middle-class tradition he himself was born into. But his prime reaction was against that tradition. His father was the third Betjeman to run the family's furniture firm (established in 1820—its fortune was founded on the tantalus, the bottlestand in which whiskey was safe from the butler's private nipping, a symbol of the Victorian bourgeoisie), and he wanted John to be the fourth. But the latter determined early to be a poet, and so to escape going into the family works. And this was connected with escaping normal manhood. At prep school, he tells us, he funked a fight with Percival Mandeville, "the perfect boy," and faked an excuse for not fighting. Thereafter he accepted his failure as a boy. At Marlborough he developed a strong sense of the *doom* of going to school—of the agony of organized games and the treachery of boys to boys. He declined the invitations of manliness, and acknowledged himself a coward and a snob. But he did not have to care, because he was also a poet, a Child of the Sun. In consequence, there were ugly scenes in the Betjeman household (vividly rendered in Chapter VIII of the autobiography) in which the father calls the son bone-lazy, and a rotten, low, deceitful little snob. The central issue is that the son will not follow the father into the family business—or into the larger model of manhood. "Yes, I'm in trade and proud of it, I am," the father says. The dignity of the son's account of these scenes is that he allows his father's version, his vision, of their relations to stand, acknowledging the impossibility of explaining. And the mother, immersed in Christian Science and sentimental novels and self-deception, can win no real respect. The boy can only say no to all that he is offered, in full knowledge of the pain he causes and of the odious role he plays.

Then Chapter IX, "Oxford," describes his release from all that tension into aesthetic happiness, innovation, experiment, *"Crome Yellow, Prancing Nigger,* Blunden, Keats." The queer mixture of the modernist and the old-fashioned in that list is very typical of Betjeman's sensibility. Jocelyn Brooke has compared him with Ronald Firbank, but also with Edward Lear.[27] His precarious dandyism is more openly vulnerable than Waugh's, and it protects and props itself more with humor.

> Those were the days when that divine baroque
> Transformed our English altars and our ways. . . .

He escaped also into new and romantic social alliances; for instance, with Randolph Churchill, Viscount Furneaux, Frank Pakenham, and the marquis of Dufferin and Ava.

> I climbed, still keeping in, I thought, with God,
> Until I reached what seemed to me the peak—
> The leisured set in Canterbury Quad.

He delighted in the aristocrats and the aesthetes but still heard his parents' reproaches.

> As Harold Acton and the punkahs wave:
> "My dears, I want to rush into the fields
> And slap raw meat with lilies.'
> And as the laughs grew loud and long I heard
> The more insistent inner voice of guilt:
> 'Stop' cried my mother from her bed of pain.
> I heard my father in his factory say:
> "Fourth generation, John, they look to you."

But he bought new Savile Row suits and Charvet ties, and kept climbing socially. (In this climbing he was only typical of all his friends, as Connolly and Green admit; snobbery was intimately related to artistic sensibility in this temperament.)

These new friends and their life-styles were, of course, incompatible not only with following his father, but with living within his own income. When the day came that he had to leave the special, protected playground of Oxford (like Waugh, he had to take a job teaching in a small boys' school) he entered a reality that he had in effect been defying for three years.

> But in the end they sent me down
> From that sweet hothouse world of bells
> And crumbling walls of golden brown
> And dotty peers and incense smells.

And he describes how he said goodbye to his friends, who could continue to live in a world of fantasy, or at least of beauty.

> I called on Ava. He was packing up
> For Ireland, for the scintillating lake,
> Its gate-lodge, woods and winding avenue
> Around the limestone walls of Clandeboye.

This is Sebastian leaving Charles Ryder for Brideshead, all over again. Betjeman, like Waugh, had now to discover whether he could maintain a dandy poise and stance without the support of a fantasy mise-en-scène.

Among the other men of letters who were at Oxford with Acton and Howard were Peter Quennell, Graham Greene, Claud Cockburn, and Alfred and Hubert Duggan. The latter pair, very rich South Americans, whose mother became Lady Curzon, were particularly friends of Evelyn Waugh. He describes Hubert as a delicate Regency dandy, Alfred as a full-blooded Restoration rake. They left Oxford early, finding it dowdy and provincial, and being too purely and surely elegant themselves to need to affront it. (They seem to have been partial literary models for Waugh often—for Peter Pastmaster, and for Anthony Blanche's background.) In later life Alfred Duggan was reclaimed from drunkenness and began a literary career, partly with Waugh's help.

Quennell, Greene, and Claud Cockburn had all gone to Berkhamstead, the public school of which Greene's father was headmaster. Greene has given us vivid accounts of his sufferings there and of his remoteness from and rebellion against his father. His situation was particularly difficult because his father was the authority against which his friends were rebelling. Most of his fictional accounts sound rather different from those in the dandy movement because of Greene's defeatist tone. But in his autobiography, *A Sort of Life,* his voice sounds strikingly like that of Evelyn Waugh. His family seems to have been of much the same kind as Waugh's, socially and culturally, and so too does his alienation from it, an alienation that precluded affection but also precluded all serious resentment. He and his father were, above all, strangers to each other. And Greene too hated gym., games, and the O.T.C. at school, and would hide away to read at the time when such things were scheduled. He remembers his boyhood reading, Rider Haggard and Henty, Beatrix Potter and E. Nesbitt. Indeed, he traces its reappearance, transformed, in his own writing.

Greene was so unhappy at school that he ran away at fifteen, was sent to a psychiatrist for a year, and attempted suicide by Russian roulette (revolving the cartridge chamber of a revolver with only one bullet in it), which he repeated later as a way to relieve his boredom. He read Lytton Strachey and *The Yellow Book* together with Peter Quennell. In 1923 he went up to Oxford, a little ahead of Quennell, but with Claud Cockburn. He and Cockburn both joined the Communist party at Oxford, although both were seen as being frivolous in their political motives—Greene tells us—by an Australian Rhodes scholar who was also a member. Greene also attended a Communist meeting in Paris, but soon got bored and went back to his hotel to read *Ulysses,* the purchase of which had been a secondary purpose of his trip. Later the two of them went on a trip into the French-controlled Palatine, as spies for the German embassy. Their contact approached them on the train on the way just as they were laughing hysterically at the absurdity of what they were doing. "We flirted with fear and began to plan a thriller together rather in the Buchan manner." We see there the element of fantasy, and frivolity, in the motives of men who were to live out as well as to describe the life of action. Greene had got an anti-French newspaper to accredit him as their representative, and he then persuaded the French to give him introductions *as* the newspaper's representative—he was being a double agent. But it was all frivolous, indeed fantastic. Ideologically he eschewed the *Sonnenkind's* exuberance, indeed chose something opposite, but there were *Sonnenkind* elements in his temperament all the time, and they have worked against the authenticity of the "maturity" he has aimed at in his ideology. The same is true, more obviously, of Malcolm Muggeridge and Claud Cockburn.

That frivolity in Greene and Cockburn, and its detection and disapproval by the Australian Rhodes scholar, is something often paralleled in the history of the group. His challenge was one they were always being presented with. In the realm of literary criticism, for instance, we see it in the hostility between the *Scrutiny* critics and the dandy writers. But, staying within the world of politics, we shall see that Philip Toynbee and John Strachey were treated very *de-haut-en-bas* by their working-class comrades in the Communist party, because they could not seem serious, however hard they tried. Correspondingly, people outside the group often felt their own seriousness a disadvantage in working within the British high-culture system. Tom Driberg gives an interesting example out of the life of Guy Burgess, who became a friend at university of Jimmy Lees, an Independent Labour party member and ex-coal-miner. Lees told Burgess:

> You will get a first because your energies are not exhausted by life, because of the class-prejudice of the examiners, and because you got here easily and aren't frightened by it all. I don't have the brilliance of ignorance. I shall do ten times as much work as you—and get a good second.

And so things in fact turned out, Driberg says.[28] The university system worked for the upper-class undergraduates and against even the virtues of the lower-class men.

Peter Quennell was already a very precocious poet by the time he arrived at Oxford. Like Brian and Harold, he had had high praise from Edith Sitwell. His parents too were litterateurs; they wrote together a famous series of books of social history for school use. His verse was very literary, very languid, but it shows genuine talent, of a Walter de la Mare kind.

> If the moon laughed at me
> I should extend my fingers—
> Silver curled fingers
> Lifted all disdainfully.

And

> O go to the South
> Where the bird calls shrill in amazement
> To see on thin horses of glamour
> Five kings hunting thistledown.

A typical theme is that of Leviathan, the monster of chaos that overwhelms Atlantis, which represents form, beauty, and pleasure. There are poems on this theme in his *Poems* of 1926, manifestoes of dandyism that quite justified Harold Acton's enthusiasm, his determination to take Quennell up.[29]

Quennell was a friend to both Acton and Howard, but a coolness developed between them even at Oxford. The latter seemed to have felt that Quennell lacked the *courage* to follow them or to develop his talent. He was the Charles Ryder they were conscious of. In fact his poetic gift did dry up very quickly, and after trying his hand at a Radiguet-style novel, he turned to writing biographies and books of literary history. He transferred his allegiance to Cyril Connolly, who was more cautious than they and who might be compared, in his Oxford manifestation, with the Collins of *Brideshead Revisited*. But from any larger point of view these splits and subdivisions are of no importance. All these writers remained in that world of the imagination that was oriented towards dandyism.

Claud Cockburn, a cousin of Waugh's, was born into a family rather like Muggeridge's, in which the fathers were radicals, in both politics and religion. (Muggeridge went to Cambridge, and then became a left wing newspaper correspondent, so his early career was remote from those of our principles. In the 1950s, as editor of *Punch,* a T.V. personality, he became a national figurehead of the dandy movement.) At Oxford he belonged to the Hypocrites' Club, saw Waugh and Betjeman, Acton and Byron, and was also a friend of Basil Murray and Peter Rodd. Cockburn went to work for *The Times* (as did Greene) and then for the *Daily Worker,* and later ran a remarkable newsletter, *The Week,* which was famous for printing inside stories no responsible newspaper would touch. Throughout his career, he, like Muggeridge, has been unable to subdue the anarchic humor of his *Sonnenkind* temperament to the exigencies of his political convictions. One is not surprised to hear that both have been lifelong devotees of Wodehouse.[30]

Tom Driberg, who had been at Lancing with Waugh, went to Christ Church, and remained quite closely in touch with the aesthetes after Oxford, even though he himself went into first journalism and then politics. He worked for the Beaverbrook paper, the *Daily Express,* 1928 to 1943, and for much of that time wrote gossip items for the "William Hickey" column. It was by this means that "bright young people" like Elizabeth Ponsonby and Stephen Tennant became national figures; their parties were read about by millions the morning after they happened. Driberg was also able to secure publicity of a more literary kind for friends like Evelyn Waugh, and he has himself wondered how large a part was played in such friendships by the useful alliances of that kind they included.[31] Later in life he became a Socialist M.P. and played quite a prominent part in the life of the parliamentary Labour party. But his earlier affiliations continued to play an important part in his life. This is symbolized by his going to Moscow to interview the defector Guy Burgess, an old friend, to write a book about him, as soon as Burgess was made accessible to Western journalists in Moscow.

Other Undergraduates

Of the writers we have already introduced, Cyril Connolly has left the fullest record of what Oxford meant to him. "We were the last generation of womanless Oxford," he says. "Men who liked women were apt to get sent down." He remarks on the beauty of "the English ephebes" in Oxford then, particularly Kenneth Clark (a hawk god), Robert Longden (an Antinous), and various Adonises. He describes Richard Pares as a Winchester and Balliol scholar of captivating charm, having the look of a Rossetti angel with a touch of Mick Jagger. Pares was Connolly's first friend at Balliol, and Waugh told him later how keen he too had been on Pares and how much jealousy he had suffered. (A. L. Rowse also fell victim to Pares' "charm and desperation.") Maurice Bowra, says Connolly, introduced them all to the art of conversation, while Urquhart, "most civilized of dons," took them on reading parties. Connolly was the one of his group who insisted on their going to the Mediterranean in the summers, and who founded the Cicada Club, with five members, for that purpose.[32]

Henry Green's account of Oxford stresses the extravagance of the life. Some undergraduates came up with £3000 a year to spend, and were therefore much sought after. The aesthetes, he said, created a mutual admiration society there, which they continued in London afterwards. It was, he implies, a closed society, making much esoteric reference to the Victoriana its members collected (glass paper-weights, baskets of eternalized flowers, pyramids of wax fruits) and to their favorite authors. One of these was William Beckford (Waugh, for instance, was a Beckford enthusiast), but the work they referred to most constantly and made use of in interpreting their own experience—as much use as the hearties made of Kipling—was Proust's *À la recherche du temps perdu.* Bowra tells us that Connolly made elaborate schemes of comparison and identification between his friends (including himself) and the characters of that novel; Bowra was Swann, Urquhart was Françoise, an unnamed friend was Albertine, the Morrells were the Verdurins, and Lord David Cecil was the duchesse de Guermantes. We shall see that Goronwy Rees, John Strachey, and others also saw themselves and their relationships in terms of that novel, in the Oxford of that decade.

Two interesting autobiographies that give us a different point of view, a working-class boy's point of view, on Oxford, are A. L. Rowse's and Goronwy Rees's. In *A Cornish Childhood* (1942), Rowse describes how he suffered at his village school and how, like Jude the Obscure, he fixed his eyes ahead on Oxford as the place that would be his home. While at school, his poems appeared in *Public School Verse,* in one issue with Quennell's, and in another, with poems by Graham Greene and Christopher Isherwood. Rowse went up to Christ Church in 1922, and found Harold Acton living on the next stairway. "I came to know him a little, never well—that would have been going too far. . . ." He describes Acton's odd, affected bearing, as he shouldered and minced his way through the mob, with carefully rolled umbrella, leading his band of aesthetes. When he went to one of Acton's parties, he felt out of it, because people were discussing subjects too modern for him, like the Sitwells, Luigi Pirandello, and D. H. Lawrence. He saw Acton even then as an ally against the philistines, but when he sought him out one night, ready to offer friendship, he found "the poet" garbed in a grey silk kimono and with his face powdered with Icilma, and fled. It is, he feels, a related fact that his own poetry has suffered all his life from being "out of date."

Many of the highly idiosyncratic opinions of *A Cornish Childhood* and *A Cornishman at Oxford* (1965) are those of a late-developing aesthete. Rowse uses the case of D. H. Lawrence to justify his own gradual disillusionment with the working class and with politics. Lawrence and he were both of the working class, and both knew it and distrusted it; Rowse attacks George Orwell and John Strachey as middle-class idolizers of that class from the outside and from ignorance. In a way one might expect from Cyril Connolly he cites dictionaries of clichés, like Flaubert's, as his favorite reading; his Book of Life. His favorite authors are Proust, Rainer Maria Rilke, and John Henry Newman, and he aligns himself with George Santayana in the latter's Latin dislike of Anglo-Saxon moralism and Protestant utilitarianism. Rowse now explicitly regrets not having joined Acton and the aesthetes, in Bowra's salon, at Edith Sitwell's lecture, and so on. In the foreword to his autobiography, he thanks Lord Berners and Lord David Cecil for reading his manuscript for him. Rowse was not a Charles Ryder, having no Oxford relation to Anthony Blanche, but he makes judgments rather similar to Waugh's as he looks back on those events of the '20s.

Goronwy Rees was born into a Welsh Presbyterian minister's family in 1909.[33] He went up to New College only in 1928, so his impressions are not quite contemporary, but he says the university was still then divided between the aesthetes and the hearties, decadence and virility, culture and barbarism. The hearties went in for beer, sports, and picking up girls on Saturday nights. Aesthetes went in for poetry, homosexuality, and a modified Baudelairian dandyism. Oxford was still an almost exclusive monopoly of the "great capitalist class" (Keynes' phrase), and its breeding ground, the public schools. Henry Green, a later friend of Rees, was, as Rees describes it, woken every day at noon by his scout with an orange and a glass of brandy; he then strolled to the Carlton Club for a grilled steak and a bottle of claret, then went to the cinema, had dinner, drank heavily, and went to bed.[34]

Rees was a Socialist and anti-English when he won his scholarship, but he soon acquired more aesthetic criteria. He found the New College Socialists too professional and puritan in their socialism, also just too humdrum and dreary. He avoided them, and his fellow Welshmen at Jesus, the College they traditionally went to. He was, he admits, extremely impressionable, quick to adopt Oxonian traits as protective devices and to discard all the habits that marked him out as different from the other undergraduates. (He took a pleasure in so performing, but felt also a strain—and consequent depression.) Thus he soon learned that term at Oxford was not a time for working but for making friends. And he kept silent about his revolutionary and apocalyptic socialism, his vision of a world ruled by the South Wales Miners' Federation, because he found that his new acquaintance had no historical imagination at all. Instead he read Proust and saw his own life through Proust's spectacles, finding among his own acquaintance a Charlus, a Bloch, a Cottard and so on. Proust, he says, became an obsession.

Oxford, he says, was still bathed in a golden glow, as of a setting sun. He found that his new public school friends all thought that they knew what their futures would be (and they *did* know—later events proved them right, while his larger perspectives of, for instance, revolution turned out to be misleading). The undergraduates were officer cadets in the great army required to rule the British Empire, which still covered a third of the world's land surface. Some intended to be artists, and some even revolutionaries, but they all expected that British society would take special care of them. They expected—and events justified them—that the rest of life would be *like* Oxford. This is, obviously, the natural training ground for *Sonnenkinder* that he is describing.

Rees also makes the point that it was an exclusively male society. The "undergraduettes" might as well not have existed. It was a nursery life, of sexual infantilism. All had their affections and ideas in the masculine gender, "in the man, that is to say themselves." The Fall of Man happened only to Eve. She was expelled, and Adam was left to enjoy the garden alone with the serpent. Men remembered Oxford in a golden glow because only *after it* came their fall from grace into heterosexual relationships. Rees himself remembers it in a golden glow, but he feels the resentment of the seduced, also.

The Dandies' Rivals and Enemies

To give ourselves a different, and contrasting, perspective on this period, let us consider the two most brilliant writers of their times, Vladimir Nabokov and D. H. Lawrence, to see the light they throw on the dandies' vocation and careers. That light is primarily of opposite kind.

Nabokov gives us the perspective of seeing what a dandy-writer *could* achieve in the world of art. Although born in 1899, Nabokov was an undergraduate at Trinity College, Cambridge, 1919–22, and so can roughly be counted as contemporaneous with Harold Acton at Oxford.[35] Nor is the conjunction so forced as it may at first seem, for Nabokov was brought up on English literature and in close contact with English culture. As a child he read the books of an English childhood, like *Alice in Wonderland,* Mayne Reid, and so on; and in fact he could speak English before he could speak Russian. He says, apropos of *Alice,* "I was an English child." And while he was at Cambridge, he was soaking himself, like any English literary undergraduate, in Rupert Brooke and the post-Keatsian lyrical poetry of the late 19th century and early 20th century. The proof of this lies in the verse he himself wrote at that time, and later.

I think we can agree with George Steiner, when he says that the aesthetic sources of *Lolita's* language are to be found "in the Cambridge which Nabokov attended as an undergraduate and in related Bloomsbury." He associates *Lolita* with the English versions of art nouveau and with the colorations of Beardsley, Wilde, and Firbank. He speaks of Nabokov's asperities and glissandoes of condescension in that novel's language and goes on to name Strachey, Beerbohm, and Waugh as masters of the same style.

> . . . the whole stance of the amateur/amatore of genius, always turning towards the golden afternoons and vintages of the past, is demonstrably late Edwardian and Georgian . . . the lilac summers of a lost, high bourgeois order, and the erotic ambiguities of Lewis Carroll.

One would not, of course, so describe the prose of *Glory,* the novel he wrote about Cambridge in 1932. It is Nabokov's later work that is so assertively dandified and aesthetic; unlike the comparable English writers he has grown more of a dandy-aesthete as he has developed. Thus it is not so much because of his inheritance as because of what he made of it that Nabokov belongs here—because he carried the dandy sensibility to heights of achievement that have to be compared with those of great novelists of very different temperament, like Leo Tolstoy and D. H. Lawrence.

However, Nabokov did belong by family, as well as by taste, to the world of Diaghilev, the world of Russian dandyism. His parents were enormously rich, highly aristocratic (although liberal) in lifestyle, and in touch with all the latest movements in art and thought. His mother was painted by Bakst, and his cousin Nikolai Nabokov composed music for a Diaghilev ballet that Pavel Tchelitchew designed. Tchelitchew, who came from the same world of rich Russian aristocrats, and who will appear again in this story as a dandy painter, shared rooms in Paris with Sergei Nabokov, the novelist's brother. And Vladimir Nabokov's play of 1938, *The Event,* concerns a man, Trostcheikin, whose paintings are so described as to sound like Tchelitchew's; the latter's career also seems to be reflected in that of another character of the play, Romanov. So we may take it that the novelist has been very conscious of the great impresario. And although he keeps private the sources of his inspiration, Nabokov has made one or two small admissions that point to Diaghilev's having been an important, if ambivalent, figure to his imagination. He has said how eagerly, as a boy, he always looked forward to new issues of Diaghilev's magazine, *The World of Art;* and he has said that he drew the corrupt aesthete in "Solus Rex" from Diaghilev, at least in terms of looks.* Since

---

* "Solus Rex" is a chapter from an unpublished novel, written in 1939 and 1940. Its narrator is an artist who, to console himself for the death of his wife, has invented an imaginary country of which he becomes king. The throne is supposed to go to his cousin, Prince Adulf, the corrupt aesthete, who is described as a stout fop and *charmeur,* with a big head and fine bulging eyes; his court is all homosexual aesthetes and playboys, and his lover a famous young acrobat, sullen and silent in social life (thus very like Nijinsky). The narra-

the figure of the corrupt aesthete recurs in so many of Nabokov's works, and in such a crucial function—as the protagonist's alter ego, on whom the novelist discharges all his self-doubt and self-disgust—this connection with Diaghilev seems very important. It suggests that Nabokov felt himself called to follow a life-path like Diaghilev's, but equally felt called to be different—to be a dandy and an aesthete who transcended dandyism and aestheticism; and that is in fact what his work is all about.

Nabokov published two volumes of verse while still at school in 1913–16. Then, in 1923, after his father's assassination, he published two more volumes. But perhaps his most significant publication in this period from our point of view is his Russian translation of *Alice in Wonderland,* which is said to be much the most successful of all Russian translations of that work. This is significant because *Alice* was such a favorite of the English dandy writers too. W. H. Auden, for instance, conjoins Lewis Carroll (and Edward Lear and Beatrix Potter) with Firbank when he makes a list of the authors he admires. They were all part, the safe part, of the heritage of the 1890s. And Nabokov's play, "The Waltz Invention," seems to show that the influence of *Alice* was still powerful on him in the late '30s.

Nabokov differs from the pattern followed by most of the men we have considered so far in that he loved and admired both his father and his mother. However, although that makes a difference, one perceptible in his work, it is not so large a one as we might expect because the significant rebellion against the father is not personal but cultural. It is not so much his personal progenitor the dandy must hate as the fathers of his culture. Nabokov's father was himself a dandy and a rebel, and his son could become the same himself and still identify with his father. (At the first Duma in 1906, the novelist's father was

---

tor is at first dazzled by the prince, but he goes to one of his parties and leaves in disgust when the behavior becomes grossly indecent. He says to himself that the prince is really only "a savage, a self-taught oaf, lacking real culture," and not fit to be king. And, in fact, Prince Adulf is assassinated, and the narrator/Nabokov becomes king in his place. This story surely hints at a very significant relation between Nabokov's idea of Diaghilev and his idea of himself.

one of the leaders of the rebellious Kadet party, but he wore a new suit every day and a tie that always refined upon that of the previous day and that other men challenged in vain. He was a brilliant and in some ways insolent figure.) But the father's rebellion took quite different forms from the son's. The father had different gifts—for public speaking, for directing committees, for surveying facts and managing men. The son translated his rebellion into terms much more intimate imaginatively and much less precise politically. Nabokov's case is also complicated by the fact that he had a younger brother, Sergei, who was always at a disadvantage compared with Vladimir (whom the latter felt he oppressed) and by the fact that this brother became a dandy-aesthete of a more flamboyant kind. Vladimir, we may guess, did not need and could not afford to be like Sergei. Attending premieres of Diaghilev ballets in London, Sergei wore a flowing black cape and carried a pommeled cane; Vladimir, who also attended, was always very elegant, but more worldly and gay, more the tennis player.

Probably these facts, and his own rich endowment of manly skills and strengths, led Nabokov to construct representative heroes for his novels who are—and this is particularly true of his early work—as far from those of Firbank and Harold Acton as can be imagined. In relation to friendship, games, women, and sexuality, the Nabokov hero is most often (take Martin Edelweiss in *Glory)* fit to be the hero of a pre-1914 novel. He is proud to be the man that he is, and Nabokov is proud of his manliness. But Nabokov always rebelled against socially established modes of seriousness (most notably, the political and the psychoanalytical), and as time has gone by that pride of self-determination has become more querulous, more bitterly irritable with the world of men, and with other things. He has become more the aesthete and more the dandy.[35]

The perspective in which D. H. Lawrence puts the dandies is primarily one of opposition, of hostility, although not entirely, as we shall see. Lawrence was always interested in *Sonnenkind* figures, like Egbert in "England, My England." But in his large novels before 1918 he was the priest of the cult of Demeter. And in the postwar period he still sometimes spoke for her, although in the modified and modulated tones of the "decent" man, the man of responsibility. The tone of *Sea and Sardinia* (1921), for instance, is very changed from the tone of *Twilight in Italy* (1916), but it is a change away from the oracular toward the conversational, not a change toward some new faith or idea. While writing in this style and mood, Lawrence often mocked the dandies of his time very effectively. Perhaps the best example of this is his "Introduction" to Maurice Magnus's *Memoirs of the Foreign Legion* (1924). This, together with the pamphlet of protest it provoked from Norman Douglas the next year,[36] amounts to a controversy between the dandy and the decent man. Or rather, Lawrence narrates, as decent man, his dealings with a dandy, Magnus, and Douglas, who is really a rogue, replies. Douglas speaks for the *Sonnenkind* movement of the '20s, and Lawrence attacks it.

But in other works of this period, we can see Lawrence in quite a different relation to that movement. In all three of his leadership novels, *Aaron's Rod, Kangaroo,* and *The Plumed Serpent,* he depicts a relationship of a man to a man that the reader is asked to take as a great source of value, a great origin of life. This relationship is in some sense erotic, and it displaces from primacy that relationship of a man to a woman that had been the great cult-object of the earlier books. The cult of this new relationship, and the mythos and ethos that derive from it, are in fact the most impressive development of the *Sonnenkind* impulse in English. Of course, Lawrence remained uninterested in dandies and rogues, and no doubt his mockery of them even in these novels explains why he has never been connected with this movement. But he *was* interested in the naïf and in the magus, which are powerful images of the *Sonnenkind* cult.

Let us look at *Aaron's Rod* in this light. Aaron is clearly a naïf—all responsiveness and seeming readiness for commitment, while shrewdly reluctant in fact to give up that availability, which is the source of his attraction to others. Lilly is a magus, a man possessed of esoteric life-wisdom, into which he is willing to induct disciples, if they will make a complete submission to him. Aaron moves through various levels of postwar England; he tests everyone by attracting them so that they declare themselves, in a bid to possess him. He finds all but Lilly inadequate, but will not submit even to him. He is tempted, therefore, to dissipate himself in casual affairs with women; he has one with Josephine and one with the Marchesa, after both of which he falls ill. Lilly rescues him. After the influenza that follows the first affair, Lilly loves Aaron, saves him from death, gives new birth to him, in the sacramental rubbing with oil. And Aaron wants to be his friend—but not his disciple.

They meet again in Florence, when the second affair takes place. The city is presented to us as "one of the world's living centres," because there men had been "at their intensest, most naked pitch"; Aaron knows this when he sees Michelangelo's *David,* white, stripped, half-shrinking, "the white, self-conscious, physical adolescent," standing near the big heavy male statues by Bandinelli, which represent "the undaunted physical nature of the heavier Florentines." In the presence of these sacred emblems of the *Sonnenkind* cult, Aaron feels a new manhood, a new life-urge, rising in him. It is clear that Lawrence means this new life-urge, so homoerotic in feeling, to explain and confirm Lilly's teaching in Aaron's mind—and in ours. But Aaron still will not submit. The novel ends inconclusively—and indeed it has never succeeded fully along the way—no doubt because Lawrence could not free himself from that dependence on Frieda that he was struggling against, which obliged him to worship Demeter instead.

But that is not our concern. What we must see is that in this, Lawrence's first postwar novel, he created a *Sonnenkind* myth—one that transcended the other imaginative expressions of that cult in England as completely as Aaron and Lilly, seen as people, transcend Francis and Angus, the Sitwell-type dandies, and Argyle, the Douglas-type rogue.* Thus even the great enemy of the dandies, even the great

---

* Of course Aaron and Lilly are not of the same temperament as Francis and Angus, and I must here anticipate the justified complaint that I have invented a "*Sonnenkind* temperament" that is really a congeries of different temperaments. In fact, I have used the word *temperament* when I needed another—but it does not, I think, exist. It seems to me that temperamental types whose cultic gods belong in the same pantheon do have some-

prophet of Demeter, was in this period a priest of the *Sonnenkind* cult. While our principals, at Oxford, were worshiping at the local and debased altars of a minor sect, the genius of their times was struggling in solitude to build a great temple of the cult.

In 1925 and 1926, those dandies began to go down from Oxford into the real world. Several left without taking any final degree, or under an academic cloud; these included Brian Howard, Evelyn Waugh, John Betjeman, Alan Pryce-Jones, Randolph Churchill, and John Strachey. None left with high honors. But the parties of farewell were lavish and hopeful, even triumphant. Brian gave one for twenty-two guests, including the Acton brothers, Patrick Balfour, Maurice Bowra, Bob Coe (a rich American), Oliver Messel, Harry Stavordale (one of Brian's peers), Henry Weymouth (another of them, later the marquis of Bath), John Sutro, and Mark Ogilvie-Grant. They were invited—on a thick, cream card, fourteen inches by ten, heavily printed in gold—to come wearing *"robes de fantaisie."*[37] Many were to be their returns to Oxford in the succeeding years and many the retrospective articles about them in Oxford magazines—as late as 1928 the *Cherwell* carried news items about their London lives and memories of their Oxford lives. They had created their legend. It inhabited Oxford and shaped the place's meaning for generations to come.

---

thing in common and may be said to constitute a group, and that group itself I have also called a temperament. What they have in common may be so subtle as to be quite insignificant from most points of view. What do the votaries of Ares have in common with the votaries of Apollo? Yet set in contrast with those who worship the Mother Goddess, or with those who worship the Sonnenkind, all those who worship the Olympian pantheon do have something in common, because ultimately they acknowledge a great Father God. Just so much do all the votaries of the Sonnenkind have in common with each other, even though some are temperamentally unlike others by most criteria. For historical examples, see this book.

Chapter Six

1925–1932: London

Brian and Harold in London

IT WAS NOT into Reality that the dandies immediately came down from Oxford. England as a whole, and especially London, was itself in the grip of the pleasure principle during the 1920s. That is, certain forms of life developed, themselves characterized by clear dandy or young-man traits, which were felt to characterize the cultural moment. Some of them have already been mentioned, like the nightclub. Then there was the cocktail party, which Alec Waugh is credited with inventing, in 1924; and the bottle party, said to have been introduced by Loelia Ponsonby in 1926—Michael Arlen took twelve bottles of pink champagne to the first one. Such parties were clearly more informal, more like dormitory feasts in style, than the stately entertainments of the fathers. If food was served at them, it was likely to be bacon and eggs, not a *bombe surprise*. Another such institution, even more adolescent in style, was the treasure hunt—

which sent its participants driving all over London and the countryside in quest of more and more extraordinary objects. This was said to have been invented by Eleanor Smith, F. E.'s daughter, and her friends, Allanah Harper and Baby and Zita Jungman. These women, prominent among the "bright young people" and great friends of Brian's, also played elaborate practical jokes, impersonating foreign dignitaries, hiding for the night in the Chamber of Horrors of Madame Tussaud's waxworks museum, and so on. There were, then, many violations of the traditional limits of mature behavior, many prolongations of adolescent styles into adult years. This was another form of what was called decadence.

The '20s also saw, as we have said, a marked violation of traditional sexual limits and roles. The styles of the time were assertively boyish for women, and for men also boyish or even effeminate. Both the brisk patter and the languid drawl of the new speech patterns offended mature dignity. Cecil Beaton says it then became smart to say "madly" and "divine" and "how terribly unfunny, darling," and to clip one's speech as one turned one's toes in. People imitated Philip Sassoon, who emphasized each syllable equally, saying, "I could-dern't care less" and "I could-dern't agree more." These new fashions were the topics of the time, and some dandies were able to make a career, even a living, by *talking* about them in print, at the same time as they practiced them.[1]

The gossip column became their preserve, as we shall see, and they also found a natural medium of expression in the magazines of high fashion. The latter were ready to print quite serious articles about art as long as art was news, and it was in the hands of the aesthetes. Thus *Vogue,* while edited by Dorothy Todd, published nearly all the writers of Bloomsbury, writing on films, theater, painting, literature, and so on. And *Harpers' Bazaar,* under Carmel Snow and under the French editor, Marie-Louise Bousquet, published many things by the dandies proper, including Brian Howard's 1932 article on Cocteau's film, *Le sang d'un poète.* And *Vanity Fair* published Edmund Wilson on jazz and on Cocteau, and Cocteau himself. While Cecil Beaton, Noel

Coward, and the Sitwells were, of course, very frequent subjects of and contributors to such magazines.

Much of this was frivolous, and deserved the scorn it provoked in such hostile observers as Wyndham Lewis, F. R. Leavis, and George Orwell. But it was also in its way pedagogical and even, paradoxically, serious. In Graves's and Hodge's *The Long Week-end,* Mayfair in those years is described as a kind of free university, in which the "bright young people" provided the sports, because there was so much learning and teaching of the new tastes going on—the taste for Picasso, the taste for jazz (a jazz band was soon earning more in a season than the prime minister in a year), and the taste for pleasure itself. Some bottle-party establishments offered free invitations to black singers, musicians, and dancers—notably the Blackbirds—because they inculcated by example and spread the right Dionysiac spirit among the other guests. In this world of hedonistic pedagogy, the Oxford dandies took a prominent place, easily. They could hope to rule here too, to have the walls of London like those of Oxford fall to their trumpet call. Their difficulties were mostly a matter of what work they were to do in the outside world—the "real" world still there at a distance; what profession to enter, how to earn a living.

England still offered traditional postuniversity careers within institutions that fostered dandyism. Most of the Oxford group tried, or at least considered, one of these careers, but of course such institutions fostered only those limited, ultimately subordinate, styles of *Sonnenkind* exuberance approved by tradition. One was the career of a regular officer in the army, if one went to Sandhurst and then into the Brigade of Guards. The Royal Military College at Sandhurst taught its upper-class trainees impeccability on parade and hooliganism off-duty, both conducted at an extravagant pitch. The Brigade of Guards was more aristocratic in style, perhaps the most aristocratic of all British institutions.

In 1959 Simon Raven analyzed the hierarchy of regiments thus: in order to join a regiment of Foot Guards, one should have a private income of at least £150 a year and have gone to Eton, Harrow, or

Winchester; in order to join one of the rifle regiments, one should have gone to any one of the six big public schools; in order to join the fusiliers, or the light infantry, to any public school. While down in the mere regiments of the line, an officer who went to Eton may even be at a disadvantage, because "too fancy," and gambling and homosexuality are frowned on just as in ordinary society. There are, in those regiments, even some grammar school officers, a thing unthinkable in the Grenadier Guards. In the Brigade of Guards the officers are gentlemen, not professionals. And this was even truer fifty years ago.

Osbert Sitwell, for instance, had become an officer in the Grenadier Guards in 1912 and had found himself happier there than he had ever been. He liked his companions, and they liked him. He was the friend of, among others, the future Viscount Alexander of Tunis, to whom Sitwell dedicated the volume of his autobiography that covers these experiences. General Alexander was himself a painter, a dandy—he wore a fur muff even in the trenches—and something of an aesthete. And the life of a Guards officer fostered these traits. They wore very expensive, very colorful, very close-fitting uniforms, whose fitting was supervised by the adjutant; and their appearance, in uniform and in mufti, was a matter of mutual and official concern. They were forced to be bodies to each other much more than men usually are.[2]

Then the life was one of alternate ritual and idleness. There was four months' annual leave for captains, five for majors, and six for colonels. Their work was to guard the palaces, the Tower of London, and other such places, and they observed certain aristocratic customs peculiar to themselves. Company orders were read at ten, but could be attended in civilian clothes; then came the commanding officer's orders; then everyone took a glass of black strap, a heavy vintage port, at noon; and then polo, cricket, or the boat club at Maidenhead, for those who were not on duty. Neither leadership nor the science of war was stressed. Those on duty at Buckingham Palace could invite men and women to lunch in the mess there, and men guests could dine. They observed a strict code of behavior in social life—a Guards officer might never carry a case or a parcel, smoke a Virginian cigarette, or reverse in waltzing—and of course more serious matters. A gentleman was defined as a man in whose presence a woman felt herself to be a lady. Shyness was not disliked, nor heartiness encouraged, and wit was welcomed, says Nigel Nicolson, in his biography of Alexander.

In the evenings the officers went to elegant parties, dressed in very splendid evening dress. The crack regiments were, and are, centers of social snobbery in the most ordinary sense. They are communities of men from great families and the great public schools, and usually with large incomes; and they allow themselves many freedoms from bourgeois prudence and decency, in matters like gambling, extravagance, and even homosexuality. Their traditions maintain a connection with the world of Brummell, a connection that still seems strong. Even in full Victorian times one can trace that connection in the myth of the Guards officer celebrated in the novels of Charles Lever, George Alfred Lawrence, and Ouida. And Cecil Beaton says that the overcoats worn by the Guards even today are cut in the taste initiated by Brummell himself. He says also that the decorations at White's and Boodle's, the two great London clubs, to which Waugh and Connolly aspired and to which they finally achieved admission, are kept in keeping with Brummell's taste—his preference for whipcord over silk and for sparse carpet, in his carriage, over furs. It is Brummell's influence, says Beaton, that keeps London a world center of men's elegance in dress.[3]

Of course those clubs and the tailors are an important part of the world of the Guards officer. It is a private world, true to its own traditions, exempt from many of the influences of "modern thought," in all periods. This is true of its serious work in time of war, as well as of its pleasures in times of peace. As late as the Second World War the Brigade of Guards was the home of leaders of private armies—the duke of Atholl's Highlanders, Lord Lovat's Scouts, and the Earl of Suffolk's men. Among our authors, Ian Fleming led a "private navy" and Evelyn Waugh served in a "private" task force led by Brigadier St. Clair Morford; the latter is described by Waugh in *Officers and Gentlemen*, where he renames Morford Ritchie-Hook.

It is by means of such institutions that societies dedicated to mature and responsible values also foster *Sonnenkinder*. But few of our dandies and rogues went into the army. Alec Waugh went to Sandhurst, but he was of an earlier generation, closer to Sitwell. Alan Pryce-Jones was intended by his family to go into the army, but he refused. James Stern was sent to Sandhurst by his father, the major, and hated it. Ian Fleming went to Sandhurst, but did not stay in the army. Roger Spence, a close friend of the aesthetes at Eton, was about the only one who did make a career of it. For the purposes of our group, the army's dandyism was too old-fashioned, too much in the service of other values.

Another traditional dandy career was in the foreign office or the foreign service. British ambassadors in this century seem to have been notorious for eccentricities like homosexuality and transvestism, which disabled them from full participation in the world of men and made them welcome *Sonnenkinder* among them. This is something that helped the careers of Guy Burgess and Donald Maclean, for instance, and Waugh's novels reflect the same facts. (Sir Ralph Brompton, in *Unconditional Surrender,* is one of those homosexual and Communist-sympathizing diplomats.) The embassies established private worlds, exempt from the laws obeyed by the greater society. Perhaps we can take an anecdote told by David Herbert, brother of the earl of Pembroke, as indicative of the curious mélange of literary and libertine elements sponsored by the diplomatic establishment. While Harold Nicolson was in the British embassy in Berlin, around 1927, David Herbert was sharing an apartment there with Christopher Sykes, also an attaché at the embassy, and Cyril Connolly wrote for them a series of "Oriental" plays, in which Herbert played a seductive slave girl, Connolly a pimp, and Sykes a carpet-seller. These entertainments were performed in the Nicolsons' apartment before an audience that included the British ambassador. The mingling of moral anarchy and political authority was very intimate.[4]

Harold Nicolson and Christopher Sykes, two figures mediatory between the dandies and the gentlemen of the Establishment, were in the diplomatic service, but also had literary ambitions. Sykes was a personal and literary friend to both Robert Byron and Evelyn Waugh, a collaborator with and adaptor of works by both and a biography of the latter; he is also the dedicatee of one of Harold Acton's books. Harold Nicolson, although not intimately involved with these men, is perhaps more generally emblematic of the relations between the dandies and the Establishment. He often wrote satirically about the public school ethos and its affiliates, and he was briefly a friend of Ronald Firbank's, but he never stood clearly with the dandies. His ambiguity is perhaps symbolized in his bisexuality and his marriage to Victoria Sackville-West, a passionate lesbian. Vita Sackville-West was a great heiress, a great aesthete, and a more "masculine" character than Nicolson himself. But he maintained a happy marriage with her, recorded in *Diaries* that avoided all admission of sexual irregularities. He himself was in the foreign service from 1909 to 1929; but his wife thought that public service was only for those who could not, as he could, be creative, so he left. He became briefly an adherent of Sir Oswald Mosley, the Fascist leader, and was later a National Labour M.P. from 1935 to 1945 and a governor of the BBC, 1931–46. His first book was on *Verlaine* (1921), an anti-Establishment subject, but it was followed by *Tennyson* in 1923, and then by *Byron* in 1924 and *Swinburne* in 1926; the subjects of these books indicate his interest in the socially disreputable, the form and style indicate his insistent disengagement. After the war he wrote on *The Congress of Vienna* (1946) and finally took to royal biography with *George V* in 1952. At the same time he was a friend of such outrageous rogues as Guy Burgess.[5]

Nicolson's career suggests better than anything else how the Establishment, in its most respectable form, intellectually, was vulnerable to the anarchic playfulness of the *Sonnenkinder*. That was demonstrated, of course, most vividly by the espionage adventures of Guy Burgess, Donald Maclean, and Kim Philby, who could occupy between them so many key positions in the diplomatic and secret services because they were so like other men in those services. Our principals, however, did not enter this profession, although Brian's friend, Eddie Gathorne-Hardy, did, and Harold says that his parents wanted him to. Harold seems to regret not having done so: "I should have made an ideal ambassador."

There were other Etonian careers, like finance. The key positions in the Bank of England, the Treasury, the Stock Exchange, and Lloyds (the famous underwriters), have traditionally been held by Etonians or similar people. Victor Sandelson, in *The Establishment,* of 1959, invents a typical city man, Sir Norman Tullis, who comes of a landed family and has gone to Eton and Trinity College, Cambridge, and who distrusts politicians and the press but trusts the "old boy" network. Sandelson cites in real life such men as Lord Kindersley, an Etonian, who was chairman of Lazards (the banking house) and Rolls-Royce, governor of the Royal Exchange Assurance Company, and a director of the Bank of England; Lord Cowdray, Eton and Christ Church, who was chairman of Pearson Industries; and two other members of the Pearson board, Lord Drogheda, Eton and Trinity, and Lord Poole, Eton and Christ Church, the latter also a member of Lloyds and chairman of the Conservative party. When Sandelson was writing, the governor of the Bank of England had gone to Eton and King's College, Cambridge; and of the court of the Bank, one member had gone to Eton and Sandhurst, another two to Eton and Trinity, another two to Marlborough and Corpus Christi, and so on. It was only the Bank Rate Tribunal of 1957, according to Sandelson, that destroyed the myth of the City, by revealing that "the whole City rested on nothing more than a criss-cross system of upper class gossip."

But our group, or at least our principals, were determined to be dandy-*aesthetes.* Brian and Harold scorned the old English institutionalizations of the *Sonnenkind* impulse. They wanted to be pure manifestations of Orpheus or Adonis, perfectly free embodiments of their idea on the stage of imperial London. They refused the careers their families proposed, Brian to become a lawyer, Harold a diplomat. "I was blind to the fact," says the latter, "that in England the poet had scant chance of survival." They were determined to dazzle the world with a series of artistic gestures, some of which would take the conventional form of a poem or a novel, but others of which would be those of the impresario and the notoriety—the gestures of a Cocteau or a Diaghilev. Thus it was that in the first two or three years after Oxford they mostly gave and attended a great many parties, and were reported in a great many gossip columns, as members of the "bright young people."

Brian Howard also stayed at Longleat with the marquis of Bath's son, Henry Weymouth (he was a bit in love with both Lord Weymouth and Daphne Vivian, who became Lady Weymouth), with Michael Rosse, already the earl of Rosse, at Birr in Ireland, and with Bryan Guiness, son of Lord Moyne. He gave a party on Tite Street, Chelsea, at which he appeared dressed as a duchess of 1905—Willy Clarkson, the theatrical costumier, had spent an hour making up his face. At one of these parties Brian's father observed him with disgust; he reported seeing him "smacking his great blubber lips." Brian was then supposed to be studying law, but he was in fact putting his energy into such things as designing the costumes and scenery for Anton Dolin's ballet, *L'escalier d'or,* danced to Debussy's *Cortège,* in a Charlot revue. He had become a great friend of Dolin's, an English dancer who joined Diaghilev's company in 1924 and became one of its great stars. Brian's friendship with him was another of the links between the English dandies and Diaghilev. Brian's father disapproved of Brian's passion for the ballet, especially his amateur ballet dancing. Brian was also being painted by John Banting, who became one of his greatest friends, and photographed by Cecil Beaton, who described him as "extremely urbane, svelte, and sophisticated. Very much of the great world of London. . . . He had a great charm, style, and an 18th century manner."[6] He even became briefly partner to a fashionable photographer, and photographed sitters wrapped up in chicken wire, rope, metal tubes, and such.

Brian and his friends burgled other friends' houses, landed illegally on the islands in the lake at the Wembley Fun Fair, played leapfrog through Selfridges, set the Thames on fire with petrol, and performed other such exploits. They organized hoaxes, like the Bruno Hat Exhibition of 1929, which introduced to the public a fake modern-

ist painter. Brian painted the pictures, Evelyn Waugh wrote the catalogue notes, Tom Mitford played Bruno Hat himself, and the party to
launch it was held by Bryan and Diana Guinness.

They went often to Rosa Lewis's hotel on Jermyn Street, made
famous in *Vile Bodies*. Rosa Lewis was basically an Edwardian phenomenon, who distributed white feathers during the war to men she
thought should be fighting and adopted the whole regiment of the
Irish Guards. She liked her dandies to be heroes too. But she fostered
any sort of rowdy rebellion against authority, and liked to hear something as twenties in style as Mark Ogilvie-Grant imitating Clara Butt
singing "Land of Hope and Glory."[7]

They made a cult of the review *The Blackbirds* and of its black performers. The star, Florence Mills, who was born in 1895, was a dignified, tasteful performer, and well-read and sophisticated in private life,
although her husband, U. S. Thompson, the comedian of the troupe,
was quite uneducated. *Blackbirds* ran in New York, and in Paris sixteen weeks, but its great success was in London, where it ran for over a
year, and was seen by the Prince of Wales twenty times. Brian Howard
and his friends saw it perhaps as often, and they got to know the performers socially. One of Connolly's memories of the parties of those
years is of the Blackbirds "inviolate" at many of them. *The Cherwell*
reported in March 1927 that the Blackbirds had been entertained at a
fancy dress party given by Oliver Messel in St. John's Wood, to which
Robert Byron had come dressed as Queen Victoria; and in May of
that year, that the climax of the Blackbirds' visit to Oxford had been a
party given for them by William Acton. One of Harold Acton's short
stories tells of an aesthete admirer of one of the male performers in
the troupe who gets beaten up by him.[8]

Such doings were reported in gossip columns like the one written
by Lady Eleanor Smith for three years in *The Weekly Dispatch*. Hannen Swaffer was the first social columnist who knew from inside the
world he wrote about. In 1926 the *Sunday Express* introduced the first
signed column, Lord Castlerosse's; in 1927 the *Weekly Dispatch* introduced Eleanor Smith's, and the *Sunday News* Lord Donegall's; and

then came Lord Kinross's column—as Patrick Balfour, Kinross had been one of the dandy circle at Oxford.

These columns sometimes reported the activities of the "Bright Young People" in shocked or disapproving tones, but they always reported them. One event was the Sailor party held at the swimming baths in Buckingham Palace Road, which was reported for *The Daily Express* by Tom Driberg. The party was given by Brian Howard, Eddie Gathorne-Hardy, Elizabeth Ponsonby, and Babe Plunket-Greene, with a black orchestra, colored lights, rubber horses, and flowers in the water. Lytton Strachey and Tallulah Bankhead were among the guests. There was a Circus party, given by the dress designer Norman Hartnell, in 1928; a Boat party, with the inner circle all dressed as stokers; a Cowboy party at William Acton's in 1929; and the Great Urban Dionysia, given by Babe Plunket-Greene for Brian Howard on his twenty-fourth birthday, on April 4, 1929. One that seems not to have taken place was a homosexual Lovers Through the Ages party, planned by Brian, Eddie Gathorne-Hardy, Lytton Strachey, Raymond Mortimer, and Sandy Baird, with music by Constant Lambert and decor by John Banting.[9] In many ways climactic was the White party of 1931, given by Sandy Baird, one of Brian's friends (Brian himself was out of the country), which ended with a young man being killed in rather scandalous circumstances.

These were the parties written about by Evelyn Waugh in *Vile Bodies,* with their elaborate invitations, their sordid aftermaths, and their conscious pathos of disillusion. Because so strong an atmosphere of despair or disappointment surrounded them, they were at least as much dandy institutions as dionysiac. (One need only think of the great rock festivals of recent years to see how different a dionysiac event is.) But they were still, like their Oxford parties, brilliant rituals of the *Sonnenkind* cult.

As time passed, however, and talents and characters developed, the Oxford group began to split up and to stand for different versions of their joint idea. Brian and Harold, whom we might call collectively Anthony Blanche (after the *Brideshead Revisited* character), contin-

ued to stand for the international modernist aesthete style, while
Waugh, Byron, Betjeman, and others began to work out a specifically
British dandyism—a difference symbolized in *Brideshead* by Ryder's
choice of Sebastian and country-house painting.

Not that even Brian and Harold were so close, however, in this
period. Harold, for instance, was a much less constant and prominent
figure on the London scene than Brian. He had been given a liberal
allowance by his parents, with which to "make good" within three
years. He tried living in Venice and in Paris, where he shunned the
writers he called "bogus Broncho Bills," with their vaunted virility,
like Hemingway and Pound—"they lived in dread of betraying their
emotions, except by hiccups." Then he came back to London, where
he stayed first with Robert Byron and later with his brother.

William Acton had rented a house in Lancaster Gate, having
decided to make a profession out of beautifying houses. This one had
a Venetian silver ballroom, which he filled with Venetian shell furniture and 18th-century mirrors, cupids, and Negro figures. He bought
bigger and bigger objects and painted Chinese panels in tempera.
His paintings had no great success, because, his brother says, William
painted for palaces in the age of the flatlet. Gradually he grew discouraged and seemed to prefer furniture to people; he finally returned to
La Pietra.

Harold Acton was also discouraged by the state of poetry in England, especially once he saw it fall into the hands of W. H. Auden and
his followers—"the hot gospellers"—who struggled with ideas and
left the words to look after themselves. They knew, he thought, that
they could get a public hearing by grafting political messages onto
Eliot's techniques. As for him, he loved experiments with words above
everything, and so he gravitated back toward Paris, toward Gertrude
Stein and James Joyce.

He had followed a suggestion of Norman Douglas's to write some
versified lives of the saints, in a modernized Richard Crashaw manner; and in 1927, Holden Inc. published his *Five Saints and an Appendix,* which was dedicated to Evelyn Waugh and Desmond Harms-

worth. (Harmsworth was another of his protégés, whom he was soon to see lost—as poet and as man—through marriage.) The individual poems are also dedicated, one to Norman Douglas, another to Edith Sitwell, another to Osbert and Sacheverell. One of the saints is Mrs. Dyer, a baby farmer who apparently strangled her charges; the others are freaks of canonization with very odd legends attached to them. The verse form is the heroic couplet; the diction and the larger style is baroquely wild; and there are aggressively modern references, for instance to George Gershwin, Irving Berlin, and Paul Whiteman.

He followed this with a novel, *Cornelian,* published by Chatto and Windus in 1928. Grant Richards and others had asked him to write an Oxford novel, but he felt that that had been done, once and for all, by Max Beerbohm. *Cornelian,* however, could be called a post-Oxford novel, drawing as it does on Firbank for its handling of the social scene and Beardsley for its style. Gertrude Stein praised it, but it really cannot be said to succeed any better than *Five Saints.* Both the design of the whole and the taste governing the choice of details seem essentially arbitrary. One can only guess at the artistic intention and at the responsive posture into which the reader is asked to put himself.

Acton, very much aware that he was not succeeding, then wrote what he regarded as a potboiler, another novel called *Humdrum.* This, which was also published in 1928, tells the story of two contrasting English sisters, typical of the contemporary contrasts—fast Linda, who lives in luxury at Cannes, and homely Joan, who stays at home with mother in Widdlehampton. They marry contrasting husbands, give contrasting parties, and so on. Linda is of the postwar England, a dandy, and Joan is of the prewar England, a dowdy, intended to be a wife and mother. She names her child Rudyard, after Kipling. Later Joan starts following Linda's pattern—betrayed by a visit to the theater, where she contracts an enthusiasm for ballet—and Linda ends up in Joan's position. The main design is promising enough for a "satirical" novel of the kind Evelyn Waugh was to write, and there are some mildly funny lines, in an Arthur Marshall, Gillie Potter style:

> Joan was not one of those modern girls who keep people
> waiting by powdering their noses. In a trice she was ready,
> bouncing in a big leather coat and jaunty motoring cap, sim-
> ply too sweet and waggish for words.

But the characterization shifts from page to page, some crucial events
in the story are slurred over, figures are insufficiently differentiated
from each other—the author clearly does not believe in what he is
doing enough to control it. And by an unlucky coincidence, *Humdrum* appeared at the same time as Waugh's *Decline and Fall,* which
was a brilliant success. Cyril Connolly reviewed the two together, in
the *New Statesman,* and demolished *Humdrum* the better to praise
Decline and Fall. Acton writes that he "sank out of sight."

He had continued to publish, however, while Brian Howard had
done practically nothing. Both were feeling the pressure of competition, as their contemporaries at Eton and Oxford, comparatively
silent and subordinate in those settings (notably Evelyn Waugh)
caught up with them and passed them in London. On the other
hand, it was scarcely more encouraging that others of their friends
and protégés seemed to have already given up the struggle for success in art.

For instance, both Graham Greene and Henry Green, rather similar
figures in their melancholia and strong sexuality, had both retreated
from the competition of London into the Midlands and drabness.
Greene worked on a newspaper in Nottingham, which he mythicized
into the capital city of all failure, all seediness, all provinciality; he
calls it a focal point of failure, a place to be resigned to, a home from
home. He (as does Green, to some extent) presents in his fiction the
negative of the dandy's vision. What he sees in a house is always how
unlike it is to the splendors of, say, Brideshead. (It is interesting that
in this period he wrote a biography, not published until 1974, of the
earl of Rochester, the Restoration dandy and rogue.) Green worked
for two years as a laborer in his father's factory in Birmingham, and
then took over directorial responsibilities. He too focused his artistic
vision on the sordid and needy.

Brian and Harold remained true to the style of Cocteau and Diaghilev, but London was *not* falling to Anthony Blanche as Oxford had—bold modernist aestheticism was not capturing the national mind. They were also feeling the pressure of parental disapproval, as their range of expenditure increased and no prospect of their supporting themselves came into view. Among their new acquaintance, moreover, there were some who were selling their talents for high prices, and who were spreading a kind of dandyism and aestheticism, however lightweight the kind was.

New Friends and Allies

Of these, one of the most prominent was Cecil Beaton, the fashion photographer and theater designer, and the story of his development will fill out our sense of the way England as a whole was changing in those years.[10] His father was a quite wealthy businessman, who was, like Arthur Waugh, an amateur actor whose "imitations" embarrassed his family and who was socially suppressed by the other members of his family. Cecil describes himself as a snob and a dandy, who hated both family life and school games. He went to the same primary school as Evelyn Waugh, and then to the same prep school as Cyril Connolly (and George Orwell)—Connolly tells us that Beaton then represented Sensibility to him as an alternative to the Character the school lived for, just as Orwell represented the Intelligence alternative.[11] Then he went to Harrow, where "any signs of intelligence were seen only out of class," and where he painted his rooms entirely blue. When he left Harrow, "I had a reputation for making people laugh, and for being sophisticated, but was anxious about a career." He hated games and family life, and was a conscious snob and a flamboyant dandy. He went to Cambridge in 1922, scared of having to live among "awful heartiness"; he found nothing there in the way of teaching, but became deeply involved with the Amateur Dramatic Company. Coming down, he had many bitter quarrels with his father over the latter's attempt to force him into a job in the City of London. But before too long, he was launched into his career as a photographer.

Beaton presents his own vocation in terms that recall the Regency dandy novel, by Catherine Grove, *Cecil, a Peer.* (That Cecil fell in love with his reflection in his mother's mirror at twelve months of age—"I looked, and became a coxcomb for life.") At three, Cecil Beaton was allowed to scramble into his mother's bed, and to play with a collection of colored photographs of female stage stars. Among the photographs he found his vocation for life; he fell in love with Lily Elsie, the star of the London production of *The Merry Widow*—or rather, he identified with her.

From Osbert Sitwell to George Orwell, everyone makes Lily Elsie the symbol of the Edwardian era. But Cecil Beaton actually met her. First, his mother and he were photographed by Miss Elsie's photographer, and Cecil tried to hold, for *his* picture, the bunch of roses he recognized as having been held by Miss Elsie for hers. And then his Aunt Jessie brought the star to her house, where Cecil and his brother Reggie sang and danced in her honor, but also in her imitation. Cecil (wearing a green nightgown) played the Merry Widow herself, Reggie Prince Danilov. "Even at such a tender age, I realized that the performance was inept, shaming, and abominable," but Miss Elsie kissed him in kind congratulation. He spent many hours practicing a calligraphy just like hers—with the appropriate result that when his father forced him to take a job as a City clerk he got into trouble because his account books were illegible.

He was in love not so much with her as with her glamour, with the theater and photography.

> So absorbed did I become in this somewhat stilted and artificial branch of photography that I cherished even its shortcomings. If an actress were caught in some particularly affected attitude, I was enchanted. Because they appeared behind my favourite's head, the out-of-focus blobs of light, like frog-spawn, which misrepresented the sky seen between the leaves of distant trees, had a magic quality for me. I was fascinated by the small stippling marks, which, I soon dis-

covered, were the results of re-touching on the negatives, and, once seen, could often be recognized at the waistline, or under the chin, of my favourites. To this day the addition of painted eyelashes on the print, a fad of this period, is a convention that delights me.

He took many photographs, at first of his mother and two sisters, all artificial, fantastic, and theatrical in quality. At St. Cyprian's, still fascinated by actresses, he drew pictures of them in the notebooks that should have been filled with history, and in school concerts sang and danced imitations of Violet Lorraine and Beatrice Lillie; after dark in the dormitory he did less inhibited imitations of "principal boys." Photographically he imitated the Baron de Meyer, a glamour-pose portrayer of Hollywood stars and dancers in *Vogue,* who continued in photography the tradition of Boldini, the painter who had so inspired Harold Acton. At Harrow, Beaton and a friend photographed each other half-naked or in Greco-Roman draperies. Once they did it early in the morning beneath their housemaster's windows, and looked up to see Major and Mrs. Freeman gazing at them in amazement. At Cambridge he became an enthusiast for the theater, in particular for the Russian Ballet. He photographed Steven Runciman and George Rylands, dandy-aesthetes who brought him to the attention of *Vogue,* the fashion magazine that published Bloomsbury writers.

He tried to get a job at the BBC, but was told that he had an over-cultured, upstage voice. (Harold Acton also says that persons like himself, who articulate clearly, and give syllables their proper values, are not wanted by the BBC.) When his interviewer imitated his way of speaking, Beaton realized with horror that he sounded like the silly ass in a musical comedy, "the one with spats, buttonhole, and eyeglass." (This is, of course, Bertie Wooster or Peter Wimsey, and with this reference our group of talents touches another cultural image of the dandy, which operated at a lower cultural level and for coarser purposes.) Beaton went to Venice in 1926, to report a pageant there, and he managed to meet Diaghilev and to get some sort of minimal approval from him of his sketches and photographs—which was "a supreme moment."

But his career, like many others, was effectively launched by the Sitwells. "The Sitwell brothers had both established a mode of aesthetic existence that completely satisfied my own taste. No detail of their way of life was ugly or humdrum." Osbert encouraged Edith, "whom I now considered the most remarkable and beautiful-looking human object I had ever seen," to pose for him, with "her etiolated Gothic bones, her hands of ivory, the pointed, delicate nose, the amused, deep-set eyes, and silken wisps of hair. . . ." Clearly this was no columbine, but equally clearly it was a *commedia* kind of beauty. Edith posed for him wearing a flowered gown, like *Primavera;* wearing a tricorne and looking like a Modigliani; and lying on the floor like a medieval tomb figure.

> At Renishaw Hall, the Sitwell house in Derbyshire, the ivy-covered ruins, stone terraces ornamented with large Italian statues, and the tapestried rooms, made wonderful backgrounds for pictures of her. Here was the apotheosis of all I loved. With an enthusiasm that I felt I could never surpass, I photographed Edith playing ring a ring of roses with her brothers. . . .

Beaton gave the Sitwells the response they wanted—created the image of them they needed and made it famous; and they did the same for him. When he gave an exhibition at the Cooling Galleries in Bond Street, Osbert wrote the catalogue preface. They were all journalists, and all knew how to create the kind of stir that got their names and their friends' names into the papers. The Sitwells' recommendation got Tom Driberg his job as a gossip columnist for the *Daily Express,* and they nearly got Harold Acton a job as reviewer for the *New Statesman.* The exhibition Beaton gave with their help in 1928 was a great success, and he got promises of work in New York; he went there and returned with a contract from Condé Nast for several thousands a year, which baffled and impressed his father. He became England's leading photographer and a brilliant figure in many branches of art and fashion. In 1931, on the Sitwells' recommendation, Duckworths published his *Book of Beauty;* and he did his first theater work on a ballet for Charles Cochran, which had a story by Osbert, music by William Walton, and choreography by Frederick Ashton.

It will be convenient to continue here our discussion of the Sitwells (before going on to figures who answer more exactly to the description of "new friends") because they were certainly allies of Beaton in terms of their influence on contemporary taste. In 1925, Sir George Sitwell had transferred his home from Renishaw to Montegufoni, where he had hitherto only spent holidays at the persistent prompting of his sons. Osbert says that only when his father was removed from the English scene were they able to pursue their vocations as artists. Sir George often warned his children against those vocations, warned them that they were offending people. And so indeed they were, quite deliberately. They wrote a great deal in this period, attacking institutions and individuals, and they provoked a reaction. Wyndham Lewis's *Apes of God,* (1930) for instance, contains hostile portraits of them. But they were succeeding; they were established figures. In 1928, Thomas Balston at Duckworths brought out *Sitwelliana,* a handlist of works by Edith, Osbert, and Sacheverell Sitwell, 1915–1927. In the same year Osbert collaborated with Nina Hamnett in *The People's Album of London Statues.* And in 1929 Edith brought out *Gold Coast Customs,* more "tragic" poetry that owed a lot to *The Waste Land* and to *The Hollow Men.* From our point of view, perhaps the most interesting Sitwell publication of these years was Sacheverell's preface to Cyril Beaumont's *History of Harlequin* of 1926. The book was written by Britain's leading balletomane, and dedicated to Osbert and Sacheverell Sitwell, and its semifantastic way of treating Harlequin as a real person is like their way of writing art history.

Sacheverell's preface, beside being a lengthy discussion of Harlequin, also makes several connections between the ballet and the *commedia.* He says we can guess from the perfection of the Diaghilev ballet company, who have danced together for only twenty years under the rule of their great impresario, what heights of art must have been reached in *commedia* companies like the Gelosi, who existed as such for a couple of generations. And he describes as the masterpiece of painting in this century the curtain Picasso painted for Cocteau's *Parade,* which adds to the usual masks of the *commedia* a Negro boxer, a Spanish guitarist, a cowboy, and a cowgirl. Sacheverell also connects Harlequin with the music hall tradition of Dan Leno and Nellie Wallace, and with the circus clowns like Grock and the Fratellini brothers.

It is perhaps worth noting that Harold Acton's novel of 1928, *Cornelian,* appeared with a cubist Harlequin with guitar on its cover; and that Lord Peter Wimsey assumed the character of Harlequin to deal with the "bright young people" in *Murder Must Advertise,* (1933). Dorothy Sayers' detective novel is quite a vivid fable of aristocratic youth's self-corruption with drink and drugs, orgies and extravagant treasure hunts, and their subsequent corruption of middle-class dullards. The moral plot is that Lord Peter, as Harlequin, outdoes the wicked in fantasy and daring, and so makes virtue glamorous again. But then he plays some beautiful cricket at a country cricket match (very fully described) at the end of the book, saving the game for his side—and the idea of England for his readers.

Finally, Harlequin was also a motif in the 1920s paintings of Pavel Tchelitchew, the Russian painter whom the Sitwells adopted as a genius during this period. Tchelitchew painted Edith Sitwell seven times, and designed dresses for her. He also painted Cecil Beaton and Harold Acton and Peter Watson. Watson, the future patron of *Horizon,* bought Tchelitchew pictures, as did Edward James, the patron of Betjeman, and Lord Berners.[12]

Other people who were making a humbler success out of some form of dandyism or aestheticism were Oliver Messel, Beverley Nichols, and Noel Coward, not to mention Beatrice Lillie and Gertrude Lawrence. And then there were the gossip columns, already mentioned, of Patrick Balfour, Eleanor Smith, and Tom Driberg.

But most of these *Sonnenkind* journalists saw themselves essentially as artists. Most of them sooner or later wrote a novel, and some of them took that vocation very seriously. For instance among the various circles of "bright young people" were always one or other of the Mitford sisters, the six daughters of Lord Redesdale, who between them acted out all the ways there were of reacting to the situation of the English aristocracy in the '20s and '30s. Lord Redesdale seems to have been a caricature of a hearty, philistine squire; as depicted in Nancy Mitford's novels, he made the principal ornament of his home the trenching tool with which he killed Germans in hand-to-hand fighting during the war. Later he became a Nazi sympathizer. Jessica became a Communist, Diana became a Fascist, Unity became a Nazi, Deborah married a duke, Nancy became a literary dandy.[13] (Pamela's career was less extravagant and the one brother Tom, a close friend to many of our principal group, died in the second war.)

It is the last, Nancy, who concerns us most. She says, "I grew up as ignorant as an owl, came out in London, and went to a great many balls." There she met many people who were not ignorant at all— "Messrs Henry Green, Evelyn Waugh, John Betjeman, Maurice Bowra, and the brilliant Lord Berners (who appeared, at his own request, in *The Pursuit of Love,* as Lord Merlin). . . . Very soon I became an intellectual snob."[14] She was to marry, in 1933, Peter Rodd, whom she describes as a man whose favorite reading was the Greek and Roman classics. She is the clearest case of someone making herself the dandies' apprentice, and in some sense their victim, for the postures they induced her to adopt are in her especially brittle and unconvincing.

She published two very Waugh-like novels within this period. *Highland Fling* (1939) describes an aesthete called Albert (Memorial) Gates, who addresses his friends as Darling, and wears crêpe de chine shirts, taffeta wraps, tartan trews, and gardenia perfume. (He is generally thought to be drawn from Hamish Erskine, one of the most frivolous dandies of the group.) Jane Dacre, who seems to represent the author, wants to marry a genius, and so falls in love with Albert, as the reader is also asked to do. There is much satire of British society and much camp praise of Victoriana. Albert is a painter whose pictures make use of real human hair. *Christmas Pudding* (1932) is dedicated to Robert

Byron and illustrated by Mark Ogilvie-Grant. The central figure is a dissipated Etonian schoolboy, who reads Firbank and Huxley, and who defeats all the representatives of sense and decency in the story.

The most striking thing about Nancy Mitford's fiction from our point of view is the satirical portrait it presents of her father (he is General Murgatroyd in *Highland Fling*, Uncle Matthew in *The Pursuit of Love*) as violently philistine and chauvinist. This is so striking partly because her father was alive and read these portraits, and remained on relatively good terms with his daughter. (She claims that he was furious to discover when she published *Mme. de Pompadour* that he was *not* portrayed in that book.) Like Osbert Sitwell's, her antipaternal jokes seem to derive from a baffling mixture of genuine outrage and "clever" gossip. Ideologically, this corresponds to a strange alternation we find in her between brilliant frivolity and old-fashioned piety. In an essay of 1962, about Captain Scott's heroic journey to the South Pole, she said that the book about the exploit, *The Worst Journey in the World,* remained one of her favorite books. "Here is the Englishman as he was when I was a child. . . . Something seems to have happened in the last fifty years to make him more practical, less idealistic, much less respectful of animals. . . ."[15] And there is a pattern in her novels that makes the red-faced philistine squire (the character most like Lord Redesdale), mocked at the beginning, turn out at the end to be the only real man around.

Another dandy novelist made a similar beginning. Anthony Powell edited a collection of family letters in 1928, and then published one novel *(Afternoon Men)* in 1931 and another *(Venusberg)* in 1932. These were both rather like Waugh's fiction; they are less purely satirical than much of his work, more like *A Handful of Dust* than *Decline and Fall,* but definitely dandy fiction. Powell's collection of family letters, moreover, corresponded to Waugh's *Rossetti,* just as later his *John Aubrey* corresponded to Waugh's *Edmund Campion;* and it is fairly certain that Powell felt himself in competition with Waugh all along. In actual form, his collection of letters corresponded more exactly to a collection made by Nancy Mitford, called *The Ladies of Alderley.*

All these books answer to Waugh's remark in *Rossetti* that biography had replaced the novel as the métier of "those young men and women who, in every age, concern themselves with providing the light reading of their more cultured friends." In *Work Suspended,* Waugh portrayed himself as a writer of detective novels, in *Brideshead Revisited,* as a painter of English country houses; these occupations, and writing travel books, were the métiers of the dandies. Notably lacking is anything large-scale, even in the dandy line—not to mention anything really serious, whether political or literary-critical.

It is striking how many of them aimed only to entertain a fashionable audience. Of course, it was in writing of that kind that the dandy precedents had been set—by Wodehouse, Wilde, and Beerbohm—and that their audience was ready for them. The Sitwells were among other things popular humorists, and besides Waugh and Powell, nearly all the "bright young people" tried their hands at "bright" articles, even someone like Daphne Vivian. Several also tried their hands at film criticism for the popular papers, like Graham Greene and John Betjeman. But it is most striking that the humorous columns of the popular Sunday and daily papers throughout this period should have expressed a public-school-and-university sense of humor. Take, for instance, the Beachcomber column in the *Daily Express,* with its Captain Foulenough character, who would belong in an Evelyn Waugh novel—and to which Waugh sometimes refers. Then there was Hannen Swaffer's "Through a Glass Darkly" column in the *Sunday Express.* And there were D. B. Wyndham-Lewis in the *Daily Mail,* Nathaniel Gubbins in the *Sunday Express*, and (still appearing) the Maudie Littlehampton cartoons that Osbert Lancaster draws for the *Daily Express*—all of them very much in the mood of Evelyn Waugh.

There were already easy and ample rewards for British dandy authors, as long as if they were willing to entertain as well as to attack. Thus one of the older-fashioned consensus authors was Mary Webb (1881–1927), who wrote minor novels in the Hardy tradition about Shropshire rural life, full of folklore and inarticulate passion. She was made into a posthumous bestseller by the prime minister's praise in

1928—by official fiat, as it were—and her novels were reprinted, with introductions by Stanley Baldwin, Buchan, Chesterton, and Robert Lynd. This may be called a literary success decreed by the fathers. But it led to the writing of Stella Gibbons's dandy-satirical novel, *Cold Comfort Farm,* which was much *more* of a popular success in 1932. It is not possible to define the precise relation between Stella Gibbons's book and Mary Webb in particular, but *Cold Comfort Farm* is quite brilliant satire of Webb's kind of novel, and an effective piece of dandy fiction in its own right. It is so because the novelist's persona, Flora Poste, is an unusually honest portrayal of the point of view from which the other figures in the novel are mocked. Flora is herself depicted with a potentially satirical pen.

Thus it was that throughout this period, including the years of political seriousness and left-wing commitment, English popular taste, even at the level of the popular press, was in alliance with the dandy aesthetes, in one important phase of sensibility, the sense of humor. The snob-aesthete Evelyn Waugh was closer to the mass audience of England than would seem to a foreigner credible.

Waugh and British Dandyism

Waugh himself had a very bad time during his first three or four years after coming down from Oxford. He was on bad terms with his father, and he could find no career for himself. He was in love with Olivia Plunkett-Greene, sister to David and Richard and one of the fast girls of the "Bright Young People" set, who yet yearned for a quite religious purity and quietude. Waugh himself was similarly split, but he had also great cleverness, energy, and ambition, and a desire to conquer the world of men, which she did not and which she did not approve in him. It seems likely, also, that he was still for some time divided and tormented in his sexual allegiances; and above all he still loved-and-hated the life of parties and drunkenness. He went to teach in a boys' school in Wales, taking with him a very *Sonnenkind* selection of books—*Alice in Wonderland,* Horace Walpole, and Sir James

Frazer's *The Golden Bough*. (The last appealed to the aesthetes as a source book for Diaghilev's "primitive" ballets.) He tried to get a job as secretary to C. K. Scott-Moncrieff, the translator of Proust, who lived in Pisa. This sounds as if it might have been an aesthetic apprenticeship like Connolly's and Clark's. When that failed and at the same time he got from Harold Acton discouraging comments on a novel he had been writing, he attempted suicide.[16]

In 1927 he met Evelyn Gardner, whose father was Lord Burghclere and whose mother was sister to that earl of Caernarvon who discovered Tutankhamen's tomb. In order to seem to her family able to support her, Waugh undertook a biography of Dante Gabriel Rossetti for Duckworth—having been recommended by Anthony Powell, who then worked there—and then wrote *Decline and Fall,* dedicated to Harold Acton "in homage and affection."

Decline and Fall is a brilliant comic-satiric fantasy, one prominent feature of which is its cruelly accurate imitation of various paternal voices—of Oxford dons, judges, prison governors, schoolteachers, vicars, literal fathers. Waugh makes the reader hear those voices pompously perverting the truth of incident after incident, as they describe it in their own language and their own interests. He explodes half society's institutions for us, creating in literature a joyful anarchy just like that created by Brian and Harold in their parties at Oxford. With this one publication, Waugh established himself as the literary leader of the *Sonnenkinder.* And his development, together with that of John Betjeman, Robert Byron, and Cyril Connolly, gives us the history of the serious side of dandyism in England—the side we can take *in some sense* seriously. It is a history full of their renunciations of or attacks on their original "idea," but then that is always the case with serious dandyism.

Decline and Fall had been offered to Duckworth, but they had asked for expurgations—against which Harold Acton encouraged Waugh to stand firm—because they had found it shocking. Its success was such that it was made Winston Churchill's Christmas present of the year. The book brought Waugh high praise (from Arnold

Bennett as well as from Connolly and Raymond Mortimer) and commissions from the *Daily Express,* the *Evening Standard,* and others to write articles on "Youth," "Censors," and such subjects. For a time he wrote a weekly article for the *Daily Mail.*

Among his articles of that kind is an interesting piece on "The Younger Generation and the War," in the *Spectator* for April 13, 1929, which is full of reactionary contempt for the new relaxation of standards in which Waugh himself so zestfully participated. It, therefore, well expresses his fundamentally ambivalent attitudes, which were detectable in *Decline and Fall,* although there the anarchy was dominant. Here Waugh says the only thing that would have saved the younger generation from anarchy (since they had no fathers) would have been a rigid school discipline. But unfortunately the schoolmasters came back from the war with a jolly tolerance of everything modern. Children who should have been whipped for disobedience were encouraged to think for themselves. They were Bolsheviks at eighteen and bored at twenty. They had nothing to rebel against. Such freedom breeds sterility. (It is impossible for us to tell, and probably for Waugh, how far his tongue was in his cheek in saying such things. That is why he was a humorist, and why his best work, like *Decline and Fall,* is both a cultic celebration of the *Sonnenkinder* and a harsh mockery of them.)

Waugh also wrote an interesting piece on Ronald Firbank. Anthony Powell had persuaded Duckworth to bring out in 1929—using the money Firbank had bequeathed for the purpose—the Rainbow Edition of all Firbank's works. Osbert Sitwell wrote a biographical introduction, and Arthur Waley (the translator from the Chinese, and a Bloomsbury figure) wrote a critical introduction.

Waugh's piece, which appeared in Osbert Sitwell's *Life and Letters* in 1930 says that Firbank owes something to Corvo and Beardsley and the '90s, but that his humor is structural whereas theirs was ornamental—he is baroque where Wilde was rococo. And so Firbank has more to give to modern writers, and *has* given more, to for instance Harold Acton, Osbert Sitwell, Carl van Vechten, and even Hemingway.

Firbank is the first modern writer to solve "the problem of fiction," that is, to release us from 19th-century forms. Waugh quotes dialogue (choosing effects very like his own,) passages of impressionism, invention of names, and above all the breaking of the cause-effect connection. Firbank thus came into his own and acquired sons and heirs. Ifan Kyrle-Fletcher published *Ronald Firbank, A Memoir*, in 1930.

In 1928, Waugh paid a visit to Renishaw, the home of the Sitwells, and Osbert describes him watching their father "in an ecstasy of observation." Sir George does indeed seem to have suited all the requirements of a dandy's father—he was tyrannical, obsessive, philistine, crazy, and clever enough to be a good enemy. In the same year, Waugh married Evelyn Gardner—the only male witnesses at the ceremony were Harold Acton and Robert Byron—and they went to live in a flat in Islington that Acton describes as like a "sparkling nursery." Evelyn Gardner seems to have had a marked character of "innocence," and Waugh himself clearly yearned back at that moment to a childish simplicity. It was a very twenties marriage. The two Evelyns looked rather alike—both like young boys. Nancy Mitford, who was a close friend to both, describes Evelyn Gardner as "even smaller than he was, resembled a ravishing boy, a page." Neither took on the weight or dignity of manhood/womanhood. Waugh at this time took lessons in carpentry (an interest that he explained to Powell as deriving from "Tolstoy and all that") and spent a lot of time making cheap and ingenious objects for their flat—pasting postage stamps decoratively over coal scuttles, and then varnishing them, for instance. Acton says he expected Waugh to start designing tiles and fabrics, and perhaps to solve "some of our pressing social ills," like another William Morris. But Waugh was more deliberately childlike than Morris. Several witnesses agree that the objects in their flat had the character of being toys, and it seems clear that Waugh was cultivating naïveté—for the first and last time in his life. No doubt just because he had been to some degree letting down the defences of sophistication, he was more than normally upset when his wife told him she was leaving him for another man. This happened in 1929 while *Vile Bodies* was being written, and the overwhelming effect it had on him can be felt in the melo-dramatic *Waste Land* atmosphere of the book's ending. The theme of a marriage betrayed by a woman's lightness remained an important theme in his later fiction, although indeed it is to be found in the very first of his Oxford stories.

The most obvious and drastic effect this had on Waugh was that from July to September, 1930, he took instruction in Roman Catholi-cism from Father d'Arcy, a Jesuit with whom Olivia Plunkett-Greene put him in touch. It is clear from remarks made later by Father d'Arcy and Douglas Woodruff that Waugh came to Catholicism mostly to find an ideology that would support an old-fashioned moral sense and a conservative politics. Only later, after studying Edmund Cam-pion, the Elizabethan martyr poet, did he come to love the Catho-lic religion in some more emotional sense. Of course he continued to live a wordly life of parties and drunkenness, to which the church provided a background of severe and eternal values, acknowledged although not lived by.

Among the new friends he made during this period the most impor-tant were probably Lady Diana Cooper and Randolph Churchill. Both belonged to the conservative wing, but to the liveliest style, of the social and political aristocracy of England. They were both Sebas-tians, to use the symbolism of *Brideshead Revisited.* Lady Diana, daughter of the duke of Rutland, was a famous beauty, who went on the stage to play the Nun and the Virgin in Max Reinhardt's *The Mir-acle,* which ran for twelve years, on and off, from 1922 to 1934. In one way, then, she stood for a certain raffishness, Bohemianism, modern-ism, but on the other hand, she was married to Duff Cooper, one of Winston Churchill's parliamentary lieutenants, a minister during the Second World War, and an ambassador afterwards. And Randolph, who had been very beautiful and brilliant during his boyhood, was turning himself into a rogue, improvident, always in trouble and a trouble to his friends. Both were flamboyant characters, and of types that Waugh loved—a great beauty and an outrageous adventurer. Both were stylistically prewar figures—Diana's wedding was the last great society occasion for which crowds of factory girls assembled. Both were to appear in Waugh's books.

Randolph Churchill deserves a word of introduction here, because he typifies the relations of the aristocratic rogue figure to aesthetes like Waugh and Betjeman.[7] He was born in 1911, into one of England's greatest families, and his godfathers were F. E. Smith and Sir Edward Grey, the Liberal Foreign Secretary. He went to prep school with Beaverbrook's son, and to Eton with Smith's; far from being embarrassed there by himself being the son of a controversial public figure, he says, he always exulted in it. He was unpopular at Eton, because he was already, as for the rest of his life, quarreling with everything said by anyone in authority and trying to win every argument by sheer force of rhetoric. But he became friends with Tom Mitford, and saw much of the Mitford sisters. Already at Eton, it is interesting to note, he collected Wodehouse novels. Professor Lindemann used often to invite Randolph from Eton to Oxford to dine at high table, while he was still a schoolboy, and to send him back with presents in a chauffeur-driven car; Roy Harrod seconded Lindemann in this deference, as in much else.

Randolph went to Oxford in 1928, and made the announcement that he intended to become president of the Union faster than anyone before him. He already knew such institutions from the inside, from the gossip of those who ran them. In fact he never achieved that ambition and always felt that Oxford had resisted him. He saw more of the dons than of the undergraduates, and says that Oxford was a valuable experience because there "one met the clever witty dons on equal terms and learned a great deal which was to prove serviceable in the battle of life." These dons were Lindemann and Harrod, Bowra, Sparrow, and Lord David Cecil. Beside these, Seymour Berry, son of Lord Camrose, Basil, the marquis of Dufferin and Ava, and Freddie Furneaux, F. E. Smith's son, were his friends. He met Waugh in 1929, and soon forged an alliance with him, but Waugh had of course long gone down from Oxford. Churchill did not stay there long, seeing better ways to advance his career. He had come to Oxford with an allowance of £400 a year, but the next year he was invited to make a lecture tour of America, where he earned $12,000 in seven months— and where he always took a suite of rooms in any hotel he stayed at. John Betjeman says that Churchill belonged to a set *above* the university—like the group described by Evelyn Waugh in his novels. But what bound *this* set together, Betjeman says, was politics. They were ministers of state in embryo. "The tutelary god in Oxford of these men was Professor Lindemann, later Lord Cherwell. In his bowler hat above his inscrutable yellow face, he was to be seen driving to the best country houses."*

Randolph loved Betjeman's poetry from the first and made him recite it at parties. He then persuaded Edward James, a rich young Etonian patron of the arts, to publish a volume of it. He even read the proofs for Betjeman, and forced many people to buy a copy. He therefore contributed significantly to the launching of Betjeman's career. Of Connolly and Quennell, on the other hand, he is said to have said that they had been allowed to join White's Club only so that they could know how "we" live. But Waugh and Betjeman he seems to have accepted as members of his world.

And it *was* the strength of their dandyism that it was so British, that it related so vividly to so many British types then vividly on the scene. There were powerful forces in the national life that made aristocratic *Sonnenkinder* and country-house eccentrics the darlings of

---

* But, as we have seen, the measures that produced a Winston Churchill before 1914 produced Randolph after 1918. The culture had weakened, in its internalized forms, too—its loyalties, values, and disciplines; and those who rebelled, in Kipling fashion, against its minor shibboleths found they had broken out of connection with its major laws too. Roy Harrod tells the story of how, in the year the Prince of Wales was suggested as a possible chancellor of Oxford, both Randolph Churchill and Basil Murray, in turn, took over Harrod's rooms in college to promote that candidacy. It was a typical cause for them—partly because it never had a chance—and they employed typical means, dispossessing Harrod and hectoring all kinds of dignitaries over the telephone. It was another "Basil Seal" episode. They failed, on that occasion, and in general. Harrod says that both were "impossible" despite their great charm and their great gifts. He says they had no "direction in life." But their direction was clear enough; what betrayed them was their temperamental irritability and contempt for the world they wished to dominate. They could not believe in it enough even to exploit it.

the English imagination just then. This was the advantage British dandyism possessed over Anthony Blanche's, which was so much more international.

Three other men, so *like* Waugh's friends, so much *of* his world, in nearly every way, deserve mention here because they also played a lurid role in English history, and thereby illuminate another side of the Children of the Sun. Guy Burgess was born in the same year as Randolph Churchill, although he did not reach Cambridge until 1932. His father had been a naval officer (the son of an admiral), and Guy was sent from Eton to Dartmouth Naval College, and then back to Eton because he did not like Dartmouth. He was very close to his mother, very handsome, and very actively homosexual. In his last years at Eton he played an Oscar Wilde role, and when he left his passions were for Proust, Firbank, and Arlen, although he had also won the Gladstone Memorial Scholarship. His first night of dining in Hall at Trinity College, Cambridge, he asked a rowing blue to sleep with him that night. His most illuminating remark about himself was that he could never travel by train because he would be obliged to seduce the engine driver. He did feel obliged, and it was always the engine driver.

One of his typical conquests was the naïve, confused (in both politics and sex) Donald Maclean, of a Presbyterian, Gladstonian, Highland family. Maclean's father, Sir Donald, had become a member of Parliament in 1906 in the Liberal landslide. He was interested in social legislation and a founder of the N.S.P.C.C. (the National Society for the Prevention of Cruelty to Children). He was a lay preacher, and the Macleans held family prayers. He became president of the Board of Education in 1931, the year before he died. That was the year Donald went up to Cambridge. He had been mocked at school as effeminate, and one of Guy's jokes against him was that to sleep with Donald—"that great white body"—"would be like going to bed with Dame Nellie Melba."* Cyril Connolly, who knew them both quite

---

* Their relationship, ideological, social, and sexual, was like that between Paul Blackenhurst and Jimmy McGrath in *The Golden Notebook*. Some of the interest of Doris Lessing's fiction derives from her intuitive fabulations of contemporary phenomena.

well, said in *The Missing Diplomats* that both showed a strong resentment of female domination, from which they were trying to break away; and their addiction to alcohol and to adolescence—that is to undergraduate informality—was a way so to escape.

Burgess and Maclean were part of a left-wing circle at Cambridge; others of its members with a notable future were Victor Rothschild, James Klugman, Anthony Blunt, John Cornford, Malcolm Dunbar, and David Haden Guest. But the most important man in their fate left Cambridge the year Guy Burgess arrived. Kim Philby went up in 1929, though only seventeen. He was shy, and stuttered, and was much in awe of his father, who was an Establishment rebel. The father, St. John Philby, had known Kipling in India and idolized him—hence the name "Kim"; and he had himself played a Kipling part in Arabia during the war. Kim's career can be seen as a more extreme, and 20th-century, version of his father's. Kim, too, was an Establishment type—he loved cricket and P. G. Wodehouse—but he needed something stronger and bigger than the British Establishment had become to belong to. His father found that *he* needed that, but in his time there were alternatives to outright treachery. In 1925, St. John Philby resigned from the British service to become Ibn Saud's political adviser—in effect, to become an Arab. He studied Arabian flora and fauna scientifically, and became a fellow of the Royal Geographical Society, and a Koran scholar; but he was also a shrewd businessman, and mixed up in Arabian politics. He had a wife and children in London, and an Arabian wife who bore him a son forty-two years after Kim was born. Like Kipling himself, St. John Philby railed against moral decline and perfidy in Britain, but he kept his membership in the Athenaeum Club, attended test matches, and wrote for *The Times*. The England he *admired* was Cromwell's England, and he hero-worshiped Ibn Saud, who belonged to one of the strictest Moslem sects, the Wahhabies. When the latter captured Mecca, they burned 100,000 hookahs as emblems of ease and luxury. St. John Philby himself used neither bed, table, nor chair while he lived in Arabia. Later he came to feel that even the young Arabs had lost their primitive virtue. It seems

BRIAN HOWARD

Brian Howard at his glittering zenith. Fancy dress was the natural costume for Children of the Sun, for they were always outshining the ordinary, and by mostly theatrical means.

Brian Howard

Brian while still at Eton, bursting the bonds of English boyhood.

RANDOLPH CHURCHILL; RUPERT BROOKE

The sons of England at their most beautiful.

THE PRINCE OF WALES; SIR OSWALD MOSLEY:

The lyric grace of Pierrot; the brutal triumph of Harlequin.

RUDYARD KIPLING AND KING GEORGE V

The fathers, against whom the sons rebelled.

LORD BEAVERBROOK (LEFT);
WINSTON CHURCHILL AND DAVID LLOYD-GEORGE

Three of those uncles who sponsored the rogues among the sons—
the rougher, tougher, more activist rebels.

**EDITH AND OSBERT SITWELL (TOP);
VIRGINIA WOOLF AND LYTTON STRACHEY**

*Some of those "uncles" who sponsored the dandies
and aesthetes among the sons.*

JEAN COCTEAU AND SERGEI DIAGHILEV (TOP);
VASLAV NIJINSKY

*Figures from abroad who inspired
the dandies and aesthetes among the sons.*

WILLIAM ACTON; OSBERT SITWELL (TOP);
BRIAN HOWARD; HAROLD ACTON

Some dandy-aesthetes in their infancy and boyhood.

BRIAN HOWARD; HAROLD ACTON; EVELYN WAUGH

Brian (top left) and Harold (top right) as seen by their contemporaries at Oxford. The cartoon of Harold was drawn by his friend and admirer, Evelyn Waugh (bottom).

Harold Acton's style showed best in motion, not camera portraits.
Here he is seen moving in counterpoint to a baroque statue, and
depicted in tapestry—sinuously inclined over a table.

We see Brian enlivening the style of his contemporaries at an Oxford party—and one assumes that before the photographer arrived they were following his lead with a little more panache. His is the only modern face among them,

his the only bold and lively pose, his the only activity (embracing his two shame-faced companions). The others are all more or less victimized by the camera, and wear their traces of saturnalia as awkwardly as so many cows decked with daisies.

NANCY CUNARD; LADY DIANA COOPER

*These were the nearest female equivalents to Brian and Harold,
affronting the conventions, the first harshly, the second playfully.*

*A party of Bright Young Things in London,
including Cyril Connolly, Cecil Beaton, and Patrick Kinross,
making contact with the proletariat.*

STEPHEN SPENDER (TOP);
CHRISTOPHER ISHERWOOD AND W. H. AUDEN

The literary dandies and naïfs of the 1930s, disguised as comrades.

EVELYN WAUGH AND RANDOLPH CHURCHILL (TOP);
J. ROBERT OPPENHEIMER AND MAJOR GENERAL
LESLIE R. GROVES (BOTTOM)

The 1939–1945 War imposed harsh tests on the Children of the Sun.

GUY BURGESS (TOP LEFT); DONALD MACLEAN (TOP RIGHT);
KIM PHILBY (BOTTOM)

Rogues and dandies serving in the English Secret Services

F. R. Leavis (top left); George Orwell (top right); Kingsley Amis (bottom)

The resistence to, and reaction against, the Children of the Sun.

certain that Kim's relations with him were full of highly charged tensions, but issued in imitation. The wife and mother died in 1956, perhaps by her own hand, and St. John in 1960, saying, "God, I'm bored." He was one of the great rogues of his generation.[18]

These men and their fathers are representative figures of Waugh's England, and his attitudes derive from and refer to them—although those attitudes are complex and ambivalent, both for and against the Children of the Sun in their rebellion against the fathers. On the whole, however, in these early years he was writing on their behalf.

Thus in *Labels* he has a brilliant passage in attack on the Morris tradition.

> The detestation of "quaintness" and "picturesque bits" which is felt by every decently constituted Englishman, is, after all, a very insular prejudice. It has developed naturally, in self-defence against arts and crafts, and the preservation of rural England, and the preservation of ancient monuments, and the transplantation of Tudor cottages, and the collection of pewter and old oak, and the reformed public houses, and the Ye Olde Inne and the Kynde Dragon and Ye Cheshire Cheese, Broadway, Stratford on Avon, folk-dancing, Nativity plays, reformed dress, free love in a cottage, glee singing, the Lyric, Hammersmith, Belloc, Ditchling, Wessex worship, village signs, local customs, heraldry, madrigals, regional cookery, Devonshire teas, letters to *The Times* about saving timbered almshouses from destruction, the preservation of the Welsh language, etc. It is inevitable that English taste, confronted with all these frightful menaces to its integrity, should have adopted an uncompromising attitude to anything the least tainted with ye oldeness.

This is what Betjeman means when he says, "At William Morris how we laughed"; and Waugh's laughter is, of course, directed at D. H. Lawrence too—"free love in a cottage"—at Demeter and Woman. In the same book Waugh remarks that the pornographic frescoes at Pompeii are "mere scribbles, no better than D. H. Lawrence's," and nothing like the elegant work in the other rooms. Waugh's major tendency (as a paradoxist, he sometimes affronted this) was to regard demonstrable technique (even in drawing) as a manifestation of taste, taste as a manifestation of reason, reason as deriving from a sound moral sense, and so on, and each as necessary to the defence of the others against corruption. Perhaps what is most remarkable is the solidity this gives to the concept "taste"—the absoluteness of judgment, the range of specification. "Taste" is always more of a reality to dandies than to other types, and Waugh works out an ideology to support that. (By a natural paradox, he much admired the "ruthless absence of good taste" at the Jesuit House on Mount Street, which he described as "superbly ill-furnished."[19] He liked to see religious values stand independent of that whole other complex of "natural" values.)

Betjeman also worked out an ideology of taste, similar although less clear and impressive. His *Ghastly Good Taste* of 1933 said it was written to dissuade the average man from distrusting his own taste, and the average architect from continuing in his profession. Like Waugh, Betjeman connected bad taste with the decay of Christianity, via the decay of civilization. Civilization lost its unity with the Reformation, and architecture can only regain coherence when Christendom is reestablished, either in the form of an ecclesiastical union or in that of the USSR. As this indicates, Betjeman was more sympathetic to the Left than Evelyn Waugh, and that phase of his development belongs in our next chapter. But the general line of his taste is very parallel to Waugh's, as a few of his chapter titles will indicate: Chapter IV, "The Upper Classes Take Over from Holy Church"— hence the excess of ornament in Jacobean buildings; Chapter V, "Educated Architecture"—in praise of Bath; Chapter VI, "Regency Architecture"—the last days of England and the best; Chapter VII, "Middle Class Architecture"—some praise for King's Cross and St. Pancras stations; Chapter VIII, "Revolt in the Middle Classes"— the death of architecture in England, from refinement, "refeenment," good taste—Morris and cottages and wholemeal bread.*

---

* It is perhaps worth remarking the artificiality of these historical schemes. Whether

In an Introduction to a reprint of the book, in 1970, Betjeman gives "An Aesthete's Apology," describing the history of his own taste. While at Marlborough, he learned about modern art from his fellow schoolboys, notably Anthony Blunt, who already knew all about Roger Fry and Clive Bell and Significant Form. But Betjeman's own taste then was already for 18th-century artificiality, particularly for grottoes. By the time he reached Oxford, he loved 18th-century and early 19th-century country houses, especially those in Ireland, where he went to stay with aristocratic friends. Only after Oxford, when Bowra got him a job on *The Architectural Review,* did he begin to read Le Corbusier and respond to modern architecture. (In literary matters his taste was still then quaint and archaizing; he frequented the Squirearchy, the circle around Jack Squire of the *Mercury,* and made friends with Arthur Waugh and Eric Gill.) Indeed, Betjeman admits that he wrote the book in a muddle—wanting to be up to date, but really preferring all other centuries to his own—and one can see a similar combination of incompatibles within the taste of nearly all Betjeman's books, and indeed Waugh's.

In *Labels,* Waugh also has a long essay on Antonio Gaudí and his Sagrada Familia cathedral in Barcelona. He is clearly much excited by the cathedral, which appeals to his taste in many mutually inconsistent ways, so many that he is unable to "approve" of it. He says it is what "art for art's sake can become when it is wholly untempered by considerations of tradition or good taste." He treats it as a kind of "Anthony Blanche" in architecture. In fact he explicitly compares Gaudí's work to Firbank's in literature, and to late UFA films in cinema, ". . . the apotheosis of all the writhing, bubbling, convoluting, convulsing soul of the Art Nouveau." Someone wrong in the head, he says, should pay for the building's completion. This exactly expresses

---

devised by Betjeman, or by Waugh, or by Connolly, or by Byron, whether Left or Right in tendency, they never begin to convince, or even to engage much interest. The taste they "justify" is another matter. But history was not a discipline the *Sonnenkinder* mastered. It belonged too much to the world of men. Their historical schemes are schoolboy paraphrases and inversions of their teachers' lessons at school, and best when most lighthearted.

Waugh's ambivalence (all the British dandies' ambivalence) about all brilliant and extravagant art—he loves it for being extravagant, but therefore cannot endorse it.

In *Remote People* (1931), Waugh's style has become genuinely Gibbonian, sustaining the note of sardonic but discreet judgment through long passages of clear and elegant exposition. Take, "Hardly had the blood congealed on Gougsa's mangled corpse, or the bereaved empress succumbed to her sudden chill, before orders had been given for the formation of this corps." And there is a fine paragraph on the Abyssinian currency in a footnote. But Waugh's paradoxical variation on Gibbon is that he bases this sensibility on Christianity, on Catholicism. He sees the church as the great clarifier of religion.

> At Debra Lebanos I suddenly saw the classic basilica and open altar as a great positive achievement, a triumph of light over darkness consciously accomplished, and I saw theology as the science of simplification by which nebulous and elusive ideas are formalized and made intelligible and exact.

He saw pre-Catholic Christianity as contaminated by "hazy and obscene nonsense . . . magical infections." And he saw how this had been defeated by the great open altars of Catholic Europe, where Mass is said "in a flood of light, high in the sight of all." The Gibbonian stress on reason (of course it is Chestertonian, in more immediate derivation) is accompanied by a stress on formalism that must remind us of Robert Byron's enthusiasm for Byzantine art, at Ravenna and Mount Athos. The Byzantinism of this period was the more severe and masculine equivalent of the baroquerie.

Byron published a good deal in this period, beginning with *Europe in the Looking Glass* in 1926. Sections of this had appeared in *The Times,* and it set a pattern—deriving from Norman Douglas ultimately—for a type of travel book that was subsequently written by many of the dandies and rogues. This is an account, written with lots of panache, of a journey by car from Grimsby to Athens, conducted—with lots of panache—by him and two friends. They traveled in considerable style and at considerable expense, quarreled with waiters and policemen, charged barricades with their car, embarrassed their hosts, got arrested in Rome, and so on. Narratively, it is full of impudent irrelevancies and personalia. He tells us that one of his friends, although he went to Eton and Oxford, is a Communist—"the misdirected outcome of sympathy for those less fortunate than himself." And he begins the book with:

> This book makes no pretentions to literary merit. It is offered to the public in the sole hope that the public will buy it. Any vestige of purpose it may contain is outlined in the last paragraph of the first chapter.

This purpose is to build a "European Consciousness," which is necessary if we are to understand (and, as he implies, to deal with) America. He speaks often of "the retrograde industrialism sprung up in a night on the other side of the Atlantic," which is so unlike our *complete* civilization. There are many anti-American anecdotes in the book. Parallel with this is the satirical treatment of the *Wandervogel* and the cult of youth, the latter an ideal, he says, which has replaced manhood. Byron was, like Waugh, a propagandist for old-fashioned kinds of aristocratic or gentlemanly power.

His *Essay on India,* which appeared in 1931 (and which Christopher Sykes says won him a great reputation in government circles),[20] developed some of the same themes. He says that he sees "the whole philosophy of Western history and culture, already thrown aside in Russia and the United States, undergoing the supreme and ultimate test of its practical value" in India. Our worst enemy is our own materialism, a philosophy bred by the scientific revolution, which makes us think of ourselves as only a fortuitous concourse of atoms, and makes us skeptical of our old values. Already in the United States,

> we perceive the nascence of a portentous barbarism, whose clamour before the Golden Calf threatens to obscure even the lesser, purely expedient virtues, such as justice and integrity, of materialistic civilization, and which pays neither lip-service nor courtesy to the Universal Truth.

Byron's style can often sound like a parody of Waugh's (in fact, it probably derives from Macaulay) and that may be another reason why Waugh's tone about Byron was acid. This brassy rhetoric, for instance, is the serious counterpart to the undergraduate magazine humorousness:

> The hard Hebroid scum of racially indeterminate, machine-worshipping, truthless little men who have laid hands on half the world since the War, stencilling the American pattern where they touch, have found no place in India.*

Byron credits the British administration with resisting that infection, and he waxes enthusiastic over the British achievement in governing India. He advocates Home Rule, but assures the reader that the Indians will want the British to stay, of their own free will. He attacks Winston Churchill for his policy of keeping India a dominion, but his attack sounds largely rhetorical, and much of what Byron has been saying about politics—and everything about his way of saying it—is very Churchillian.

There are seven pages of invective against Churchill, which one cannot help suspecting were written for the man himself to read. They are written very much in Churchill's own language, and were surely meant to evoke the response, "I like your style, young man; why don't you fight with me, instead of against me." In 1938, seeing the Nazi menace, Byron was to become an ardent Churchillite, and temperamentally he had belonged with men like Robert Boothby and Randolph Churchill all along. This suggests to us the thought that the

---

* Byron's use of this kind of language of course makes it impossible for us to take him seriously as a thinker in any sense. But he did not seem so completely disqualified to others in his group, and the truth is that they all suffered from similar disqualifications. Waugh never wrote so badly as Byron, true, but the real problem with all of them is the sense they give that they wrote to impress, to "dazzle and confuse those they despise," as Waugh says, and they could not write any other way, even in moments of sincerity. This is the intellectual aspect of the *Sonnenkind* phenomenon. Thought, as much as history, was the property of the mature man, in the gift of Apollo, and they *could* not submit to its inner disciplines. They loved their amateur status too well, and amateurs they remained.

insults to America should be read in the same way. Byron knew very little about America when he wrote them. What he was responding to, almost explicitly, was America's overtopping of England—England's overshadowing and diminution. Consciously or unconsciously, he was surely aching for an offer of a "special relationship," both on the personal and national levels. Byron was always ready to join the "big boys," whether they were called Winston Churchill or the United States of America. His way of getting asked was to cheek them.

The same pattern can be seen in Randolph Churchill's attitude to America, and in that of most of the rogues. Waugh was less political, and had more intellectual integrity—he was consistent in his anti-Americanism. All of them saw America as the enemy of "culture," as they understood it. They believed in the specialty of special people and resented American efforts to treat everyone alike. Those efforts were, after all, part of America's assertively normal, family based, father-and-mother-worshiping culture. Implicitly, the English allowed the Americans to usurp normality, masculinity, size, but thereafter they wanted no intimate contact with them. If the Americans had taken over civilization, then the English would content themselves with culture, and would arm themselves with *cultural* standards, which their enemies would find pretty severe in their way—or so the *Sonnenkinder* intimated. This was, of course, an old pattern of anti-Americanism, and always acute in dandies. Diaghilev had hated the "hail-fellow-well-met" equality he had met in America in 1915.

One symbol of the American size, which can be shown oppressing the English imagination, was the American woman; she appears in book after dandy book as psychologically brawny and gross, threatening or demanding. Following the example of Oscar Wilde and P. G. Wodehouse, Osbert Sitwell and Alan Pryce-Jones and Robert Byron and Dorothy Sayers often portray such women—seen, loudly assertive and self-assertive, across a hotel lobby. John Betjeman plays with the image of the threatening woman erotically, and uses hearty English girls. But more typically that figure is American, in the first twenty years of our period, and then, after the second war began, Russian or proto-Russian. Waugh during the war confessed to the nightmare of being wounded, captured, and tended by a Communist *woman* doctor, and Lord Birkenhead in his account of his mission to Yugoslavia dwells on the huge and brawny *women* soldiers. It is surely likely that the physical size is culturally symbolic, and that the English dandies felt threatened by it in all kinds of ways. Nancy Mitford says, "Russians, like Americans, tend to hate me on sight."[21]

Harold Acton and Brian Howard were in a special position, becauwse of their American families—and because of the hope they placed in American innovations like cocktails and jazz as means to subvert the old structures. Early on, in *The Eton Candle* days, they inclined to idealize America. Brian described it in one of his *Candle* essays as "a sort of paradise for that enormous legion in Art of the deserving unappreciated," while Harold seems to have seen it as the land of Walt Whitman, the home of sexual energy. It was *then* a refuge from the oppression of England. But later on the indications are that their attitudes changed, as England shrank to harmlessness and America swelled to become Reality. It is significant that Harold never felt he could settle there, despite invitations and offers of financial help from his uncle Guy Mitchell if he would do so. The *Sonnenkinder* were probably the major shapers of England's "cultural" anti-Americanism throughout this period.

Byron also published *The Station,* in 1928. This was another travel book, about a journey with friends to Mount Athos, but it was also a book about the monastery itself and its treasures of Byzantine art. It was reviewed by D. H. Lawrence, who treated it as an expression of "young England," which he defined as the postwar generation influenced mostly by the Sitwells. Basically he approved of the book for its determined youthfulness and impudence—its *Sonnenkinderei.* He specifically preferred it to the kind of book a German professor would have made out of the subject; the professor represents the fathers in the life of the mind.[22] But Byron took his interest in Byzantine art very seriously, and he made himself something of an authority on it. He published *The Byzantine Achievement* in 1929 and *The Birth of*

Western Painting, again about the influence of Byzantium, in 1930.

El Greco, who derived so much from Byzantine sources, was perhaps the biggest painting "discovery" of the period, and there developed a certain fashion for Byzantine studies. One of Byron's companions on his trip to Mount Athos was David Talbot Rice, who devoted much of his subsequent career as an art historian to Byzantium. Rice published *Byzantine Art* in 1935 and followed it with a series of related studies, on icons and Russian Byzantine art. And Steven Runciman, an Eton and Cambridge aesthete (Cecil Beaton tells stories of his stylishness at Cambridge), began a lifetime of Byzantine studies with *Byzantine Civilization* in 1933. One can see that a marked preoccupation with formalized art and culture, all metaphorically encrusted with gold and jewellery, would appeal to the dandies—perhaps particularly to those with more "masculine" taste, who found the rococo too lightweight.

The number of Byron's publications in itself was a publication. He wrote a review of Henry Green's first novel, *Blindness,* in 1926, in which he exulted in the number of books already published by former members of the Eton Society of Arts. And he pestered Harold Acton to write down, and sell in article form, the thoughts that Acton was wasting in conversation. In 1932, Byron published *The Appreciation of Architecture,* along the lines of Betjeman's *Ghastly Good Taste.* Byron was to the others an embodiment of that need to produce, to achieve, to compete, that was beginning to haunt them all, and about which Cyril Connolly has written best.

Cyril Connolly had become secretary to Logan Pearsall Smith in 1926, and he stayed with Smith until 1929, when he wanted to get married, a wish that his patron, he tells us, found "abnormal." Smith was Berenson's brother-in-law, and a scholar-aesthete of Berenson's type—a duller and narrower Berenson of bibliography. Connolly's place was later taken by Robert Gathorne-Hardy, for Smith formed the practice of paying a young man of promise a few pounds a week for some help with his scholarly projects, while encouraging him to pursue his own literary career. Connolly tells us, in his essay on Smith,

that he needed Smith to teach him to enjoy Paris, and worldly pleasures in general—he had been one for long walks and ruins and reading. Literarily, he had intended to revive the epic as a poetic form and
to write a novel about archaic Greece; these rather unreal-sounding
schemes must surely have been inherited from Eton and Oxford days,
when he still saw writing in 19th-century terms, and before he accepted
himself as one of the dandy generation. For many years he published
only as a book reviewer, and his later work expresses the agonies of
those years—the fear that he was being passed in the race, and that
he had nothing really to give. The dandies helped each other to get
published and noticed—for they were in alliance against the outside
world still—but necessarily they also competed against each other.
Connolly, as we have seen, praised *Decline and Fall* at the expense of
Cornelian; and Raymond Mortimer, then literary editor of the *New
Statesman,* interviewed Harold Acton about reviewing but gave the
job to Peter Quennell.

Connolly differed from Waugh, Betjeman, and Byron in that he
gradually developed toward more sympathy with modernism and aestheticism, while they retreated from such ideas to make various alliances with older and more patriarchal forces. But then he had further
to come toward novelty and boldness in the first place, because of what
he calls his "academicism and timidity," at Oxford and later. One could
not say that he met the other three at some middle point, but rather
perhaps that the careers of the four of them cut lines that enclose a
middle space—the space that represents specifically British dandyism.

Enemies and Rivals

Among those who offered some resistance to that dandyism, D. H. Lawrence may be mentioned first, though
not strictly speaking a new enemy. Lawrence produced in
this period two novels, one in service of the *Sonnenkind, The
Plumed Serpent,* and one in denial of it, *Lady Chatterley's Lover.*
The Plumed Serpent is his most sustained exploration of the

Sonnenkind religion, inviting the reader to find in Don Ramon charisma of the kind the world needs and cannot get outside a *Sonnenkind* cult. Lawrence imagines a whole national culture being built up, in modern times, around the worship of the life-force incarnate in a priest-king's body, a magus. (Don Ramon is a kind of matured and full-blown Osiris.) But despite the extraordinary efforts Lawrence put into this imagining (comparable to Hardy's efforts to enter into the Demetrian blood-consciousness), in fact this novel is much inferior to his others. The imaginative venture quite clearly breaks down before the insistent skepticism of one of the characters, Kate—who represents Frieda.

The second novel, *Lady Chatterley's Lover,* is written in celebration of Demeter again, of the marriage relationship, of fertility, birth, and renewal in Nature. The *Sonnenkind* figures here are dandies or rogues, figures out of modern British life, like Sir Clifford and his sister, who are often compared with the Sitwells. They are satirically represented as dandies in the most limited sense, who turn their backs on normal marriage only because they cannot measure up to it—not because, like Don Ramon, they know of something better. Thus at the end of his life, Lawrence turned his back decisively on that *Sonnenkind* idea that had excited him as well as other Englishmen (although him differently) in the 1920s. But we should continue to associate him with that idea, in its most adventurous form. It is symbolically apt that the D. H. Lawrence commemorative issue of *The New Adelphi,* June–August 1930, included a long and glowing review of Ludwig Klages' *Science and Character,* which makes it clear that Klages was a name well-known to readers of that magazine. As we shall see, Klages was the ideologist of a young-man movement in Germany. This issue of the *Adelphi,* which contained several pieces by and about D. H. Lawrence, was the last one edited by John Middleton Murry. He had founded the magazine to give Lawrence a platform, and now that Lawrence had died, Murry turned to other projects. Under the new editors, Max Plowman and Richard Rees, the magazine began to publish pieces by George Orwell.

With Orwell's first publications, and those of F. R. Leavis, which were roughly contemporaneous, the effective resistance to dandyism began. Unlike say J. B. Priestley, these two men mobilized the best consciousness of the contemporaries, the best intellectual and moral forces, in support of maturity and responsibility of taste and temperament. And unlike D. H. Lawrence for instance, they committed all their energies to that resistance movement, they made their careers out of it. Their work was at first overlooked, as mere reaction, mere rearguard action, merely embittered nay-saying. It seemed to have no understanding of nor response to any new ideas or new art. But that they were making such a response gradually became clear over the next twenty years, as their attitudes proved themselves to be in alliance with nearly all the serious forces on the national scene, with nearly all the political and social *events* that had serious meaning. Whenever people took realistic action, or thought realistically, about national events, they prepared themselves to share Orwell's and Levis's view of literature. But, in the atmosphere of the '20s, it took effort and time for these two men to win acceptance for their views, and indeed to win their own ways to those views. It still took time for Eric Blair to become George Orwell.

Eric Blair had come back from Burma on leave in 1927, and he refused to return, despite his father's disapproval.[23] (He was no closer to his father than the dandies were to theirs; indeed his relations with his family were very like theirs.) He had determined to become a writer, and he committed himself to enormous efforts to do so, living on and with his sister and passing long hours at the typewriter without remarkable results. Ruth Pitter, the poet, who was one of his literary consultants then, says that his writing was then only sub-Maugham prose and sub-Housman verse, and she was sure that he would never make a writer.

In 1928 he went to live in Paris (a traditional gesture for the aesthete writer since the days of George Moore and before). While he was there, between the spring of 1928 and the summer of the next year, he wrote two novels, never published, three stories, and about twelve articles. The novels, we can guess, were "aesthetic" to some degree, and if so almost certainly unsuccessful, for Eric Blair was temperamentally unqualified for such writing. But he also began to let himself down into the life of the lower social and economic levels, which had always fascinated him as the locus of failure; and when he returned to England he continued to do so, disguising himself as a tramp. In doing so, he gradually found his way to experiences and convictions that gave him something to write about—that is, he found his way to a non-dandy identity. For writing about such subjects, both the voice of the dandy and that of the old-fashioned humanist gentleman were inappropriate. It was the average adult man that Orwell became. (He did not seek his identity among the *Sonnenkind* alternatives to the dandy; he shows no interest in what attracted Lawrence so much.) And having found the appropriate voice, Orwell found more and more subjects to which it was appropriate, and sharper and sharper ways to reproach and repudiate those other two voices and the attitudes they implied. He gradually accepted the fact that he could not write modernist fiction, although in *Down and Out in Paris and London* there are episodes that employ those techniques. But other changes in the mood of the country—growing seriousness about Britain's position both nationally and internationally—gave him assurance that there were readers for what he had to say. Only a minority audience, of course, but that suited Orwell.

Among the major political-economic events of the period were the General Strike of 1926 and the Depression, which at its peak held 3,000,000 out of work in Britain—and none in Russia. During this period Communism and Russia began to exert a powerful fascination over British intellectuals. In 1931, George Bernard Shaw and Lady Astor paid a much-publicized visit to Russia, Sidney and Beatrice Webb went soon after, and all wrote about their experiences. Harold Laski's *Communism* came out in 1927, and Hugh McDiarmid's "First Hymn to Lenin" in 1931. The Fabian Society's research department, founded by H. G. Wells in 1912 and headed by Shaw until 1918, was mostly staffed by ex-Guild Socialists, and their sympathies were very much with Russia. The intellectuals began to turn to Russia en bloc. But the meaning of all this was barely visible to the literary eye in the 1920s.[24]

Orwell, for instance, entered the left-wing movement only gradually. *The Adelphi,* his first place of publication (he first appeared there in 1930), kept under its new editors the character John Middleton Murry had given it. It still conducted a quite "naïve" search for new guidelines in literature, politics, morals, and even religion. It was not revolutionary in the new Marxist style. And in literary terms, Orwell began by using some of the devices of old-fashioned aestheticism. But before long he had found his way to his own voice.

The other anti-dandy, F. R. Leavis, founded his critical quarterly, *Scrutiny,* in 1932. He too only gradually came into full command of his own voice, and he never entered the left-wing movement, although in sympathy with it. The equivalent of socialism for him was Lawrentianism—D. H. Lawrence's novels, his Demetrianism, his supreme genius. This fighting faith of Leavis's was to prove of immense value to the life of literature and culture in England, but he came by it gradually. In 1930 he wrote a pamphlet on Lawrence that followed T. S. Eliot's "classical" attitude to literature by recoiling from Lawrence's "romanticism." And in the opening issue of *Scrutiny* he declared that it was the artist, not the prophet in Lawrence who was important. But in the second issue, discussing the volume of Lawrence's letters just published, he called the letters "sane to the point of genius," and spoke of the healthy poise of Lawrence's intelligence and the rare talent for personal relations displayed in the letters. Soon he was recommending Lawrence at every opportunity in preference to Eliot as a life-exemplar.

This is of crucial importance to us because Leavis was to make Lawrence the most powerful criterion by which to judge and reprove the current literary scene in England. One of the major charges he brought against Eliot was that the latter would not fight against the cliques that ran the magazines and publishers' offices and literary columns in the papers. These cliques, which created reputations and determined rewards and punishments, were made up—though Leavis only implies this word—of dandies. Eliot in effect, passively allied himself with those cliques, and so Leavis became his enemy. And in that war Leavis made admirable use of Lawrence. He insisted that Lawrence's genius had been slighted in England and on the inaccessibility of his achievement to readers of dandy temperament. (In 1938, in *Enemies of Promise,* Cyril Connolly described Lawrence as one of those heroes of 1928 who ten years later were dead and seemed as if they had never been; another novel by Lawrence at that point would have been a nightmare.) And in defending Lawrence, Leavis gradually came into more and more of his vocation as the expounder of all that heritage of maturity and responsibility that modern literature and modern England had turned away from.

But the anti-dandiacal voices, the new Victorians, were to come into power later. At the end of the '20s they were only just beginning to be heard; and all across Europe, and America, their enemies seemed to be still in full flush of confident creativity.

During this period Diaghilev produced a ballet, *The Triumph of Neptune* in 1926, for which Lord Berners provided the music and Sacheverell Sitwell the story. This was one of the very few balletic collaborations between Diaghilev and Englishmen, and it is interesting to note its specifically English and Victorian kind of pantomime—the decor was taken from early Victorian prints. It was a taking up by Diaghilev of that Oxford camp-Victorianism that Acton and Byron had developed. The choreography, however, was by George Balanchine, who had joined the company less than two years before.

And the best part of Diaghilev's heritage was to be developed in a quite different direction. His ballet-master for the last period of his life, George Balanchine, was in many ways Diaghilev's true heir. Balanchine has said, "It is because of Diaghilev that I am whatever I am," and, like Stravinsky, he has several times declared (as late as the 1970s) how much he learned from Diaghilev and how important what he learned still is to him. At the same time, again like Stravinsky, Balanchine's own work expresses a much cooler, more modest, more consistently "classical" temperament than Diaghilev's. The composer and the choreographer have created, both in their independent and in their cooperative careers, more purely Apollonian bodies of work than Diaghilev did.

It was both a very representative and a highly symbolic work on which all three first cooperated—the *Apollon Musagete* of 1928. Working on this classic and Apollonian subject, Balanchine first achieved his classical style—it was "the turning point of my life," he has said. Both Stravinsky and Diaghilev helped him to achieve that and saluted it when the ballet was created. And *The Prodigal Son* of 1929 (Balanchine, Prokofiev, and Rouault) announced the return of the Diaghilev company to dramatic dancing and to the great subjects. Diaghilev was saying, "Assez de musiquette." Balanchine has said that he thinks he would have continued to be Diaghilev's ballet-master, instead of striking out independently, if the latter had lived. If so, the Diaghilev company might have become the great center of that modernist classicism that in historical fact has been the achievement of the New York City Ballet.[25]

Balanchine in choreography, Stravinsky in music, and Nabokov in fiction, each in his own way continued and transformed the tradition of Diaghilev. They followed the lead of taste, the boldest taste, wherever it led them—even into defiance of important *forms* of moral seriousness, but without becoming indifferent to the sources of life of that seriousness. They found their various ways through the modernist and aesthete maze, where the English artists lost their ways and retreated.

Brian's and Harold's Careers

Measured against such achievements, Harold Acton and Brian Howard were doing nothing. In 1930, Leonard Woolf commissioned Brian to edit an anthology of postwar poets, but it was never done. He did, however, become a reviewer for the *New Statesman;* and he began, typically, with insolently phrased enthusiasm for

Eliot's *Ash Wednesday* and a disparagement of more traditional verse, which involved him immediately in controversy with representatives of the past in poetry.

And both Children of the Sun did publish volumes of verse, at the Hours Press in Paris. Harold Acton's volume, which was called *This Chaos,* came out in 1930. It is chiefly remarkable for a series of auto-erotic poems about lying in his bath—"Narcissus to His Sponge," and so on. Brian's first and only volume, *God Save the King,* came out in 1931. The first poem, "Conversation," was a dialogue in which the other (unnamed) speaker was Harold Acton. Perhaps the most interesting of the poems was "She," about mothers:

> Across each Rhodes, besides each sea
> the maddened statue of maternity.
> The two smooth stones that are her eyes
> are not allowed to show surprise.
> She is the pelican that broke her breast
> to feed the treason in her nest.

The Hours Press was run by their old friend Nancy Cunard.[26] Both Brian and Harold seem to have been a little in love with Nancy, who was a muse to many of the young modernist artists of England and France. Born in 1896, she came out in 1914, and knew everybody in the world of the arts because her mother, Emerald, was a fashionable hostess, a close friend to Sir Thomas Beecham and to George Moore. Nancy was herself a poet, and was published in the Sitwells' *Wheels,* as well as inspiring other poets, like Robert Nichols. She was the model for figures of modern womanhood in novels by Michael Arlen, Aldous Huxley, and Evelyn Waugh. In all of these portraits she appears as a heartbreaker and more or less (depending on the novelist) heartbroken herself. Huxley had an affair with her in 1922 and was very badly treated, so in his portraits she is quite viciously cruel. And because he was *the* fashionable intellectual novelist of the '20s, she assumed great symbolic importance, as a modern Columbine. (Since Arlen's *The Green Hat* was an enormous popular success, as novel, play, and film, Nancy's image reached the nonintellectual public too.) When she went to live in Paris in the early 1920s, she inspired sculpture by Constantin Brancusi, paintings by Oskar Kokoschka, John Banting, and Eugene McCowan, drawings by Wyndham Lewis, and she was passionately admired by Louis Aragon and Tristan Tzara. She was the modern girl supreme, as Brian Howard declared in a newspaper article on the English girl. He did not depict Nancy as cruel; indeed, in his diary account of their relations, she appears rather as the one in love with him.

Before the war, Nancy had moved in the same set as Diana Cooper (then Manners). They were socialites intoxicated with the arts, and in particular with the ballet, who went to balls dressed as sylphides, Cossacks, swans, firebirds, or Siberian peasants. Their mothers were friends. Both were beautiful, brilliant, and heartbreakers—Columbine figures. They were rivals as girls, like Brian and Howard, and their postwar development into, in some ways, opposite types of women is parallel to the development of Brian and Harold away from each other. Nancy, and Brian, developed left-wing views, and a recklessly aggressive and self-destructive pattern of behavior. Diana, and Harold, became more conservative as time went by, more diplomatic and generally amiable, and more frankly part of a privileged class. The limitations of these changes, of this politicization, in both pairs are also comparable. Neither was as left-wing revolutionary, or as right-wing ambassadorial, as they seemed—neither really moved far from their dandy origins. Nancy at the Hours Press, for instance, published Louis Aragon, the surrealist, but the work was a translation of "The Hunting of the Snark"; Aragon was claiming Carroll for surrealism, but the poem is, after all, as dandy a piece of literature as any Nancy began by liking. Similarly, Evelyn Waugh used to read *The Wind in the Willows* aloud to Diana during her hours of rest while she was on tour in *The Miracle,* and she too remained basically apolitical.

But Nancy certainly rebelled against her mother and society, in political as well as aesthetic terms. After she took Henry Crowder as her lover, she published a pamphlet attacking her mother, called *Black Man and White Ladyship* (1931), and an anthology, almost an encyclopaedia of black culture, called *Negro* (1934). At the same time, she remained a close friend of both Norman Douglas and Harold Acton, neither of whom took Nancy's or any other left-wing politics seriously. And indeed her rebellion suggests personal and temperamental forces beneath and separate from its political language. The same was to be true of Brian Howard's.

Brian's path had begun to diverge significantly from Harold's, as a result of a new influence that he had come under. In 1927, when he had wanted to go to Greece with Robert Byron, his mother had forced him to go to Frankfurt instead to be psychoanalyzed by Dr. Hans Prinzhorn, who had been recommended to her by a friend, Sybil Bolitho. This Dr. Prinzhorn was an ally and principal lieutenant of Ludwig Klages, the Nietzschean, and so a spokesman for "Life" and "the Earth," who saw the problems of both individuals and humanity in terms of a struggle between Mind and Soul, in which the Soul needs every assistance from the Will. Prinzhorn edited the *Festschrift* for Klages' sixtieth birthday in 1932, and his own contribution was called "Gemeinschaft und Führertum" (Community and Leadership), and advanced a biocentric theory of society. It is an attack on individuality and leadership as ideas, an attack on Prometheanism. Every *Führertat,* act of leadership, is a crime against community, against the maternal *Wachstumkräfte,* powers of growth. In other words, Prinzhorn's was a philosophy cognate with that of D. H. Lawrence, and most difficult to accommodate to a temperament like Brian Howard's. Perhaps for this reason, once Brian had grasped it, this idea had a very powerful appeal to him. He wrote to his mother that Prinzhorn had taught him that

> nothing in this earth matters but the one necessity of getting into contact with Life. The Life that there is pulsing out of the Sun and the Mountains. The Life that is the rhythm behind the great money exchanges. The Life that animates great music. It is all we have on this earth. There is only that. Once one feels it, gets into it, devotes oneself to it—one is right, to a certain extent, whatever one does. Even if one happens to devote oneself to it by committing murders—almost.

Because one is doing. To do with the mind is nothing. To do
with the soul, *which is Life,* is everything. . . . Because man
thinks, gradually, more, and *lives,* gradually, less, do you see,
he becomes more and more of a tiny, separated, egotistical,
plotting creature, and less of a part of life? . . . Birkenhead
and modern Christianity and Cézanne and Daddy and Mr.
and Mrs. McGrath are *Geist.* Mind. They will go, when they
go, for good. You and I (hard, shrill, prejudiced, extravagant
ME,) are *Leben-Seele-*Life-Soul.

It is of interest that Dr. Prinzhorn's life companion had been Mary
Wigman, the dancer and choreographer, the founder of Absolute
Dance. She did no miming, and danced without music or with only
flute and percussion. Her work, both solo and group, was thematic—
the themes being Elegy, Motherhood, Landscape, and so on. Dance
for her was about man in relation to his environment, and to his fellow men. Her moods were somber—fate and sacrifice and death—
and she often used primitive masks. She kneeled, crouched, crept,
struggled and often ended the dance clutching Mother Earth. Quite
often her dances expressed phases of Motherhood or Womanhood.
Her most famous individual work was an antiwar pageant, *Totenmal,*
which she danced in Munich in 1930 and again in Berlin in 1936. The
latter performance, in defiance of the Nazis, lost her her state subsidy,
and in 1937 her group was disbanded. She had studied with Emile-
Jacques-Dalcroze and Rudolf von Laban, the anti-ballet dance masters, and appeared on her own in 1918. Her great success, outside Germany, was in America, the only other country without a ballet
tradition. Her work was an opposite to Diaghilev's, in everything
from the organization of the group of dancers to the use of music.
(Diaghilev said, in reference to her among others, that Germany had
learned how to move but had forgotten how to dance.) Clearly her
work was related to Isadora Duncan's; it may be said that both were
matriarchal, but Wigman's style was Demetrian to Duncan's Aphro-
diteanism, for Wigman added direction to Duncan's inspiration and
used the *limits* of the space in which she had to dance. She represented

the Motherhood of Mother Earth, and this was the kind of female strength that Brian Howard and the dandies never came to terms with, so it is appropriate that she should have been part of the Prinzhorn experience for Brian.

In 1927–28, then, we see the dandy intoxicated with a new philosophy, which demanded he build himself a new temperament. This new philosophy and temperament were still in service of the *Sonnenkind* cult, but profoundly different from those of the dandy—a difference like that between the temperament of the Apollo-worshiper and that of the Ares-worshiper among the cultists of the Olympian pantheon. In order to become a *life-worshiping* Child of the Sun, Brian would have to become a naïf. This is what Auden and Isherwood were soon to try to do, with somewhat more success than Brian Howard. They called the naïf the "pure-in-heart," as we shall see.

Brian was soon planning with Prinzhorn that they should write a joint novel about an Indian maharajah who tries to become an English gentleman. It was to be called *The Cow Jumped Over the Moon,* in which the cow would represent India, a maharajah, Nietzsche, and the élan vital, while the moon—dead planet—would represent England, the gentleman, Christianity, and materialism. Brian now read D. H. Lawrence enthusiastically, and on the party invitations for the Great Urban Dionysia of 1929, where he listed a number of items under *J'accuse* and *J'adore,* we find Lawrence, Intuition, Germany, Spengler, Yes, Love, and Nietzsche under *J'adore* (though also Cocteau and Diaghilev), and Intellect, No, Elgar, Belloc, Anglo-Catholicism, and Nationalism under *J'accuse.*

The Cow Jumped Over the Moon might remind us of the philosophy of Byron's *Essay on India,* and in fact Brian and Byron worked closely together for some months in this period (just before Byron's essay was written). They planned to produce together a volume called *Values,* or *Value,* which, if successful, might become an annual event. They thought Chapman and Hall, the Waugh publishing firm, might bring it out in a gift-book format. It was to propose that the idea of Value should take the central position that had been held by the idea of Truth, and that works of art should be categorized as not good or bad, but alive or dead. It was to be organized into five "conversations," in which Harold Acton, Cyril Connolly, Henry Green, Patrick Monkhouse, Peter Quennell, Tom Driberg, Timothy Coughlin, Evelyn Waugh, and William Acton—all of them old Oxonians and old friends—would discuss values of various kinds. Harold and Quennell were to discuss Values in Poetry, Waugh and Connolly, Values in Criticism, and so on. The volume was to be dedicated to T. E. Lawrence, as hero, and its doctrines might loosely be called cultural Fascism or Mosleyitism. More strictly they were Prinzhornism. Man is divided between Body-Soul and Mind; Mind has no existence save as a check and a means of expression; the Life-Force of the Body-Soul consists of the natural instincts and appetites, and intuition is, when strong enough, genius. It is all very far from the '90s, and it is no wonder that Brian wrote to a friend, "Harold no longer understands us. I foresee him passing out of our lives." *Values* was to be "the first concerted move on the part of our generation . . . carrying on the spirit of the *Candle* [six of the contributors were Old Etonians] . . . we are a collection of people full of talent, and it would be a pity not to do something of the sort. . . . " But the project failed.[27]

Harold Acton had gone back to Florence, deeply discouraged, and began to translate an unpublished document he found in a library there. It was a scandalous record of the scandalous life of Gian Castone, last Medici prince of Florence. Acton said he had from youth loved the Uffizi Gallery's portrait bust of Gian Castone, with its pouched eyes, heavy jowl, pursed blubbery lips, and portentous passivity. "As a piece of decoration it is superb: the wig alone is like a swollen sea; but as a bust of a human being it is gruesome. Decay has set in, and the maggots will soon be nibbling. . . ." Clearly this was to be no act of life-worship, but rather the opposite. Norman Douglas wrote an introduction when the translation appeared in 1930.

The subject Acton had chosen, like the Sitwells' King Bomba of Naples, was a Pulcinello historical grotesque. He, and they, were attracted to the back alleys of history. We might cite here a quotation

Acton himself makes from J. A. Symonds's remarks about Gozzi, the Venetian decadent, who also attracted him:

> . . . the decadence of Venetian society in a putrid mass of political corruption, Brummagem French philosophy aped by Italians with no revolutionary force inside them, prostitution, literary cabals, vain efforts to rehabilitate Dante in the city of Casanova, Baffo, and the Doge Renier, bad style, bad morals, effeminacy, hypocrisy, sloth, *doppocagine* of every sort . . . all this is so irrelevant to the main current of world-history, so bizarre, so involved in masses of petty details which have lost the accent of humanity, that I despair of making anything out of my work.

Perhaps Symonds was more ambivalent than he here admits—he had after all *chosen* this subject, chosen to translate Gozzi's *Memoirs;* but certainly Acton and the Sitwells were positively attracted by the features he here protests against, and by the atmosphere of a noisome back alley.

In 1932 appeared *The Last Medici,* Acton's historical account of Gian Castone and his immediate predecessors, the last and decadent Medici. It had furthered Acton's interest in Gian Castone to discover that despite the scandals of degeneracy surrounding him, he had been a patron of peace and learning. But in 1958, when the book was reprinted, Acton, in the preface, wrote,

> To be candid, I was fascinated by the prodigious pageantry as well as by the ferment of the fine arts of 17th century Italy . . . with all the enthusiasm of a neophyte I rallied to the still-disputed cause of the baroque. And I wished to produce a baroque piece of literature.

And in *Memoirs of an Aesthete* he says, "I hoped to raise a monument of baroque prose. . . . I detested the chirpy manner of most modern historians." Whatever new line Brian might pursue, Harold was still faithful to the Sitwells and the early '20s. Most readers, he tells us in 1958, had been shocked by *The Last Medici's* "moral detachment." Indeed, one of the book's major interests, and the source of most of its humor, is the desperate effort made by Gian Castone, his father Cosimo, and his uncle Francesco Maria to generate an heir—despite extremely distasteful wives. But Acton set no hope on this volume's recapturing for him the positions or the vocation he had lost, for in January 1932 he set sail for China. He felt he had been defeated in England and would be mocked.

The career competitiveness between the members of this group of friends seems to have been quite peculiarly keen and cruel—a fact that one can perhaps ascribe to their knowing each other so very intimately from school on, and also to their being dandies and not really believing in those other perspectives, those other values and commitments that introduce corridors of air and light between other competing friends.*Although not often mentioned, this is perhaps one of the worst—the most impoverishing—features of "decadence." Brian was very jealous of Waugh and Powell and Connolly, particularly after Waugh and Connolly started to portray him in their satirical pieces. He declared that Byron, Pryce-Jones, and Quennell were the real talents of the group. But there was as much malice to his friendliness as to his hostility, a fact that is caught in one anecdote that Harold Acton gives us. Quennell allegedly thought of himself as another Shelley and acted out the idea by, among other things, letting a lock of his hair fall carelessly across his brow. Brian one day said, "My dear, you can't think how démodé you look, with that tumbling jonquil. So greenery-yallery. It just isn't done these days. Where is your comb?" And although Quennell resisted the offer of Brian's help, he ever after combed his hair smoothly back, and gave up thinking of himself as a Romantic poet.

One of the sharpest phrasings of this competitiveness comes in Connolly's novel, *The Rock Pool* (1936). The hero reflects that all his friends seem like galley slaves, working desperately to get ahead, or like fossils, ossifying in various stages of snobbery.

---

* It was one of the achievements of Edmund Wilson's career that his ideological and historical enthusiasms did open such windows, did let fresh air and light into his emotional life. He did assimilate the modes of being of the world of men enough to escape—not for ever, but again and again—that cruel closeness of competition with his literary friends.

They all seemed to be playing a game of grandmother's steps, in which, whenever he looked round at them, they were somehow blandly and innocently nearer the social success which was their universal goal. And their vulgarity and pot-boiling, their rowdy charm, taking small liberties with each other to see if they could get away with them, calling each other "old" so-and-so, since "old" implied impotence . . . their implication that they could not afford to quarrel or make enemies, that all that kind of thing was rather silly, their mistaking of verbal twists for epigrams, of epigrams for wit; products of a system of education which had sent them out into the world with the opportune belief that there existed to every worthwhile experience a short-cut which, like the back way into their colleges, they alone knew how to take—and their smell of self-advancement, like the stench that rises from publishers' advertisements on Sunday mornings!

The people he is referring to might be Powell in his publisher's office, Tom Driberg in his gossip column, Connolly himself in his reviews, Robert Byron writing about Henry Green, Alan Pryce-Jones writing about Brian Howard, Cecil Beaton photographing Evelyn Waugh for his book of notables, Peter Quennell writing a text to accompany the photographs, and so on. These were the careers the new dandies had substituted for the army, the diplomatic corps, and the other professions into which their predecessors had gone. And the quarreling they said they could not afford was not with each other, but with outsiders in literary authority, those with literary patronage to dispense, like J. C. Squire and Arnold Bennett, Harold Nicolson, and Leonard Woolf.

This taste of group self-disgust is detectable also in Powell's *Afternoon Men* and is more vigorously rendered in Waugh's unfinished novel, *Work Suspended,* in which he describes himself and his group of friends in a much more realistic style than elsewhere. The central figure, John Plant, who clearly resembles Waugh, "deals with" his friends by means of tricks and plots and challenges and betrayals that seem to preclude any ordinary trust or warmth. They are mutually suspicious and malicious appraisers of each other's social manner, life-style, and ideology.

> There was little love, and less trust, between my friends. . . .
> Moreover we were bored; each knew the other so well that it
> was only by making our relationship into a kind of competi-
> tive parlour game that we kept it alive at all. . . .

Their one chance of purposeful cooperation had come in 1931, with Mosley's formation of his New Party. He had been a junior minister in Ramsay MacDonald's second Labour government, and had drawn up a scheme of public works and extended pensions to cure the unemployment of the Depression. When this was turned down by his minister, J. H. Thomas, in 1930, Mosley and five other M.P.s rebelled against the Labour party and four of the rebels joined Mosley's New Party, formed the following year. In October 1931 his publication *Action* began, with Harold Nicolson as editor; it called for discipline and dynamic order in the nation. Although it ran for only three months, Peter Quennell, Raymond Mortimer, Alan Pryce-Jones, Osbert Sitwell, John Strachey, Christopher Isherwood, and Francis Birrell, were among the contributors. The Sitwells held a giant rally for the party at Renishaw, and Mosley's close links with other branches of the *Sonnenkind* movement are symbolized by his later marriage to Diana Mitford.

Byronic, Napoleonic, Nietzschean, Mosley was certainly the nearest thing to a political leader that the British *Sonnenkinder* found, and his politics expressed their temperament, in its emphasis on athletics and fighting, and uniforms, military comradeship, contempt for squeamish liberalism and ineffectual intellectualism, rough practical jokes, the worship of young male heroes and nostalgia for a primitive past. This is what the intellectuals of the time were looking for, a young man's politics, and in many ways the appeal of Communism and its affiliated groups during the 1930s was very similar. It was the appeal of fresh faced young comrades marching together to smash the bastions of privilege, the banks and barracks of the old men. But for young intellectuals the ideological superstructure of Marxism, which surrounded and masked that appeal, was vastly more attractive than that of Fascism. And for non-intellectuals in England, unlike Germany and Italy, the style of the fathers still inspired confidence in politics, and Mosley's style was too different. Over a period of ten years (1922–1932) he was successively a Conservative, an Independent, a Liberal, a Socialist, a New Party man, and a Fascist. Very few intellectuals followed him into the British Union of Fascists; the equivalent there of John Strachey and Harold Nicolson was William Joyce, who later broadcast for the Nazis to England. Even his closest adherents had come to doubt him by 1932—to doubt at least his power to *seem* trustworthy to others.

A conservative consensus, an anti-imaginative consensus, seemed to have established itself in the country at the end of this period, and it can be symbolized in an entertainment event and a political event. In October 1931 Noel Coward produced *Cavalcade,* a nostalgic and sentimental celebration of "England" from 1899 to 1930, threaded on a string of popular songs, and built around a woman "like my own mother." Her final speech was a toast to "the hope that one day this country of ours which we love so much will find dignity and greatness and peace again." It had enormous matriarchal success—it made Evelyn Waugh's mother feel that "she was seeing the whole of her life passing before her eyes," as Alec Waugh tells us in *A Year to Remember*—and was run as a serial by the *Daily Mail.* It ended with a "decadent" nightclub blues, which was drowned out by a "God Save the King," in which the whole company joined. The royal family attended the second night.

Two weeks later a National government was elected, containing representatives of all the major parties in coalition. It commanded 554 votes out of the 615 in Parliament, which was the largest majority ever. Ramsay MacDonald, the Socialist, was premier until 1935, then Baldwin, the symbol of "England," and then Neville Chamberlain, from 1937 until he was replaced by Churchill during the war. Alec Waugh tells us that the feeling of national dedication and rebirth was very little less than it was to be after Dunkirk.* Against this massive consensus the various minorities were helpless, even though they comprised nearly all the country's intelligentsia, in one way or another. For instance, Oswald Mosley was driven out of regular politics, and his magazine *Action* discontinued publication that year, although during the summer Churchill had still been trying to enlist Mosley among his "tough Tories." And there were many other signs of reaction against twenties extremism and experiment—against *Sonnenkinder* styles. There was a consolidation of traditional temperaments, not at the level of the lively imagination, but in mere conservatism.

The thirties styles in dress were much more conservative, more manly and womanly, than those of the twenties—and less imaginative. Even the new ideologies propagated by revolutionaries like Auden and Isherwood were temperamentally conservative. The young men enthusiastic for Freud and Marx tended to wear corduroy trousers and beards and to present themselves as "workers." The fact that they were *Sonnenkinder* underneath did not appear immediately. They appeared to be, in imaginative terms, allies of "the average Englishman."

The consensus began to seem invincible to the twenties dandies. In at least one of its devices, the revival of "country" feeling, the dandies were gradually to participate themselves. (Not Acton or Howard, but Waugh and Byron; and this return to gentlemanly "Englishness" was another aspect of the fatal Sebastian-choice.) But country feeling was generally anti-dandy. J. W. Robertson founded *The Countryman* magazine in 1927, and S. L. Bensusan's books on the peace of Essex and A. G. Street's book, *Farmer's Glory* (1932), were very popular. And the Batsford series of illustrated books on the English heritage began about this time.

A popular *new* consensus author was J. B. Priestley, a friend of J. C.

---

* Alec Waugh ascribes the preceding mood of anxiety and depression to England's going off the gold standard in September 1931. "For me, as I suppose for most Britons born before 1910, the announcement on that Monday morning was the biggest shock that we had known or were to know. . . . 'Safe as the Rock of Gibraltar,' 'Safe as the Bank of England,' these had been the 'two main pillars vaulted high' that sustained our way of life."

Squire, Robert Lynd, Hilaire Belloc—the old guard. He published the very successful Dickensian novel, *The Good Companion,* in 1929. An incident of 1932 makes an interesting connection between him and the dandy writers. When Graham Greene had a success with *Stamboul Train,* which became a Book Society choice that year, Priestley threatened to sue because he thought he was the subject of the book's satirical portrait of a popular novelist. However popular the dandy novelists became, they never felt themselves to be "popular" in the degrading sense that fitted Priestley and Hugh Walpole.

But despite such portents as *Cavalcade* and J. B. Priestley, the world of the arts and entertainment at least still belonged to dandies; and, except among Auden, Isherwood and their friends, not even the naïf was yet an established cultural type, and Germany, its place of provenance, was still not fashionable. Most literary young men would probably have still agreed with Harold Acton's analysis in his *Memoirs:*

> Intellectually, Paris was the capital of the world, and the judgement of Paris was final. The *Entente Cordiale* in the fine arts had never been stronger. Bloomsbury was only an extension of Montparnasse, and its prophet Clive Bell wrote in a language that was nearer French than English
> .... Our standards were increasingly Gallic. In their exuberant moments, T. S. Eliot wrote French verse about "M. l'Editeur du Spectateur," Nancy Cunard about the Sitwells; ... Aldous Huxley was saturated by Laforgue ... the best of our younger critics, Raymond Mortimer, Francis Birrell, and Richard Aldington, were primarily concerned with the diffusion of French criteria in England.

The ballet had gone French, and Cocteau was acknowledged as a great arbiter of taste. "To my mind," Acton said, "Cocteau's line was often more expressive than Picasso's."

Acton's sense of any dissent from this on the part of his friends is not of anything substantial.

> Evelyn Waugh winced at the sound of a French word, and Robert Byron rolled a censorious Victorian eye when I spoke

of Cocteau. . . . "Come to Paddington!" wrote Robert. Paddington is the symbol of all that Bloomsbury is not. In place of the refined peace of those mausoleum streets, here are public houses, fun-fairs, buses, tubes, and vulgar posters.

Englishness of this kind is closely related to Betjeman's architectural nostalgia, and anti-cosmopolitanism of this kind is like Charles Ryder's rejection of Anthony Blanche in *Brideshead Revisited*. Waugh and Byron and Betjeman were still believers in the "European Mind." Acton is clearly not aware of a dissent from his Francophile much more powerful than theirs—a dissent so rooted in temperament that it could not enter into dialogue with his assertions. This is the mark of temperamental differences, that they make dialogue, even listening, almost impossible. That is why there is so much exasperation and so much bewilderment, so little mutual understanding, between the men of the dandy temperament and the opponents who were soon to attack them.

Chapter Seven

1932–1939:
Chinese Philosophy
and German Politics

Brian and Harold in the '30s

AS EVERYONE KNOWS, the 1930s was not a decade favorable to dandyism. In England and everywhere else the political situation and mood were both grim. Even in the literary life the old dandy style had to be abandoned. But this did not mean that the resistance led by Leavis and Orwell triumphed. The temperament that lay behind the old dandy style found itself a new style, superficially the opposite, and continued to flourish. Its underground presence was betrayed in the hypertrophied sense of humor and the humor-infected sensibility that still marked the new radicals, marked them off from their would-be comrades and brothers and united them with their would-be ideological enemies—united Auden and Isherwood, let's say, with Acton and Howard, and not with Harry Pollitt and Palme Dutt (the Communist party leaders). More time had to pass, a new generation had to come to flowering, before the temperament rooted in maturity and responsibility could displace that of "decadence." But at the time it seemed that an enormous change had occurred—and indeed it had, in non-literary parts of the culture.

During the 1930s, half of England came to feel that both its national and its international situation were matters for grave concern.[1] In Glasgow half the population was out of work in 1933. And the structure of the general consciousness shifted, as people became more aware that 74 percent of British families were working class, earning about £4 a week; 21 percent were middle class, earning about £4–10; and only 5 percent were upper class, earning more than £10. The dandies' sense of discrimination had operated almost exclusively within the 5 percent, separating the lively from the decaying there. Now a different kind of book was wanted. J. B. Priestley published *English Journey* in 1933, Walter Greenwood *Love on the Dole,* also in 1933, and George Orwell *The Road to Wigan Pier* in 1936, all accounts of poverty and deprivation and their causes.

There were hunger marches in 1932 and 1934, which had a big effect on opinion in the universities; Oxford undergraduates began to go to spend weekends in the Rhondda, among the unemployed Welsh miners, and to march with them in protests and demonstrations. In December 1931 an October Club was founded at Oxford, to study Communism; by January 1933 it had 300 members, and in October of that year it began a campaign against O.T.C.s. In 1934 this club gained control of the Oxford Labour Club and hung a giant picture of Lenin in the meetinghouse. In some ways at least, this was a very different Oxford from Brian's and Harold's. Even in 1929 a new seriousness had been detectable at the Union, so that when Osbert Lancaster came down to take part in a frivolous debate about duelling, it was interrupted in favor of a serious discussion of unemployment. This was the seriousness that made the Union so inhospitable to Randolph Churchill.

Nineteen thirty-six was the crucial year of the decade, from our point of view, because it was the year of the start of the Spanish Civil

War, of the Jarrow March of the unemployed to London, of Virginia Woolf writing for the *Daily Worker,* and of the birth of the Left Book Club, which sent its members a left-wing book every month for 2s.6d. The last soon had a membership of 60,000. Beside the Left, there grew up a Right and a Liberal Book Club, and there was already a Book Society, which propagated the consensus "Baldwin" taste (its committee included George Gordon, Hugh Walpole, Edmund Blunden, and Clemence Dane)—but none of these others had anything like the success of the Left. In addition to the books, the organization sent out *Left News* and held weekend seminars, Russian language courses, and many special groups and centers; the Poetry Group published a magazine with a circulation of 1,000; and the Musicians' Group organized musical pageants, in which choral groups sang a Marxist interpretation of English history. Victor Gollancz, the publisher, organized the club; he asked John Strachey and Harold Laski to help him choose the books, and offered Brian Howard a job too.

And there were many other left-oriented groups of artists and intellectuals; the Artists' International, founded in 1933; the Writers' International, founded the same year; and more than one drama group. John Grierson's film unit, at first serving the Empire Marketing Board and then the General Post Office, made documentaries that celebrated man working (with considerable social and political criticism), on some of which Auden, Benjamin Britten, and Robert Medley worked. And in the *Spectator* Anthony Blunt's art criticism was frankly left-wing in its tendencies.

In their early years many of these organizations served Russian Communist policy fairly openly and directly, but between 1935 and 1938 they modified their organization and their ideology, to suit the policy of creating a Popular Front, which would unite large numbers against fascism. This policy was reflected in the composition of the Communist party itself. In 1930 the British Communist party had only 1,300 members, but in 1938 it had 15,500; and its Agitprop department set up a supervisory section in 1935, run by Emile Burns and Ralph Fox, which was very tolerant of individual experiments and even controversy. And the thirties mood was not only a matter of direct political conviction. 1937 was the founding year of Mass Observation, an organization for the study of popular culture. It was founded by Charles Madge, Humphrey Jennings, and Tom Harrisson, and soon had 1,300 observers, who all sent in reports regularly on every kind of social phenomenon, reports that were then collated to form an objective document. Among their most striking publications was *May 12,* about Coronation Day, in 1937, when George VI was crowned, and the Oxford Collective Poem, written by twelve undergraduates collectively. All these institutions seemed to bear witness to a stiffening of the moral fiber of the intellectual life in England, a new social responsibility and a new aesthetic realism, far from the dandy frivolities and fantasies of the '20s. They corresponded to the changed general sense of a national crisis.

The persistence of massive unemployment and the decline of major industries on the one hand, the rise to power of Nazi Germany and the stabilization of Soviet Russia on the other, made the British status quo seem to some insecure and to others not worth securing. And this coincided with a disillusionment about the possibilities of dandy defiance within the arts; the brilliance of Harold Acton and Brian Howard now seemed to have been false, and the success of Evelyn Waugh's fiction or Edith Sitwell's poetry was not of the kind on which a major literature could be based. No one was exploring the possibilities of the dandy imagination for England the way Nabokov was doing for Russia. Other dandies *were* being successful—Cecil Beaton, Oliver Messel, Noel Coward—but their success was minor where it wasn't trivial. And finally, although perhaps most significantly, the iconography of the *commedia* was worn out. Pierrot and Harlequin, and the range of feelings associated with them, had come to evoke feelings of how much they had already been used, of things completed and unrepeatable. (The iconography of the new movement was to be political—tractors, shutdown factories, the Red Flag—an iconography of the world of men.)

So for these and other reasons a new group of writers came to prominence in England, professing a new ideology, asserting a new tone, and claiming a new temperament, almost the reverse of the dandies'. It will be our argument that this reversal was more apparent than real—that the new writers too were Children of the Sun, devotees of Narcissus and Adonis. They were not really comrades or party members, they never intended—at the level of temperamental sincerity—to serve the great patriarchal enterprise they spoke of. They were naïfs, who saw themselves as forever about to commit themselves, forever being converted and repudiating the false gods that had enslaved them and their fathers. Indeed, time was to show that many were even as much dandies as naïfs.

And although their failure (understandable and honorable as it was) could not invalidate the rest of the country's efforts to achieve "manhood," still, because they were the voices of their time, that failure did become a liability for the age. We shall note several times how an individual artist's dandyism assumes the importance of a cultural symptom even when it might seem more "fair" to call it a purely personal aberration. This is particularly true in retrospective diagnosis. The artist writes the record, and future readers find in what he has written not just what he intended to write, but the "true" history of his times. This is often quite unlike the "actual" history of the statistics of institutions and mass movements; the "true" history of Auden's poetry, for instance, is quite unlike the "actual" history recorded in, say, the records of the Left Book Club. For our purposes, the purposes of imaginative history, the former is the more important, although we keep an eye on the latter.

But still, an important reversal of intention did establish itself. Of our two principals, only one accommodated himself to it. Brian Howard, like several of his dandy friends, took on new interests and new convictions, a new seriousness and openness of tone, "went Left." Harold Acton, like Waugh and the Sitwells, stayed a dandy of the Right. He might fairly claim to have been not so much right-wing as apolitical; he might fairly accuse Brian Howard of being equally apolitical, at the level of authentic temperament; but at the level of behavior—and effective behavior—Brian became actively of the Left, while Harold stayed passively on the Right. Because of this, and because he spent these years in China, Acton is a less representative figure, less relevant to our general concerns during the period, and we shall deal with him briefly and preliminarily. His action as a whole in going to China is profoundly relevant to our theme, but the detail of just how he spent those seven years is not.

It was by an act of generosity of his American uncle, Guy Mitchell, that Acton could leave Florence in January 1932 for America and China. He had long wanted to go to China in order to achieve personal integration. He had felt that if he did not make some such effort, he would remain "an unbaked mould." He had been finding that he suffered from "treacherous moods" at home. And in Peking he in fact felt in harmony with the atmosphere. "I belonged to myself again." On the way he visited American dandies like Carl van Vechten and Muriel Draper—often seen in Florence before the war—and nineties' institutions like Mrs. Gardner's Fenway Court villa in Boston. He visited various Mitchell cousins, including the very rich Dillinghams, citizen-rulers of Honolulu, and slowly made his way through Indochina to China. He found Peking very like Florence in its expatriate society, and was determined to get deeper into "China" than that. He bought a Chinese house, adopted Chinese clothes and customs, and cultivated Chinese thoughts.

On the whole it seems that he succeeded in his enterprise—that he changed his social temperament in the direction of more general amiability, courtliness, scholarliness, away from the insolent panache and overweening ambition of his earlier years. It seems that he learned how to disperse dangerous concentrations of anger and desire, how to cultivate diffuseness and distraction of interests. We might take Osbert Sitwell's summary of the "Chinese" temperament, which stressed its subordination of will and purpose, as indicating what it meant to Harold Acton.

> The essential oneness and harmony of man with the universe is a sentiment which permeates much of the greatest Chinese art and poetry, for in the Chinese, as in perhaps no

other people, has been developed a keen consciousness of the rhythms of nature, the rotation of the seasons. This subordination of man's will has prevented China from achieving a science. *(Escape with Me,* London, 1939)

Sitwell came out to China while Acton was there, and stayed with him in Peking. For him too the idea of "China" and of "Chinese culture" had long been an important and attractive part of his cultural geography; "Chinese sensuality," for instance, means to him something especially innocent, merry, and (one suspects) infantile in the way of sensuality. Sitwell was to become more and more of a model to Acton, and indeed they were not dissimilar men.

One can also get some clue to Acton's "China" from Harriet Monroe, who visited him there in 1935. In *Poetry,* April 1935, she describes this China in terms of buildings. The Temple of Heaven in the Forbidden City is one of the masterpieces of the world, but its circular marble altar is open to the sun and stars and rises less than twenty feet above the park, although mounted on three marble terraces. There are three marble rings of balustrades, one carved with the dragon of the earth, one with the phoenix of the air, and one with the cloud-forms of the sky, but there is no image of God; "as though, beyond this triple marble circle, beyond the square wall tipped with blue and the round wall tipped with green, beyond the battlemented Tartar Wall, and the far-away Chinese Wall, lay the vast acres of immortal life." Something of this openness, this lack of walls and gods and duties, this sense of space and fluidity and quiet, one imagines Harold Acton absorbing and cultivating.

His novel about China, *Peonies and Ponies,* (1941) which describes the expatriate society, is full of malicious satire in the old style—as his subsequent fiction also has been; but that seems to be because the writing of fiction, the action of writing as a whole, does not work from the "Chinese" center in him. At least not from any sense of spiritual peace. But other aspects of his life seem to show that he did successfully cultivate such a center, and for that reason has survived into the '70s with considerably more serenity than most of his contemporaries.

He of course began to study Chinese history and to collect objects of Chinese art, and one of the subjects that most engaged him was Chinese theater. He was fascinated by the importance of female impersonators in that theater. Mei Lan-fang, he tells us, was the Sarah Bernhardt of China, and he applies to him Francisque Sarcey's words about her, "She whose movements are disciplined, she who is a living harmony, a lyric in flesh and blood." Moreover, Chinese theater is a combination of ballet and opera and the *commedia,* of everything that is best in theater, although Acton saw a deplorable Western influence toward realism becoming paramount while he was there. But in the classical Chinese theater, art triumphs over nature far more brilliantly than in Western drama. It was that highly formal and elegant synthesis of all the arts that he had been seeking—what the ballet only approached. He delighted in the actors' falsetto singing, which he compared with that of Farinelli, the 18th-century castrato, a favorite subject of the Sitwells. And the art of the female impersonator he called "a genuine triumph of art over nature." In other words, he found in that theater a further development of Diaghilev's work.

Harold Acton remained in China until 1939, with the exception of one brief visit to Florence in 1936, where he saw much of Norman Douglas with great pleasure, but otherwise felt no desire to return to Italy permanently. It seems likely that he could have lived contentedly in China for the rest of his days (but for its conquest by Japan) and that he could have successfully cultivated the role he had assigned himself of intermediary between Chinese and Western cultures. He saw himself as an ambassador of culture. But because of international politics he had to leave, to sacrifice his home and his "things" (he compares himself in his *Memoirs* with Mrs. Gereth in James's "The Spoils of Poynton") and to return to London—where he lived first in Robert Byron's rooms—to await the outbreak of war with Germany.

Meanwhile Brian Howard had made friends in Germany in 1931 with Klaus Mann (a friend of Dr. Prinzhorn's), then with Erika Mann and the whole Mann family. He was still intoxicated with Prinzhorn's ideas, and reading Nietzsche and Lawrence. The journal he kept in

Obergurgl, in the Tirol, in 1931 reads very like both of those authors. He was in fact planning a long poem, to be called a *Song of Zarathustra;* and his analysis of his relations with his lover of the moment is written in terms that recall the last scenes of *Women in Love.* He uses vivid snow and ice imagery for the states of their souls, and one reads such resolutions as, "I will apply *every* energy to simple, soft, interior, personal *growth.* I *will let all else go.* . . . I want him to come out to me spiritually, and come out with me occasionally, to eat together the beauty of the place." About writing he declares that technique is nothing, attitude everything—all one needs is to see honestly, and that he resolves to do. But for someone like Brian there was very little chance of keeping such resolutions. He was visited in Obergurgl by Nancy Cunard and her black lover, Henry Crowder, and the relations between them all grew very complicated (Brian believed Nancy loved him) and the behavior very wild and destructive. Brian had really no resources for living the new life that his creed prescribed. He was bound to seek a way to resume his old life with greater ideological dynamism, and he found that way.

Erika Mann was then master of ceremonies of the Peppermill satirical cabaret in Munich, which she later took to other cities in Europe and finally to America. She was a brilliant figure of modern womanhood—actress, journalist, racing car driver, theatrical producer, and an anti-Nazi. The whole Mann family was much involved in German politics, and they taught Brian about the Nazis. Erika, who was like Nancy Cunard much attracted to Brian, described him as the first Englishman to recognize the full immensity of the Nazi peril and to foresee, with shuddering horror, what was to come. Brian said it was a politically ignorant remark he made at the Mann dinner table, or the fact that everyone found it so shocking, that led him to investigate politics. He immediately became an ardent left-winger. "The whole capitalist system is beginning its death-throes," he wrote in a letter to his mother. "It has been admitted for years now that Church, State, and Finance are spiritual shams. But the thing is that they're material shams too. . . . Russia is the one beacon of progress." He also told her that Hitler's voice on the radio sounded like his father's in a rage.

Holding these convictions, he had a topical point of view to offer in his writings, and he became a prolific contributor to the *New States-man,* writing over seventy quite long pieces for it between 1930 and 1947 (beside several for the *News Chronicle,* under assumed names, and a play for the BBC), the majority of which dealt specifically with the Nazi threat. For instance, he had a revealing interview with Hit-ler's friend, Ernst Hanfstaengl, which he reported for the *New States-man* in 1933, and he should have had an interview with Hitler himself, except that at the last minute Unity Mitford, who had arranged it, refused to present him. His articles were sufficiently committed and knowledgeable for the German embassy in London to serve notice on him not to return to Germany unless he changed his attitude.

Brian thus illustrates quite vividly the temperamental paradox of the '30s, and the penetration of even the principal organs of the new ideas by representatives of the old temperament. When Brian Howard was to be found in the *New Statesman* and the Left Book Club, when the message of anti-fascism was delivered in Brian Howard's voice, an unre-ality pervaded the politics. For within the Carlylean prophet of war and revolution, the old Brian lived. When Cyril Connolly and his wife, Jean, met him in Athens in the summer of 1932, they found him "for-midable and fascinating," in the old destructive dandy style. Connolly compared him with Brummell in exile at Calais. He says, "Both Jean and I were rather infatuated with Brian," and speaks of his looking deli-ciously handsome and distinguished, and playing his voice like a guitar; also of his dressing up as Madame Sosostris, and playing dangerous and cruel practical jokes. Another anecdote of this period is of an escapade in Paris. Brian woke up in a male brothel to find all his clothes stolen; he could not even beg the money for a telephone call for help, so he borrowed a maid's frilly apron and wore that in front of his nudity as he made his way to the Café des Deux Magots. (He never returned the apron, saying, "I cannot remember in which of these silly little streets is that *maison de passe,* and anyway, my dear, I *like* having a souvenir so *very* inappropriate to that night's adventure.") To everyone who knew him, Brian continued to be an archetype of "decadence."

Even his *New Statesman* reviews reveal clearly enough the dandy substratum to his criticism of British capitalism. When he welcomes a week full of "seditious" novels—and exults in the fact that all contemporary fiction makes the same "seditious" assumptions—one sees the *New Statesman* writer at whom Orwell aimed so much of his anger. Orwell had after all known Brian Howard at Eton, and some of his phrases, like "shrieking little poseurs," refer themselves very vividly to that target. Orwell too was finding a message and a role in the political exigencies of the times. But he was taking the opportunity to rebuild a temperament also, which Brian Howard could not do; so Orwell became an authentic Socialist, and Brian Howard did not. And because *Brian* was the one who wrote for the *New Statesman* and such periodicals, the very institutions and careers of anti-fascism in England were tainted with unreality. Orwell and Leavis saw and felt this immediately, other people more gradually.

Orwell went to Spain in 1936, and Brian did not. But that is not the crux of the difference. Auden also went to Spain, but his poem about it could, as Julian Symons points out, have been written by someone who had not gone.[2] It is a fine poem, but not fine in the manner of *Homage to Catalonia,* which *does* derive from Orwell's having gone. Brian Howard's poem about Spain, which is not bad, is also Audenesque, for he and Auden were close friends then. And both were sincerely left-wing about Spain. But neither was building the sort of temperament that the experience of Spain and the war could nurture—as they did nurture Orwell's temperament.*

---

* The contrast between Orwell and Howard was in some sense typical and must remind us of the general contrast between Englishmen before 1914 and Englishmen after. Using the imaginative terms of Conrad's *Nostromo,* one of the fullest celebrations of the pre-1914 Englishman in fiction, one might say that Orwell adapted his new socialist ideas to the old English-temperament tradition of Charles Gould, the ascetic and idealistic mine-manager of Conrad's novel, while Brian's style was more that of Colonel Sotillo, the mountebank insurrectionist. To make their ideology effective, the English Socialists of the '30s should have cultivated Gould's and Orwell's acute sense of manly responsibility; but temperamentally they were—insofar as they were represented

In 1934, Brian spent the summer in Bavaria again, seeing the Manns and writing articles about the concentration camps. Later he shared the Amsterdam pension of Christopher Isherwood, where Klaus Mann also lived and edited his anti-Nazi magazine, *Die Sammlung.* It seems to have been there that Brian first took cocaine as well as opium. He saw Auden off, when the latter left Paris for Spain, to be an ambulance driver. The summer of 1936 Brian spent near Salzburg again. He helped Nancy Cunard, in June 1937, to put out her appeal to the poets of the world to help the anti-Franco forces in Spain. His poem about Spain appeared in the sixth in her series of leaflets and was reprinted in *Poems for Spain* in 1939, edited by John Lehmann and Stephen Spender.

He lived with Auden while the latter taught at Colwall, the Quaker school near Malvern. Together they planned to write a book to be called *The Divorce of Heaven and Hell,* a treatise on the intellectual symptoms and dangers of authoritarianism, with examples from modern popular reading. There were to be studies of Housman (the treasonable highbrow), Ruby M. Ayres (the popular women's novelist), Henry Williamson (the "fascist" nature writer), and John Buchan (or perhaps P. C. Wren, the creator of Beau Geste, or "Sapper," the creator of Bulldog Drummond.) The idea was to expose all of these as dangerously fascist influences. In the case of Buchan, the studies would probe into his ideas of good and evil, and reveal that his stories' villains are all dark intellectuals and their heroes vicious models to imitate. There were to be some "Mass Observation" accounts of these books as wish-fulfillments, by means of interviews with large numbers of their readers. The publisher Robert Hale was interested in the book, but it was never written.

In 1937 in Salzburg, Brian also became great friends with Guy Burgess, who was in many ways of a very similar temperament. The two alternately attacked and admired each other. But as it became clear that war was impending, for England too, Brian had to consider his

---

by Brian—so many Sotillos, hectically flamboyant and febrile poseurs. England had changed, and even the serious ideas had passed into the hands of "Latin dandy" types.

own course of action. He joined the Independent Labour party when it declared against war in 1938, and told Nancy Cunard that he would run away if it came to war. He agreed, he said, with Aldous Huxley (the leading pacifist then) that the things that matter can not be defended, or imposed, by means of force. He decided that he would go to America if war broke out. But when it happened, he was living in France, and his German boy friend was put into an internment camp in Toulon. Brian went to great lengths to get him released, but finally had to leave France himself when the Germans advanced on Paris.

Men of the '30s

One of the books that Brian reviewed early in his career with the *New Statesman* was John Strachey's *The Coming Struggle for Power* of 1932. This book spread the ideas of *struggle* and *power,* two concepts that meant much more to the intellectuals of the 1930s than to those of the '20s. Strachey praised Nietzsche because Nietzsche had recommended violence, and condemned Wells and Shaw, as well as Proust, Eliot, and Joyce, for not being really committed to communism. Strachey's book is generally considered to have had more effect than any other in causing the large-scale swing to the left of the English intelligentsia in the '30s. His political books in general sold in large numbers and were very influential. His *Theory and Practice of Socialism,* for instance, sold 40,000 copies in its Left Book Club edition alone, and his *Why You Should Be a Socialist* sold 300,000 in a week in 1938. At the same time he was enough in sympathy with the older dandyism to recommend Evelyn Waugh, even in *The Coming Struggle,* as the most accurate and most insightful of all historians of modern England. It is therefore of interest to see the ways and the degrees in which Strachey conforms to the pattern we have been drawing.

His father, St. Loe Strachey, was editor of the *Spectator* from 1878 to 1925, and a leading patriotic and moral Liberal journalist.[3] He was an ebullient and dominantly "masculine" character, a friend of Theodore Roosevelt. It was he who raised a scandal over the moral tone of Wells' emancipated-woman novel, *Ann Veronica,* and he quarrelled with his cousin Lytton Strachey in 1917 over the treatment the latter gave in *Eminent Victorians* to the colonial administrator, Lord Cromer. Cromer, one of the 19th-century fathers debunked by Bloomsbury, was in fact John Strachey's godfather and namesake. St. Loe Strachey was then a vigorous representative of pre-1914 England. But he was forty-one when his son John was born in 1901, and they were never close to each other. An older son, born in 1889, died in 1907, and John received his crucial early affection from his nurse and his older sister, Amabel.

John went to Eton and was unhappy there. He afterwards said that he became a Communist because he had failed to get onto the Eton cricket XI and he seriously believed that his chance on the team had been denied him because of his unconventionality and unpopularity. He was always extremely keen on playing and winning games (he is cited by Stephen Potter in *Gamesmanship),* so his remark need not be taken as entirely a joke. He was another public school rebel against the public school system.

Moreover, while at Oxford (1920–1923), he was apparently a bit of a dandy and an aesthete himself. He wrote poetry, played cricket in a ribboned woman's hat, and breakfasted at noon on chocolate cake and crème de menthe. He wrote to his friend, John Rothenstein, "We have got to give up this 90-ish way in which we have been living." We even find him described as a Beardsley character—as looking like the drawing of the fop in *Under the Hill*—in one of Carrington's letters to Lytton Strachey. Even later, to many people he seemed to be an effete Oxford aesthete, of a pre-Harold Acton vintage. He kept all his life the thin, high Bloomsbury voice associated with his friends Lord David Cecil and Edward Sackville-West, and some of those verbal mannerisms; thus, in a letter, "My dear, the measles is too bad. I know it can be a simply vile disease." During his period of being infatuated with Proust, he identified himself with Odette, and his girl-friend with Swann. And perhaps the most emblematic detail of all is that during those years, and as late as 1929, his name was Evelyn. He changed his name to John later, after he went into politics.

In his Oxford days he was a conservative politically, and belonged to the Carlton Club. He was and remained a close friend of Robert Boothby, always a staunch Conservative, and of Elizabeth Ponsonby, one of the "bright young people" and a putative model for Waugh's character, Agatha Runcible (in *Decline and Fall*). Later he was one of Nancy Cunard's admirers and one of her circle.

Nevertheless, these dandy traits are not to be called the "real" John Strachey, on which the man of socialist convictions was superimposed—not even in the highly qualified sense in which that could be said of Brian Howard. Strachey seems to have been a true naïf, an always potential personality, never fully actualized, always in subjection to some idea outside himself. Oswald Mosley said that Strachey belonged to Freud from the neck down, to Marx from the neck up, and nowhere to John Strachey. And his sister Amabel wrote to the Frenchwoman with whom he had an affair in the early '20s,

> His head is extremely mature but, in his affections, he still has, at bottom, all the self-protecting coldness which lies under the enthusiasms of adolescence. He won't have a heart for years yet, I expect. . . . He has grown up very irregularly.

These traits add up to a very familiar syndrome, often labeled "the intellectual." The type was often portrayed in novels of the period by Aldous Huxley, who himself exemplified it to other people's minds, both in physique and in spirit. It is the type Orwell often castigates, as having lost touch with common experience, and often deplores, as dominating the general public's image of Socialism. The "intellectual" is thus one of the Children of the Sun, in revolt against both father and mother qualities, but he is seen from an unsympathetic point of view. I shall continue to subsume this type in the naïf category.

For seven years Strachey was a disciple and follower of Oswald Mosley, who seems to have dominated him, as he did so many others. Strachey expounded Mosley's plan for national development in 1925,

Revolution by Reason (Mosley published a paper of the same title in the same year) and dedicated it to "O.M., who may some day do the things of which we dream." He was Mosley's intellectual aide, as Harold Nicolson was his diplomatic aide—Nicolson brought into Mosley's orbit Peter Howard, rugby-football captain of Oxford and then of England. Through him quite a band of university hearties joined the New Party. (Nicolson wrote in his diary of October 19, 1930: "I find myself having day-dreams of power and youth," and the homoerotic element in his attraction to Mosley's politics is perceptible in others, too.) But there were limits to these men's desire to be dominated, and to see others dominated, limits which Mosley was crossing.

When Strachey left the New party in 1931, Osbert Sitwell wrote, "Those who know Mr. Strachey are aware that his spiritual home is in Moscow rather than in London." But in fact Mosley's own thought, as much as Strachey's, drew heavily on the Marxist analysis of social problems. What made his policies fascist was his reliance on personal leadership and personal bravura as a solution to these problems, the stress on youth and fieriness, and the implicit continuance of the country squire's hostility to the industrial city. (The Mosley family had a long standing quarrel with Manchester and its Jewish businessmen.) What Strachey rebelled against was Mosley's increasing dominance as a personality.

Strachey apprenticed himself to Palme Dutt and the Communist party in Great Britain from the moment that he left Mosley and the New Party. This immediacy and totality of commitment was characteristic of him. With the switch came a switch in wives. In 1929 he had married a dandy wife; she was the sister to Gerald Murphy, the man Fitzgerald had portrayed as Dick Diver in *Tender is the Night,* and she belonged to another such set of rich expatriate Americans in France. She was also clever, dominant, ugly, and lesbian. This made an unhappy, although brilliant, marriage for Strachey, and it could not survive his change of political allegiance. In 1931 he left Esther Murphy for Celia Simpson, an English vicar's daughter and a committed socialist, who soon became a Communist party member—

something Strachey himself never did. (A German Communist friend described Celia as "the better man of the two.") After their marriage, both underwent a three-year-long psychoanalysis. Strachey was accepting all the disciplines of Reality, and of manhood. He had children, led a respectable family life, and put his son down for Eton. But he remained always only an apprentice to manhood, in the eyes of, for instance, his Communist party bosses. They seem to have taken always a very tough line with him, talking as realized men (normal, hard-working, serious men) to an unrealized man. They took this line with Philip Toynbee too, and with Stephen Spender, at least judging by the latter's account of his relations with Harry Pollitt in *The God that Failed,* the 1930 collection of essays by ex-converts to Communism. R. H. S. Crossman, the editor of that collection, says that the Communist party leaders not only resented and suspected their intellectual converts, but deliberately oppressed them. This would fit our sense that the party had a temperament as well as an ideology, and that it was one alien to its *Sonnenkind* converts.* (A similar hostility in their dealings with intellectuals is attributed to party leaders in *The Golden Notebook.*) And indeed it happened that the moment Strachey lost his faith in the party, he reverted to a Bohemian-decadent style of life, giving up patriarchal manliness.

There were many striking cases in the '30s of rebellion against the public school ethos, in the name of Socialism but in the spirit of that ethos itself. One central figure is Esmond Romilly, nephew of Winston Churchill.[4] His father was a colonel in the Guards, and he and his brother Giles were sent to Seacliffe prep school, which was all Scouts, Sunday walks, and the reading of John Buchan, Rider Haggard, and bound volumes of Punch. In 1930 they were sent to Wellington, a public school with strong military traditions. Giles rebelled by stealing, by masturbating, and by resigning from the O.T.C., after a long struggle with the authorities to get the right to do so. Esmond,

---

* In Alan Pryce-Jones' novel, *Pink Danube,* the hero runs over all the career advantages he would derive, as a writer, from becoming a Communist, but decides against it because party men are "punctilious in a narrow space . . . good solid infantry men of the class war . . . who despise the liberal worm"—and he seems to have been right.

the younger, was the dominant brother. He was rougher and tougher than Giles or anyone else, and gloried in being so. In their joint autobiographical volume (Esmond was under twenty when he wrote his share of it), he often describes himself as having been, at some point or other, "furious," "enraged," or "violently incensed," or having just had a ten-hour quarrel with his mother. He also often claims to have cheated his antagonist, who may well be also his friend, and to be intensely competitive. "I, myself, am always prepared to argue for the sake of arguing." In other words he was—and the testimony of his friends supports his own account—a pure example of the rogue.

Like his cousin Randolph Churchill, he was very conscious of the successes of his rogue uncle, Winston, and for a long time he had also a great admiration for Mosley. But in 1933 he got interested in Communism, and wrote articles attacking the O.T.C., in the *Student Vanguard* magazine for public schoolboys. (A Scotland Yard official wrote to the headmaster of Wellington, warning him about these articles.) Esmond also sent in to the organization *The Friends of the Soviet Union,* the names of some of the Wellington masters, as people wanting to receive Soviet propaganda. In 1934, when he was sixteen, he ran away from school, and hid from police and family in a room above a left-wing bookshop in Bloomsbury. From there he edited and published a magazine for rebellious public schoolboys, called *Out of Bounds,* the public school journal against Fascism, Militarism, and Reaction. It was fifty pages long, and its circulation varied between 1,000 and 3,000. It sold best at Eton. News of these doings brought *Daily Express* and *Sunday Graphic* publicity to Wellington, and there were articles on "The Red Menace" in the *Daily Mail.* Esmond was interviewed secretly by the press, visited other schools to propagandize them, confronted recalcitrant headmasters, and so on.

Philip Toynbee, son of Arnold Toynbee, grandson of Gilbert Murray, ran away from Rugby to join the Out of Bounds movement, and was, by his own account, dominated by Esmond from the moment they met, even though Esmond was a year younger. Esmond told Toynbee to smoke Craven A cigarettes, for instance, and several years

later the latter noticed that he had never tried anything else. Expelled
from Rugby for his rebellion, Toynbee was sent to Ampleforth and
then to Oxford, where he became the first Communist president of
the Union in 1938. Esmond, on the other hand, was sent to a remand
home, and then to the experimental school Bedales, but refused to go
to a university. He went to Spain to report the Civil War, and while
there got involved in perhaps the most typifying of his exploits. He
encouraged a homosexual M.P.—there on a fact-finding mission—to
make sexual advances to him, and then blackmailed him into promising to speak for the Loyalist cause in England, on pain of public exposure. (Toynbee emphasizes how manipulative Esmond was, and says
"I was Verlaine to his Rimbaud." The Rimbaud model was important
to all the *Sonnenkinder*.) When Esmond returned from Spain to England, he met Jessica Mitford, a distant cousin, and eloped with her. He
was then seventeen, she eighteen.

Jessica was the younger sister of the Nazi Unity and the Fascist
Diana (Lady Mosley), but she was in rebellion against her family and
class. It was, of course, a rebellion as much in the *spirit* of her own
class as Esmond's own. Toynbee tells of hearing her ask a Birmingham
workingman,* "Could you be absolutely sweet and tell us where we
could get some delicious tea?"—"in the curiously cadenced singsong
of her world and family." She and Esmond ran away together to Spain,
were pursued by Nancy and Peter Rodd in a British destroyer, and
married in France. Esmond was, his wife says, part adventurer, part bad
boy, beneath his political convictions and commitments. He invented
a gambling system to make their fortune, borrowed friends' cars and
abandoned them, ran up bills and absconded, and devised ways of
cheating and bullying people. He loved being a silk-stocking salesman
and forcing women to buy stockings they did not need. Jessica speaks
fondly of the "strong streak of delinquency which I found so attractive." (This is clearly also what her sister Nancy had found attractive

---

* Of the prominent intellectual radicals of the '30s, seven came from families with
strong Liberal traditions—Spender, Strachey, Lehmann, Maclean, Toynbee, Haldane,
and Ivor Montagu. Four had prominent journalists as fathers—Lehmann, Spender,
Strachey, and Christopher Caudwell.

in Peter Rodd. He too had provoked comparisons with Rimbaud, and had taken part in revolutions in South America after a glamorous career at Oxford.) Esmond was a good hater, she says approvingly, and resistant to all discipline. She explains their joint rebellion as the effect of too much security plus too much discipline as children, but it seems clear that larger cultural forces were involved.[5]

Philip Toynbee is of great interest, independently of his connection with Esmond Romilly, as a representative figure of his times and in relation to the *Sonnenkind* temperament. As an adolescent he had greatly admired Basil Murray, who was his uncle though only five or six years older, and the other model for Evelyn Waugh's Basil Seal beside Peter Rodd. Toynbee admired Murray for his insolent rebellion against his parents. Murray would say to his father (Professor Gilbert Murray), "Your wife tells me . . . ," and to his mother, "Your husband seems to think . . . ," with a panache that delighted Toynbee. Murray later became a journalist for the *Evening Standard,* which was one of Beaverbrook's papers and therefore anathema to his Liberal parents. And he wrote a biography of Lloyd George, again a villain to them, because they followed Asquith. Toynbee's knowing Basil Murray as a boy obviously prepared him to appreciate Esmond Romilly later—just as knowing Peter Rodd as a brother-in-law may have prepared Jessica to appreciate Esmond. The latter thus inherited admirers from both of Basil Seal's models. And if reading about the character Basil Seal may be said to have prepared all England to admire Guy Burgess, then certain families, like the Mitfords, preceded and prefigured the national experience.

In his *Friends Apart* (1954) Toynbee contrasts Romilly with the other friend who had a great influence on him in the '30s. Both died in the Second World War. The other friend, Jasper Ridley, was an Etonian dandy-aesthete—at one point Toynbee explains him as typical of Eton and its handsome "fascinators"—although allied to Bloomsbury rather than to our group of dandies. Toynbee first met Ridley when he was seventeen, at Castle Howard, a great house where one dined in the Canaletto Room, with windows open on wide lawns, yew hedges, and a statue of Atlas in a fountain. Toynbee was then in love with Laura Bonham-Carter, whose family (one of the great Liberal families) owned the place, and Ridley was to marry her sister Cressida. The girls of that family and the Asquith and Sinclair girls, the "liberal girls," all adored Ridley, Toynbee says, and soon he too was captivated by him. Ridley was personally beautiful, and his conversation had the mad humorous logic of *Alice in Wonderland,* quietly but brilliantly crazy.

At Oxford, Ridley refused to work and formed, with about ten of his friends, a colony of privacy in Beaumont Street. It was a Cambridge-Bloomsbury world, whose prime values were emotional integrity and personal relations. Two second-generation Bloomsbury figures in it were Ben Nicolson and Jeremy Hutchinson. They were all discreet, indirect, playful, fastidious, overrefined, and given to fantasy. Ridley in particular was a moral and artistic puritan, who found any action difficult. (In this he was the opposite of Esmond Romilly, and Toynbee was torn between the influence of his two models, the rogue and the dandy. Toynbee describes the Etonian side of Ridley as "just what Esmond had so long lovingly hated.") After Oxford he was supposed to take bar examinations, but he rebelled too deeply against his parents' expectations, and against the career they foresaw for him, and he ended up reviewing books about dogs.

Toynbee became organizing secretary of the Oxford University Communist party, which had about 200 members, half of whom left it quickly. Of those who remained, Toynbee says, half were toughminded lower middle-class types, who despised him for choosing to live his social life among the Christ Church smarties. But those toughminded ones were not the ones who later wrote the books. The literary record is filled by *Sonnenkinder.* Toynbee much admired and liked his party boss, Abe Lazarus ("Bill Firestone," to use his party name), who was a Cockney Jewish proletarian and who brought a breath of fatherly manliness into his life. But like Strachey, Toynbee himself remained quite a *Sonnenkind* in temperament. He compares the experience of being in the party with that of being at a good school—highly disciplined and meaningful, where you believed in the school spirit and respected the teachers, but were conscious of being treated like a child. And leaving the party was like leaving such a school, except of course that it must be a leaving in disgrace. (One might compare this attitude to the party, as representing Reality, with Waugh's attitude to the church—compare Abe Lazarus with Father d'Arcy or Monsignor Knox. In both cases the refugee from literal laxity sincerely respected the new seriousness he had sought out, but remained emotionally alien to it and rebellious against its disciplines.)

Romilly visited Toynbee at Oxford, selling his silk stockings, and bringing Jessica with him. Frank Pakenham, the mildly socialist don, took the Romillys and Toynbee for an afternoon drive, and was persuaded by Esmond to call unannounced on a rich viscount, who professed socialist convictions. Esmond then forced an invitation to dinner; and then another to stay the night. He and Jessica stole the host's cigarettes, in quantities, exacted extra meals and inordinate service from the staff, and even planned to steal the curtains from their bedroom. Toynbee writes, "I was delighted with their behaviour," and clearly it was its temperamental style as much as its ideological bearing that delighted him. And he did not resent the fact that the same brutality was directed against everyone, including himself. Later, when they lived in Rotherhithe, Romilly dropped a quart of beer that Toynbee had bought him, demanded 2s. 6d. to buy himself another, refused to return the change, and when they fought, bit Toynbee till he wept. The characterizing style of Esmond's behavior was always this assertion of his own manhood at the expense of other people's. He never wanted to join the Communist party, being too purely the rogue. At the same time no one doubted that he had genuine and extreme political convictions and was willing to sacrifice a great deal for them.

That he and Jasper Ridley could play such parallel though opposite roles in Toynbee's life is another indication of how powerful our pattern of cultural vectors was. But we should note that this time the dandy and the rogue were not mutually complementary, as in the Ambrose Silk-Basil Seal pattern. This time they were two partners in a troika, the dandy, the rogue, and the naïf.

Another pattern is the mutual complementarity of rogue and naïf, Burgess and Maclean.[6] The rogue whose life story most luridly illustrates our pattern is, of course, Guy Burgess. He seemed to quarrel with his Communist friends in Cambridge, and to renounce his Communist faith, in the early '30s. He became, among other things, financial adviser to one of the Rothschilds. He also became secretary to a right-wing homosexual M.P., whom he took to a *Hitlerjugend* camp, and on to Budapest, where they fell in with another homosexual, this time a wealthy Anglican ecclesiastic, and with Tom Wylie, private secretary to the Under Secretary for War—notorious for the wild parties he used to give in the War Office itself. With these men he was involved in a series of ludicrous misadventures, which formed the basis for Guy's anecdotes for years to come. Nearly all the stories of his life are plots for Evelyn Waugh novels, and Guy was the most outrageous of all the real-life Basil Seals, and a center of London's maelstroms of laughter during these years, as protagonist of that hypertrophied national sense of humor for which Waugh found the fictional analogue. Moreover, Burgess was a great appreciator of those novels. When he died in Moscow, among his reading matter were several signed first editions of Evelyn Waugh. At the same time, like Waugh himself, Burgess loved the relics and the memories of England's 19th-century greatness. He loved the Reform Club, *Middlemarch,* Lord Salisbury, the 19th-century statesman, and the British navy. He always wanted to write the missing last volume of Salisbury's biography; he kept models of ships in his flat; and he constantly reread *Middlemarch* and preferred it to all 20th-century fiction. He despised all but Anglo-Saxon countries, and loved the architecture and furniture of the age when Britain was powerful, was technically and politically progressive and expansive. He loved power and scorned for instance Orwell's attitude to the Spanish war as "sentimentalist" and as sabotaging the Republican cause.

It seems clear enough that Soviet Russia was to him, among other things, a reincarnation of Victorian England; whereas 20th-century

England was a country that could make no claims on his loyalty or affection. He remained a compulsive drunkard, completely promiscuous, and a neurotic and grubby nail-biter when he got to Moscow, but the serious part of his mind was at rest there. In London only the frivolous and anarchic part of his mind had felt at home. But his influence on his friends never relaxed or failed, says Goronwy Rees.[7] Burgess was "childishly" persistent, knowing he would get what he wanted if he behaved "badly" enough. And we cannot doubt, reading Rees's account, that the contemporary cultural vectors helped him to dazzle and confuse his victims, giving both him and them a sense of the authenticity of his style. When he told Rees that he was a Comintern agent, Rees "didn't know whether to believe him," not only in the sense of doubting the proposition, but being unable to make any imaginative connection between Burgess' personality and such behavior.

In some ways the most genuine expression of *dandy* political feeling in the '30s was the sympathy with the Negro cause, which climaxed in Nancy Cunard's 900-page anthology, *Negro,* published in 1934. This *was* politics, although of a very unorthodox kind. As she herself said, she was no Communist, but she could be called an anarchist. Among the people who contributed to her anthology were Norman Douglas and Harold Acton, and in a way this too was appropriate. Harold Acton had a genuine response to black music and black dancing, as had Firbank and van Vechten. Nancy Cunard's visits to America were in 1931, when she came with her black lover, Henry Crowder, and in 1932, with John Banting, the painter, who was later Brian Howard's lover, and who wrote about black dancing. This was a politics that shaded fast into aesthetics and erotics, but it did not entirely cease to be politics. The intense love of the Dionysiac aspects of black culture, this was something the dandies genuinely felt, and it was much more *their* politics than, say, Spain. The Spanish cause belonged to men like Orwell, who—contrariwise—was no lover of black dancing. (He professed himself bored by the Blackbirds.) Waugh's attitude was, as so often, paradoxical. He seems to have appreciated jazz and black music, at least to begin with, but he professed brutal racist opinions—saying, for instance, that he could only enjoy his food when it was served to him by black waiters.

Another striking example of anti-imperialist negrophilia was Geoffrey Gorer's *Africa Dances,* of 1935. This book begins with Tchelitchew introducing the author to Féral Benga, a black dancer at the Folies Bergères. Gorer (born 1905, Charterhouse and Cambridge), who had been devoted to art, theater, and ballet, and who had just written a book about de Sade, was invited by Benga on a trip to West Africa while Benga assembled a dance company. But while there Gorer became concerned with the whole culture, or cultures, of West African Negroes, and his book is about a lot more than dance. Moreover, it brought him to the attention of Ruth Benedict and Margaret Mead, and he went to train in America as a social anthropologist, and so escaped the "bright young Englishman" confines of the group we are discussing. But this book is largely written in their "faunlet" prose, although it vies with Isherwood's *Lions and Shadows* for the honor of being the best in that kind; despite its impudent naïveté, its resonances are clear, strong, and complex, in the realms of politics and ideas in general. (The old master of this "young-man" prose is E. M. Forster, in such essays as "What I Believe.")

Auden and Company

The two imaginative writers who, by general consent, did most to influence their contemporary writers to adopt the political mood of the '30s, were W. H. Auden and Christopher Isherwood. These were also the two to whom Brian Howard was personally closest. There is more than accident to that coincidence, for much of the connoisseur's flair is for recognizing the talent that the moment demands, and for accommodating himself to it and associating himself with it.

Auden was born only two years later than Howard, and went to a public school, Gresham's—about which he said, in 1934, that the best reason he had for being a socialist was that at school he had lived in a fascist state. (This suggests the thought that one factor that differentiated the twenties dandies from the thirties activists was that the latter did not go to Eton, but to some more backward and reactionary institution. They consequently reacted more fervently both for and against the public school ethos, and above all they had no easy and early induction into dandy-aestheticism.) In 1934, Auden described himself as having been while at school, and in most respects still being "mentally precocious, physically backward, short-sighted, a rabbit at all games, very untidy and grubby, a nail-biter, a physical coward, dishonest, sentimental, with no community sense whatever, in fact a typical little highbrow and difficult child." Talking about the Oxford he went up to, he said in 1965 that it was the same as Evelyn Waugh's, the same as that described in Mackenzie's *Sinister Street*. Girls were still in purdah, and politics were not yet in fashion. Auden never opened a newspaper before 1930. In *Letters from Iceland,* 1937, he wrote We were the tail, a sort of poor relation

> To that debauched, eccentric generation
> That grew up with their fathers at the War
> And made new glosses on the noun Amor.

And in his poem of 1960, "To Professor Neville Coghill upon his retirement," he sketches a dandy and *commedia* Oxford as his own.

> For a columbine season
> we are free to play
> swains of a pasture
> where neither love nor money
> nor clocks are cogent
> time to wear odd clothing
> behave with panache
> and talk nonsense, as I did.

He therefore found that Leonard Woolf's Cambridge (he reviewed the autobiographies of Waugh and Woolf together in 1965) sounded very "serious-minded" by contrast with the university life he had known. He called his 1965 essay on the two autobiographies "As It Seemed To Us," and added some account of his own life, to make the point that they were all three remarkably similar in their major determinants. But it is with Waugh, the dandy, that the similarities are most striking. Unlike Woolf, but like Waugh, Auden felt loved by his mother (who sang the love-duet from *Tristan* with him when he was eight) but not by his father.[8]

Nevertheless, Auden's group at Oxford seems to have felt itself entirely separate from Acton's, and quite hostile. They dismissed Harold and his poetry as frivolous. Perhaps that feeling was a matter of intention—Auden's intention—deriving from his sense that prominent features of the other group's style were outworn, especially the iconography of the *Commedia* and the moods associated therewith. In any case by 1928 (after Oxford) the Auden group existed as a separate and very self-conscious entity, and was known as "the gang," "the happy few," or "the Lads of the Earth." Auden, and the earlier members, kept recruiting new ones. Auden brought in Gabriel Carritt, the son of an Oxford don, Derek Kahn, A. J. P. Taylor, and Hugh Gaitskell; Spender brought in Isaiah Berlin, an intellectual historian, and Richard Goodman, a poet; Day Lewis brought in Rex Warner; and so on. Several dons were associated with the group, like Maurice Bowra, Neville Coghill, and R. H. S. Crossman. Various members edited the magazines, *Oxford Outlook* and *Oxford Poetry* and made the group's power felt.[9]

Auden's group at Oxford were still, in their early years, aesthetes. Auden, for instance, worked always by artificial light, wore eccentric hats, carried a loaded starting pistol with him, and went always for the same walk along the canal behind the gasworks. These are eccentricities of dandyism compared with the orthodox elegancies of Acton and Howard, so sumptuous in clothes and decor, but Auden as much as the latter pair was a phenomenon of self-stylization. He was also an aesthete about literature. He said a poet must have no opinions and must feel *less* strongly than other people, that a poem's subject was only a peg to hang the poetry on, that the poet was a chemist mixing words and meanings to produce a reaction, and so on. This seems to show that in essential matters he was not far from the earlier group.

As late as *Letters from Iceland* (1937) he also said that he would like to write like Firbank, Beatrix Potter, Carroll, and Lear, just the writers Waugh might have cited. Both admired, for example, P. G. Wodehouse and Max Beerbohm. (In a late essay on *Alice in Wonderland,* Auden declares that Alice as a person is what every human being should try to be like—"what, after many years and countless follies and errors, one would like, in the end, to become.") And Auden distrusted his own enjoyment of such authors in the same way as Waugh. Waugh's distrust is implicit in *Brideshead Revisited,* in the fable of how Ryder is artistically ruined by his love for Sebastian. Auden's is explicit in an essay on Beerbohm, in which he warns all English artists against the cosy and minor charm of such authors.

> The great cultural danger for the English is, to my mind, their tendency to judge the arts by the values appropriate to the conduct of family life. Among brothers and sisters it is becoming to entertain each other with witty remarks, hoaxes, family games and jokes, unbecoming to be solemn, to monopolize the conversation, to talk shop, to create emotional scenes. But no art, major or minor, can be governed by the rules of social amenity. The English have a greater talent than any other people for creating an agreeable family life; that is why it is such a threat to their artistic and intellectual life. If the atmosphere were not so charming, it would be less of a temptation.

To grow up, Auden's theory and career imply, an English writer has to go abroad—if he stays inside English culture he will be trapped in some immature, adolescent, style.[10]

These are some of the symptoms of that British dandyism that was always there and self-aware in Auden. But of course he gave the best of his conscious energies to projects of quite opposite tendency, in the '30s. Like Brian Howard, he was converted in Germany first to naïveté and then to political seriousness. He went to Berlin for a year in 1928, and met John Layard, a Jungian analyst much influenced by Homer Lane.

Part came from Lane, and part from D. H. Lawrence:

> Gide, though I didn't know it then, gave part.
> They taught me to express my deep abhorrence
> If I caught anyone preferring Art
> To Life and Love and being Pure in Heart. . .
> I lived with crooks but seldom was molested;
> The Pure-in-Heart can never be arrested.
> He's gay; no bludgeonings of chance can spoil it,
> The Pure-in-Heart loves all men on a par,
> And has no trouble with his private toilet;
> The Pure-in-Heart is never ill; catarrh
> Would be the yellow streak, the brush of tar;
> Determined to be loving and forgiving,
> I came back here to try and earn my living.[11]

This ideal, which derived much of its power from its partial actualization in the Weimar Germany around him, was transformed into something more political as that Germany was first threatened and then crushed by Hitler and as Spain was conquered by or for Franco.

This was a crucial experience for the Auden group, who set about the business of proletarianizing themselves. Auden wore a worker's cap, dropped his "aitches," and ate his peas with a knife; Isherwood drank bad tea and ate chocolates, in order to ruin his too-good teeth; Spender let himself be cheated by unemployed workers; Gabriel Carritt changed his name to Bill. It was a crucial experience also for other British intellectuals who visited Germany between 1928 and 1932—for instance Alan Bush, the composer; Felicia Browne, the artist; Rupert Doone, the dancer; Naomi Mitchison and Arthur Calder-Marshall, the novelists.

Auden and his group began to publish nationally in the *New Signatures* anthology, edited by Michael Roberts in 1931. Their poetry was aggressively different—they put no titles to their poems, for instance, but only Roman numerals. Roberts announced the new poetics by saying that the poets of the '20s (meaning Eliot and Edith Sitwell) had been unwilling to accept the responsibilities of leadership in society, and had written esoteric poetry for a small audience; whereas the poets of the '30s would write about the machines all about us and would be leaders of society. (This "Kiplingesque" feature of their poetry, its tough and threatening tone, its giving of orders, is what I called elsewhere a disguised Harlequinism. The poetry of the '30s was new in that it shifted its center from Pierrot to Harlequin, but a Harlequin made new in Marxist costume and slogans.) In the second Roberts anthology, *New Country* (1933), he demanded a new social system, and said that his poets would "prepare the way for an English Lenin." This indicates the kind of unsustainable heroics into which the group were betrayed, and their poems were in fact full of exhortations to conspire against society.[12]

Auden went to Spain and served in the ambulances, and he married Erika Mann, to give her the protection of a British passport and so help her to escape from Germany. But it was always clear, to those who knew him, that the patriarchal modes of operation, of politics and armies and administration and revolution, were not natural in him. He spoke out boldly for left-wing politics, both at home and abroad, but in 1939 when war became inevitable, he left England for America.

So did Christopher Isherwood, as well as Benjamin Britten and Peter Pears, James Stern, Louis MacNeice, and others. Isherwood's autobiography, *Lions and Shadows* (1938), is of quite extraordinary interest in extending our pattern. His father was a professional soldier, who was killed in the war, and his own relations with his mother, while passionate and intimate, were always difficult. In *Down Here on a Visit* (1962), he says of himself, "his strongest negative motivation is ancestor-hatred. He has vowed to disappoint, disgrace, and disown his ancestors." This is clearly one of the *Sonnenkind* impulses carried through to a tragic extreme. In *Prater Violet* (1945), Isherwood depicts himself living in London in the '30s, disaffiliated from his natural family, but finding a new father in the Jewish film director (in real life Friedrich Viertel) who has "all Central Europe in his face." He tries to become a son to this man, so as to inherit his manhood. This represents perhaps Isherwood's nearest approach to true naïveté, his openest approach to self-affiliation, and it was a brief and unsuccessful episode—in art and in life. In his most brilliant work, the autobiography and the Berlin stories, he is really a faux-naïf, using naïve tones to say subtle and sardonic things.

Lions and Shadows covers his life up to 1929, when he went to Germany, on Auden's recommendation. He describes the book as narrating "the education of a novelist," but we could as well call it the education of a Narcissus—from being a distressed dandy to being a naïf; one with putative Marxist convictions, of course, and also one with a lethal power of cynicism.

He tells us a lot about his public school, Repton, where he arrived,

> thoroughly sick of masters . . . having been emotionally messed about by them at my prep, school, where the war had given full license to every sort of dishonest cant about loyalty, selfishness, patriotism, playing the game and dishonouring the dead.

He remembered with resentment "those fatherly 'pi-jaws' and the resultant floods of masochistic tears," and he made friends with the rebels at his new school. His principal friend, "Chalmers" (in real life Edward Upward), hated all authority, and referred to the school habitually as Hell.

But the history master there, "Mr. Holmes," made favorites of both "Chalmers" and Isherwood, intrigued to get them into the history sixth form and later into Cambridge. He was a man who fully appreciated all their gestures of rebellion, all their mockery of the established, and yet himself belonged to the public school system, body and soul. Mr. Holmes is a brilliant study in practical cynicism, in effective treachery, and the first of a series of such portraits by Isherwood, which includes Mr. Norris. Isherwood's fascination with this kind of mature and discreet cynicism complements his fascination with young flamboyant corruption (seen in the Berlin stories and in *Down Here on a Visit*), and together they alert the reader to the subtle and deceitful resonances ever present in Isherwood's naively candid prose.

At Cambridge, he and "Chalmers" developed a private mythological world called Mortmere, which made fun of the university and the dons and everything else. But in his dreams, Isherwood tells us, he was still an austere young prefect who fought "slackness" and homosexuality at his public school, and emerged a man. He exercised in private with a chest expander, and bought a motorcycle in 1924 as another version of "the test." Like Connolly, Waugh, and the other *Sonnenkinder,* Isherwood was permanently imprinted by his school experiences. It is the naïveté of these confessions that establish the book's character of being "naïf."

But when Isherwood describes Auden ("Hugh Weston") he presents him very much as another dandy-rebel. They had gone to the same prep school, and when they met again (Christmas, 1925) they revived the old jokes and imitations of the masters, and laughed themselves to tears. Auden, as Isherwood presents him, was all eccentric interests and opinions, exaggerated and insisted on, fantastically clever, and underneath very boyish. Their friendship, like that between Isherwood and "Chalmers," was based on dandy fantasy—take, for instance, Auden's hats. Auden wore a broad-brimmed black hat, an opera hat, a workman's cap, a panama with black ribbons ("which presented Weston as lunatic clergyman"), and a mortarboard. Isherwood's judgment, "I will never, as long as I live, accept any of Weston's hats," is one of the few moments when the Oscar Wilde tone suddenly rings through his voice without disguise. And Auden's interest in Norse sagas Isherwood connects with the similarity between the sagas' heroes—their feuds, their riddles, their jokes—and prep school boys.

Like so many of the others, Isherwood got a private school teaching job through Gabbitas and Thring, the teachers' agency; he felt the same despair as so many—for instance, Evelyn Waugh; like Waugh, Isherwood contemplated suicide, and bought a pistol for that purpose. But "Chalmers" found in Marx the formulas for relating Mortmere to the real world, and "Weston" found in Berlin the way to be

"Pure-in-Heart" and told Isherwood to go to Germany. So it was to Berlin that he went at the end of *Lions and Shadows*.

What he found there is best described in Stephen Spender's autobiography, *World Within World*. Spender was presented to Isherwood in 1929 by Auden (who had recruited him at Oxford for his "gang" of poets—a quite open and undisguised recruitment), and Isherwood told *him* to go to Germany. He told him that that was the country where all the obstructions and the complexities of this life were cut through. Spender went first to Hamburg and then to Berlin, to live with Isherwood. He says that he realized later that he had lived three years off the excitement of being with Isherwood, but the experience of Germany was in itself all that he had been promised. He found that

> to these young Germans the life of the senses was a sunlit garden from which sin was excluded. The sun was a primary social force in this Germany. Thousands of people went to the open-air swimming-baths or lay down on the shores of the rivers and lakes, almost nude, and sometimes quite nude. . . . Their lives flowed easily into the movements of art, literature and painting, which surrounded them. . . . Modernism in this Germany was a mass-movement. Roofless houses, expressionist painting, atonal music, bars for homosexuals, nudism, sun-bathing, camping, all were accepted. . . . Drums and flags seemed to march through my brain; it was as though my blood were a river of music.

This was the Aphroditean society that the anarchist Otto Gross had struggled to set up in Germany before the war, and it was an intoxicating release to these young Englishmen, as the last sentence quoted shows. The sun, the nudity, and the interflow of life and art are all signs of the fathers' defeat. To some degree these banners of youth triumphant reached England too—the hiking, sun-bathing, pacifism, the youth hostels, the unisex hiking costume, the concertinas and mandolins; some of these manifestations, particularly those with "Fascist" connections, even found favor with the authorities. In 1936, Parliament sent a team of observers to Germany to look at the Strength Through

Joy movement; it reported enthusiastically, and its recommendations were incorporated into a physical fitness bill and a festival of youth. But the sun-bathing of individual freedom was something to be associated with pre-Nazi Germany, rather than with English holiday camps or the *Hitlerjugend*. The fact that it was only precariously established, that there was another Germany there all the time—the fathers' Germany, like the one the Englishmen knew at home, only grimmer—added to the excitement and the satisfaction. Spender remarks on the architecture of Berlin, "the long straight grey uniform streets, expressing Prussian domination . . . the cynical relation between the grim architecture and the feckless population. . . ." This cynical relation is what is dramatized so brilliantly in Isherwood's *Berlin Stories*.

Another source of the Englishman's excitement in Berlin was the open invitation extended there to express their homosexuality. They were able to behave there, and publicly, as they could only talk in London, and privately. Thus we find Isherwood writing to congratulate Brian Howard on two of his poems, "just a mad wave of my fan, my dear." But none of the others were as ready as he to reverse their naïveté, and flaunt the dandy lining. Spender, for instance, was much more thoroughly a naïf. He was awkward, gangling, and blushing with the others; Auden told him he could become a poet because of his capacity for humiliation, and Isiah Berlin called him the Child of Nature.

Of course, this is not to say that he was only naive. Connolly described him in 1951 as really two people: one, an "inspired simpleton, a great big silly goose, a holy Russian idiot, large, generous, gullible, ignorant, affectionate, idealistic—living for friendship and beauty;" the other, "shrewd and ambitious, aggressive and ruthless, a publicity-seeking intellectual full of administrative energy and rentier asperity."[13]

Spender's general formation corresponds well to our pattern. His father, Harold Spender, was a Liberal journalist (and in 1923 the Liberal parliamentary candidate for Bath), and his uncle A. J. Spender was editor of the *Westminster Gazette*. Stephen was early "horrified" at his father's "unreality." He found his father "all rhetoric," his life all "scenes written by a hectic journalist." Harold Spender imposed large moral

significances on everything, so that discipline, purity, and duty were
fiery ideals, and his children's examinations, for instance, were Alps
they had to scale. And his own experiences were dramatized just as
falsely. When his wife died, he said to his children, "My little ones,
you are all your old father has left. . . . These are the words of a dying
man."[14] This self-pitying patriarchal melodrama was a habit of Virginia Woolf's father and Evelyn Waugh's father, while Harold Spender's position in British society was very like that of John Strachey's
father and John Lehmann's father. He was interested in ideas and politics exclusively. His interest in art was conventional, and he called all
modern art a cynical leg pull, a fraud perpetrated on a gullible public. Augustus John, Van Gogh, Lytton Strachey, Bernard Shaw, we
are told, for him symbolized a diabolic depravity. Even his brother
Alfred, who was a friend of Henry James and Rupert Brooke, Oscar
Wilde and R. L. Stevenson, thought all art was in the last analysis an
extravagance. But he (Alfred) had at least some realistic conception of
politics. Of Harold, his son says,

> His conception of politics was confined to high ideals, hav-
> ing our name in the newspapers, and journalistic discussion
> of political personalities. Unlike my uncle, he had little con-
> ception of the task of being a public administrator or of the
> responsibility of pursuing a realistic policy.

Thus Stephen Spender too could rebel against his own father and
the England of the fathers in the same action. He was unhappy at prep,
school, but not at his public school, University College School, London, because it was a day school and had working-class boys there too.
At Oxford he felt out of the main stream, because he was at University
College, not one of the important colleges (New, Balliol, Magdalen,
or Christ Church), and it seems to have meant little more to him than
Eton did to Orwell. Only Auden offered him an encounter of any significance. He describes Auden as carrying a cane and wearing a monocle, and taking an icily haughty and dictatorial tone with the "gang"
he was assembling, despite the boyish fantasies he openly indulged.

By 1933, Spender was established as one of the new poets of the '30s, partly as a result of Auden's favor. He had contributed to *New Signatures* in 1932, and in 1933 contributed to *New Country* and published his own *Poems.* After his time in Germany, he began to spend six months of each year regularly in Vienna, and in 1937 he published *Forwards from Liberalism,* which became a selection of the Left Book Club and was widely hailed as an important contribution to the movement to commit the British intelligentsia to socialism. (In his case, and in that of most of the literary dandies, the idea of Liberalism was very personally related to the literal father.*) Brian Howard reviewed Spender's book, very favorably, in the *New Statesman* in January 1937. G. M. Young, the historian, had reproved Spender for historical inaccuracy, so Howard said that what people like them needed was "less a text which elderly beaks should be unable to blue-pencil, than an answer by one of themselves to the question as to *what they are to do* about a world that is rapidly becoming fit for tyrants to live in." Later Spender and Howard dedicated poems to each other, and were friends and allies.

Among families like the Harold Spenders—in fact, friends with the Spenders—were the Rudolph Lehmanns, whose children, John, Rosamond, and Beatrix, all played fairly prominent public roles in the years we are describing. John in particular is important for our story.[15]

Rudolph Lehmann wrote for *Punch* up to 1919. For thirty years nearly every week something appeared over his initials in its columns. He used there the stories his children wrote, printed with all their misspellings, and wrote about them, for his readers' delight. His children loved their father's writing, and learned the social and political history of England from the bound volumes of *Punch* in his library. Some of the masters at John's school, Summer Fields, were also fans of Rudolph Lehmann, who was also a Liberal journalist, an M.P. for a time after 1906, and an expert boxer, fencer, and above all a rower. He was nearly fifty when John was born.

---

* Of the prominent intellectual radicals of the '30s, seven came from families with strong Liberal traditions—Spender, Strachey, Lehmann, Maclean, Toynbee, Haldane, and Ivor Montagu. Four had prominent journalists as fathers—Lehmann, Spender, Strachey, and Christopher Caudwell.

John was at Eton—the top scholar of his year in college—when Connolly was there, but John took the official ethos much more seriously. He thought Connolly a bad influence on the other boys, "notoriously dangerous, shocking, and exciting." He associated Connolly with Turkish cigarettes, powerful liqueurs, avant-garde books, and nightclubs. His own reactions to Eton seem to have been very conventional. He says the provost gave the impression of thinking all rules and examinations ridiculous, and "the faces of the beautiful young 18th-century gentlemen looked out of their treasured canvases on the walls and smiled their silent 'of course.' " John thought some of the Eton athletes like "Greek warriors," and particularly adored Connolly's friend, Godfrey Meynell. When the latter had borrowed a chair from Lehmann's room, that chair when returned "seemed to glow with invisible sacred fire." We can take John Lehmann to represent naïveté much more completely than the others—to stand at the opposite extreme from Isherwood, on the other side of Spender.

He went to Cambridge, became a friend of Julian Bell, Clive Bell's son, and apprenticed himself to Bloomsbury, going to work for Leonard Woolf at the Hogarth Press. He had tried for some time to be a poet, but he was insecure about his talent. The Lehmanns all wanted to practice the arts, but they got in each other's way. Rosamond published a novel, *Dusty Answer,* in 1927, and it became a best seller, thanks partly to a review by the aging poet, Alfred Noyes. John says that all the Lehmanns considered this "our book," because "so much of it was an imaginative transposition of the world we all grew up in." And Julian Bell remarked on the similarity between John's and his sister's imaginative work: "You've both got a same quality, midsummer in gardens—trees—water and parties, I should label it." John could not compete with Rosamond, or find a creative mode in which he would not need to compete with her.

John Lehmann was certainly not a dandy nor a rogue. The edges of his mind were not hard or sharp enough to make him any kind of *Sonnenkind,* but he was closer to the naïf than to any other type. He grew up too encompassed by first his father and then his sister to develop a personality of his own. But he is of interest to us as an impresario of British letters in the '30s. He met Spender in 1930, and the latter told him he should go to Germany, because that country had escaped through defeat the fate overtaking the rest of Western civilization. "There youth had started to live again, free of the shackles of the past, a life without inhibition, inspired by hope, natural humanity and brotherhood in the springs of being." This was the gospel of naïveté, of the Holy Land of Weimar Germany, handed down from Auden to Isherwood, from Isherwood to Spender, and from Spender to Lehmann. It is a process very like that by which the gospel of aestheticism, of the Holy Land of Southern Baroque Italy, was handed down from Acton and the Sitwells to Waugh and Betjeman and Connolly, in the Oxford of the '20s.

Lehmann became a socialist and got Isherwood's first novel, *The Memorial,* published by the Hogarth Press. He edited the *Year's Poetry* in 1934, and again in 1935, and in 1936 he began the serial anthology, *New Writing,* using some of his mother's money. He used this anthology to publish the work of Auden, Isherwood, Spender and their friends. This was how he began his long career as Britain's major literary editor, and impresario of the socialist writers. He saw himself as joining a political movement, and ceasing to be merely aesthetic, and he published some proletarians, like George Garrett, B. L. Coombes, Leslie Ackward, and Willie Goldman, besides the public school socialists. Spender and Isherwood were advisory editors to *New Writing,* and Isherwood became a friend of Beatrix Lehmann. John felt personally betrayed when Auden and Isherwood went to America in 1939.

Other writers sometimes grouped with the "thirties poets," notably Louis MacNeice and Cecil Day Lewis, are much less relevant to our interest here. If they were dandies at all, it was in a whimsical style that was independent of the social pattern we are tracing. MacNeice's autobiography gives us some glimpses of the Oxford we have seen before. "I discovered that in Oxford homosexuality and 'intelligence,' heterosexuality and brawn, were almost inexorably paired. This left me out in the cold, and I took to drink." The jaunty tone seems to indicate that he was able to turn his back on the problem, as few Englishmen were, and we can conjecture that his Irish heritage helped him to do so, since we find something similar in Lewis's account of himself.[16] These men might be aligned rather with Robert Graves than either Auden or Acton. They were gentlemen, and only marginally and moderately affected by the fascinations of dandyism, or by the bracing airs of anti-dandyism. But most of the men of the '30s, we have surely shown, were quite crucially affected by those forces. They cultivated—however hidden this was at the time—one or other of the three main styles of *Sonnenkind* temperament.

Old Friends

Among figures we have met before, Cyril Connolly became converted to a kind of socialism as the decade wore on, although it mixed uneasily with his aestheticism and only carried real conviction insofar as, like Brian Howard's, it was a rebellion against Englishness. In *Enemies of Promise* he called for a literary dandyism of the Left, for plays politically true but having the elegance of *Love for Love* or *The Importance of Being Earnest*.

In 1937, Connolly published a satire—one of the genres at which Connolly excels—entitled "Where Engels Fear to Tread," a spoof review of *From Oscar to Stalin*, an autobiography by Christian de Clavering. Quite apart from the use of Brian's middle names, it is clear that it is he who is principally aimed at, from the presentation of Christian de Clavering's parental situation, his exotic homes, and his father's "shady" occupation. Brian is depicted as patronizing Evelyn (Waugh), John (Betjeman), Robert (Byron), Peter (Quennell) at Oxford, and then going to Greece to write, where he meets Stephen (Spender), Wystan (Auden), Cecil (Day Lewis), and Christopher (Isherwood). From them he picks up the idea that all writers now must be socialist and proletarian, and he changes his name to Cris Clay and starts threatening his literary rivals and potential reviewers like Connolly with political punishment. "A line is being drawn.... Those lines mean something. Tatatat! Yes, my dears, bullets—real bullets, the kind of bullets they keep for reviewers who step across the party line." In the last scene he is depicted going on a protest march through London, rather dismayed at seeing Peter and Robert and Evelyn now standing at the window of White's Club with the peers he used to dominate and patronize. But then he finds some foreign nobility in the march with him, so happily begins instructing them in correct proletarian dress and manners. Connolly was, of course, only putting into writing the feelings of most of Brian's friends who had known him first as a dandy, on finding him now a revolutionary. This spoof is Connolly's equivalent for Orwell's more serious disgust.[17]

Turning to frankly non-socialist dandies, we find that Anthony Powell had left Duckworths in 1936, and was devoting more of his energies to his vocation as a novelist. In 1938–39 he was already planning his *Music of Time* series, because he foresaw the war that was coming, and also foresaw a postwar world in which the people he wanted to write about would have disappeared, so that he would be lost—without his bearings as a novelist. In other words, he needed a dandy subject, and he feared it would disappear, as history punished his generation's frivolity.[18]

Peter Quennell wrote an essay-review in 1939 of Samuel Dill's *Roman Society in the Last Century of the Western Empire,* in which he pushed the silver age and age-of-decay idea to extremes.[19] This essay was entitled "This Is the Way the World Ends . . . ," and it remarked on the resemblance of that last Roman century to the situation in which Quennell and his readers were living. Those cultured and leisured aristocrats of the 4th and 5th centuries, who lived on immense and beautiful estates above the Rhone and the Garonne, and those Silver Age scholars like Symmachus, Ausonius, and Apollinaris Sidonius, their vitality sapped by centuries of cultural inbreeding—such melancholy images expressed much of the aesthetes' deeper feelings about life at the end of the '30s, as we can see also in Osbert Sitwell's evocation of the Rome of Gregorovius in *Escape with Me* (1939).

Some, of course, continued in exactly the same style as they had begun in the '20s. Cecil Beaton in these years set up his establishment at Ashcombe in Wiltshire, which he decorated in rococo style, and which became a frequent meeting place for his friends from twenties days. It was a modern English version of those French pavilions of the 18th century that so delighted him and his friends.[20]

In 1939, Beaton was first asked to photograph the queen, at Buckingham Palace, and one can see a similar movement toward respectability and conservatism—toward the gentleman and away from the dandy and rogue—in the career of Robert Byron. He and Michael Rosse founded the Georgian Society, to preserve Georgian buildings from destruction, and he published his *Appreciation of Architecture,* to teach the public to appreciate good building and to defend their heritage. He thus joined one of the conservative movements of the '30s. Connolly has remarked on how "besotted with architecture" were his Oxford friends—Byron, Clark, Waugh, Powell, Quennell, and Betjeman—and on the invention of a new profession in England, that of architectural critic. What happened in the '30s was that these men's taste turned to *English* buildings in *English* settings, and became conservative, in more than one sense. John Betjeman, the aesthete, joined forces with J. C. Squire, the cricket-player of literature. Betjeman and John Piper edited a series of Shell Country Guides, for which Byron wrote the volume on Wiltshire in 1935, and Betjeman wrote on Devon and Cornwall. The Batsford books, for which Sacheverell Sitwell wrote, began their work of depicting and describing the beauties of the English scene. And beside Beaton, Waugh and many others established homes in secluded country houses. This marked an alliance between the dandy and country gentleman, which was also something of a psychic transition from the one to the other. British dandyism was a style that stressed both personae.

Waugh's work in the '30s included some travel books, *Black Mischief,* and *Edmund Campion,* all of which illustrated *his* move towards the political Right and Catholic orthodoxy. He also wrote *Lawless Roads* for the Catholic Book Club, and was one of the very few writers to answer Nancy Cunard's questionnaire about the Spanish war by declaring his sympathy with Franco (another was Eleanor Smith). *Scoop* was his only really brilliant comic fantasy in the old style. But he tried his hand at what he later called *Work Suspended,* a fairly realistic and uncomfortably sardonic novel about a group of people very like his own friends. It is perhaps fair to associate this with the new stability that entered his life when he got married again in 1937. He was trying to look back on his premarried life with detachment and distance.

His stay in Abyssinia had led him to his first serious politics. He was enthusiastic about the new roads the Italians built there, which he saw as a continuation of the road-building and civilizing work of the Romans. The last words of *Waugh in Abyssinia* praise "the inestimable gifts of fine workmanship and clear judgement—the two determining qualities of the human spirit, by which alone, under God, man grows and flourishes." He saw these as in the gift of the Fascists.

Before then Waugh's political pronouncements had been largely calculated to win him publicity or to express a reaction against orthodox enthusiasms. Even now, they and their artistic "application" were hard to take seriously. Waugh tells us that in 1935, when he visited Jerusalem, he felt proud of being English, because of Allenby's superbly modest entry into Jerusalem in 1918. This was a moment that much struck the English imagination when it happened, although by 1935 not many were still thinking of it. England had then created in the Holy Land "the purest and most benevolent government the land had known since Constantine." Waugh conceived of a large-scale literary project, which might amount to his lifetime's work.

> I was of an age then—32—when, after I had struck lucky with three or four light novels, it did not seem entirely absurd, at any rate to myself, to look about for a suitable "life's work"; (one learns later that life itself is work enough.) So elated was I by the beauties about me that I then and there began vaguely planning a series of books—semi-historic, semi-poetic fiction, I did not quite know what—about the long,

intricate, intimate association between England and the Holy Places. The list of great and strange Britons who from time to time embodied the association—Helena, Richard Lionheart, Stratford Canning, Gordon. . . .[21]

The only one he wrote was *Helena,* but that can give us some idea of what "great and strange Britons" meant to Waugh. It is a novel Waugh remained very fond of, perhaps because in it he managed to escape the satiric mode more completely than elsewhere—to make the transition from dandy to country gentleman as writer—to take Lady Circumference seriously. But, as Waugh himself admitted, it was not successful in inducing readers to take up the imaginative posture required for enjoying it. And one cannot help reflecting how unlike any literary scheme of Nabokov's this of Waugh's was. And it persisted. On the very day of his death, in 1966, Waugh canceled a contract to write a book on the Crusades. This lifework project expresses Waugh's neo-Victorianism. It is his *Idylls of the King,* and it should perhaps be regarded as a respectable final fruit of that camp-Victorianism of Oxford in 1922. But there is a paradox, a tour de force, at the heart of Waugh's aesthetics, as there is at the heart of his religion. He boasted of the blunt simplicity and realism of his creed, while plainly rejoicing in its exoticism and mystical authority; and he set out to create positive heroes, exemplars of decency for his readers' edification, while his talent and taste ran all to the extravagant and preposterous.

Aesthetes and Anti-Aesthetes

Meanwhile Nabokov published *Despair* (1934), in which the central character, Hermann, finds a man who is his physical double, and murders him in order to change legal identities with him and so to escape his own life. This was a story that Nabokov was to develop into many forms and make much use of later. It affords a plot-framework to his thematic concern with the dandy's self-hatred—the self-condemnation of the man of overweening imaginative pride. In this instance, the authorial voice executes some brilliant complex maneuvers, which are all ultimately in attack on the stupidity of the normal world, but which will not finally relinquish the claim to represent a higher morality.

In 1935 came *Invitation to a Beheading,* which takes on a political theme and treats it with dangerous hauteur and levity—insisting on the superior rights of the imaginative writer, blending the aesthete's categories of boredom and vulgarity with the political man's themes of tyranny and injustice. Thus, everyone in the hero's life (including his wife and mother) being inauthentic, they are shown as either (literally) playing parts or as able (literally) to be disassembled like puppets. They are bad works of art. In 1937 came *The Gift,* a brilliant novel that includes a mocking biography of Chernyshevsky, the father-figure of socialist realism in Russian literature. This biography could be called another battle in Diaghilev's war against Chernyshevsky's influence on Russian art. The hero of *The Gift,* who writes this biography, is a poet and aesthete, and he causes a scandal amongst Russian émigrés by his condescension to its subject, whom he treats as essentially an absurd figure. And in real life, the scandal did occur. *The Gift* was serialized in a Berlin Russian newspaper, but the biography had to be omitted because of protests. This was Nabokov's attempt at a serious dialogue with his critics, with the representatives of anti-dandyism in Russian culture. By means of this biography he shows them his interest in, sympathy and even affection for, Chernyshevsky, but also his incapacity to find him anything but wrong-headed, hopelessly limited, and hopelessly inferior—someone who did not know enough about beauty or art by experience to theorize about them to any point. (As Diaghilev had put it in the *World of Art,* "Chernyshevsky wishes to make logarithmic tables out of pictures, touching art with unwashed hands, and out of poems he would concoct prescriptions for all the nasty ills of civilization."[22]) And this is just one battle in Nabokov's hero's war against the forces of both well-meaning and ill-meaning stupidity that surround him in the Russian colony in Berlin.

Finally, in 1938, came *The Eye,* where the challenges to the reader's sense of normality and reality (not to mention realism and decency) are even more acute. For in *The Eye* the hero is beaten up by his mistress's husband (the mistress herself and that relationship are dismissed with a contemptuous phrase) and so shoots himself (also thrown away as a subject) and then *imagines* himself recovering and reentering the normal world, giving an account that the reader begins by believing and only gradually realizes to be fantasy. Later, "life tries to prove to him that it is real." But he resists that attempt, and defeats it. Gradually he becomes happy, having realized that the only happiness there is is to observe, to spy, to watch. "What does it matter that I am a bit cheap, a bit foul, and that no one appreciates all the wonderful things about me—my fantasy, my erudition, my literary gifts. . . ." The hero stakes everything on his imagination—against the world, against life—and he wins his bet. Again and again Nabokov was to show how a writer could blaspheme against the sense of decency and the sense of reality (in ideological terms, against the seriousness of Marx and the seriousness of Freud) and yet write great imaginative fiction. His books are cultic celebrations of the dandy and aesthete, but at the same time serious works of art.

George Balanchine, meanwhile, had gone to America. He had worked for a while in London, in Edward James's *Les Ballets,* but then was persuaded by Lincoln Kirstein to found the school and company that eventually became the New York City Ballet. Kirstein was a patron of several arts, and he played something of the role in relation to the Balanchine company that Diaghilev had played in his day—but less flamboyantly and despotically, and less in rebellion against the culture's dominant values. He was less the dandy and the aesthete, and brought a concern for American and democratic themes and styles into harmony with the classicism and modernism of Balanchine's work. (Before they engaged on this ballet enterprise, Kirstein and his friend Edward Warburg had founded the Harvard Society of Contemporary Art, and Kirstein had, while still a student, founded a literary magazine, *Hound and Horn;* it is worth reflecting on the success of these ventures compared with the somewhat parallel English pair, Brian Howard and Harold Acton.)

Tchelitchew made a great impression on Kirstein and a considerable one on Balanchine, and his influence brought something of the febrile and outrageous quality of Diaghilev's other side to the New York Ballet for a time. But the great artistic personalities of that ballet, Balanchine and Stravinsky, who intensified each other's influence by their mutual admiration, were powerfully sane, objective, Apollonian. It is no mere coincidence that both remained adherents of the Orthodox Church. Equally it is no accident that Stravinsky's opinions, and even his prose, was in his late years so like Nabokov's; that cool, proud, personally reserved, intellectually exuberant *intelligence* is the final triumph of the Diaghilev inheritance, dandyism finally wedded again to a serene Apollonianism.[23]

Among the anti-dandies, we can note a new name, Julian Symons. He was a South Londoner, who did not go to a public school and whose comments on the public school socialists of the time are sharpened by his alienation from them. He ran a magazine called *20th Century Verse,* together with Derek Savage and H. W. B. Mallalieu. They and their friends felt alien to the circle of "university wits" around Auden. Symons and Geoffrey Grigson (who ran the rather similar magazine, *New Verse)* were described as being both of them concerned about *the situation* and *poetry* in that order—in other words, as being non-aesthetes. Symons quotes such a description of them in his autobiography and seems to accept its judgment; it continues that Symons and Grigson were both younger sons in large and respectable families, both were swots grown prefectorial, and both enjoyed playing patron and district magistrate to young poets.[24] Such a description, of course, implies a temperamental *manhood,* described in a rather Kiplingesque vocabulary. Symons described his and Grigson's magazines, when they both ceased publication in 1939, as having been a movement for *common-sense* standards in English letters. He was long a prominent enemy of the Sitwells, especially Edith, and all dandy-fantasists. Grigson was one of those who pointed out how much Edith had stolen from Leavis's *New Bearings in English Poetry* for her *Aspects of Modern Poetry.*

It is worth noting something of Symons' relations with his family also. His brother, A. J. Symons, born 1901, was an aesthete quite like those we have been studying, although he never went to Eton or anywhere like it. He was a self-made dandy. He modeled himself on Disraeli, wore a monocle and carried a malacca cane, read books on etiquette, wore elaborate lavender suits, and practiced an elaborate old-fashioned calligraphy. He made a mystery of his name and origins to friends—concealing his Jewishness—and in fact found the "A. J." he decided to be known by in a Raffles story. Intellectually, too, he made himself a link between the '90s and the '20s—like Firbank, only in a more urbane and scholarly, less personally extremist, way. He founded a First Edition Club in 1922, and made friends with Lord Alfred Douglas and Vyvyan Holland, respectively Wilde's lover and son. He worked for a long time at a bibliography of nineties writing, and at a biography of Oscar Wilde, without completing either. (His *Quest for Corvo,* of 1934—about "Baron Corvo," the nineties novelist—is an elegant and completed exercise in nineties biography.) In 1933 he founded a Wine and Food Society, belonged to many other clubs, collected musical boxes, and so on.

A. J. was twelve years older than Julian, who evidently devised his own style in reaction against his brother, just as the latter had devised his style in reaction against their father (whom Julian describes as a great family man, and of a Victorian severity in sexual matters). Julian derided his brother's urbanity, dressed with conscientious untidiness, and describes himself as an emotional puritan. A. J. called him a bloodthirsty philistine, and was on Connolly's side when Julian engaged in controversy with the latter. One can see that, among contemporary critics, Connolly would be *his* man. Julian's hero, of course, was Orwell. This family imbroglio exemplifies for us the 20th-century English dialectic, in which dandyism was the cultural thesis and the antithesis was represented by Orwellism.

Orwell published several novels in the '30s, of which *Keep the Aspidistra Flying* and *Coming Up for Air* best illustrate our argument. In the first, Gordon Comstock's "economic" interpretation of the world (he sees money and capitalism as the explanation of everything) is meant to become tiresome and unconvincing to the reader as the book goes on, so that at the end one should accept Gordon's entry into domesticity and wage-earning with confident hope as well as relief. His "Marxism" should have revealed itself as an aesthete's strategy of disengagement, so that the reader will accept the Lawrencianism at the book's end as justified by all that preceded it. But this does not happen, and the reason—beside Orwell's general weakness as a novelist—is that he has too great a sympathy with Gordon's aestheticism and "Marxism." He is Lawrencian by intention, but not by experience; his experience, which he now seeks to repudiate, has been Gordon's.

But in *Coming Up for Air* Orwell takes a fat, jolly, average man for hero, and creates a "normal" voice for his England. The character George Bowling is strikingly like a character in *Keep the Aspidistra Flying,* a fat commercial traveler called Flaxman, whom Gordon recoils from in horror and envy of such blatant enjoyment of life. Of the two, Gordon was certainly the more like Orwell, or at least Eric Blair, in the latter's early conversations with himself as a would-be writer; but Bowling was much closer to the common-sense voice Orwell developed in his critical essays. There is some evidence to suggest that Orwell was fascinated for personal reasons by the Don Quixote-Sancho Panza dichotomy of human types, that his own life-enterprise was to stop being the first and become the second. The great writer from whom he learned so much, James Joyce, had achieved his aristic salvation by a similar transition in fictional heroes; from Stephen Dedalus to Leopold Bloom; and although Orwell's was a smaller achievement, it was a solid one. The image of England he gives us in *Coming Up for Air* is much more authoritative than that of *Keep the Aspidistra Flying.* It belongs, I think, with Waugh's very different images of country-house decadence, among the authoritative images of England then. Both authors show us large houses, with small people rattling around in them; both make the same implicit diagnosis—of a country of little, light-weight suburbanites, shrimps and small crabs sleeping through the storm of history in the protective shells, now much too large for them, that fitted their genial, solid, and vigorous grandfathers.*

Outside fiction, Orwell found his voice in two splendid books, *Homage to Catalonia,* about the Spanish war, and *The Road to Wigan Pier,* a Left Book Club description of the life of the unemployed in the north of England. Here the factual exposition, the practical-man tone, and the clear, sharp polemic serve a very complex and vigorous consciousness behind them. In these books the "experience," the unhappiness, which overbalanced the *Aspidistra's* enterprise, is only the material for his purposeful intelligence, and so the decent man can use everything he knows and is. Moreover, Orwell's genre of "cultural criticism"—of asking not what the socialist creed is, but what sort of men socialists are—became the most powerful weapon in the hands of the anti-dandies. This "culture criticism" (to which "temperament criticism" is perhaps the natural successor) had in the 19th century been directed primarily against the philistinism of the world of men. But in the 20th century it has directed itself rather against the dandies and aesthetes.

Orwell was also becoming a fine literary critic, in essays like the one on Dickens, that on Dali, and that on Henry Miller. And even more than a literary critic he became a culture critic, and in essays like those on boys' magazines and on comic postcards he taught

---

* It is interesting that Waugh more than once characterized modern Englishmen as impostors—pretending to be full-size men like their fathers—and preferred his dandy-aesthetes as being at least conscious impostors, or even impresarios of imposture. In Put Out More Flags, Ambrose Silk talks about the Victorian fog, out of which Victorian England spoke like the Voice in Sinai, until electricity replaced coal and the fog dispersed. "It was a carnival ball, my dear, which when the guests unmasked at midnight was found to be composed entirely of impostors." And in Brideshead Revisited Anthony Blanche is described as a kind of Diaghilev of the Oxford scene, whose departure left the young aristocrats disenchanted, magicless, looking suburban in the common light of day. "The Charity matinee was over, I felt; the impresario had buttoned his astrakhan coat and taken his fee and the disconsolate ladies of the company were without a leader. . . . For a few happy hours of rehearsal, for a few ecstatic minutes of performance, they had played splendid parts, their own great ancestors, the famous paintings they were thought to resemble; now it was over. . . ." Orwell, of course, was not interested in magic or theater; but he had just as clear a sense of the disenchanted drabness of contemporary Englishmen.

an eager, although discriminating, response to popular culture. In all these ways he was building a temperamental alternative to the dandy, the rogue, the naïf, and the magus—a barrier against all those attractions that had proved so dangerous to Eric Blair and all his generation.

Orwell's effective ally, *Scrutiny,* was busy undermining the prestige of the dandies and of those the dandies admired—undermining their literary reputations on strictly literary grounds. *Scrutiny* also, of course, engaged in intellectual and cultural criticism, but an important feature of its strategies was its concentration on literary criticism as an irreplaceable and intrinsic discipline, which could deal with aestheticism and aesthetes on their own terms. Thus *Scrutiny* critics attacked Lord David Cecil for his graces of style—his "sentences which mean nothing" and are all embroidery and music—and warned readers against him as a dangerous model. And they attacked taking Aldous Huxley as a model of "intelligence" and blamed Bloomsbury for touting him as such. Q. D. (Mrs.) Leavis commented that E. M. Forster was not much better than Bloomsbury, and F. R. Leavis commented on how Auden's group, or "gang," protected their master, and each other, from the criticism he and they needed.[25]

"Criticism" meant something very concrete and demonstrable to the *Scrutiny* writers, and they condemned other scholars and appraisers of literature for offering something so merely personal and feelingful under that name; but it was also for them something with important implied and extended meanings. In fact, "criticism" was the intellectual activity that trained men to be mature and responsible. It was a play or discipline of the mind, involving much knowledge and intellectual techniques, which yet carried with it powerful determinants of temperament; it was to the cult of maturity and decency what Christian theology was to Christian worship. Every cult must develop related activities (for example, church history, church music, and church social life) that are only indirectly, but significantly, religious. Some of these are intellectual, and "criticism" was decency's equivalent for these.

Mrs. Leavis also had a long attack, in 1937, on Dorothy Sayers and those who made a literary cult of her detective novels, and
we can connect this with *Scrutiny's* attack on P. G. Wodehouse. In
1939, Oxford awarded Wodehouse an honorary doctorate. Evelyn
Waugh wrote in *The Tablet* that the university had redeemed itself
in so doing, and cited Belloc's praise of Wodehouse as a prose styl-
ist. He described Wodehouse as the equal of Beerbohm and Knox
and as "high in the historic succession of the master craftsmen of his
trade." He pointed out—and one supposes that he was pointing to
one source of his own delight in Wodehouse—that the latter's characters all live, year after year, in their robust middle twenties, and
their desperate, transitory, romantic passions have no connection of
either hope or fear with "procreation."[26] *Scrutiny's* editorial comment
was that the whole point of Wodehouse's humor was its shamefaced
rejection of the standards of maturity—they thus saw much the same
thing in him as Waugh, but valued it differently—and that Oxford's
honoring of him was the mark of that university's final decadence. In
this and the attack on Dorothy Sayers, we see how clearly *Scrutiny*
understood the plan of the cultural battlefield, recognizing how the
detective novel and the humorous novel were in those days the allies
of the serious dandy writers.

The weaker side of the *Scrutiny* writers appears in their remarks
about Picasso, the ballet, surrealism, and other manifestations of modernism to which they were temperamentally opposed, but in which
they recognized artistic achievement. Their tone tends to become
priggish and their maneuvering clumsy—they were maneuvering for a
way to preserve their own consistency and yet make some genial contact with these phenomena. Thus we read, in a 1937 issue, that Picasso
had to destroy old values in order to create new ones; that is the saving
purpose that redeems his iconoclasm, although we gather that he was
unconscious of this purpose, and that *Scrutiny* is finding it for him.
Indeed, a correlation *can* be established between his art and a sickness
in the modern soul, the argument goes, but we are not to say simply
that he is "sick." Anyway, he is the *last* of the moderns; no more can be

done along the lines of disintegration. (This is the tactic Leavis took toward Joyce's *Ulysses,* too.) The ballet criticism is less self-constricting, for it does emphatically prefer Diaghilev both to dilettantism of the Duncan and Dalcroze variety and to pure classical dancing. And it can joyfully attack inadequate styles of ballet criticism as mere word-painting, mere impressionism, and so on. But one senses an embarrassment—what else could there be?—before the task of reconciling Diaghilev's whole enterprise with *Scrutiny's,* of making the two out to be in any sense allies.[27]

Here we come up against the stonewall limitations of Leavis's (and Orwell's) adventure of ideas, the paradox of any largely rearguard action in art. In fact Picasso's paintings and Diaghilev's ballets were icons of the *Sonnenkind* cult, and therefore "decadent" from the point of view of the two great spokesmen for maturity. To contemplate them could not confirm the temperament the Leavises were inculcating. To have been significantly consistent, *Scrutiny* should have dealt with both the way L. C. Knights dealt with Restoration comedy and its admirers, in another issue of 1937. He found the genre trivial, gross, and dull, its language too limitedly upper-class to be rich, and its attack on the institution of marriage dull. (It is, of course, my contention that what offended Knights really was that Restoration comedy is the genre of dandies and rogues.) And on another matter of literary culture, in 1938, Q. D. Leavis attacked Virginia Woolf for not being serious, for reacting against the seriousness of the 19th century, and for "letting our servants live for us." Discreetly, but firmly, Mrs. Leavis let it be known that she herself was a wife and mother as well as an intellectual, and that she objected to Virginia Woolf's feminist rebellion against the former roles because she herself had succeeded in combining those with the other. She was the critic as married woman; something similar was implied—usually it was not explicit—in all *Scrutiny* criticism; F. R. Leavis wrote as "the married man" as much as Lawrence did in his introduction to the Magnus memoir. So did Orwell, explicitly in *Homage to Catalonia.* The *Sonnenkinder,* of course, did not.

In 1939, Mrs. Leavis wrote an interesting essay called "The Background of 20th Century Letters," in which she reviewed Cyril Connolly's memoirs together with those of Logan Pearsall Smith, Edward Marsh, and Louis MacNeice. She contrasted the picture presented by all of them with that presented by the Americans Malcolm Cowley and Lincoln Steffens. In the latter's memoirs we see a gradual evolution out of cultural chaos toward standards and health. However, in England, she says, the "odious little spoilt boys of Mr. Connolly's schooldays move in a body up to the universities to become inane pretentious young men, and from there move into the literary quarters vacated by the last batch. These who get the jobs are the most fashionable boys in the school, or those with feline charm, or a sensual mouth and long eyelashes." The particular interest of these last phrases for us is that she is quoting them from Connolly's description of Brian Howard; it is the dandy she is attacking, and his prevalence, his dominance, in English letters. Moreover, one can be sure that she would not have been moved to withdraw her charge by being told that Howard was now a politically committed writer. It was the dandy *temperament* she was concentrating on—and blaming for the evils of the British situation. "The advantages Americans enjoy in having no Public School system, no ancient universities, etc., can hardly be exaggerated." They do not have schoolboys and playboys in charge of their literary life. Brian Howard represented the evil the Leavises warred against, and from which they hoped to rescue a saving remnant of Englishmen. He and the dandies were one pole of the cultural field. D. H. Lawrence was the other.

Chapter Eight

1939–1945:
The War

Harold and the Patriots

I
N THIS PERIOD, we must consider the national mood created
by the war before turning to the fate of the intellectual *Sonnenkinder,* because the latter now had to deal with new and alien
conditions of life, which affected them much more intimately and
unfavorably than the new ideas of the '30s had done. So adverse were
these conditions that they were almost deprived of their identity as
a group in various ways. Not only were the British dandies separated
from Anthony Blanche, but Brian and Harold quarreled between
themselves and for good, while Waugh, Betjeman, Byron, and Connolly all went very separate ways. Waugh became a soldier, Betjeman ensconced himself in neutral Ireland, Byron became a war correspondent, and Connolly edited an aesthetes' magazine. Moreover,
although only Waugh fought and only Byron was killed, all six were
largely silenced, their energies taken up by some war-work or war-life

enterprise. Waugh alone did "work of his own" of any importance. The unfriendliness of war conditions to any dandy-aesthete style of life or work was, of course, predictable from the first, but the full extent of their destructiveness only gradually became apparent.

The impact of the war on English social life, as measured in the lives of the *Sonnenkinder,* seems to have fallen into two stages: a preliminary period of genial anarchy, in which the dandies could triumph to some degree in the defeat of the country's old Reality principle; and then a longer period, during which a new and sterner Reality principle came to dominate the national life much more completely than the old one, and in which the dandies felt themselves the least valued and needed of all members of society. These stages correspond to those mirrored in the fiction of Evelyn Waugh, in this as in so much else our best imaginative historian. He presents the first stage in the appropriately anarchic and genial satire, *Put Out More Flags.* Then, in the war trilogy beginning with *Men at Arms,* he presents the whole story in the more realistic manner appropriate to its second half. But even for Waugh, who at the end of the first novel had welcomed the triumph of Reality and the end of the "phony war," the second half was deeply depressing and disappointing.

England in the grip of Reality was even less a homeland for dandies and rogues than it had been. Of course, the war brought back to political power the rogue "uncles," like Churchill, Beaverbrook, Lindemann, who had been exiled to the wings of national life during peace. They were retroactively redeemed; Baldwin and Chamberlain, the fathers, were repudiated. And a certain amount of protection and patronage did filter down from them to their "nephews," the post-1918 *Sonnenkinder.* In Churchill's case, the conduit of this patronage seems most often to have been his close associate, Brendan Bracken, and those two do seem to have acted on behalf of Waugh, Randolph Churchill, and Cecil Beaton in their war careers. But few of the men of letters, or men of the other arts, seem to have benefited significantly. They nearly all made *some* kind of special deal, through friends in high places, but not a good enough one to save them from the general fate. They were not the types the nation wanted and needed then.

Of the people we have much discussed, only Oswald and Diana Mosley were literally put in prison. They were there from 1940 to 1943, although Churchill personally did what he could to improve his old friends' lot. Most of our subjects, however, felt themselves in a metaphorical prison.

The new Reality principle called itself the "war effort," and it dominated national life by means of the rhetoric of official speeches and publications, propaganda, and censorship, but also by means of new institutions and regulations, which in wartime interfered much more than before in the major and minor features of everyone's experience. The army, naturally, came to count for much more in the complex of the national life, and civilian life changed in the direction of becoming more like the army. This could not be pleasant for *Sonnenkinder,* who always rebel against institutions, and especially those with a severe discipline. Of course, armies themselves are institutions that have traditionally found room and scope for brilliant individualists. The British army, as we have seen, had its own traditions of dandyism, and also of individualism of T. E. Lawrence's kind; and the wars of Elizabethan England evoke images, at least in the uninstructed imagination, of Children of the Sun triumphant everywhere, from Sidney and Raleigh to Leicester and Essex. And there *were,* in the second war, one or two fields of action for adventurous *Sonnenkinder*—the private armies, which we have already mentioned, and the secret services, which we will say something about. But this does not seem to have been *their* war—there was no T. E. Lawrence and no Compton Mackenzie this time; and certainly it was not the dandy-aesthetes' war. One reason was that the army and the navy were overshadowed in action by the air force, the most technological and least aristocratic of the armed services. Another, related reason was that official propaganda presented this as a "people's war," and emphasized the proletarian ordinariness of its heroes. (Evelyn Waugh satirizes this and the air force in *Officers and Gentlemen.)* Thus the pilots of the Battle of Britain, the nearest thing to a corps of *Sonnenkinder,* were not presented as brilliant or elegant figures. Exceptions like the poet-pilot Richard Hillary seemed old-fashioned beside the much more prosaic Douglas Bader.

In many ways, civilian England during the war does not evoke the image of an army so much as of a school. It was a war of rules and regulations, of solicited sacrifices and exhortations to show the right spirit. One heard as much of civilian as of military sufferings, and in fact only 750 Old Etonian servicemen died in this war, although the same number served as in the first one, when 1,150 died. And the civilian sufferings derived from rationing, regulations, and regulators, as much as from bombs. The civil service, which in 1939 employed 387,000 people, had in 1943 710,000 employees. Harold Acton says, "Bliss was it then for politicians and bureaucrats to be alive, for they enjoyed the kudos of earthly divinities." Their intellects could burgeon as never in peacetime.

The dandies in particular felt that they were back in an institutional atmosphere just like the one they had so joyfully escaped at the beginning of the '20s—an atmosphere of do's and don'ts, of punishments and reports, of lights out and school meals and pedagogical praise and blame. They were back in many senses. Just to be stuck in England again was a kind of imprisonment to Brian and Harold, who had sought the freedom they needed abroad; now they were trapped in England for the duration of the war, and the "normal" dullards, whose disapproval they had flouted, were suddenly in a position to punish them. One vivid example of that in Brian's and Harold's lives was their official air force dossiers; both had millstones round their necks in the form of hostile official reports that they could not get rid of and which prevented their promotion. This must have reminded them vividly of school experience—that aspect of it that they had hated and that in the years since Eton they had triumphed over in wit and scorn. Now suddenly the whole nation was a school again, and school prefect types like Sir William (later Lord) Beveridge were running their lives.

Beveridge had no direct contact with Howard or Acton, but he is worth examining as a public representative of the Reality principle, a public servant of the world of the fathers.[1] He was a virtuous dowdy, the opposite of the dandy-aesthete in every way. He was an aesetic saint of planning and statistics, a social-scientist social worker, dedicated selflessly to the service of his community; he avoided personal flamboyance himself by virtue of indifference and broke down traditional forms of splendor (and inequity) by rational analysis and experiment. A friend of the Webbs and brother-in-law of R. H. Tawney, Beveridge worked first at the East End settlement, Toynbee Hall, and then went to the board of trade. During the first war he worked out and pushed through a national unemployment insurance scheme. In 1919 he became director of the London School of Economics, and continued his work of compiling national social statistics throughout the interwar years. During the second war he worked out his plan for a welfare state in England—the famous Beveridge Report of 1942, which was the basis for the postwar Labour government's attempt to socialize the country. Winston Churchill, although a former patron of Beveridge, a user of his statistics, tried to smother the report when it came out; an army pamphlet that summarized it as a subject for educational debate among the troops was officially withdrawn. Temperamentally, as well as ideologically, Churchill hated a womb-to-tomb planned life. So did Evelyn Waugh, who took occasion more than once to insult Beveridge in public. Indeed, one can take the character of Sir Wilfred Lucas-Dockery in Waugh's *Decline and Fall* as a satire on exactly Beveridge's kind of man. To Children of the Sun, men like Beveridge seem bloodless pedagogues, sexless state functionaries, servants of system, with no life or style of their own and an unconscious hatred of life and style in others. And these were the men who rose to power in time of war. This fact, more than anything the Germans did, made the war years in England so miserable for the dandies.

When Harold Acton arrived back in London in 1939, he found his friends awaiting the war in various postures. He saw much of picturesque dandies like Lord Berners, who kept a spinet in his Rolls-Royce (also a porcelain tortoise) and attracted attention in restaurants by blowing bubbles at other diners, and Robin de la Condamine, an actor who specialized in luridly evil parts and whom Acton had known in Florence. The latter's home reminded Acton of *À rebours:* "alabaster bowls of semi-precious stones, rose quartz, and smoky topaz, and iridescent black amber from Catania. . . . The amber he described as resin from Hell's volcanoes.—'I bought it when I was down there on a visit.'" But Acton also saw the more warlike Robert Byron and Evelyn Waugh. Byron had bought a gas mask and helmet before war broke out, and was building himself an air-raid shelter in his garden, when Acton arrived. Waugh was recently married—Acton described his wife as "hardly more than a child, with celestial, trusting eyes"— and was ready again to be friends with Acton. Waugh and Byron were now seriously estranged. Waugh tells of their meeting in a restaurant, when Byron came over to his table and hissed malevolently, "In uniform, I see, like Billy Clonmore," a phrase that he managed to imbue with significant venom. (Billy Clonmore, an Irish peer, was a friend of both since Oxford, and Byron seems to have been implying that Waugh was playing some game of competitive snobbery by joining the army.)[2] In both rogues the idiosyncrasies and irritabilities were growing so intense as to get out of control, and so their old rivalry was becoming hatred.

Acton applied to the War Office for a job, but was given nothing; so he went to Italy, for the British Council, to lecture on Anglo-Italian relations. He was wounded to discover that his parents were afraid that he would make a fool of himself as a lecturer. They had not seen him since 1936, and he realized that they had never believed in him as an adult. This was particularly true of his father, who stood in much the same skeptical relation to Harold as Sir George Sitwell did to Osbert or Francis Howard to Brian. Moreover, Arthur Acton was indifferent to literature and looked down on writers. Nor did he want his son's companionship—all he wanted was pretty faces and prattle and flattery.

> The knowledge that I was a disappointment to my father proved a barrier to complete enjoyment of home life. I greatly admired his fine taste and intuitive flair for painting,

sculpture and architecture; had I not been his son I am sure we would have been the best of friends. Unfortunately he expected my brother and me to live *in statu pupillari* under his permanent supervision and control. . . . My mother was the most angelic of companions. . . . I owe everything to her instinctive understanding.

His father never believed in Harold's manhood; and his mother offered him only "understanding." It is a sad story that Acton has to tell of his relations with his parents in the second volume of his *Memoirs;* and it is a sad story that Marie-Jacqueline Lancaster's book about Brian Howard tells of *his* relations with *his* parents. Their fathers had never been convinced by their gestures of independence—their young-man style still seemed to need "permanent supervision and control" by a man—and by 1939 others apparently thought that the fathers had been right all along. By 1945 that was to seem incontrovertible.

William Acton, meanwhile, had refused to become a war artist, as Harold had urged him to do, and finally was put into the Pioneer Corps without a commission. He had been disappointed in his career as an artist, and in life generally. He was irritable with his brother when the latter returned to London and went to stay with him. William had a studio in Tite Street in Chelsea, but he was painting very little by 1939. He had become in some sense a fashionable painter of portraits; his sitters included the duchess of Kent, Phyllis de Jantze, Anne Messel, and other fashionable beauties from the dandies' circle, and during the war he painted the marchesa Casati. But his works were never successful in art circles. Harold calls his brother's work unconscious surrealism, and the heads of these beauties *can* remind one of heads in Dali's paintings, for they are rendered like wax models, very brightly lit and colored, and are suspended from above by ribbons or superimposed upon some theater-backdrop landscape. But if his painting fits into the same category as that of Dali or Tchelitchew, William Acton's stops as far short of the significant design one can trace in theirs, as his brother's novel *Cornelian* stops short of, say, Nabokov's *Pale Fire*.

Harold Acton returned to London in May 1940, and lectured on Italy to members of the W.R.N.S. (Women's Royal Naval Service), who, he says, hated him and his lectures. When Mussolini entered the war, his parents found themselves briefly arrested, and Mrs. Acton had to spend three days in prison. Finally, by means of bribery, they escaped detention and emigrated to Switzerland, to Vévey, but they had been severely shaken by the experience, and also by the indifference or malice of Italian neighbors they had thought their friends. Mrs. Acton declared she would never return to Florence, but Mr. Acton spent his war days gathering every scrap of information he could get about the fate of his possessions and intriguing for their safety from a distance. Both generations, then, began to realize that this second war was going to be harder on aesthetes than the last one.

In London there were two types of response to the war among Acton's friends (discounting eccentrics like Berners and de la Condamine); the more orthodox response was exemplified by Cecil Beaton ("under a lackadaisical manner, he was a determined dynamo, and a stalwart patriot," says Acton) and the other by Brian Howard. Brian returned from France in June 1940 and by November had got a job in M.I.5, the secret service agency, which had already enrolled several of his left-wing friends. This was on the surface a kind of patriotic activity too, but it turned out to be less orthodoxly so than Cecil Beaton's. Brian talked to everyone about M.I.5, as if he had joined some very exclusive club, or some secret Star Chamber court. Acton says, "he had begun to look at me with pitying condescension, as at one of the doomed." Brian saw the war, in these first months of official anti-fascist enthusiasm (which was to some extent anti-right-wing in general) as a chance for his left-wing friends to exert power over the Conservative half of their acquaintance, whether dandy or hearty. Among these newly powerful friends of his, "parlour-pink cronies" as Acton calls them, the most vindictive, we are told, was Guy Burgess. Brian and Guy saw a lot of each other in those months, and Acton describes them as epitomes of "this muddled intelligentsia."

There was an obvious current of sympathy between Burgess and Brian, who fulminated against *rentiers* and Money Men in his latest role, but at bottom he remained a hedonist and a snob [and a dandy, in speech as well as clothes]. . . . Sitting in the Gargoyle or the Cafe Royal, he could still impose himself by his superior command of language. While others hemmed and hawed he spoke with precision.

We hear from other sources too that Brian, while working for M.I.5, used to bully people even in nightclubs, threatening to have them "put inside," by turning in information he had collected about them. "I've got it all here," he would say, tapping his briefcase, "Call yourself a gentleman, I think I smell a Fascist, hmmmmmmm? . . ."

At the same time, he was still very indiscreet and hostile to all authority, and especially to all *British* authority, and became more so as the years of the war passed. Gerald Hamilton (the original of the corrupt Mr. Norris in Isherwood's Berlin stories) was with Guy Burgess and Brian when the latter was, as often, discussing official secrets in a loud voice in public. A policeman approached them and asked Brian to give him his name and address. He replied, "I am Brian Howard and I live in Mayfair. No doubt *you* come from some dreary suburb."* Hamilton says he "remarked to Guy Burgess that, in my experience, this was a *most* tactless way of receiving the attentions of the civil arm."[3] (Sometimes Hamilton sounds like a caricature of Harold Acton.)

On another occasion Brian was asked for his name and service number in the Ritz Bar, where he had again been talking very loudly and critically about national policy. He was then an aircraftsman, of the lowest rank, and it was an officer who spoke to him; but Brian replied over his shoulder, "Mrs. Smith to you, darling," still defying author-

---

* It is worth comparing an anecdote about Randolph Churchill in Athens in 1944. Someone told him he only got away with his rudeness because he was his father's son, and he replied, "I don't see why you have to bring MY father into this discussion. I never would bring in your father, even if I knew him, which I don't. I can but assume you do. . . . As a matter of fact, I am bloody sure he's an utterly dreary, middle class bore. . . ." The insult direct is emblematic of a number of things that unite Howard and Churchill, and so many others. Dandy and rogue are in this matter indistinguishable.

ity. Like Firbank in the first war, Brian came to see the prevalence of the army as the triumph of all his life enemies. He came to hate the sight of a uniform, and could not prevent himself from insulting those who wore it, even taunting army officers with the retreat from Dunkirk while this was being presented to the public as a British victory. Finally (for their relationship), Brian grew angry with Harold and threw a cocktail in his face, again in the Ritz Bar, because the latter was wearing an officer's uniform. This was the last time they ever met, although they did exchange letters again later.

Acton meanwhile had been sent to Blackpool for several months in 1940 to teach the English language to Free Polish airmen. He was unhappy: "Maybe I was presumptuous, but I could not be satisfied with this occupation." In May 1941 he was finally accepted into the R.A.F. himself, which he welcomed because he hoped that it would be the means by which he might be sent to represent Britain in China—he thought he could "clear the air of distrust between the two nations." "Absurd as it may sound in retrospect, I had a sense of vocation that was almost mystical; I could almost compare my experience to Joan of Arc's voices."

This ambassadorial vocation was Acton's solution to the problem of combining patriotic convictions with the dandy-aesthete temperament, although in him by this time that temperament was much modified by the qualities of the connoisseur and the scholar. And his style in describing those convictions reveals the difficulty of making that combination.

However, he entered the R.A.F. with enthusiasm, or with a determination to be enthusiastic. He speaks of the airmen as "these legendary heroes," and asks, "couldn't it be said of the R.A.F. that the spirit burned with a hard, gem-like flame?" "My admiration for these fellows amounted to hero-worship. . . ." He became the intelligence officer attached to a squadron. "Laughter irrigated our relationship though I never became proficient in their patois. . . . I could never exclaim 'Wizard show!' or 'It's a piece of cake!' without acute embarrassment." He jested and sang with them, "more actor than Acton."

Finally in 1942 he was sent abroad, and arrived in Barrack-pore in India, where he was set to collecting news items for propaganda purposes. He hoped he was on his way to China. But he found his senior officers so secretive with him that he grew discouraged. He was kept in a "lowly secretarial capacity," answering telephones and filing documents, "couched in an execrable English which I was not allowed to correct." "I was never invited to any conference. . . . I had the unpleasant feeling that I was not trusted." Then he found in an embassy file a gross libel on his character (apparently he was described as "a scandalous debauchee"), as well as a statement that he was not persona grata and must never be allowed to get to China.

This discovery was obviously a great shock to him. The schoolmaster primness and prejudice he had thought he had escaped for ever had returned with even more power to punish him. In the introduction to *More Memoirs,* he deals with the matter quite grandly, saying that his calumniator was "evidently some epicene dunderhead from the Foreign Office. His rage against my independent way of life was that of the perennial snake in the grass, the envious Philistine." But at the time, it is evident, such verbal exuberance could not salve the wound dealt him. The snakes in the grass were in power. "In time of peace I was beyond his bite; in time of war I was poisoned by it, and the wound continued to fester."

He got himself transferred to Delhi as press liaison officer, and then, having to have an operation, was sent home, where he rejoined the society of Emerald Cunard, Randolph Churchill, Duff and Diana Cooper, and all his friends in London. He worked as press censor at the supreme headquarters of the Allied Expeditionary Forces Unit in Bloomsbury, until in October 1944 he was sent to do the same work in Paris. There he met Cocteau, Bérard, and the Diaghilev dancers Kochno and Lifar again. (Their reputations were then besmirched with accusations of treachery—of collaboration—as some of Burgess and Maclean's friends in England were later to be.) Cocteau was still a major inspiration for Acton. The latter describes him as "a poet in whatever he did . . . the symbolic Harlequin . . . always rejuvenating himself," and as a brilliant talker, who could not help wanting to please. He thought the new literary star, Jean-Paul Sartre, only another Cocteau, expunged of poetry.

While he was in Paris, Acton was sought out by George Orwell, who came there as a war correspondent. Acton says,

> He remembered me from Eton, and I vaguely remembered him as a stork-like figure, prematurely adult, fluttering about the school-yard in his black gown. . . . [To me, he] was as amiable as he could be, in his dry, frustrated way. . . . I was impressed by his mournful dignity. . . . He looked like a soul in pain in spite of his puzzling moustache, but he was more complex, more ingrown, than a Latin intellectual suffering from similar sorrows." All these phrases evoke Orwell's strategic self-concealments, as well as Acton's strategic theory of Englishness as "dry and frustrated."

Each one's strategies were designed to protect himself against the other, but their meeting was apparently a success. "Altogether he kindled my sympathy," says Acton, "And he must have found me agreeable to seek my company." Apparently Orwell shared most of his meals in Paris with Acton.

I think we can assume that he would not have so sought out Brian Howard. But Harold Acton was a figure who suited Orwell's intellectual categories—in rather the same way as he suited Waugh's. For both of them Acton was the man who had devoted himself to art and beauty, and so was ineffectual in other areas of life where *they* were effective—his life demonstrated the necessity of the choice *they* had made, although he had taken the opposite option. Orwell wrote warmly of such men, even of Osbert Sitwell—but not of men like Howard and Auden, who tried to be effective in politics as well as in literature. Unlike Waugh, Orwell had no easy means of converse with Acton, no way to exchange affection, but he had, we can believe, liking and respect for him.

Among others who visited Acton in Paris was Cecil Beaton. (They went to see *Huis Clos* together.) Beaton's war career had been like an immensely more successful version of Acton's. He had been attached to the R.A.F., to take photographs of airmen and airplanes. He had held exhibitions of those photographs, and published books of them, as well as of people in power and of ruined streets in the blitzed cities. He now photographed very different subjects, in a very different style. Instead of debutantes, reflected upside down in tin foil, or apparently beheaded, he showed the nation bandaged babies, courageous old Cockneys, and unself-consciously heroic firemen and trawlermen, portrayed with reverent pathos and in the simplest of settings. Like Acton, Beaton seems genuinely to have felt the patriotic emotions appropriate to his activities and to have laid aside his dandy persona insofar as that was possible—not without pain, but without grudge and with some success.

He too treated the soldiers, sailors, and airmen as "heroes," although proletarian heroes, and their lack of style in *his* sense, the gulf between them and him, he sincerely though inauthentically interpreted to their advantage. (Ironically, he himself suffered from the prescriptiveness of the proletarian style he helped to spread. In New York in 1945, one of his friends in the British intelligence services told him they could not use him as a representative because, "You give the impression of being a beau, and the office wants to show that the British are really very like the Americans." Dandies were to be hidden away out of sight.) Like his photographs, Beaton's chapters about the young airmen in *The Years Between*[4] are very like Noel Coward's depiction of young sailors in *In Which We Serve*. Between them, these two dandies did more than anyone else to fix the official image of cheery, hearty, proletarian England at war. The two had been rather hostile to each other, but in 1942 they met at John Sutro's, and were reconciled. It was a rather grotesque encounter, as Beaton presents it. When the latter said he had not understood why Coward had shown no interest in him, the latter replied, "Don't you believe it, sister, I've been madly interested in you! But I've been a fool, I've misjudged you." Now, convinced by Beaton's record in war work, he embraced him. ". . . People like us should be friends rather than enemies because we really have so much in common—powers of observation, wit, industriousness and professionalism."

The most poignant case in Beaton's memoirs of the confusion between the dandy persona and the war work comes in an anecdote about his photographing a Spitfire formation from one of the planes.

> The wind blew my eyelashes into my eyes, and it was difficult to focus. Suddenly, I saw myself reflected in the view-finder of my camera. The crow's feet around my eyes were those of an old man. Oh God! was there no escape from oneself even under these unusual conditions?

These are rather like the feelings Waugh ascribes to Cedric Lyne in *Put Out More Flags.* But Beaton was England's official photographer. He gave the nation its visual images of the king and the prime minister, and the cabinet.

In 1942, Randolph Churchill persuaded Brendan Bracken to send Beaton to Cairo, where he photographed the heroes of the desert war, and from there he was sent to India, Burma, and China. He was in America in 1945, when the war ended, and his comments express a general British attitude to Americans then, attributing to them a greater sexual and vital potency. He had already described meeting "sexy" American soldiers—"They do not seem to contaminate the gum they chew." Now he was driven to Connecticut from New York, through streets

> filled with cars dashing so smoothly to the overpopulated countryside. Sexy, apricot-coloured husbands with their arrogant wives, their dyed hair blowing in the wind, paid no attention to the nest-full of children sucking goodies in the back of the car. Everyone seemed so independent and carefree, so self-assured in taking so much luxury for granted. The gargantuan Sunday joint we enjoyed would have used up a six months ration ticket book at home.

That surely expresses very vividly the Britishers' sense of the Americans' greater size, a sense that was at the end of the second war even sharper than at the end of the first. The English faced an even more difficult problem in finding a national style and identity, if they were not to feel simply inferior.

Beaton, of course, could not offer them such a style, torn as he was between the old ones. The climax of *The Years Between* is a description of how he broke down on hearing the news of his friend Rex Whistler's death—on that weekend in Connecticut. His own career successes all became unreal to him, and he felt guilty: "Of course Rex is dead and I'm alive. It's so bloody unfair! I've been messing about doing a rotten, piddling little job that's only an alibi. I'm not capable of making any real effort as Rex had done. I started to bellow." It is notable how the vocabulary of St. Cyprian's, both verbal and ethical, returns to Beaton in this moment of crisis. In the crunch, at the moment of death and love it was the old values of action and war that counted. The dandy adventure had been only a holiday.

Brian and the Traitors

Notable among those who refused to accommodate themselves to the public roles assigned them was Brian Howard. In June 1942 he was dismissed from the war office, and when he was thereupon conscripted as an airman, there was a note in his dossier at the air ministry that he was never to be given a commission. His and Harold Acton's dossiers, being so like the school reports of their youth, symbolized the fearful regression into the shadows of childhood, into imprisonment by the fathers, that the war as a whole meant to the dandies. Brian became a clerk in Bomber Command, at High Wycombe; he was under the command of Squadron Leader Alan Clutton-Brock, his old ally and disciple at Eton, a member of the Society of Arts there. He used to impose himself on the Clutton-Brocks socially. Transferred to another post, Brian formed the habit of referring to his commander as "Colonel Cutie" (something Basil Seal does in *Put Out More Flags*) and so aroused his hostility. Finally he was given a medical discharge in December 1944.

He had by then acquired the love-companion he was to keep till his death. This was an Irishman called Sam, who served in Air-Sea Rescue, and who was fond enough of Brian to form a stable relationship with him, even though he was often treated abominably. It was now that Brian undertook to write a biography of Norman Douglas, for the publishers Home and Van Thal. He was still writing reviews for the *New Statesman* and scripts for the BBC (five of the latter in 1942). But his behavior was wilder and more destructive, his health was worse, and his cruelty to others was more intolerable than ever before.

Often there was enough panache to his style to make the cruelty funny. Thus he is reported to have taken sudden offense at a bishop he met in the Authors' Club, and to have pulled his nose in public, saying, "Oh, so you're one of those matey, cocktail-drinking padres, are you? Don't think I didn't see you winking at that young waiter. What did you say? I've a good mind to pull your nose. I think I will." But his attacks on old friends and lovers were more intimately vindictive and ugly.

Two men whose experience of the war began by being somewhat similar to Brian's were John Strachey and Guy Burgess. Strachey had been disillusioned with Communism and with Russia by the Nazi–Soviet pact of 1939, and with his usual speed in switching sides he had sold his Russian bonds and bought General Motors stock instead. His wife, Celia, took their children to Canada for safety when the war broke out, and he turned Bohemian again, released from both personal and ideological pressures to be a respectable family man. He picked up a girl friend who had been one of the "bright young people," and went to live with Guy Burgess in Victor Rothschild's house in Bentinck Street. This house became, as we shall see, a center of quite orgiastic self-release for quite a lot of people, some of whom were quite highly placed. Burgess introduced Strachey to the delights of music, and also spent a lot of time discussing politics with him, as well as indulging in rowdier pleasures.

But Strachey moved out of the house before too long. He became an adjutant in the R.A.F., and wrote patriotic war-effort essays like *A Faith to Fight For.* He loved his men in the R.A.F., and adored his squadron leaders, Gleed and Smallwood. He persuaded Gleed to write *Arise to Conquer,* another patriotic clarion call. The R.A.F. apparently replaced the Communist party for Strachey; Air Marshal Slessor replaced Palme Dutt as a father-figure. Strachey reentered the Establishment and reassumed responsibility and maturity. When Celia returned from Canada with the children in 1943, he resumed family life, and in 1945 he became M.P. for Dundee. Typically, Strachey during the elections dined with his Liberal opponent (in a private room, to elude the gaze of his supporters) because he despised his fellow Labour candidate. And on the train back to London after winning, he secretly joined Robert Boothby, the Conservative, to drink champagne, as soon as they were safely away from his station. He had more in common temperamentally with such ideological enemies than he had with his Labour constituents and allies, and these were subdued gestures of defiance. But his behavior as a whole was adjusted to public demands—as was *not* true of Brian Howard and Guy Burgess.

Burgess had continued his career in the secret services after Howard had been fired. He also continued his undercover career as a Russian agent in that paradoxically congenial setting: Here we must give some sketch of the British secret services during the war, both so that the reader can follow Guy Burgess's career in particular, and so as to illuminate one of the main loci of the rogues and dandies in general.[5] (It was thither they flocked, when the war broke out, as to their own holiday camp. These services were the great anti-institutional institutions of the war, where *Sonnenkinder* exacted a half-conscious revenge for the humiliations they suffered elsewhere.) Everyone who was in the secret services during the war (at least during its first years) takes the same tone of sardonic and destructive cynicism in writing about them. It is the tone of adolescent schoolboys about their masters at a very inefficient school; it is the tone of *Sonnenkinder* about the world of the fathers at its most absurd. In England then there seems to have been both a large number of *Sonnenkinder* working in those services, and a high incidence of feebleness in the permanent members who temperamentally accepted the system.

There had long been bitter rivalry and jealousy between M.I.5. (intelligence) and M.I.6. (counterintelligence). They were new and almost exclusively peacetime institutions. The head of the former from its founding in 1909 had been Sir Vernon Kell, until he was replaced by Sir Joseph Ball, a man who promoted Burgess's career considerably. The head of the latter had been Mansfield Cumming, from its founding in 1911 until Sir Stewart Menzies took over in 1939. The latter was an Old Etonian blue-blood, three times married into the aristocracy, and decorated with the K.C.B., K.C.M.G., D.S.O., and M.C. He represented the world of power and privilege, in old-fashioned gentlemanly style. He spent much of his time conferring in the bar at White's Club, and left much of the power to his two mutually hostile assistants, Valentine Vivian and Sir Claude Dancey. As presented in various memoirs, they seem to have been quite classically a dandy and a rogue; Vivian was lean and elegant, with crinkled hair and a monocle, while Dancey was tough and bear-like, anti-intellectual and "a bounder."

Among these men at M.I.6, between M.I.6 as a whole and M.I.5, and among the other secret services, there was much competition and mutual betrayal, which seems to have amounted to a more real war than that waged against the Germans—more real both psychologically, in the hostile passions of those involved, and practically, in the shrewdness and destructiveness of the moves made. And observing all this were the temporary personnel, many of them writers of the group we have been following.

All the men of letters who have worked for the British secret services form in some ways a recognizable literary group, but there are important differences between earlier and later members. Kipling may have spied, Buchan certainly did, and A. E. W. Mason and Compton Mackenzie (we might take Mackenzie, and Somerset Maugham, in the first war, as transitional between the earlier and the later figures), and then Graham Greene, Malcolm Muggeridge, Dennis Wheatley, John Le Carré, and Ian Fleming. What unites them all is that their literary work presents itself as fantasy, even when it is drawn from their real-life activities. (Their unity becomes apparent as soon as you contrast them with authors in the range from George Eliot to D. H. Lawrence.) On the other hand, the differences between Kipling's *Kim* and Greene's *Our Man in Havana* suggest all the differences between the England and English manhood of before 1914 and those of after 1918. In *Kim* the secret servicemen believe in what they are doing and derive moral health from doing it. After 1918 the services gradually became—in literary image but also apparently in literal fact—a grotesque and preposterous fantasy that bred cynicism and unhealth. The general form of English life had grown so shaky that the subordination of rogue and dandy values to gentlemanly ones had broken down.

Some of the stories told about the chaos in M.I. 5 during the war almost exceed belief. The organization took over Wormwood Scrubs prison, but moved in before all the prisoners had moved out, and a chaplain who had been left behind continued to preach to his new congregation about the civic responsibilities that they would shortly be facing, once they had paid their debt to society. (Even if such anecdotes were apocryphal, they were also current, and that tells us that M.I.5 lived in an Evelyn Waugh world.) Kell had always hired upper-class girls (applicants were asked whether they had titles), many of whom could not type or file, and some of whom could not spell. They took their jobs as fantasy, and at lunchtime ate their sandwiches out of baskets, perched on shooting sticks, as if they were at the races. In the mornings the bus conductor would call "All change for M.I.5," when the bus reached the prison, although it was supposed to be secret. And the girls dined out on stories of the absurdities of their work; that all Smiths were filed under Schmidt, and that there was a special file on "Suspect Servants in the United Kingdom," and so on. Appropriately enough, Brian Howard frequented Wormwood Scrubs in his War Office days, and M.-J. Lancaster, one of the girls who worked there, tells of meeting him, splendidly attired and mannered, in its corridors, and being unable to guess whether his claims to be an official employee were true. A bomb destroyed all the files in 1940, and when the photocopies (which had been stored elsewhere) were examined, it was found that they had been so badly prepared as to be illegible. It was as a result of this that the whole section was reorganized, and, after some time, the efficient Dick White became its head. (White was the man who finally, much later, secured Philby's dismissal.)

The history of these events has been written by journalists, typically, who were investigating the background to the treachery of Burgess, Maclean, and Philby, and who had to rely on unofficial sources. It is therefore hard to cite absolutely established facts that are of clearly defined importance; some qualification is always necessary to either the establishment of the fact or the definition of its importance. The reader is convinced by the *number* of anecdotes, the *variety* of their sources, and the *unanimity* of their testimony, because all those anecdotes prove the existence of at least an unofficial/official interpretation of the security services of the utmost cynicism. Thus Page, Leith, and Knightley, in their book on Philby, say that one of the people lavishly supported by M.I.5 during the war was Peter Pollock, one of Guy Burgess's young protégés. When Guy met him, in 1938, Peter Pollock was seventeen, ten years younger than Guy himself, so he may have been under twenty-one when he was living in the Dorchester Hotel on M.I.5 pay, "keeping an eye on aliens—especially Hungarians." And Leith reports an interview with a veteran of the security services, in which he (Leith) commented that "an amazing amount of crooks" had got into those services during the war. The veteran agreed, observing that in such times one had to take what one could get. But, Leith replied, these men had been hired in the bar at White's. Well, what else would you find there? replied the veteran. "Where were you recruited?" "Boodle's." Obviously, this is pretty trivial, both in the facts reported (or alleged) and in the attitudes expressed toward them. But what the testimony unanimously intimates is that trivial facts were predominant, and trivial feelings were the only true ones, in that context. Any official account, by giving dignity to that context, would falsify it.

To return to Burgess at the beginning of the war. He had resigned from the BBC in December 1938, to join Section D of M.I.6, which had just been formed, under Colonel Lawrence Grand, to organize sabotage and propaganda. The section developed some very ambitious schemes and was for a time very busy. Later Burgess and Isaiah Berlin set off for Moscow, on behalf of the section, to persuade Russia to supply arms to various underground movements in Europe. But Burgess was recalled while in America, still on the way, because he and Colonel Grand had been fired. In 1940 he was again working for the secret services; he gave M.I.5 information that led to the arrest of Anna Wolkov and Tyler Kent, who had photographed Churchill/ Roosevelt letters in the American embassy files and given copies to Russia. Later he worked in the news department of the Foreign Office (where one of his colleagues was the dandy cartoonist, Osbert Lancaster) and from there rose to become, in 1946, personal secretary to Hector McNeil, the minister of state there. Socially, he saw a lot of Brian Howard and Gerald Hamilton and Dylan Thomas.

He lived for a time at the Rothschild house in Bentinck Street, which, together with Guy's other quarters, temporarily became a center of Dionysianism for highly placed people in wartime London. Anthony Blunt the art critic lived with him, and other people, like John Strachey, stayed there for a time. Frequent visitors included Guy Liddell and Desmond Vesey, both of the secret services, and Goronwy Rees, who was involved in the planning of D-Day. Another prominent feature of the establishment was the presence of working-class boys, who participated in the homosexual stripteases and drink-and-drug orgies. It is said that Burgess took compromising photographs of Donald Maclean there; certainly he exerted blackmailing pressure on his own former lovers, and kept compromising letters from them for that purpose.*

---

* Malcolm Muggeridge visited this "millionaire's nest," which sheltered "a whole revolutionary *Who's Who*" and he describes it in *The Infernal Grove*. He says that all these men—he includes J. D. Bernal, the scientist—were in some sense grouped around Burgess, "the sick toast of a sick society, as beloved along the Foreign Office corridors ... as among the pimps and ponces and street pick-ups. ... A true hero of our times . . . hip before hipsters, Rolling before the Stones, acid-head before LSD." Lord Rothschild was a socialist and a scientist, as well as being immensely rich and one of the heads of the international Rothschild connection. Muggeridge describes him as mor-

Donald Maclean, who had married an American girl in 1940, went to Washington in 1944. His work at the British embassy in Washington led him to deal with the classified secret material about atomic fission, and he passed much of this information on to Russian agents. The C.I.A. early formed suspicions of him, partly from information given them by a Russian defector, and they warned the British Foreign Office against Maclean before 1951.

Kim Philby worked for Section D of M.I.6 in 1940, and when in 1942 this partially merged with the war office, he went into a counterespionage section of S.I.S. (Secret Intelligence Services). He put this section in touch with a Russian ring of spies in Switzerland, which brought in much useful information. Then his father, who was an old friend of Valentine Vivian, one of the chiefs of M.I.6, recommended him into that organization. He ran the Iberian department there (he has since been suspected of engineering the mysterious death of General Sikorsky in Gibraltar in 1943) and was much admired. He was in control of sixty agents, who included Graham Greene and Malcolm Muggeridge.*

After the Yalta Conference, Philby was made the head of the anti-Russian section of S.I.S. Because of this position he was able to block the defection to the British embassy in Istanbul of a disaffected Russian official—and no doubt did more beside. After that, he went to the British embassy in Washington, as undercover head of M.I.6 in America, and linkman with the C.I.A.

Among the many members of the British intellectual establishment who worked with Philby and liked him was Hugh Trevor-Roper, the

---

ally and ideologically bewildered, floundering between White's Club and the Ark of the Covenant, between the Kremlin and the House of Lords. Burgess was the will-o'-the-wisp of Rothschild's bewilderment, as of so many other Englishmen's.

* Muggeridge says that Philby was the dominating personality in his section of S.I.S. at St. Albans, where he (Philby) habitually wore his father's First World War army tunic. (Muggeridge sees all his contemporaries' experience of the second war as haunted by their nostalgia for the first.) Philby always spoke of Burgess in adulatory terms, and it is Muggeridge's theory that his deeper loyalties did not go to any kind of politics, but to every kind of bucaneering—"boozers, womanizers, violence in all its manifestations, recklessness however directed, he found irresistible." Like Burgess, moreover, Philby was in love with the *process* of deceit, the *machinery* of treachery, and unlike Burgess, he was able to carry out the work of espionage efficiently and impressively.

Oxford historian. Like so many men of letters, Trevor-Roper felt he recognized in Philby someone of his own kind, as compared with the average secret serviceman. Trevor-Roper is very satirical in his account of Vivian and Dancey, "the Aaron and Hur who, from right and left (but with eyes steadily averted from each other) held up the labouring hands of our Moses." (Moses was Sir Stewart Menzies, known as "C"—from whom Ian Fleming drew "M" in the James Bond stories— the head of M.I.6.) Trevor-Roper insists, as does Graham Greene, and every other writer on the subject, that M.I.6 was very inefficient, and survived largely because it got the credit for good work done by the General Code and Cypher School.[6] This work's combination of fantasy (remoteness from all the categories of the mature and responsible imagination) with inefficiency (breakdown in the machinery of the fathers' world) made these services the perfect locus of activity for the rogues and dandies. Harold Acton says "Apparently members of the Secret Services enjoyed a special license to misbehave: there was always some hidden motive as an excuse." He says this apropos of Brian Howard and Guy Burgess, but they were far from being isolated phenomena. That was the spirit of those services, that was their *point*.

The Manhattan Project

Among the secret information passed on to the Russians from Washington by Donald Maclean there were some atomic fission reports. Some of this espionage was done in the period of the next chapter, but much of the research itself was done during the war; moreover, the whole story of the Manhattan Project deserves some of our attention here. It bears on our theme because of its striking contrast with the story of the British secret services—a contrast between two organizations of intellectuals, two ways men of imagination were integrated into the war effort—and because it involves larger contrasts between England and America, in imaginative temperament. The dialectic of temperamental types developed along very different lines in America—obviously because that country was in its phase of dominance in the dialectic of world power—and the difference throws light on the shape of events in England.

To work on the Manhattan Project was, by the accounts in the various books about it, a "magnificent" experience ("magnificent" is the word witnesses keep coming back to), an experience of extremely hard but creative and, in some sense, self-creative work. There, as in the British secret services, people were working sixteen hours a day seven days a week—and at projects very unlike their usual ones, and in a lifestyle very unlike the one they had chosen to live in. Moreover, at Los Alamos, "the Mesa," there were again many men of intellect and intellectual pride—indeed men of greater intellect than the British writers in the Secret Services; but over them all was a philosopher-king, J. Robert Oppenheimer, a figure head of nobility, beauty, and profundity. Robert Jungk says, in *Brighter Than a Thousand Suns,* "It was probably the first time in history that so brilliant a group of minds had voluntarily undertaken to adopt a mode of work and existence so unlike their normal way of life." And James Tuck, an English scientist who came to work on the project, says:

> Here at Los Alamos I found a spirit of Athens, of Plato, of an ideal republic. . . . I've never seen a place less ordinary. So many people doing a damned difficult job wresting the secrets from nature. Oppenheimer had to concert the fullest effort of the best minds of the Western world. Los Alamos is a phenomenon unique in history.

And about Oppenheimer, Tuck says, "The people who had been gathered here from so many parts of the world needed a great gentleman to serve under. I think that's why they remember that golden time with enormous emotion."[7] The project's military director, Gen. Leslie R. Groves, on the other hand, put it differently: "At great expense we have assembled here the largest collection of crackpots ever seen." His philistinism and hostility are also parts of the story of the achievement, as we shall see.

Tuck described the Mesa then as "the most exclusive club in the world," and this may remind us of M.I.5 and M.I.6 just enough to point the contrast. The exclusiveness of *those* clubs derived from different criteria of membership; and in no one's account of them is there any glowing celebration of the work done, the effort made, or the genius deployed. And although it is unfair from many points of view to take the secret services as typically British, or the Manhattan Project as typically American, history persuades us to do so. There are many other contrasts between the two countries that are emblemized in this one. And there are many forces, quite independent of those we are concerned with, that push things into such a pattern—for instance, the fact that the British work on atomic fission was from 1942 on sacrificed to the American effort, was absorbed into the latter and lost to Britain. We are bound to feel, however justifiable we may be in calling it unfair, that these differences are *typical* of England and America then.

Size was an American dimension, and science was an American field, in this period. Stephane Groueff describes the Manhattan Project as "a superb illustration of the way the American system operated in the early 1940s," and as "the greatest single achievement of organized human effort in history." One might easily dissent from that— but not so easily imagine a comparable enthusiasm for the British secret services, even as something to dissent from.

And an important aspect of the project *was* the enormous effort of engineering, organization, construction, and bureaucracy of the American system that went into it. Dupont, Chrysler, Kellogg, Westinghouse, Allis-Chalmers, many huge corporations were involved. Three new cities were constructed, Hanford, Los Alamos, and Oak Ridge. Some 150,000 employees were put to work, the sum of $2 billion was spent. And because of the scale of the job, it was given to General Groves, the man who had just finished building the Pentagon, to administer.

Groves appears in the memoirs of the project as a "Widmerpool" figure—all drive and push and achievement, with no wit, imagination, taste, or style, belonging exclusively to the world of men, and absurd by the standards of Adonis. His father had been a Presbyterian chaplain in the army, a very severe and hard-working man, who allowed no drinking, smoking, nor swearing in his family and imposed a strict Sabbath. The son grew up with a harsh and aggressive manner, and extraordinary powers of work and command, but also with some marked infantile traits—like the greed for the chocolates kept in his safe, which an aide had to replenish constantly—and a crude ignorance about all ideas. He once declared that his scientists were not yet sure whether plutonium was solid, liquid, or electric. But he imposed the yoke of the fathers' values on them much more successfully than Sir Stewart Menzies did on his writers.

Of course, the nature of scientific work as it has developed in the West over the last three centuries has tended to promote in scientists a temperament adapted to the world of men. Science has put an emphasis on teamwork in laboratories, on alliance with technology, on progressive thought about public affairs, and so on. Men in the arts have had less training of this kind, and we recognize Los Alamos as Oppenheimer described it (in his trial testimony in 1954) as much more likely to be a scientists' than a humanists' enterprise.

> . . . a remarkable community, inspired by a high sense of mission, of duty and of destiny, coherent, dedicated, and remarkably selfless. There was plenty in the life of Los Alamos to cause irritation; the security restrictions . . . the inadequacies . . . and in the lab. itself the shifting emphasis . . . ; but I have never known a group more understanding and more devoted to a common purpose, more willing to lay aside personal convenience and prestige, more understanding of the role that they were playing in their country's history. . . . We worked by night and by day; and in the end the many jobs were done.

But Los Alamos was much more than an ordinary community of scientists, and the contrast between it and the British secret services was much more than a contrast between that and a community of humanists. It bore the marks of all the many contrasts between two national cultures in disparate phases of growth.

There was one great scientist, and a massive cultural presence (in the normal and hearty style), in England in the first years of our period.

That was Lord Rutherford, and he had come to England from New Zealand. He and his "boys" at the Cavendish Laboratories in Cambridge—they included the Japanese Shimisu, the Australian Oliphant, the Russian Kapitsa, who had left their native countries to practice their science in England, then a big country—formed a team that took Nature on as if she were a reigning football team. They had the biggest and best machines in the world, and by means of them they would master her.

It is appropriate that Rutherford was a New Zealander rather than an Englishman, for that zestful normality, that "heartiness," was even in those years to be expected rather from the newer countries. And it was appropriate that his favorite pupil, and spiritual heir, was Peter Kapitsa, the Russian, who was also full of jokes and physical vigor and loved "big bangs." And we find an equally extrovert type, although a less great scientist, in the American Ernest Lawrence, who built up the laboratories at Berkeley to rival those at the Cavendish, and to excel them in the size and power of their machines. Russia and America, the big countries, were the countries of science.

Lawrence, like Kapitsa, made his scientific career out of accelerating particles to enormous speeds by means of applying enormous voltages—in the hope of splitting the atom. His first cyclotron weighed two tons, the next eighty-five, the next four thousand. In 1932 he created a magnetic field of a million volts. These projects necessitated huge buildings and equipment, and so huge sums of money. But Lawrence was also an expert at selling his ideas to the rich individuals and the institutional committees who were needed to finance these machines. He was America's most prominent scientist in the 1930s—his picture was on the cover of *Time* magazine in 1937—and it was he who, at the end of 1941, persuaded James Conant that the country should make a major effort to build an atomic bomb.

Lawrence made his Radiation Laboratory at Berkeley into a college of the simple manly temperament, just as Rutherford did with the Cavendish. But he also made friends there with J. Robert Oppenheimer, a man of very different personality. It was of course Oppenheimer who eventually headed the Manhattan Project, the great harnessing of science to the state, and his incongruity in that position—which is an important part of our story—makes it worth studying the contrast between the two men. Lawrence was three years older, being born in 1900, and arrived at Berkeley in 1929, the year before Oppenheimer. He was for a few years much the more successful, in the public aspects of science, but he did not succeed in impressing the great physicists on the world scene. He was, for instance, humiliated at an international physicists' meeting in 1933, because the Englishman James Chadwick showed everyone that he had misread his experimental results; and the Frenchman Frédéric Joliot later showed what he *should* have been using his machines for.

Of course, Lawrence was an experimental physicist and Oppenheimer, in those days, a theoretician, but that difference was one of many similar ones, all rooted in temperament—intentional temperament. Lawrence *went in for* simplicity, Oppenheimer *went in for* subtlety; although both had great social charm and force, Lawrence's style was naive—it claimed to be all spontaneous exuberance—while Oppenheimer's was stylish. Oppenheimer's students could be *seen* imitating him—his walk, his pauses between sentences, his jumping up to light other people's cigarettes, and so on. Lawrence said he believed in his own character (he knew that some of his subordinates had better minds than he had), which is a characteristic hearty's remark. Oppenheimer read Dante and Sanskrit poetry, quoted Proust and Dostoevsky. He was *cultured,* in a T. S. Eliot style. When asked by the dean at Berkeley what had made him accept their offer of a job, he said, "Just a few old books. I was enchanted by the collection of 16th and 17th century poetry in the university library." Oppenheimer was, as this suggests, a dandy-aesthete, and although he gradually developed more Apollonian traits, became more the philosopher-king, he was always a phenomenon of style.

Even at Los Alamos he retained some *Sonnenkind* and even *commedia* traits. The photograph of him in a broad-brimmed hat standing next to General Groves at the Trinity Testing Ground, the one so concave and elegant and curving, the other so convex, gross, steady, is one of the classic pictures on a naïf Pierrot and his brutal antagonist. *Naïf* does not mean the opposite of subtle, of course, but open to every experience, constantly and essentially responsive and potential. *Naïve,* in its vulgarer sense, meaning a hearty, fits Lawrence much better, but he was not really open to new impressions. He was committed to the world of men and its establishment in America from very early on; his political loyalties, for instance, were orthodox and unshakable. As Oppenheimer said about the two of them, "Between us was always the distance of different temperaments. But even so, we were very close."

The conflict between them was tragic, and a national tragedy. Their temperaments trapped them into playing opposite roles in America's brutal dialectic of temperamental types in the '50s. As a dandy-aesthete, Oppenheimer was marked down to be a victim, and Lawrence was induced to make himself into another General Groves and attack him.

Los Alamos was an attempt to change the imaginative style of science in America; and in its petty and preposterous way Wormwood Scrubs was doing something comparable to the style of "intelligence" in England. But while the latter's effect was corruptive and destructive, the former was creative, expansive, and civilizing. It was redeeming American science from philistinism. Ernest Lawrence's laboratory had belonged to the America of big corporations and big football teams. Oppenheimer was building something that could remind people of Plato—or of his own Göttingen. He had been a student at Göttingen in the 1920s, during the great period of creative physics, when Max Born, James Franck, and David Hilbert were teaching there and Werner Heisenberg, Paul Dirac, Norbert Wiener were students. Oppenheimer has described that period in physics as a time of patient work in the lab., of crucial experiments and daring action, of many false starts and many untenable conjectures. It was a time of earnest correspondence and hurried conferences, of debate, criticism, and brilliant mathematical improvisation. For those who participated it was a time of creation. There was terror as well as exaltation in their new insight.

And the German physicist Pascal Jordan has said,

> Everyone was filled with such tension that it almost took
> their breath away. The ice had been broken. . . . It became
> more and more clear that in this connection we had stum-
> bled upon a quite unexpected and deeply embedded layer of
> the secrets of Nature."[8]

This wonderful experience was ended in 1933, when Hitler had seven
Jewish professors fired from Göttingen. It seems likely that what
Oppenheimer tried to create in Los Alamos, with the help of many
refugees from Nazi and other oppression in Europe, was a recreation
of Göttingen. He was trying (and largely succeeding) to devise a
handsomer imaginative style for American science. And he had got
what seemed a god-given chance when the government decided to
fund atomic research on a huge scale.

Groves admired Lawrence (I. I. Rabi has said that the two men
had much in common), but he picked Oppenheimer to head Los
Alamos. "Find me another Ernest Lawrence," he said, "and we'll
appoint him. But where do you find such a man? With Oppenheimer, we at least have a first rate theoretician and an extremely
brilliant mind. As for the administration, *I* will see that it works."[9]
This suggests one reason he may have chosen Oppenheimer—that
he would be the better able to interfere.

Once in the post at the project, however, Oppenheimer displayed
remarkable gifts of organization and administration that no one had
hitherto suspected in him. It was not surprising that he was able to woo
scientists from all over the country to join the project, for his magne-
tism, his imagination, and his tact were well-known early. But he proved
able also to organize a complicated operation, to harmonize his subordinates' efforts and to reconcile their conflicts when they got there. He
even reversed his work-pattern, to the extent of rising at dawn and working before anyone else got up, whereas at Berkeley he had refused to lecture before 11 A.M. Rising at dawn was Lawrence's pattern all along.

Oppenheimer acquired Lawrence's virtues, then, and harnessed all
his intellectuals to the service of the state, of the world of corpora-

tions, armies, and administrations. Of course he was still distrusted in that world, because his looks and manners still also promised that he would be its enemy. He still looked—seen in repose, seen from another angle—the sensitive poet, the stricken deer. His looks were ambiguous. And the big symbol of what he and his Platonic republic achieved was the very ambiguous one of the bomb, with the appalling problems of how to use it and how to use nuclear power. But although he and many others wished later that this harnessing of the mind to the state had never happened, it gave to America, to science, to intellectuals in America, an experience of working together that was the reverse of that which British intellectuals had in the secret services. America's experience in those years was the opposite of England's. That was the destiny of the two nations—that is what national destiny means. What Americans saw and felt as "the way life works out" was the opposite of what Englishmen saw and felt. On the whole Americans felt that if you made a big effort, you got the return you deserved; that is, even if the return were unfavorable, it would be *big*. A great deal is implicit in the simple facts that the American Widmerpool was General Groves, the American Pierrot was J. Robert Oppenheimer. To recognize such cultural images in such contexts of enormousness gives them a potency that is just what was lacking from the British equivalents. The British scene was a fit theater rather for Evelyn Waugh's imagination.

Waugh and Old Friends

Waugh may be said to have passed 1939 and 1940 in one of his anti-dandy phases; his faith in the Allied cause, in England, and in old-fashioned manliness were all renewed together. He, of course, despised Auden and Isherwood and those friends of theirs who went to America in 1939 to avoid the war. He also cut himself off from the group of his old friends and allies around Cyril Connolly at *Horizon*, which included Peter Quennell and Stephen Spender. Waugh developed a contempt and almost a hatred for this group (Connolly was a partial exception, because Waugh did respect the latter's taste and intelligence), and he began a systematic persecution of Quennell in particular. He told friends that it was what Quennell "stood for" that he hated. Indeed, he complained of all these men's "war and marital records"—in a word, their unmanliness—and pursued them with defamation and direct insult. He was on scarcely any better terms with the other leaders of British dandyism. He quarrelled bitterly with both Robert Byron and Randolph Churchill in the course of the war. And, of course, Brian Howard had been condemned long before. In Waugh's particular case one can see the splitting up of the general movement under the stress of war conditions.

Of course, Waugh, like Orwell, had welcomed the outbreak of the war. In an unpublished essay called "Writers at War," he describes a soldier as being his rulers' natural enemy, and as being immune from the emotions of the crowd.

> But he battens on the individual lives of his fellowmen. . . .
> Army life with its humour, surprises and loyalties, its ferocious internal dissensions and its lack of all hate for the ostensible enemy, comprises the very essence of human intercourse and in an age of scant opportunity for adventure serves to dissipate literary vapours.

The last idea is predictable enough, but the first is surely odd, and interesting, as an image of the "very essence of human intercourse"—an image surely derived from the young-man phase of life, when the fathers' affairs arouse mostly irony. Here Waugh speaks more as rogue than as gentleman, and the jarring of the two personalities within him was not in fact resolved by the war.

Indeed, it was a long time before Waugh could get any military employment, in part because of his age, but in part also because of his irritability and arrogance. He fought in Crete in 1941, but between 1941 and 1943 he was again kept from the battlefields. His commander in Crete, Robert Laycock, whom he admired, left Waugh behind when he sailed for North Africa. Waugh was unpopular with his men as well as with his fellow officers, and Laycock said he was afraid that when the shooting started Waugh (and Randolph Churchill) would get "accidentally" shot by their own men. The rogues proved as unemployable as the dandies, and found the army a disappointment. Waugh's diary, and his war novels, suggest that although he admired Laycock, he also resented the latter's army professionalism and careerism, his keeping out of trouble, his not being really a rogue or a rebel. Ritchie-Hook, the great soldier of the novels, has struggled all his life against the military bureaucracy.

During these months of idleness, Waugh reacted bitterly against the official mood of the country. As a member of the BBC "Brains Trust" in 1942, he insulted the other members, Professor Joad, Commander Campbell, and Sir William Beveridge. They had been claiming to feel that the private soldiers in the army were perfectly their own equals. Waugh invited them to validate this claim by handing back their fees for the broadcast and taking a soldier's pay instead. He was becoming obsessed by his hatred of current pieties, which were, as we have seen, especially egalitarian during the war. In particular he hated the idea, and the phrase, of the "Century of the Common Man," which he associated in particular with J. B. Priestley. (The phrase can be called a conceptual equivalent to Beaton's photographs and Coward's films of proletarian heroes.)

After a quarrel with Lord Lovat, in August 1943 Waugh had to resign from the former's commando brigade, and in January 1944 he was given six months leave from the Army to write a novel, which became *Brideshead Revisited*. He had just finished the novel, on June 28, 1944, when Randolph Churchill sought him out to go with him on a military mission to Yugoslavia, to make official British contact with the partisans fighting against the Germans there. It sounded like a congenial adventure to both of them, a rogues' mission. And in fact they enjoyed its dangers and were agreed in hostility to Tito, and to Britain's policy of alliance with him. But they also quarreled with each other.

Churchill, like Waugh (and Basil Seal), had entered the army with enthusiasm, and had been polite and charming to his commanders to begin with, but he soon became bored and insulted his colleagues and indulged his passion for intrigue. Both were temperamentally unsuited to cooperative functioning. Waugh has some poignant diary entries about their boredom and irritation with each other in the close quarters and unrelieved companionship they had to endure in Yugoslavia. On October 23, 1944, he wrote (of Churchill and Lord Birkenhead, who had joined them there):

> At luncheon Randolph and Freddie became jocular. They do not make new jests or even repeat their own. Of conversation as I love it [here Waugh sounds very like Ambrose Silk in *Put Out More Flags*]—a fantasy growing in the telling, apt repartee, argument based on accepted postulates, spontaneous reminiscence and quotation—they know nothing. All their noise and laughter is in the re-telling of memorable sayings of their respective fathers or other public figures; even with this vast repertoire they repeat themselves every day or two—sometimes within an hour. They also recite with great zest the more hackneyed passages of Macaulay, the poems of John Betjeman, Belloc, and other classics. . . . [Randolph] is not a good companion for a long period, but the conclusion is always the same—that no one else would have chosen me nor would anyone else have accepted him. We are both at the end of our tether as far as war work is concerned and must make what we can of it.

In such passages we see how the rogues as much as the dandies suffered from the disciplines imposed by the nation at war.

Waugh's general disillusionment with the army and the life of action must have played a part—as indeed *Brideshead Revisited* makes clear—in Charles Ryder's sense of having made the wrong choices in life. In both the novel and his diary Waugh names the right choice as Catholicism; but there are some indications that aestheticism was the most authentic element in that lost opportunity. For instance, some of the phrasing of the passage last quoted—"Betjeman's poems and other classics," and "conversation as I love it"—hint at a nostalgia for

Harold Acton and his aestheticism. And Waugh soon after began to define himself as an aesthete. In *Life,* in 1946, he said that it would now be the work of a very few writers to save the English language.

> Now I see writing as an end in itself. Most European writers suffer a climacteric at the age of forty. . . . After that they either become prophets or hacks or aesthetes. I am no prophet, and, I hope, no hack. . . . The artist's only service to the disintegrated society of today is to create little independent systems of order of his own. I foresee in the dark age opening that the scribes may play the part of the monks after the first barbarian victories.

Here Waugh clearly speaks with the voice of Ambrose Silk and not of Basil Seal. The truth is, of course, that he was completely ambivalent on these issues. He was passionately both for and against Ambrose Silk and his aestheticism, and out of that passionate ambivalence comes his best humorous writing.

Anthony Powell also spent the war as an officer, but most of the men whose lives we have followed were civilians. Cyril Connolly, with Stephen Spender's help, ran *Horizon,* which began, on Peter Watson's money, in 1939. John Lehmann, who had expected Spender's help, ran *New Writing* at first in conjunction with the Woolfs' Hogarth Press, and later with Penguin Books Ltd. Between them, these two Old Etonians controlled the market of magazine publication for young writers in England. Both magazines reflected the common man ethos of the war, but had deeper impulses that were quite opposite in tendency. In Connolly the dandy can be seen struggling resentfully against the responsible citizen; and although Lehmann was so eclectic, still his dominant taste was clearly parallel in tendency. He was always in tune with what Connolly/Spender and Auden/Isherwood would think of what he published, and he brought, for instance, the aesthete Henry Green into the Hogarth Press. Indeed, he consulted with Harold Acton about his magazine, and published him in it even during the war.

Connolly wrote a petulant "Letter From A Civilian" for *Horizon,* which Brian Howard said made him the best writer of his generation.

It might, indeed, have been written by Howard himself. It is addressed to the Civilian's old friend, Victor, now a soldier, in resentment of the latter's enthusiasm for the war.

> I could have slapped your face. I could have slapped so many people's faces and I never have. That is why I am a civilian. . . . The civilians who remain grow more and more hunted and disagreeable, each sweating and palpitating like a toad under his particular stone. Social life is non-existent, and those few and petty amenities which are the salt of civilian life—friendship, manners, conversation, mutual esteem—seem now extinct for ever. . . . You may liberate Europe, but you cannot liberate me. And when the Party is really over and you come home and marry your Tank [Connolly has fantasized a romantic relationship between the soldier and his beautiful new Tank, and the war as a Party for them.] don't send a wedding invitation, for he will have underground, to your bald, bitter, shabby old playmate, Civilian.[10]

Although it can scarcely be called dignified, this writing does express more of the dandies' experience during the war, their oppression by the war ethos as well as by material conditions—it does remain truer to their deepest identities—than the writing of, say, Cecil Beaton. And although the latter's experience was no doubt genuinely different from Connolly's and Brian Howard's, still Connolly's tone was the more authentic; it was the adult equivalent of those bitter jokes against the public schools that had first given all these people their identities and bound them together.

Stephen Spender has observed that *Horizon's* strength lay in Connolly's vivacity and idiosyncrasy as an editor. In that function he was—as he was as a writer—wayward, inconsistent, petulant, careless, but always about to tell the truth. He published what he *chose,* rather arbitrarily, and flirted with his readers and his writers both, but he was always pursued by the thought of saving his intellectual soul. Spender himself passed the war as a fire fighter, as well as poet and editor. Peter Quennell shared a flat with Connolly, and wrote a text for a volume of

Beaton's photographs of the previous decades. This text stresses Quennell's sense of an equivalence between Beaton's photographic style and the artificial and luxurious subjects he chose to photograph—also his sense that those days of dandyism and pleasure-seeking were gone for ever now, so that their decadence, their "artificiality," could be forgiven and forgotten. The fathers' values reigned again.[11]

Orwell and Old Enemies

Among the anti-dandies, Julian Symons says that up to 1942, when the army claimed him, the war was "one of the happiest periods of my life." One suspects that Orwell might have said the same thing. So Connolly (*The Evening Colonnade*) at least implies: "He felt enormously at home in the Blitz, among the bombs, the bravery, the rubble, the shortages, the homeless, the signs of rising revolutionary temper." To this degree even those wedded by intention to the Reality principle can share the irresponsibility of the dandies.

Symons (and again Orwell) admired George Woodcock and his anarchist magazine, *Now*. They preferred that to both the "Bohemian caperings" of Tambimuttu's *Poetry London* and the "hedonism" of Connolly's *Horizon*. These magazines symbolized the alternatives available in literature then, and the anti-dandies recognized their enemies. Symons describes *Horizon* as "keeping a flag flying for a social as well as a cultural elite." He was invited to meet Connolly, but found the "refined" air of that magazine unbreathable for long, without a retreat to a football match or a pub.

The conjunction of Symons and Orwell helps us to realize how much more difficult, or complex, the latter's position must have been, just because he knew Connolly and the *Horizon* writers so intimately. For instance, he and Connolly shared the same editor at Secker and Warburg, Roger Senhouse, who had been at Eton with them, and who had gone on to be Lytton Strachey's lover. Senhouse passed on to Connolly Orwell's failure to be moved at the news of the death of Bobbie Longden, who had also been at school with them.[12] Orwell was caught in this very close web of old acquaintance and institutional gossip at the same time as he was writing about such cultural phenomena from an immense distance, both of life-style and of political sympathy.

It must have been much easier for Symons to feel that he and *Horizon* belonged on opposite sides, and that "this battle of players against gentlemen, puritans against hedonists, Goths against silver-age Romans, is a permanent one in 20th century Britain. . . ." To him, it could not be clearer. He wrote that in 1972, and continued, "Today the gentlemen are on the defensive, but there are still reasons for being miffed about (to take a small instance) the seriousness with which a book about the talentless Brian Howard, talentless perhaps but amusing, and *one of us,* was recently treated."[13] This refers to M.-J. Lancaster's book, *Portrait of a Failure,* and the image of Brian Howard that the book evokes is one to which "talentless" represents a very narrow response. But Symons had adopted the opposite temperament, and consequently could not hear the voice, the idea or the drama of Brian Howard and his ilk.

During this period Orwell wrote regularly for the *Tribune,* and composed some of his most brilliant essays, including "Inside the Whale," the second part of which describes the intellectual atmosphere of his times. He defines that atmosphere as being dominated by the Communism of people who had lost faith in "patriotism, religion, the Empire, the family, the sanctity of marriage, the Old School Tie, birth, breeding, honour, discipline." They have lost that faith, and are looking for an equivalent of it in Communism. (We have already said that this seems to have been true of Guy Burgess, for instance.) Orwell's implication seems to be that he himself has not lost that faith; this is puzzling if we consult the items on his list, but not if we think rather of the temperament of having faith or the capacity for it. We can see that Orwell could claim to have kept the capacity to believe in things like responsibility and justice. Whereas people like Auden, he says, have forgotten what life is like, and so their words are weightless. His implication seems to be that those who went *looking for* faith (in Communism) had forgotten what faith was like. And "England, Your

England" relates the intellectuals to the Colonel Blimps, as two opposite branches of the same family—the wrong family to be in control of England—who are both equally remote from ordinary manly experience. The Socialist as much as the Tory disbelieves in the ordinary manliness that alone makes democracy work. There is a curious passage in a letter from John Strachey to Robert Boothby in 1928, which seems to bear out Orwell's remark. Strachey writes as a socialist to Boothby, a Conservative, who was then Churchill's parliamentary private secretary; he says that every upper-class socialist is a neurotic and secretly jealous of him (Boothby), and that he (Strachey) knows that he will have to pay later for this "faith" he so enjoys having and has so longed for.[14] This seems to indicate a willed and inauthentic belief in socialism—a faith for the sake of faith. It was Orwell's great vocation to authenticate a socialist faith, to build a democratic temperament.

Scrutiny did not comment on the war, nor was affected by it directly. Indirectly, it suffered from the reduced allocations of printing paper, from the reduced number and quality of the students at Cambridge, and from the conscription and dispersal of its natural audience of Cambridge graduates. But it gradually benefited a great deal from the greater seriousness of reading taste among educated people, and the general revulsion from dandyism, as the Reality principle established its grip on the nation's mind.

Q. D. Leavis wrote a series of essays in elucidation of Jane Austen, in the course of which she took several occasions to dissociate the latter from Bloomsbury.[15] Mrs. Leavis said that members of Bloomsbury used to claim Jane Austen as a precursor of theirs—as an 18th-century David Garnett. Or her novels were said to be like Huxley's *Crome Yellow* or *Antic Hay*. This Mrs. Leavis found to be as monstrous as to compare Norman Douglas's *South Wind* with the satirical romances of Thomas Love Peacock. Peacock and Jane Austen were fundamentally mature and responsible minds; and the modern figures were not. Jane Austen did not have Bloomsbury's "witty" outlook on life, its sophisticated cynicism; a taste for her humor cannot be assimilated to a taste for P. G. Wodehouse.

One should note that *Scrutiny* often named its enemy as Bloomsbury when aiming at quite a range of targets, including the dandies
proper; this was because Bloomsbury had written more on *Scrutiny's*
subjects and claimed intellectual respectability by the old standards.
This "defense" of Jane Austen was very characteristic. *Scrutiny* was
always fighting off the claims of unworthy modern writers to appropriate the great men of the past. It intended to pass on to young readers a great past—uncontaminated by the debasing uses that past was
being put to by degenerate contemporaries—as a criterion by which
to criticize modern life and literature. It also fought off that debase-
ment of the critical vocabulary that resulted inevitably from the social
closeness of the dandy cliques. The women writers of those cliques in
particular were heavily overpraised—Nancy Mitford by Cyril Connolly, Nancy Cunard by George Moore, Diana Cooper by Evelyn
Waugh, Harold Nicolson, the *Times Literary Supplement,* everybody.

Another interesting example of *Scrutiny's* strategies was Martin
Turnell's attack on Maurice Bowra's book on symbolism. This said
that, compared with Edmund Wilson *(Axel's Castle* is on the same
subject), Bowra was no critic and (a related point) that his "mystical"
view of poetry was simply false. Turnell disliked the idea of a school
of symbolism. He thought it made more sense to speak of the school
of Baudelaire than of "the Symbolists." And he went on to reproach
Baudelaire for having created much confusion by identifying the poet
with the dandy in the latter's quarrel with the bourgeois.[16] For Turnell, for all *Scrutiny* writers, the poet has no such quarrel, or at least
no more quarrel with the bourgeois than with the dandy himself. The
tendency of the Cambridge critics was almost to claim the artist *for*
the bourgeois, as his natural ally against dandies and aesthetes; if not
for the bourgeois, certainly for the moralist.

Also, in 1945, Cyril Connolly was attacked for sponsoring Aragon,
a writer who had been overrated because of the school he was said to
represent. Aragon needed to be *judged,* in and for himself, but only
Scrutiny maintained the traditional duties of judgment. Connolly was
also reproached with belonging to the tradition of "fine writing"—the

tradition of Moore, Pater, and Virginia Woolf that parades the "sensitiveness" of both writers and readers. This tends to make the study of literature into a cult of aesthetes, which it must not be. Thus *Scrutiny* struggled, at the level of literary principle and practice, to prevent various enemies from appropriating literature and culture and making them islands of Circe for the seduction of the young, where they would forget manliness in aesthetic lotus-eating.

Chapter Nine

1945–1951:
Exile and the
Decay of Hope

The National Trauma

DURING THE FIRST years after the war, England seems to have been more than usually describable in terms of a split personality. On the one hand, it had a Labour government with a large majority, and with large schemes for nationalizing the country's industries, which were put into effect energetically. Moreover, great hope was placed in social renewal by means of education, discussion groups, and every kind of planning. And rationing controls were retained, even in some instances intensified, at a time when other countries were relaxing them. All these were signs of a seriousness of mood, one of democratic responsibility, which found its climactic symbol in the Festival of Britain in 1951. The Festival aimed to recapture the seriousness of the Victorian Great Exhibition in London of 1851, but without the ornate, overstuffed, and self-aggrandizing aspects of the Victorian style, employing a more democratic and "Scandinavian" taste.

Even in the world of the imagination, in literature, two of George Orwell's books became successes and big sellers—*Animal Farm* in 1945 and *1984* in 1949—and there were other examples of such "puritan" and "proletarian" writing, while in the realm of literary and cultural theory F. R. Leavis began to be recognized as the important British critic. There were internal differences, and even contradictions, between the components of this mature and responsible "personality," but taken in the context of England as a whole, they all stood for a common effort at community seriousness.

On the other hand there was, in the more fanciful spheres of imaginative life, a marked cult of the frivolous, the elaborate, and the playful—seen at one level in the New Look of 1947 in women's dress, and at another level in the revival of Oscar Wilde plays. (It is symbolic that the Labour minister, Sir Stafford Cripps, appealed to English women not to follow the New Look, because of its extravagance.) And in literature successes even greater than Orwell's were won by Waugh with *Brideshead Revisited* (1945) and *The Loved One* (1948), while the first volume of Nancy Mitford's trilogy (also a popular success) came out in 1945 and the first volume of Anthony Powell's novel sequence in 1951. Osbert Sitwell began his many-volumed autobiography (again a huge success) in 1945, with *The Cruel Month,* and Harold Acton's *Memoirs of an Aesthete* came out in 1948. At a lower imaginative level, Angela Thirkell's celebrations of snobbery and nostalgia in fiction were enormously popular. It was partly a simple matter of age; the dandy generation were now in their forties, and had inherited the executive desks in the literary establishment. But it was partly an idea, a movement of taste; Acton predicted in his *Memoirs* that perhaps by the time his book was out his word *aesthete* might have become a general favorite even in England.

These two "personalities," two forms of cultural life, are clearly enough rooted in the dandy and the anti-dandy temperaments, which had been in conflict since 1918. But a change had come over that conflict. Feelings were intensified on both sides, and in particular the anti-dandies now felt themselves politically able to crush their enemies. The tone of Lord Beveridge's autobiography, published in 1953, and even more that of his wife's book of the succeeding year, was triumphal. There was a general increase in political seriousness in the mood of 1945, compared with that of 1918, especially among the voters of the ruled classes.

This was easiest to discern in the armed services. The dominant service in the second war had been as we have seen, the air force, the least public-school and dandified, the most "technical-college" in its style. In the election of 1945, 60 percent of the men still in uniform voted, whereas in 1918 only 25 percent did; and the A.B.C.A. (the Army Bureau of Current Affairs) had done a great deal of political education, which tended to build up "seriousness" and "responsibility." Everyone in 1945 seemed to know about the Beveridge Report of 1942 on how to turn Britain into a welfare state; and a great many people wanted to put it into effect. There was a great deal more serious reading and listening to serious music than there had been before the war, and institutions to foster high culture for the public were founded. The BBC created its Third Programme in 1946, and J. M. Keynes started the Arts Council. J. B. Priestley, C. P. Snow, and Nigel Balchin were popular "technical-college" authors, and Neville Shute, who had been an engineer and aeronautical designer, was the Angela Thirkell of this half of England.

People and institutions might be on opposite sides of the split in successive years. Thus the Oxford Union had a more serious tone immediately after the war, and several undergraduates were also candidates for parliamentary election. The undergraduates were less interested than those of the interwar period in inviting famous men from London to speak at the Union, in the hope of thus finding a patron for their own careers. The Union symbolically refused a gift of Oscar Wilde's poems for its library. But the man elected as its secretary in 1948 was Kenneth Tynan, the future theater critic, already a dandy famous for wearing a purple doeskin suit and a gold satin shirt; and from the time of his election on, the Union Chamber was again a scene of pranks and performances. These were natural enough reactions against the depressing sequences of English public life, from the British Restaurants meals to the fiasco of the Groundnut Scheme. The latter, one of the large efforts of socialist government planning, began in 1946, as a sort of African Tennessee Valley Authority, and more than 100,000 Englishmen volunteered to go to East Africa to work for it—to join the "Nut Army," as the papers came to call it. By 1953 it had cost £36.5 million, and was plainly doomed to failure. Oxford dandyism was as natural a protest against England's failure in the world of men—and against America's abundant success there—as the dandyism of thirty years before.[1]

The two "personalities" could be found in the same families; they went in close alternation and sometimes dependence on each other; but above all they were opposites, and opposed in taste and temperament as well as in ideology. When Parliament assembled after the 1945 election, the Tory members greeted Churchill's entry by singing "For He's a Jolly Good Fellow," and the Labour members responded by singing "The Red Flag." Within nine months the Labour government introduced seventy-five bills, and fifty-five of them received the royal assent—any one of which, said Clement Attlee, the prime minister, would have taken a year to debate before. Figures of Orwellian virtue like Sir William Beveridge and Sir Stafford Cripps even took on a public *glamour* of a Labour kind, the opposite of Churchill's and Eden's Tory glamour. Cripps exhibited the same virtues as Beveridge in a more public way. He was the best man in the government at giving some moral panache to austerity and planning. He rose at 4:30 A.M., worked a fourteen-hour day, and ate a vegetarian lunch out of a box. And for a time this was a dominant imaginative *style;* the alternative was characterized by the categorically shady—the Spivs, the black marketeers, the slum landlords, and the army deserters still hiding out in bomb ruins. Virtue was Socialist, and the nonsocialist was nonvirtuous.

But there was also, unofficially, a widespread mood of exhaustion and depression, one source and expression of which was a resentful feeling of inferiority to America. England was now not merely inferior, but in a lower class as world power. Edmund Wilson's *Europe Without Baedeker* described England as being now, for Americans, only a collection of interesting ruins, like another Greece or Italy. On the trip he describes in that book, Wilson had a hostile encounter with Evelyn Waugh; and Harold Acton tells us that Waugh was, in Italy, lectured by Sinclair Lewis on England's literary impotence, compared with America's potency. In the 1948 Olympic Games, America won thirty-eight events, Britain three. On the musical-comedy stage, *Oklahoma* played to audiences adding up to two million in London, and drove into obscurity the native musical *Bless the Bride.* Such phenomena made it seem that the moral superiority of England's socialism was hypocritical and compensatory. Harold Acton says that there was a certain self-righteousness about English asceticism, about the meek English "queuing up."

The dandies, especially, found America overwhelming. We have already cited Cecil Beaton's comments on the greater potency of New York, and Connolly wrote after his postwar visit there that in England

> the ego is at half-pressure; most of us are not men or women but members of a vast seedy, over-worked neuter class, with our drab clothes, our ration books and murder stories, our envious, stricken, old-world apathies and resentments—a careworn people. And the symbol of this mood is London, now the largest, saddest, and dirtiest of great cities, with its miles of unpainted half-inhabited houses, its chopless chop-houses, its beerless pubs, its once vivid quarters losing all personality, its squares bereft of elegance, its dandies in exile . . . its crowds moving round the stained green wicker of the cafeterias in their shabby rain-coats, under a sky permanently dull and lowering like a metal dish-cover.

He still preferred the Mediterranean countries to America, but New York was the opposite of London, and a world-center of vitality.[2]

London was a world-center of impotence, even for anti-dandy writers like George Orwell and Doris Lessing, as they portray it in *1984* and *The Four-Gated City*. The handsome buildings inherited from the past only mocked the decrepitude and sordidness of the present; even when not handsome, the past had been *big*. Betjeman and Waugh, too, for once coincided with Orwell and Lessing in the feeling for London and England and exhaustion. Dandy and anti-dandy felt decay all around them.

English films and novels came to rely on the American youngman, the *Sonnenkind* visiting England, to provide a hero valuable enough to recompense the heroine for her sufferings. (Doris Lessing makes the most distinguished imaginative use of this myth in *The Golden Notebook.*) Even in Evelyn Waugh's war trilogy that figure (called "The Loot") is perceptibly more potent and attractive than the young Englishmen around, even though Waugh is hostile to him. And in real life we could take the Kennedy family as symbolizing—a little later—all those qualities that made the American personality *bigger* than the English. It was not only that they had more vigor, more beauty, more ease, more range, but that they possessed these qualities in such an easy relation to adulthood. Although they were palpably *Sonnenkinder*—radiant with youth, fulfilled as young—they moved on with every confidence toward being fathers and rulers. They were what England's golden lads of 1914 had been, a living promise that one could combine the gods of the young man with those of maturity. But England produced no more such young men.

Waugh was the most anti-American of the older dandies, although his satires on America's vulgarity and inanity cannot hide his feeling that everything there was bigger, brighter, more alive. Still, his tone was bitter, and his feelings seem to have been complicated rather than complex; at least they seem to have baffled his powers of observation, for *The Loved One* is very mediocre satire by his standards. Its enormous success (it was published by Connolly as an issue of *Horizon* before it became a book) shows the voracity of England's appetite for satire against America then. Soon after, Waugh welcomed Thomas Merton's religious autobiography, *Elected Silence,* generously, and as a specifically American work. He did some editing of the manuscript before it appeared, in 1949, and responded to it in his Foreword with some enthusiasm. But his generosity to American monasticism included, quite essentially, a recoil from *secular* America. "Americans no longer become expatriates in their quest for full cultural development. They are learning to draw away from what is distracting in their own civilization while remaining in their own borders." They do this, he says, by means of Catholicism. The contemplative life has till now drawn few Americans, but he thinks that there will be a great monastic revival there. "In the natural order the world is rapidly being made uninhabitable by the scientists and politicians." Nowadays the Devil can only tempt us with power, since elegance and beauty are no longer available. (Waugh recognizes only past forms of elegance and beauty.) He compares his own period with that after the fall of Rome: "As in the Dark Ages the cloister offers the sanest and most civilized way of life." In Waugh, more clearly than in anybody else, anti-Americanism was connected with anti-humanism, but in nearly everyone it seemed connected with depression and defeat. Even in the heroes of moral activism, Leavis and Orwell, those two elements could both be detected, and a connection between them.

In a collection of essays called *Age of Austerity,* David Pryce-Jones describes the literature of England between 1945 and 1951, under the title "Towards the Cocktail Party."[3] He takes Eliot's anti-humanist play *(The Cocktail Party)* as a representative work for England, and crystallizes the general contrast with American writing of that time by contrasting Norman Mailer's *The Naked and the Dead* with Angela Thirkell's *Love Among the Ruins,* both of 1948. (Waugh published a short novel with Thirkell's title at about the same time—the phrase is a symptom in itself.) In Thirkell's book one of the characters says, with the author's approval, "We have seen the end of a civilization, we are out of date." And there is talk of "the deliberate under-nourishment of the people of England, to make them too listless to resist petty tyranny." This was typical of Angela Thirkell's anti-socialist message in all her books, which sold enormously.

All the dandy writers were, as was to be expected, skeptical about the Festival of Britain of 1951. In his Epilogue to *Unconditional Surrender*, Waugh wrote,

> . . . the government decreed a Festival. Monstrous constructions appeared on the South Bank of the Thames, the foundation stone was solemnly laid for a National Theatre, but there was little popular exuberance among the straitened people, and dollar-bearing tourists curtailed their visits and sped to the countries of the Continent, where. . . .

Michael Frayn, in his essay "Festival," also in the *Age of Austerity,* says that this was the climactic achievement of a decade of English life inimical to the interests of the "Carnivore" group—the Tory ruling class. The Festival was the work of the "Herbivores," the radical-liberal middle classes, the people to be associated with the BBC, the *News Chronicle,* the Crown Film Unit, the rationing system, and the British Restaurants—the people who stood for seriousness and responsibility. But festivity was not their forte, and mounting the Festival was the furthest reach of that movement, the moment of the "Herbivores" frail triumph. It was almost immediately followed by the return to power of the Conservative party, and the country realized that the balance of power and privilege within it had not shifted as much as had appeared. (Intellectually, in the serious enthusiasm for Orwell and Leavis, the "Herbivores" triumph lasted longer.)

Harold Acton and the Right

Among the dandy writers, there was a consolidation against their newly powerful enemy. Right and Left reconciled their differences, Anthony Blanche joined ranks with the British dandies. Let us take the Right Wing and Blanche first.

Harold Acton published his most successful book, *Memoirs of an Aesthete,* in 1948. He introduces his memories by saying that half his friends have disapproved of his calling himself an aesthete. But, "the label of aesthete has clung to me since I left school." Moreover, he welcomes it, defiantly.

> It is undeniable, however, that I love beauty. For me, beauty is the vital influence pervading the universe—glistening in stars, glowing in flowers, moving with clouds, flowing with water, permeating nature and mankind. By contemplating the myriad manifestations of this vital principle we expand into something greater than we were born. Art is the mirror that reflects these expansions, sometimes for a moment, sometimes for perpetuity.

This is the doctrine of the Berensonian aestheticism to which he had held over the years. He says that since he returned to Europe from China he has felt a cold wind blowing, a general hostility to all he stands for, a universal philosophy of, at best, utilitarianism.

> But we had a culture which war interrupted, and it was nourished by a few people like myself, citizens of the world. We citizens of the world are neither famous nor spectacular. But there is a slow fire burning within us, and it is time for our latent energies to well forth anew. . . . [Just because he had been silent] I am quite a rare person. Politicians everywhere, booming and thumping! All the more reason for me to raise my gentle voice. . . . [so] let me glory in the name of aesthete. . . . Let me fling it in the teeth of the Philistines.

Acton's hostility to politicians, like Waugh's, was particularly sharp in this period in which the dominant political mood was anti-dandy. At its best, as in the paragraph I now quote, Acton's writing can remind us of Nabokov. Of course the "statement," or "situation," of this paragraph is very like many in Nabokov's books, in its railway-carriage yearning for a land of beauty, of golden perfection, a yearning already crystalized by being remembered. But it is also the mode of the statement that reminds us of Nabokov, the choice of words and images—for instance in the second sentence.

> Oh the gay rhythm of the train as we disembogued from a
> dark tunnel into the sudden summer of white casinos among
> the palms and orange trees! The rattling window-pane of
> my compartment was misted over with my tense breathing.
> I kept wiping it with my handkerchief and gazing, rapt, at
> every passing village, house, tree, as if to print it for ever on
> my soul. From Pisa on I hardly uttered. Here in December
> the sky was still bright blue. How beautifully proportioned
> were these yellow farmhouses among the vineyards. Even the
> humblest villages had buildings which could be dignified as
> architecture. Finally I paid no more attention to the warn-
> ing; "*e pericoloso sporghersi*." Opening the window with a jerk
> I leaned out and drank the Tuscan air in great gulps like a
> draught of wine.

Harold dedicated his memoirs to the memory of his brother William, for when he returned to Florence in 1945, it was to find that his
brother had died nearby in Ferrara, under mysterious circumstances
that suggested a voluntary or involuntary suicide—perhaps through
overindulgence in drugs. It was also to find his parents prostrated by
their loss. William had resembled their father, in talents and temperament. He was all nervous vitality and impulsive sociability, and was
better liked (than Harold) by people in general and their parents in
particular.

> He had always been their favourite, and I was well aware that
> I could never be a substitute in their affection or in any other
> way. My mother was inconsolable. Never demonstrative or
> confidential, she could not bear to see anybody. She shut her-
> self up in her hotel room, completely prostrated. . . . I was
> alarmed by her pallor, the sorrow of her expression when she
> saw me. She could not smile; she could not pretend to look
> pleased, for she was still too deeply upset and her recent drive
> by motor from Switzerland had unnerved her. I realized that
> she could not bear to speak of my brother, and what a vast
> difference it would have made if he had returned in my stead.

... My father still talked as if I should have been responsible
for his welfare.... It would be an exaggeration to say that I
was left out in the cold, but that was how I felt. I was no real
comfort to either of them though I tried to be.

Harold found even that his parents did not want to hear about his
war experiences. "I seemed to be talking as a stranger to indifferent
strangers, but we were all benumbed by our loss." It is a very moving
account of the rejection by mother and father of the young man—
not young by years so much as by life-choice. Arthur Acton immediately became very busy in the retrieving, reclaiming, and restoring of
objects that had been stolen or mutilated in one or other of his villas.
From this work, too, he excluded his son.

Comparatively speaking, La Pietra had suffered little. A powerful
cardinal had taken it under his protection, and the Italian and German officers who had been quartered there had treated the place and
the collection with respect. In fact, such damage as had occurred had
been done by the Allied officers at the end of the war. Still, there was
much to do. The elaborate gardens had been badly neglected; the great
cedar tree had been cut down and burned for firewood, the peacocks
had been killed and eaten for food, and the statues had been castrated
by philistines or vandals. But the house, the furniture, above all the
paintings, had survived. The Tuscan primitives, which were the great
treasure of the collection, were unharmed, and nearly everything that
had been damaged could be restored. The work of restoration could
have reunited and reinvigorated the family, if it had been shared; but
the father did not trust the son.

> Suspicious and secretive, he would never take me entirely into
> his confidence. For hours he remained closeted with dealers
> I did not trust.... I was aware of their covert hostility to me
> as an obstacle to their schemes ... more than one picture and
> statue fell into their eager clutches.

It seems that Harold, although he does not say this in the book, had
also to fear the influence that other women were exerting over his

father on behalf of their illegitimate sons by him, to make them partial heirs of the collection.

Harold had intended to leave Italy to return to Peking and resume his chosen immersion in Chinese culture, but after his stay at La Pietra, he felt undecided. He saw that his mother was still deeply upset by the loss of his brother and needed her family about her. He also saw that his father might bequeath the patrimony to somebody else, or make away with it, if Harold were far away and out of touch. He consulted Osbert Sitwell, who lived nearby at Montegufoni, and he advised him to stay at La Pietra. He also saw a lot of Bernard Berenson, at I Tatti.

> At home I did not feel as welcome as at I Tatti. My father resented my writing as an unprofitable hobby, 'scribble, scribble, scribble' . . . and though we did not quarrel openly I suffered from frequent pinpricks since his longing for grandchildren had been frustrated. Yet I could not visualize him as a contented grandfather, for he had never been suited to the role of family man; few art-collectors are.

Harold was at work writing his memoirs, and one of his father's pinpricks was the question, "Who do you think will read your book?" Another was the suggestion that he should move out of La Pietra and go to live by himself at one of the smaller Acton villas. Harold refused to budge, even though he had in effect to fight for his inheritance. "Ultimately everything at home revolved around the collection, of which the gardens were an open-air extension." Arthur Acton's dramas all took place on a stage set by Henry James.

Harold tried to get a job with the British Council in Italy, but found that unfriendly people were now in charge. In Rome the council representative was now Ronald Bottrall, a student and disciple of F. R. Leavis. Harold found his enunciation almost incomprehensible. Roger Hinks (an old Eton acquaintance, who was also in the council) was more suave, but he too, Harold found, wore an air of supercilious arrogance, like most critics of his generation. Like Cecil Beaton in New York, Harold was made to feel that he was the wrong type to represent the new England abroad—too affected and fancy, too aesthetic and dandified.

In 1946, having finished writing his memoirs, he took his mother on a trip to America. His uncle, Guy Mitchell, offered to give him a house there if he would settle down in America. But Harold found that his chances of a career there as a writer did not look good. His name meant nothing to the American publishers he met, and at the Metropolitan Museum a former friend, who no doubt thought that Harold was seeking a job, spoke to him in a tone to which he was not accustomed. He spent some time in California, living with a friend from his Chinese days, and wrote a fantasy-novelette, called *Prince Isidore.* But then he went home.

He based himself firmly at La Pietra, although he began to spend more and more time in Naples, the old family home of the Actons. He was beginning to write a history of the Bourbon rulers of that city, which was to be the major work of his postwar years.[4] The choice of city and of subject was profoundly symbolic. The Bourbon dynasty produced some fine historical grotesques—*commedia* grotesques, as we have said of King Bomba. (Tiberius, on Capri, is another of these figures, this one a favorite of Norman Douglas.) And Naples stands, in general history as in the family history of the Actons, for a mode of life quite different from that of Florence. Ruskin and Gladstone, very typically, both disapproved of the city, much as they loved Italy. The Neapolitan mode—and *Prince Isidore* also is a Neapolitan fantasy—is much more southern and priapic, much more relaxed and unrespectable, much less formal, scholarly, dedicated, much more baroquely anarchic than the Florentine. Naples replaced Peking for Harold. He attended the performances of Eduardo de Filippo's troupe at the San Ferdinando theater, and describes that actor-manager as the last mask surviving from the *commedia,* a Pulcinello grown older, sadder, and wiser.

His publications had no great success in England. His memoirs offended Cyril Connolly and Peter Quennell, and did not impress the world at large in the way that Osbert Sitwell's parallel work did.

Prince Isidore, as Acton says, "lacked that earnest social consciousness for which the critics pined." It is a historical fantasy a little like
Orlando in design, although the taste that governs the details is more
like Beardsley's than Virginia Woolf's. Isidore himself is another *commedia* grotesque, a young Pulcinello. The story is quite like Brian
Howard's *Baronness Ada,* published in *The Eton Candle,* or his *Emerald Park,* of the same vintage.

Prince Isidore has the fatal gift of the evil eye, with which he quite
involuntarily brings misfortune upon those near him. Thus his mistress, Lisette, grows fat and old in enormous spurts, each of which
follows upon one of his embraces, and his new son-in-law, up till then
a triumphant Don Juan, suddenly falls impotent. The story is set in
Napoleonic Naples, and in the Introduction Acton talks about the
city and praises John Horne Burns's homosexual novel, *The Gallery,*
as one of the few authentically Neapolitan novels. To some degree
he himself was setting out to become a Neapolitan author in these
years. It is no wonder that the "Herbivore" side of British society, the
"decent men," found his work not to their taste. But Evelyn Waugh
told Acton that he had found *Prince Isidore* "a huge pleasure, and so
much more welcome for being all against the spirit of the times," and
Christopher Sykes adapted it for a BBC radio dramatization. (Sykes
also adapted Waugh's *Helena).*

Among the dandies we might group with Acton, the Sitwells were
having the greatest success in these postwar years. This success was
both popular and critical. Their lecture tours in America, which
began in 1948 and were hugely attended, were taken as dandy performances in the Oscar Wilde tradition, but at the same time Edith was
widely referred to as a major poet of the same stature as T. S. Eliot.
Maurice Bowra published a Lyrebird pamphlet about her, and *Horizon* dedicated its issue of July 1947 to the three of them, with a section
of Osbert's autobiography and an essay on Edith's poetry by Kenneth
Clark. In 1948 appeared *A Celebration for Edith Sitwell,* with contributions by Maurice Bowra, Kenneth Clark, Stephen Spender, John
Piper, and John Lehmann. When Cyril Connolly wrote an introduc-

tion in 1949 to a reissue of *Enemies of Promise,* he said that the literary values discussed therein had remained unchanged over the intervening decade, except that "the Sitwells have since 1938 grown enormously in stature."

Osbert's autobiography was an amplification of Harold's.[5] It began by saying that this was the only literary genre that could be practiced at that time. All purely imaginative works of art are

> pulled out of the future. But in this cruel and meaningless epoch, behind the bars of which I now write, neither past nor future seems to have any existence; only the present which contains the dead ashes of the past. . . . I had the fortune to be born towards the sunset hour of one of the great calms of history.

Again we sense the aesthete's hostility to politics and history; and this was the dominant imaginative mood in 1945. "Art is the dividing line between ape and man, and I want this to be a work of art." He cited a letter to the *Spectator* of 1940, which had urged the bombing of Rome by English planes, on the grounds that the working men of England wanted the war over as quickly as possible and only bloated capitalists cared about art treasures. This represented the mood Sitwell set himself in opposition to, by the form as well as the content of this book. "The aim of this book is to beguile, and not to improve, the mind. . . . In addition, I should like to emphasize that I *want* my memoirs to be old-fashioned and extravagant—as they are; I *want* this book to be full of detail. . . . I *want* this to be gothic, complicated in its surface and crammed with turrets and with pinnacles, for that is its nature." He wants to bring out the *fantasy* of England, just as in an earlier book he had brought out the fantasy of China.

In *Noble Essences,* the 1950 volume of the autobiographical series, he had a lot to say about the relations of art and individuality, "by which alone man can be saved." On the other hand, he detests literary criticism. This no doubt reflects the fact that F. R. Leavis had made criticism, judgment, his central activity. But it also reflects Sitwell's preference for fantasy in art, and for art in life. He attacked the "proletarian" and politically serious movement in literature, saying that he himself was in closer touch with working-class experience, via his servants, than the city-bred, middle-class poets of that movement.

The Sitwells' aestheticism was formulated also in Sacheverell's *Splendours and Miseries* of 1943, which Edith cited as "one of the greatest books written in our time." Sacheverell too was concerned with the threat offered to the imaginative life by democracy. He describes the Anti-Christ as being already born,

> in a flat, or in a summer bungalow, where the asphalt ends in nothing, and the new houses are not yet built. In a caravan or trailer. Under a piece of sackcloth propped on sticks; or in a town of petrol tins. . . . The beggar king marching out of the slums, or up out of the mines. He and his men have everything to gain and nothing to lose, meaning that in the end they will lose everything and gain nothing.
>
> Are there no colors in this world of ours?
>
> There are none, none, none. Only the love, or bravery, of the common man.

In passages like this the reader is reminded equally of T. S. Eliot and of Evelyn Waugh, and it was one of the Sitwells' strengths, as a force on the scene, that they did reflect and so unite and reinforce so many otherwise disparate points of view—all those with any trace of dandy and aesthete elements; by the same token, one is reminded by such passages of both Orwell and Leavis, as their enemies.

Also active and successful in these years was Cecil Beaton. He designed some of the Wilde revival productions, and even acted in *Lady Windermere's Fan.* He designed John Gielgud's production of that play, in 1945, in typically lavish and extravagant fashion, and in 1946 he designed a New York production of *An Ideal Husband.* Later he designed some ballet productions. He worked with Lord Berners and Frederick Ashton on a version of Ouida's *Moths,* and on a *Camille,* for Markova, about which he consulted Tchelitchew. His best-known work of this kind was, no doubt, to design the lavish production of *My Fair Lady.* All this cult of luxury and extravagance derived ultimately from the dandy movement.[6]

In the world of literature, Alan Pryce-Jones became editor of the *Times Literary Supplement,* a position of great power. Even though his conduct of that power seems to have been playful, it legitimately increased the Leavises' feeling of being isolated in a world of letters dominated by dandies. And Anthony Powell began his *Music of Time* novel sequence. In the volumes that describe this period,[7] he recounts the marriage of Widmerpool to Stringham's niece, Pamela. She is a beautiful but destructive vamp, fit fate for Widmerpool, and the two accuse each other of having caused the death of Peter Templer, the other of the narrator's friends at Eton when the story begins. Pamela is also Stringham's heir, since he has died in a Japanese prison camp. Thus the novel shows Widmerpool clearing the ground of his rivals and superiors, and falling heir to their property; in standard melodramatic fashion, the plot shows the destruction of all that was beautiful and the triumph of everything evil—the beautiful and the evil being defined from a dandy's standpoint.

Evelyn Waugh had a great success with *Brideshead Revisited,* which sold out in its first week of publication in England and became a Book-of-the-Month in America; this meant, Waugh calculated, £10,000 down and a chance of another £10,000. He had always been a popular writer, and there had been cheap reprints of his books since 1937. But in 1947–49 a Uniform Edition was put out, and in 1951, Penguin Books brought out ten of his titles—he was the only writer to be sold in such numbers, apart from Shaw and Wells.

Brian Howard and the Left

For Brian Howard these were years of wandering, both geographical and spiritual. He was occupied in self-destruction. However, he continued to review for the *New Statesman,* and one of his funniest and most typical articles appeared there on Feb. 23, 1946. He began by describing the lady-reader for whom most British writers write. He characterized her by her hat and coat and two scraps of her conversation in a bookshop, and she is obviously a version of his mother's friends. He concludes that the book she is looking for is a "hot water-bottle for her tiny, chilly, lady-brains." "And this is why, meanwhile, our novels are so terribly cosy, so terribly aloof, and so terrible." In such pieces we see the dandy as an effective social and cultural critic.

Brian also wrote a review of Osbert Lancaster's book on Greece in 1947; it was quite magisterially severe on the author's scholarship, tone, politics, everything. And the literary editors of the *New Statesman* wrote to him in the most flattering terms, begging him to write for them—Raymond Mortimer wrote thus in 1947, and T. C. Worsley in 1949—while Spender wrote in 1954, as the editor of *Encounter*. But short pieces of this kind were the only islands of purposeful achievement in the chaos of his life.

He was often abroad. He spent May and June of 1948 in Ischia with Auden, and Auden's poem "Ischia" is dedicated to him. In 1949, his mother persuaded him and Sam to go abroad to live, and they looked for a house in the south of France. In August 1950, the police of Monaco expelled them from that state, and forbade them to reenter. Both of them were taking drugs and drinking heavily, and Brian ran up heavy debts, insulted people, and seduced young men wherever he went. He also had the habit of making a sexual present of Sam to his visitors (he said he only allowed him to sleep with Old Etonians). The pair were readmitted to France, but then rearrested. Their dossier noted "moralité douteux." Going to Italy, Brian wrote to Harold Acton, asking for help in setting up a home there; but, to the latter's relief, they did not meet. Brian was still working on the biography of Norman Douglas that he had begun in 1946, and in 1952 he went to talk to Max Beerbohm about it. Writing was again his major interest, or at least politics were so no longer. In this sense, even he rejoined the band of dandies beleaguered by "responsibility." He wrote to Harold Acton in 1951 that he could no longer take any interest in politics, which were all ennui to him, and that henceforth he was going to dedicate every moment to love and art. But in fact very few moments were so dedicated, and the others were passed in the ways that got him expelled from Monaco, France, Italy, and Spain, one after another.

The other left-wing writers also were in this period effectively non-political, and more clearly dandies than before. Cyril Connolly, for instance, wrote a socialist editorial in *Horizon* in 1945 (scathingly reviewed by Waugh as "Palinurus in Never-Never Land"[7]), but soon thereafter he told Waugh that he was no longer a socialist, being released from the need to rebel by the death of his father. He, and his constituency, rejoined Waugh, Powell, and Betjeman and all their old friends. Left-wing convictions no longer even seemed to have redeemed them from their class limitations. To simplify matters, we will not pursue the life-stories or the literary histories of those writers who went abroad. In the case of Auden and Isherwood, we could point to interesting developments of the same kind in this period, but they were still effectively authors-in-exile, not fully part of the British scene.

But John Lehmann's autobiography gives us interesting details of the publishing history of those years, which bear on Connolly's career as well as his own, and which show one way the group kept a hegemony over the British imaginative temperament in those years.[8] In 1945, Lehmann lost control of the Hogarth Press, but he kept *Penguin New Writing* and *New Writing and Daylight,* both of which were important places of publication for young writers. He also set himself up as John Lehmann Ltd., publisher, on £10,000, contributed partly by his sisters and his mother. He had found a west-country printer, Purnell, with a large enough official allotment of paper to allow for publishing books in editions of up to 10,000, and he promised Lehmann enough for twelve new titles every twelve months. Thus an important kind of power passed into Lehmann's hands, comparable to that of the state publishing houses in people's republics. There was still a reading boom in 1946, and *Penguin New Writing* still had a first printing order of 100,000, but the paper shortage meant that very few manuscripts could get printed, and a very few publishers could decide what they should be. Here the two opposed halves of British culture came together. The machinery was that appropriate to the serious and political half—the conscientious socialism that was part of Lehmann's ideology; but the direction of his taste in choosing the books was more appropriate to his naïf and dandy side, reflected his temperament.

He then killed *New Writing and Daylight,* and substituted for it *Orpheus, a* magazine of all the arts. The latter was quite sumptuously produced, with illustrations in color; Harold Acton, for instance, wrote an essay for it on Mexican painting. *Orpheus* appeared in two volumes in 1947, and it clearly marks Lehmann's turn back toward aestheticism and dandyism. By then books were selling less well, and he sold out his investment in John Lehmann Ltd., remaining in the firm as managing editor, with his sister Rosamond as reader. He formed a Library of Art and Travel, which reprinted Robert Byron's *The Station* and Sacheverell Sitwell's *The Gothick North,* and a Holiday Library, which reprinted Anthony Powell, Rosamond Lehmann, Edith Sitwell, Rose Macaulay, and others. Thus the styles of the 1920s reemerged.

By the end of 1948 the first printing of *Penguin New Writing* had dropped from 100,000 to 40,000. Penguin Books first reduced the size of the magazine, then allowed only two issues a year, and then, in 1950, only one. The serious phase in general reading was coming to an end, together with the Labour government's term of office. The 1950 issue of *Penguin New Writing* proved to be the last; it contained, incidentally, pieces by Lionel Trilling, J. F. Powers, Nelson Algren, Saul Bellow, Tennessee Williams, and Eudora Welty. Lehmann had gone to America in 1948 and had signed on several new American authors for both his publishing firm and his magazine. As well as those mentioned, Paul Bowles and Gore Vidal were among his new book writers. Prominent in these lists are the names of American dandy writers, to whom Lehmann was introduced through Isherwood and Auden. Cecil Beaton too was soon a friend and ally of Truman Capote and Carson McCullers, and Harold Acton met Gore Vidal and Tennessee

Williams at the American embassy in Rome. Hand in hand with the decline for "serious" reading came the rise of these American dandies in the literary world. They gave the English reader a livelier and less dated dandyism than their British equivalents, like Muriel Spark and Angus Wilson.

This then was Lehmann's achievement in these years. He presided over the transition in British taste back from the "serious" to the "frivolous," from the socialist naïf to the gentleman-dandy. And if it was he who presided, it was because he was in such close touch with the feelings of everyone in his constituency. Lehmann's was essentially a protean mind, and the consistency to his taste throughout these years was imparted by his intense susceptibility to the suggestions of others in his group.

Guy Burgess and Politics

On the political side, John Strachey was made under secretary for air in the Labour government in 1945, and minister of food in 1946. In the latter office, he was much involved in the Groundnuts Scheme, the one spectacular failure of socialist planning. And in 1950 he was made secretary for war. He was now a figure far removed from his anarchic and Bohemian phase.

But the extraordinary political news was made by a figure who had been close to Strachey in those days and who had continued to perform in that style—Guy Burgess. Burgess and Maclean fled to Moscow on May 25, 1951.

In 1947, Guy had become established in the civil service, as a personal secretary to Hector McNeil, who was minister of state at the foreign office. McNeil, who was young, a working-class boy, and had only recently ceased being a journalist in Glasgow, by general agreement treated Guy as something of an oracle. He loved drinks and jokes and social life, but he was not used to such stylish forms of the latter as Guy provided, and so was dazzled by him. He laughed at his jokes and his anecdotes and listened to Guy's opinions with deference, although

Guy was as disorderly and shiftless as ever. This was another coming together of two opposite sides of England, and again the frivolous and anarchic side took command. (It is worth mentioning here an anecdote in A. J. P. Taylor's *Beaverbrook.* When Attlee became prime minister, he sent a memo to all his ministers, saying that they would find him involuntarily shy and should make an effort to get to know him; while they would find Lord Beaverbrook the reverse of shy and should protect themselves against the seductions of his flattery and gaiety. Beaverbrook and Burgess stand together, as rogues, against the conscientious seriousness, the piety, of Attlee. Hector McNeil was the man, himself a new minister, who brought the news of this minute to Beaverbrook—to share the joke.)

The office in the Foreign Office building that Guy shared with McNeil's private secretary was always littered with newspapers and files in confusion, and with Guy's caricatures and the other man's doggerel verse. The minister's bell was petulantly ignored or complained of, while they chatted of their sexual adventures in brothels and nightclubs. Goronwy Rees says, "All this was a reflection of Guy's basic attitude that established institutions were created for his own convenience and use; he regarded them with a mixture of contempt, indulgence and amusement as if fundamentally they were playthings which only children could take seriously." (Of course it was specifically British institutions he so regarded—not Russian.) Guy owned an early copy of the Kinsey Report, which Rees wanted to see. To get it from its hiding place Guy led him into a plush and mahogany office—"It's the Foreign Secretary's," he explained. "I thought you'd like to see it. Do you love it? I do." He explained that the book was safe, being hidden right on the minister's desk. "If Ernie found it he wouldn't know what it was about."

Ernie was Ernest Bevin, the great trade-union leader, who became foreign secretary when Labour was returned to power in 1945, and who was both the most authentically proletarian and the most widely respected of the new ministers. He was a major strength of the Socialist government. Such a patriarchal figure naturally seemed asexual to Guy and his friends, because their own sexuality was so different in style, so priapic. In this contact with Bevin and with McNeil, the working-class boy new to power and privilege, Guy's roguery is seen most sharply defined.

According to Rees, some of Guy's closest friends were men still working for the security services, who still talked to him quite often about their work. Every Monday, he, an official of M.I.5, an official of M.I.6, and two women always went to the Chelsea Palace Music Hall on the King's Road together.

He was also still as indiscreet as ever. But in 1950, although openly and virulently anti-American, he was sent to the British embassy in Washington, where Philby was officially second secretary and unofficially head of M.I.6 in America. Donald Maclean was then head of the American department at the Foreign Office, after recovering from a bad nervous breakdown in Cairo, perhaps brought on by Philby's forcing him to resume spying.

Guy was as reckless in his behavior in America as elsewhere, and in 1951 he was arrested in Virginia for having a pick-up drive his car too fast, and then claimed diplomatic immunity from arrest. There were official complaints against him to the British minister, and he was sent back to England in May 1951. He told his friends he was getting a job on the *Daily Telegraph,* which belonged to his Etonian friend Seymour Berry, but he had also been commissioned—presumably by Philby—to warn Maclean of the investigations against him. On the day an official warrant was drawn up against the latter, the two of them fled the country together. Partly because Burgess himself was in no danger, it is believed that they fled as they did in order to create as much publicity and scandal as possible.

Whatever the motives behind their action, the ensuing affair certainly did serve Moscow—by humiliating Britain and exacerbating its relations with America. Britain became identified in the eyes of other governments as the country of dandies and rogues and not of gentlemen; the country of decadent *Sonnenkinder,* not men of maturity and responsibility. No doubt it was already known that the British diplomatic and secret services were infiltrated by such types, but by means of the scandal Russia brought home to America—another country in which such types were much more rigorously distanced from the seats of power—how dangerous this situation was. It thus contributed to the drama of temperamental conflict in America. The feverish McCarthy search for Communists in government circles was clearly a search for *potential* traitors as much as for actual ones, a search for security *risks,* for people of the wrong *temperament* to handle power; it was a temperamental witch-hunt by servants of the fathers' world. While in England itself the effect was, as Purdy and Sutherland in their *Burgess and Maclean* say, to crumble the image that the Establishment had always presented to the rest of the country—the image of a group of men so deeply and a priori "all right" that their undeniable eccentricities could be ignored or indulged. Those eccentricities of manner and manhood turned out to be major mutations in temperament.

The Americans suspected that Philby was responsible for the flight of the other two. They demanded that he be fired, and he was, but soon he was officially cleared in Parliament of the suspicion of being the "Third Man" involved; and later he was unofficially rehired, to Washington's disgust. What the Americans now thought of Britain was presumably along the lines of what Goronwy Rees felt.

> The whole of my association with Guy . . . had by now left me with an incurable disposition to doubt and suspect all impeccable authorities [in England]. . . . Our security services, in fact, seemed to me a microcosm of that "great capitalist class," now in the process of internal disintegration, whose structure and organization, modes of behaviour and thought, I had found so alien when I first went to Oxford.

The English ruling class was disintegrating, Rees decided. The sons who should have succeeded to their fathers' responsibilities consciously or unconsciously preferred irresponsibility. They remained "the 'committee of management' of the country of which they were the most privileged citizens," but they were temperamentally incapable of discharging the duties of management. Rees says, ". . . the worm in the apple was the inordinate value ascribed to personal relation-ships. This was the mark of a society incapable of mastering the prob-lems of the real world." This inordinate value ascribed to personal relationships—Rees points to E. M. Forster and Bloomsbury as its ideological source—certainly is a feature of the culture in which the traitors flourished. But that phrase applies itself as well, perhaps bet-ter, to a different kind of political indifference, and to people among whom these rogues and dandies did not flourish. I am thinking of D. H. Lawrence and his followers—the world of Woman. The cult of Demeter too is devoted to personal relations, by contrast with the world of men. But, as developed in England, it has been much more devoted to maturity and responsibility, much more averse from "dec-adence," than the cult of the *Sonnenkind*. It was the latter that pro-duced Guy Burgess and his friends and sympathizers.

The friends and sympathizers played an important part in developing the scandal—by their efforts to hush it up. For instance, when Goronwy Rees told mutual friends of his suspicions that Burgess's and Maclean's disappearance from London was not just a drunken absence without leave but a political defection, all those friends tried to dissuade him from even suggesting this to M.I.5. One of them, in his agitation, made Rees promise to wait till he could come and see him; and when he came (a long journey) he not only reproached him with betraying Guy but warned him that M.I.5 would give him and his news a suspicious wel-come. The friend, who had been in M.I.5 himself during the war, Rees describes as the Cambridge liberal conscience at its best—"firm in his faith in personal relations." Moreover, Rees found that M.I.5. *was* suspi-cious of his motives and incredulous of his suggestion. They—and the whole English Establishment of which they formed a part—were not able to rationally consider the probability of the proposition, because they were not able to take treachery seriously.

In Waugh's second novel about the war, *Officers and Gentlemen,* he is concerned with various acts of treachery to Britain, and with the collu-sion of the Establishment in protecting the traitors from punishment. In the main case, Ivor Claire's desertion of his men on Crete, Ivor's treachery is later abetted and compounded by Julia Stitch, the wife of the British minister in Egypt. She is herself the Palladium of British Establishment values, but she pulls every official string to save her friend from his deserved exposure and punishment, and so breaks Guy's faith in that Establishment.* Ivor is not her lover, but she is devoted to him, because of the impeccable elegance of his personal style. So is Guy, Waugh's representative in the novel, and so is Waugh, even as narrator. Ivor has earlier been described as a young prince, as a perfect dandy, and as "quintessential England." That is what makes his treachery a major tragedy, for Guy and for Waugh. But Julia's loyalties are personal or aesthetic—to the style she admires—and larger moral issues, or military duty, or patriotic honor count for nothing in comparison. The only man with whom they do count, the man who would take action against Ivor, is that pre-1914 Englishman, Ritchie-Hook. The novel's other great betrayal is Virginia Troy's marital betrayal of Guy; and although she may be said to act out of some highly personal morality, it is a kind of dandyism again—it is her own dandy style that alone commands her loyalties and constrains her actions. Thus Waugh connects acts of treachery with the personal relations of *dandyism,* specifically; and it may be significant that this novel was published in 1955, and so written during the years just after the Burgess-Maclean scandal. (In his third war novel, *Unconditional Surrender,* Waugh also treats the themes of treachery, *homosexual* and *Communist* treachery, but they are kept separate from dandyism and from his story's major action. The separation in Waugh's books of what was so unified in Burgess's life may help account for something fragmentary and unachieved in the whole trilogy.) I think we can take Harold Nicolson's comment on the scandal, in his diary for June 8, 1951, as representative of the opinions of the more cultured gentlemen of the Establishment, as revelatory of *their* temperament.

> Everyone is discussing the Maclean/Burgess affair. I mind dreadfully. (1) Because it shames my dear old profession: (2) because it will enrage the Americans: (3) because it will make

---

* Lady Diana Cooper, from whom Julia Stitch was drawn, is said to have admitted that she certainly would have done what Julia did for Ivor, had the occasion arisen.

everyone suspicious of quite innocent people: (4) because I
fear poor Guy will be rendered very unhappy in the end. If he
has done a bunk to Russia, they will only use him for a month
or so, and then shove him quietly into some salt-mine. During my dreams, his absurd face stares at me with drunken,
unseeing eyes.

Nicolson was twenty years in the foreign service, ten years an M.P.,
five years a governor of the BBC, and also a literary scholar, with honorary doctorates from five universities; he was a central member of
the intellectual establishment. The tone of his statement, and its ignorance, is surely inadequate to its subject—to say nothing of the speaker's dignity.

We might guess that such attitudes in real life were what Waugh
satirized in fiction under the name of Sir Ralph Brompton (in *Unconditional Surrender*). Nicolson *cannot* take Guy's flight as anything
more than a naughtiness, a nursery prank by a boy whom one loves
the more therefore. He *cannot* see anything more involved than rules
being broken, and he is patently about to be wise and sympathetic
about rules being there to *be* broken. When the gentlemen of England
took roguery as lovingly as this, the rogues may well have been driven
on to more provocation. One remembers Auden's remark about Guy's
going to Russia, and his own going to America, that these actions were
necessary as the only ways finally to effectively insult England.

The resultant scandal in England involved nearly everyone whose
life-story we have been following. Cyril Connolly was a friend of
Maclean's, and wrote articles about him and Burgess for *The Observer,*
articles later published as a book with a preface by Peter Quennell,
who had of course also known them. Tom Driberg went to Moscow to
interview Burgess, who was of course an old friend, and wrote a book
about that. John Lehmann quarreled with Stephen Spender because
the latter had betrayed to the press a connection between Guy and
the Lehmann family. Philip Toynbee was a great friend of Maclean's
and had been involved in one of the latter's scandalous drinking bouts
in Cairo. Auden was questioned because he was not only a good

friend of Burgess's but the man Guy had tried to phone immediately before his flight. Both Harold Acton and Brian Howard were, separately, involved in mistaken identifications of Guy Burgess in flight, in rumors reported to the police or press abroad seeking the missing diplomats. And when Kim Philby was finally identified as the "Third Man," in 1963, when he too fled to Moscow (intensifying the disrepute of the British diplomatic and secret services), Graham Greene, Malcolm Muggeridge, and Claud Cockburn were also involved.

These people were themselves troubled by these events—by the popular publicity, by the problem of finding the right tone for comment, but also, it seems, by something more substantial. It was, of course, no surprise to such people that roguery and dandyism had been at work in high places. What disconcerted them was that these three men had guided their behavior, as distinct from their manner, by loyalty to a patriarchy—and a foreign patriarchy. This was what Evelyn Waugh had *said* he was doing, but he had withdrawn from his old friends to do. Now *these* three were revealed as having been, secretly and more seriously, traitors to the gentlemanly Establishment and to dandyism at the same time. The reactions of those "left behind" were complex; but probably the dominant feeling was unwilling admiration—Burgess and Maclean had escaped the categories of explanation that had seemed to confine them.

The Manhattan Project

Turning to the contrasting Manhattan Project in America, we find a period of trouble and scandal there too, but not of the same kind. There was a crisis of conscience among the scientists at Los Alamos after 1945.

Leo Szilard led a crusade to prevent passage by Congress of the May-Johnson Bill, which would have left all decisions about the use of atomic energy in the hands of the military. He and others formed a Federation of Atomic Scientists in 1945, which lobbied Congressmen and finally secured the passage of a bill nearer to the scientists' own wishes (the McMahon Bill) in July 1946. Oppenheimer was by then regarded by many of his colleagues as having sold out to the administration in return for the prestige and power that were lavished upon him. (The day he was heard referring to General Marshall as George was the day some of his colleagues turned against him.) He had not opposed the May-Johnson Bill, and in October 1945 he resigned from Los Alamos and returned to Berkeley.[9]

In the summer of 1946 came the atomic bomb tests on Bikini Atoll. And as the original scientists left Los Alamos for peaceful and academic work, German scientists began to arrive in America, to carry on the work wanted by the Department of Defense. A group of Chicago scientists led by Eugene Rabinowitch and Hyman H. Goldsmith founded *The Bulletin of Atomic Scientists,* which kept the public informed about the danger of tests and about the government's unpublicized activities. Thus, in antithesis to the British equivalents, the American intellectuals became as a group all the more involved in decisions of political principle and practice, although now in opposition to established authority.

Then in August 1949 the Russians exploded an atomic bomb, long before that had been expected in the West, and this gave Edward Teller the opportunity to demand that work should begin on developing a thermonuclear bomb for America. Oppenheimer, now head of Princeton Institute for Advanced Study, had led opposition to Teller's plan, on the ground that they had no adequate solutions to the practical problems involved. But after the news of the Russian explosion, Ernest Lawrence, Luis Alvarez, and Wendell Latimer flew to Los Alamos to consult with Teller and to give him their support. Teller tried to assemble a team to work on the project, like Oppenheimer's old team, and solicited the cooperation of Hans Bethe, then at Cornell. The latter had problems of conscience, and consulted Oppenheimer, who still opposed the idea, so Bethe refused Teller.

But in January 1950, Klaus Fuchs was arrested in England as a spy for the Russians, who had gained access to American military secrets in 1945 while a member of a British team of scientists working at Los

Alamos. This caused a big outcry of treachery in America. General Groves protested that he personally had always done everything in his power to prevent all the British from learning anything important when they were allowed into American scientific establishments. There had already been incidents (for instance, the case of Allan Nunn May, a friend of Burgess and Maclean) in which American military secrets had been leaked to the Russians through the British. This whole area of atomic research was, like the corresponding area of Diplomatic security, a sensitive one for Anglo-American relations, and it seems likely that the Russians exploited every possibility of irritation and distrust between the allies.

Thus it has often been speculated that the Russians themselves denounced Fuchs to the British for the sake of the ensuing scandal. And when, later in 1950, Bruno Pontecorvo left the British atomic research station at Harwell and flew to Moscow, it was in a way that dramatized for America the failure of British Security yet again. (The Russians kept his presence in Moscow secret until the moment when it would have the sharpest effect on Anglo-American relations—when a British delegation came to Washington to try again to negotiate America's sharing of its atomic secrets.) And only six months after that came the much more flamboyant case of Burgess and Maclean. The Americans began to feel that British traitors were *decadent* in a way that the American equivalents (e.g., the Rosenbergs and David Greenglass) were not; and to feel even more strongly that the British security services that failed to check the traitors were themselves decadent. Consequently they felt that it must be a sick society that produced and harbored and protected such traitors. (The irritation worked both ways, of course. The British were disgusted by the philistinism, the chauvinism, and the security hysteria of the Americans, patriarchal vices they were glad to have cured in themselves since 1918.)

The effect of these acts of treachery on the course of the Cold War was very direct—the effect of their discovery, that is. Four days after Fuchs' arrest in London, and the day after he confessed to having passed on atomic secrets, President Truman ordered a go-ahead on work on "Super," as Teller's thermonuclear device was called. Hans Bethe was still unconvinced, and led a number of scientists in protest against this work until June 1950, when the outbreak of the Korean War convinced him that there was an international crisis and a national emergency. He then joined Teller at Los Alamos, and the same atmosphere of all-out cooperative urgency was generated there as during the war. Clearly it had much more uneasiness behind it and much less creative exhilaration within it, but the men sat at computers in shifts, for instance, keeping them going for twenty-four hours a day. And in October 1952 a thermonuclear device was exploded at Eniwetok in the Pacific.

Oppenheimer's opposition to this work had restored him to a position of leadership among the liberal-minded scientists, and had made him an object of suspicion to the Establishment. And in other ways too the stage was being set for his accusation and trial, which was a crystallization of the more diffuse major crisis in the American intellectual community as a whole—the crisis caused by the threat to freedom emanating from the paranoia of the fathers. For instance, Ernest Lawrence had secured large funds after the war to build a Materials Testing Accelerator (M.T.A.), which was designed to bombard uranium-238 with protons to transmute it into plutonium. This was a natural extension of his schemes involving big machines of prewar days. But by 1946 most scientists were profoundly skeptical about the value of these machines, and only his colleagues at Berkeley supported his application for funds with enthusiasm. The application had to go to the General Advisory committee of the Atomic Energy Commission, and the head of the committee was Oppenheimer. This twice reported against Lawrence's application in 1947. Lawrence was already jealous of the other man, who had outstripped him in the race for power, and from this time on he was Oppenheimer's bitter enemy. He fired Oppenheimer's brother, Frank, who had been working for him, in simple anger and retaliation.

Because of his allies and admirers in the power establishment, Lawrence did get funds and did build his machine, in Livermore, California. But by 1950 it was clear that it would never do the work he had hoped, and from that time on Lawrence's self-confidence, good-humor, and health all began to fail. He turned actively against Oppenheimer, and it was easy for him to find others who were suspicious of the latter as a "security risk." (This phrase, like that other indictment of temperament, "soft on Communism," was to dominate the next few years.)

The contrast between the American and the British crises cannot lead one to a simple preference. But the American dramas were *larger,* in terms of the money and machines involved and of the death and destruction that hung in the balance, but also in terms of the moral options embodied in the participants—the size of Oppenheimer versus the size of Burgess. That is where the large dramas were, in America and not in England. Of course the major point for us is that the threat to life came in the one case from the fathers, in the other from the sons.

Aesthetes and Anti-Aesthetes

To turn to dandy art, in Nabokov's life this period corresponded to his first few years at Cornell, the years of *Bend Sinister, Pnin, Speak, Memory,* and his first *New Yorker* successes. He had been achieving his work as dandy author for some time, independent of the currents of world opinion, but now he achieved public success, at least with American sophisticated audiences, which were now ready for dandy-aestheticism.

Bend Sinister (1947) presents us with a Nabokov-figure, Adam Krug, who is persecuted and killed by a Hitler-figure, Paduk, because of Krug's innate superiority of being. At school, where they were contemporaries, Krug sat on Paduk's face every day; and yet, or and so, one day in the dark he felt Paduk kiss his hand secretly. In later life, and in political terms, the same transactions take place. When Krug meets brute force, in Paduk's soldiers, he remembers "other imbeciles he and she [his dead wife] had studied, a study conducted with a kind of gloating enthusiastic disgust. Men who got drunk on beer in sloppy bars, the process of thought satisfactorily replaced by swine-toned radio-music. Murderers. . . ." In such catalogues, as in all Nabokov's art, force and violence are aligned with other forms of stupidity and bad taste, and so made eligible for dismissal on aesthetic grounds. When Krug in danger of his life is summoned into the presence of Paduk, now dictator, he is so completely indifferent to the powers at the latter's disposal, that it is the dictator who must plead to be taken seriously.

In *Pnin* we find one of the great successes of dandy humor and tenderness, so much richer and livelier than, say, Max Beerbohm's essays in that direction. And *Speak, Memory* surpasses Osbert Sitwell's autobiographical extravaganza on its own terms in the first few pages. Indeed, one may say that a single short story, "Spring in Fialta," is worth all that the English dandies achieved in art put together. It is understandable that Nabokov, like Wallace Stevens, should have been neglected in Cambridge, where so much of the serious literary sensibility was engaged in an anti-dandy enterprise. But it is an intellectual scandal that the English dandies themselves should have been unable to recognize or unwilling to praise the one great contemporary artist of their party.

In England the anti-dandies were also having their success. Orwell was very ill much of this period. He went to live on Jura, an island of the Inner Hebrides, as soon as the war finished, although he was suffering from tuberculosis. But *Animal Farm* and even *1984* were great successes, and it is easy to see why even readers like Evelyn Waugh could appreciate their message; Orwell's vision of Russia, and for that matter of postwar London in *1984,* was very similar to the dandies' vision. His attack on totalitarianism in general, and on Russian Communism in particular, reassured many who had been alienated by his bitterness of tone before, and his personal style was quite suddenly accepted as quintessentially English. In fact there was a change of tone in those books—a reactionary change in the image of politics that both project—and even in his (always much finer) essays, Orwell was taking a more "aesthetic" tone about cultural values than before. As

far as his immediate reputation and readership went, these books provided a happy ending to Orwell's career; they made sense and comfort out of that career for his readers, by revealing that he had been
all along tilting not at them but at foreign dictators and un-English
ideologies.

We might take *The God that Failed,* the book by ex-Communist converts edited by R. H. S. Crossman in 1949, as an extension of Orwell's
final attitudes, and a demonstration of his new influence. Crossman,
born in 1907 and a friend of Auden's at Oxford, was a leading left-
wing intellectual; he had spent eight years as an Oxford don, became
an M.P., and then a *New Statesman* editor. He describes all six of the
converts who wrote for him as having been hysterical in their sacrifice
of middle-class liberties in exchange for Communist disciplines, and
suggests that they had been perversely attracted by the humiliation
to their minds and wills. He also suggests that England had suffered
fewer such conversions because its culture was more resistant, more
Protestant, more private. His pattern of interpretations and value-
stresses was very Orwellian. It was anti-ideological and almost apolitical, certainly rooted in the categories of culture criticism rather than
those of politics.

Of course the major stresses of Orwell's message, and of his voice,
remained the same—the stresses on decency, normality, work, fidelity, and private judgment. These might be said to be the stresses of
Waugh's message too, although not always of his voice, and it is of
interest that the two men "came together" at the end of Orwell's life.
Anthony Powell and Malcolm Muggeridge visited Orwell in Stroud
Sanatorium in his final illness; they suggested to Waugh that he too
might go, so that he was one of the last visitors before Orwell died in
1950. Moreover, the latter had undertaken to write a 5,000-word essay
for *Partisan Review* on Waugh, whom he intended to defend against
the large-scale attacks on *Brideshead Revisited.* The two men remained,
of course, ideologically opposite, and perhaps these gestures of reconciliation were insignificant; but it is possible that they felt, and could
have developed, the affinity between them that certainly appears to

the onlooker. The virtues that Harold Acton ascribed to Waugh, when the latter died—truth, fidelity, honor, patriotism, soldierly courage— these were certainly Orwell's. It is no coincidence that they both disapproved the same figures on the intellectual scene—notably Brian Howard—and for the same reasons. The modifications that Waugh had gradually introduced into his dandyism and the modifications that Orwell had gradually introduced into his anti-dandyism had returned each toward the other.

One cannot, of course, predict what Orwell's career would have been if he had gone on living, but it seems likely that he would have become more conservative, more like Waugh, more resistant to the modern world, and so have offered less in the way of new life to the English intellectuals. On the other hand, it is quite possible that that conservatism of temperament could have fostered a fruitful criticism and maturity of judgment of his own kind, just as Leavis's continued to do.

In 1946 *Scrutiny* published another attack on Maurice Bowra, particularly on his exaltation of Apollinaire to the status of important "modernist."[10] Ideas like modernism and symbolism were uncongenial to the *Scrutiny* critics, because they implied that there was a kind of literature specific to modern times, rather than a "great tradition." Also because they mixed writers whose quality, whose power of mature imagination, the *Scrutiny* critics approved together with others they disapproved, and gave an excessive importance to their "ideas." Eliot as a poet and Lawrence as a novelist must be read, *Scrutiny* said, in relation to the great English traditions they drew on and the debased English contemporaries they transcended, not in relation to French or Russian ideologues. Connolly, of course, was a long-time theorist of the "modern movement," as he called it, and he included John Betjeman as one of his modernist poets; but *Scrutiny's* anti-modernism was not simply directed at people like Connolly nor Betjeman, but in defense of its own moral-intellectual life, which consisted of acts of qualitative judgment, as we have seen. To read was not to enjoy or to learn but to judge—and on behalf of the whole culture. As a method, this was both provincial and conservative, although not merely that.

The magazine took a savage tone toward Osbert Sitwell and the English Association, of which he was, in 1946, president elect. It cited many examples of the praises lavished on the Sitwells in those years, for instance John Hayward's British Council pamphlet on English prose, which cited them, and also Connolly and Bowra, as masters of style. The Association and the Council were some of the many usurpers of literature and culture. In the 1950 volume there was a sharp comment on Maynard Keynes, and the Arts Council that he had created, which *Scrutiny* saw as a decadence of the old Cambridge tradition out of which he came. There was also a sharp mockery of Stephen Spender's autobiography—mocked also by Evelyn Waugh, from the other side—that focused especially on his fulsome praises of Virginia Woolf. The Leavises regarded themselves as carrying on old Victorian Cambridge traditions of seriousness, which had been betrayed by people like Virginia Woolf and Maynard Keynes. They almost explicitly regarded themselves as the true spiritual children of Leslie Stephen and Henry Sidgwick (the latter was the hero of the earlier generations of the Keynes family). The natural children were degenerate, and the heritage had gone to adoptive children. In this way, *Scrutiny* gave criticism a cultural root and a historical tradition, so that the mature temperament should be made more visible, a standard to which all the resisters of dandyism might rally.

In 1947, F. R. Leavis attacked Auden as an *undergraduate* intellectual, "permanently undergraduate and representing an immaturity which the ancient universities *not so long ago* expected their better undergraduates to transcend." Auden, unlike earlier English poets, did not *want* to become mature. Such a judgment implies—if one cares to work out the implications—this book's whole theory of temperaments and their relation to the cultural history of England during this period. And in 1951 an attack on Dylan Thomas remarked that poet's rejection of criticism, a related charge. Criticism had become for the Leavises the major manifestation of "maturity" in the world of letters. The poets' rejection of it was a sign of their preferring an immature temperament, whether Dionysian or *Sonnenkind*. Criticism, which

Scrutiny could fairly claim to *own,* as far as England went, was the literary mode in which moral and intellectual judgment most completely dominated the power of fantasy, the purely "creative" and irresponsible element in literature, and so if literature was to serve maturity, it would have to submit to criticism. It was this theory, or the attitude it implied, which *Scrutiny* was beginning to imprint on most of "serious" England, that spelled defeat for the aesthetes.

Chapter Ten

1951–1957:
Aging and Suicide

Acton and Howard and England

D URING THIS PERIOD, England showed signs of establishing an anti-dandy center to its imaginative life. In the world of high culture, the influence of Leavis and Orwell was growing. The realm of criticism proper was gradually being penetrated by Leavisites, and it was foreseeable that the old established reputations and styles would eventually fall before them, having no effective answer to their attack. Even on theater programs, of Shakespeare productions but also of satire shows, actors and directors would lay claim, in their biographical notes, to having studied with Leavis at Cambridge. And the Angry Young Men (novelists, critics, poets, and playwrights) attempted to translate Orwell's anti-dandy insights into an imaginative vision, to complete the fragmentary success of *Coming Up for Air,* to devise an ampler dialectic of resistance to the Establishment, containing aesthetic, humorous, and erotic dimensions. These writers' attacks on the Establishment differed from the attacks of the thirties writers on the twenties writers, in that this *was* a quarrel of temperaments, an attack of anti-dandies on gentlemen-and-dandies. Indeed, one might say that there was no ideological content to the conflict, nothing but temperament, which made some commentators think it was phony. The aggressiveness of Kingsley Amis's *Lucky Jim* and other novels like it was essentially a matter of "culture," any political implications being of secondary importance. Amis's humor was felt to be "uncivilized" (it was so described by Nancy Mitford and Somerset Maugham, for instance), and it was meant to be so felt, granted the old definition of civilization—it was meant to be an attack on the Establishment. But it could not be translated into a vigorous political statement.

In the world of politics and administration, England had a Conservative government. Churchill was returned to power in 1951. But even there the mood was not one of a happy return to old traditions; indeed there was a general call for England to give up its political reliance on "gentlemen" and gentlemanly amateurishness. This mood owed much quite directly to the scandal over Burgess and Maclean, amplified by the "Third Man" scandal over Philby, and reinforced by the national humiliation over Suez in 1956. The last was more appropriately blamed on "gentlemen," while Burgess and Maclean were obviously recusants from that faith; but insofar as gentlemen constituted a class and not a creed, they could be blamed also for that pair; for the evil derived from that class's acceptance of, penetration by, dandies, rogues, and naïfs. (We saw that acceptance in Harold Nicolson's remarks about Guy Burgess.) Justly or not, "The Establishment" was blamed for most of Britain's ills, and the words became one of the catchphrases of the time, used in the titles of a dozen books, the point of a thousand satirical jokes, and even the name of a satirical nightclub.

Mockery of an Establishment must always be a dandy activity, and sympathetic to *Sonnenkinder*. Malcolm Muggeridge became editor of *Punch* in 1953, and attacked Sir Anthony Eden, Suez, and the royal family vigorously. He brought John Betjeman and Christopher Hollis to write for the magazine too. But most of the group we have been studying were by now past the age to join in quite comfortably; they had made their compromises and alliances with institutions and figures in power. Moreover, at least the British dandies among them had developed each a kind of conservative ideology, or a pattern of gestures approaching the firmness of an ideology. Most important, the voices now raised in mockery of the Establishment seemed, in these years, to have been tutored by Leavis and Orwell. It seemed to be a crowd of decent men who now rattled the gates of the palace, not a gang of rogues and dandies. For all these reasons, the group of our subjects felt not relieved but more besieged as the laughter of "satire" grew louder in the streets.

Abroad, meanwhile, Brian Howard's life followed the same pattern, in these its last six years, as it had in the preceding six. These were the times that made Auden say that Brian was "the most desperately unhappy person I have ever known." He moved from place to place in France and Italy, always creating unhappiness for himself and others, always creating scandal. He was nearly always ill, and dependent on drink and drugs. He had quarreled with, or victimized, nearly all his old friends. Yet he was still active literarily, and even on the edge of politics. In 1954 he was diagnosed as having tuberculosis and took a cure at Zurich. The Mann family was there, and Brian composed a letter to *The Times* of London, protesting against the rearmament of Germany, which was to be signed by Thomas Mann, Albert Einstein, Albert Schweitzer, and perhaps by E. M. Forster, Arnold Toynbee, and Bertrand Russell.

He conducted very intimate and loving but quarrelsome relations with his mother right up to the time of his own death; his father died in 1954. Francis Howard's pictures and furniture were sold at Christie's for over £50,000, and he also left money invested in America. Half of his fortune went to his wife, and so eventually to Brian, the other half to his mistress, Rose Elsie Peache. Brian's coevals and friends were beginning to die also. In 1956, Peter Watson died, leaving Brian £2,000. Tchelitchew died in 1957. Brian came back to England briefly in that year.

He was trying to get help from high quarters for Sam, who was having trouble keeping his French visa, because of his drug addiction. Brian saw many old friends, the Dribergs, the Sutros, the Harrods, and gave a party replete with noble guests for his old friend, Eddie Gathorne-Hardy, when the latter retired from the Foreign Office.

He seems to have felt that England in 1957 was even less a place for him than England in earlier moments. The inclement concentration camp, he called it, and he looked quite ghastly while he was there. But France too was no longer hospitable, as we have seen. And on January 11, 1958, Sam accidentally gassed himself to death in their house in France. Brian seems to have quickly made up his mind to commit suicide himself, and to have a double funeral. He kept Sam's body lying in state in the house, and played early jazz and the *Liebestod* in its honor. Four days later, without having eaten anything since Sam's death, he deliberately took an overdose of drugs and died. No doubt he had thought of suicide often before that. In 1951 he had written a poem for Klaus Mann, when the latter killed himself, a poem he later recited for Erika Mann in a voice "shaken by sobs." Alan Pryce-Jones wrote his obituary for *The Times*:

> In the small world of Eton and Oxford during the 1920s, it seemed inevitable that Brian Howard would emerge as one of the eminent figures of his generation. Exotically handsome, after the manner of a Disraeli hero, rich, brilliant in conversation, and endowed with great physical courage, he only needed the right spur to set him on the ladder of fame . . . had he cared, he might have become an English Jean Cocteau.

These are the half-truths of obituary convention. In fact, nobody could have cared more than Brian to succeed in general and in particular to become the English Cocteau. And he applied *every* spur to set himself on the ladder of fame. What ruined his efforts were inner conflicts, set off perhaps by too many such self-spurrings.

A better epitaph is suggested by what he wrote in a diary in Munich on January 21, 1955.

In a month, I shall be fifty. What has kept me from writing, hitherto, was—first—too much self-criticism, perfectionism. Secondly, a swelling guilt, I have it as others have elephantiasis [We remember his earlier description of this guilt as "life's gift to those who are selfish, know it, and hate it"]. . . . Once I had not only talent, but what English people call "character." By which, they mean the power to refrain. Now I have neither. Will has left me and the capacity truthfully to imagine—vision—is leaving. I consider myself damned.

This is a true aesthete's tragedy.

Arthur Acton had died the year before Francis Howard, a father's death much closer to the son in its effects—and apparently much more dramatic, in that the dying man, long serenely agnostic, grew very depressed and fearful as death approached. From then on, Harold, having finally successfully inherited his patrimony, lived mostly at La Pietra until his mother died in 1962, when she was nearly ninety. He wrote about her with unqualified love and pain. "Her mind had never grown old, and to me she was eternally beautiful. This was the greatest grief I have endured, and still endure, and I am unable to put it into words." Brian Howard often took a very different tone in talking about his mother, but one can guess at reticences in both cases, and at depths of feeling, that make them alike. Bachofen tells us that the *Sonnenkind,* despite his brave show of independence, defiance, and brilliant innovation, really holds his power always by grace of the mother behind him, and that certainly seems to have been true of our two principal figures, and perhaps of Guy Burgess, who remained close to his mother, even after his flight to Russia.

Harold Acton attended a Mardi Gras ball given by Marie-Louise de Noailles in 1956 (dressed in the character of the dandy-aesthete Beckford) and in 1962 attended the commemorative performance of Edith Sitwell's poetry at Festival Hall, on the occasion of the poet's 75th birthday. Looking back over his life in *More Memoirs,* he summed up the great influences on him, the debts he owed, thus: Norman Douglas had sent him to the East before the war, Osbert Sitwell had kept him in Italy after it, Beerbohm had taught him to recognize his own limits, and Berenson had taught him to preserve the heritage of La Pietra. These influences were, of course, all modifiers and deflectors of that original dandy impulse, which one might call his own idea— these were counsels of prudence that had saved him from disaster. One might compare them with those influences on Charles Ryder in *Brideshead,* which deflected him from aestheticism.

More Memoirs was not published until 1970, but in this period Acton wrote quite a few articles and book reviews, for *The London Magazine, Books and Bookmen,* and other periodicals. He also gave lectures and wrote short stories. For instance, in June 1958, in *The London Magazine,* he had an article on "Neapolitan Outsiders," in which he discussed books about Naples, praising most highly again Burns's *The Gallery,* and saying,

> "I love no people like the Neapolitans.... Naples is pre-eminently a city where life is intensely lived, where in the darkest alleys, so grim to those who lack imagination, so sordid to those without aesthetic values, life is considered the greatest good and death the greatest evil... all the strong love life."

There for a moment one hears the dandy-aesthete speaking, the old Acton.

He also wrote about Eduardo de Filippo and his *commedia*-style troupe of actors;[1] and he wrote the introduction to Gozzi's memoirs, which again took him back into the history of the *commedia* and the artists who derived from it. Thus the themes of his scholarly interests in these late years returned to those of his first brave dandyism.

Waugh and the Others

If Brian and Harold were both exiled from England, in more senses than one, their old friends could fairly claim to dominate the literary scene. Waugh as novelist, Connolly as critic, Betjeman as poet, these were the writers the book-buying public of England read and enjoyed. They were not, of course, favorites with the avant-garde, or with the most serious readers. But they wrote what the average educated Englishman loved to read. The voice of the literature-and-arts pages of the dominant weeklies, even the most politically progressive, was still a dandy voice, as Leavis insisted. Connolly's review counted for more than anything else in the sales of a serious book. In that sense the *Sonnenkinder* were still dominant.

Waugh wrote the first volumes of his war trilogy, his life of Ronald Knox, and—most interesting from a biographer's point of view—*The Ordeal of Gilbert Pinfold*. The first ten pages of this last are a most remarkable example of a dandy's ruthless scrutiny of himself. Waugh describes himself thus:

> . . . with the eyes of a drill sergeant inspecting an awkward squad, bulging with wrath that was half-facetious, and half-simulated incredulity. . . . When he ceased to be alone, when he swung into his club or stumped up the nursery stairs, he left half of himself behind and the other half swelled to fill its place.

It had always been discernible that Waugh held a severe interrogation of himself, quite as severe as his interrogation of others; this self-interrogation is one thing he had in common with Orwell, both in its severity and in its secrecy. But it had previously seemed that this part of his self was separate from and incompatible with his dandy self. Now we see the two fused—both in the sense that Waugh still saw himself *as* a dandy, and that the self-interrogation seemed to have dandy-limits. The questions were ruthless, but once they had a ruthless answer, the interrogation ceased. The questioner was satisfied—in some sense— even though anyone else would surely have felt that he was just at the beginning of the investigation. Taste warned him that to go any further would imperil his style. Something similar can be detected in Waugh's religious and political faiths, insofar as he revealed those—a notable honesty and sincerity, which had yet no power to convince or persuade anyone else to hold the same faith, because of their psychological unreality, their inauthenticity. He told the truth about himself but that self was, by ordinary standards, a construct of the will, or at least an organism so drilled as to be unnaturally rigid.

We might note that among the criticism of *Gilbert Pinfold,* which was generally hostile, was one piece entitled "What's Wrong with Pinfold?" which intimated that Waugh had gone mad, in deserved retribution for his political and social perversity; the author was J. B. Priestley. Waugh replied, vigorously. The jousts and tourneys of the old cultural dialectic continued.

In one respect, *Gilbert Pinfold* and the war trilogy can be compared with Nabokov's work. We note that Waugh at the end of his life engaged in depicting fictional situations unlike those he had before chosen to write about, and like those that Nabokov *had* chosen— situations for which Nabokov had worked out a series of elaborate strategies. The two I have in mind are the situation of the corrupt aesthete and the situation of an authorial persona's hallucinations. The corrupt aesthete is clearly a shadow version of the author himself, and he has to be destroyed, in expiation of the author's own dangerous aestheticism, the freedom from ordinary limits of morality and imagination that he has allowed himself. Perhaps the simplest example from Nabokov's work is the figure of Clare Quilty in *Lolita,* whom the author's persona, Humbert Humbert, has to kill, but who is very like him; in Nabokov's work there are many such figures. In Waugh's work there is one—Major Ludovic in *Unconditional Surrender,* who has written a bad romantic novel that sounds significantly like Waugh's own *Brideshead Revisited.* He also represents, by his proletarian vulgarity, other of Waugh's guilts and shames. And Major Ludovic's physical and psychological condition is unhealthy, unwholesome, unmanly, just like Clare Quilty's. He is even a murderer, like Quilty. The figure, then, is the same, but in Waugh's novel that figure has no context, no dialectic in which to move, comparable to that which Nabokov gives his.

Similarly, the hallucinations of Gilbert Pinfold are odd without being interesting and so contrast very vividly with the hallucinations the reader has to struggle with in the reading of Nabokov's *Pale Fire,* and indeed in *Lolita* again. The reader has no problems with Waugh's visions, except the problem of being interested. Clearly a dandy-aesthete novelist will be likely to confront themes in his inner life— themes arising from his insolent defiance of common sense and common decency, maturity and responsibility—that can find expression in fictional situations such as these. Equally clearly, it took a modernist novelist like Nabokov to devise ways of exploiting such situations to their utmost—ways to baffle, enchant, and seduce the reader without ceasing an opposite process of sharp moral probing. Waugh had never ventured upon artistic enterprises of such complexity and explorativeness, of such moral and aesthetic risk. And when he came face to face with such situations, at the end of his life, he handled them unsuccessfully—either, as in *Gilbert Pinfold,* evoking so common sense a world that no reader was engaged by the hallucinatory one, or, as in *Unconditional Surrender,* failing to create the complexity of fictional transaction in which his self-interrogation could acquire dimension and movement.

This helps us to understand Waugh's "Act of Homage and Reparation to P. G. Wodehouse" in 1961, in which he preferred Wodehouse even to Firbank because of the "excellence of his technique." And his description of the comic sketch-writer, W. W. Jacobs, as a "pure artist." These were ways of showing that his own had been a Silver Age of literature. In *Gilbert Pinfold* he says that Dickens and Balzac had been "daemonic masters," but that the 20th century's English novelists will be valued for "elegance and variety of contrivance." Thus Wodehouse's "sheer hard work" had made him one of the finest literary artists of the century. Such are the blindnesses and fatuities to which British dandyism finally led Waugh.[2]

We are therefore not surprised that Waugh disapproved the great modernist experiment in literature. "Experiment? God forbid!" he said, in his *Paris Review* interview of 1962, "Look at the results of experiment in the work of a writer like Joyce. He started off writing very well, then you can watch him going mad with vanity. He ends up a lunatic." He went on to say that he no longer enjoyed reading even Firbank. The reading he enjoyed was, beside Wodehouse, Powell, Ronald Knox, and Erle Stanley Gardner.

In the same interview he said,

> I regard writing not as an investigation of character, but as an exercise in the use of language, and with this I am obsessed. I have no technical psychological interest. It is drama, speech, and events that interest me.... I think entirely in words, not pictures or ideas.

Of course it is clear that Waugh did have a very acute sense of language, and wonderful skills in narrative. Nevertheless, his remark might deceive a reader into attributing to him a wider intellectual ambition than he had. His interest in language was not of the kind active then in critical circles. Waugh found no profit in criticism, specifying that of Edmund Wilson—who had praised him—and dismissing American critics as a whole. And Leavis, of course, was anathema to him: "Naturally I abhor the Cambridge movement of criticism, with its horror of elegance, and its members mutually encouraging uncouth writing." Waugh's interest in language expressed itself rather in a constant consultation of Fowler's *Modern English Usage* and the Oxford English Dictionary. Like Nabokov, but on a much smaller scale, he was a pedant. Like Randolph Churchill, he thought there was a "correct English," which was everywhere being betrayed and from which the American nation as a whole had lapsed. His concern for language must be taken as another example of that old-fashioned provinciality that he perversely cultivated.

And of course if he knew that *he* was not a major writer, he also knew that nobody else among his acquaintances was. He could be generous to individuals, but not to bold enterprises. This led him, not infrequently, into foolish judgments. He dismissed Joyce, he in effect dismissed Nabokov, while it is hard to believe that he ever encountered D. H. Lawrence. Among the new writers he protected, the most literary was another Catholic dandy, Muriel Spark, and the most substantial was Angus Wilson, another dandy. Reviewing the latter's

Hemlock and After, Waugh said that here was the first new writer for a long time—that in England people were still reading exactly the same writers, in every bunch of writing, as they had ten years later but here was something novel. But what would have struck most readers of Angus Wilson would surely have been how similar he was to the dandy writers of the '20s.

Waugh was still quarreling with his old friends and gradually becoming alienated from them. In his reviews of, for instance, John Betjeman, Waugh betrayed an exasperation and contempt that must have seemed unforgivable to all the members of the British dandy group. He reviewed Betjeman's book of essays, *First and Last Loves* (1952) and observed that thirteen of the essays were broadcasts and "still bear the awful stains of their birth—the jauntiness, the intrusive false intimacy, the sentimentality—which seem inseparable from this medium." He says that Betjeman now denounced suburban mediocrity, but that he himself had been

> a leader of the fashionable flight from Greatness, away from the traditional hierarchy of classic genius, away from the library to the third box of the second-hand bookseller, away from the Mediterranean to the Isle of Man, away from the Universal Church into odd sects and schisms, away from historic palaces into odd corners of Aberdeen.

He remarked to his diary, and no doubt to common acquaintances, that Betjeman would have lived a much more honorable life if he *had* gone into his father's carpentry works and *had not* insisted on becoming a poet. This strikes directly at the crucial choice, the Oxford entry into aestheticism—the moment depicted in so many dandy novels (comically at the beginning of *Decline and Fall,* and again and again elsewhere)—the crucial moment for each member of the dandy group.[3]

Waugh's critical attention had perhaps been drawn to Betjeman by the latter's sudden success in these years. He had become a familiar and popular figure on television, discussing old buildings and places of architectural interest, and this popularity was to be transferred to his poetry. His *Selected Poems* of 1948, with a preface by John Sparrow, had done well, and the *Collected Poems* of 1958, introduced by Lord Birkenhead, sold over 70,000 copies. The last book of poems to have enjoyed such a success in England was John Masefield's *Everlasting Mercy* of 1911. The dandy-aesthete—a much modified dandy by this time—had finally supplanted the manly bard in popular esteem.

The *Collected Poems* volume was severely attacked by critics of the new persuasion, like Bernard Bergonzi, and Betjeman was still not a literary man's poet. Neither was Waugh a literary man's novelist, of course. Serious critics had never found anything to say about them— beyond a few lines of dismissal—even though the educated public of England feasted on their work. Betjeman's poetic autobiography, *Summoned by Bells* (1960), was again a great popular success.

Waugh and Betjeman still had a great deal in common, of course. They still stood in exactly the same position in the cultural dialectic. Both were obsessed with hatred of the "century of the common man," that phrase for—as they saw it—the democratization and flattening out of life that they associated particularly with J. B. Priestley. In *First and Last Loves,* Betjeman's first piece, "Love Is Dead," is about the uglification of England in the age of the common or suburban man, that historical phenomenon who has himself ruled by "experts and committees." And looking to the higher ranks of the besieging army of "decency," both Betjeman and Waugh were increasingly, in these years, aware of the disapproval of Leavis and *Scrutiny.* Betjeman says in his autobiography that he always wanted to be a poet,

> Even today,
> When all the way from Cambridge comes a wind
> To blow the lamps out every time they're lit.

This is just like Waugh's abhorrence of the Cambridge movement; in his autobiography he calls the *Scrutiny* people "state-trained pro-fessional critics, with their harsh jargon and narrow tastes." For all the personal, and even ideological, conflicts among Waugh, Betjeman, and Connolly, they stood together in taste and temperament against Leavis.

New Voices

These writers, however, had begun to sound out of date to the young readers of the time. A new idiom seemed to be establishing itself as the voice of the new England, and it was quite aggressively unlike the dandy's. In an essay, "This Gale-Swept Chip," that we will discuss again in the next chapter, Cyril Connolly said that England was no longer recognizable as the country he had rebelled against as a young man. That England was now like a parent who had suffered his first stroke and needed protection instead of defiance. "Can this be the ferocious figure who tried to bend us to his will—the England of the '30s, the Establishment a group of poker-faced prefects who know there is going to be a beating?" In his day, *every* Englishman had hated Stravinsky's music, Joyce's *Ulysses,* and the paintings of D. H. Lawrence and had been confident that they and all they stood for was nonsense. English character had been a mixture of complacent philistinism, smug superiority, and latent cruelty. They could afford to wait, those fathers, for the sons to get into trouble as a result of their new-fangled antics. He could only understand England as the homeland of such fathers. Now he was just bewildered.[4]

The parent against whom Connolly and his friends had rebelled had been above all a *threat* to them. This may remind us of the motive Isherwood ascribed to himself in *Down There on a Visit,* the desire to disown and disgrace his ancestors. It was precisely against any such desire, and the congeries of dandy-aesthete motives that related themselves to it, that the new fiction of the Angry Young Men set itself. The heroes of Kingsley Amis's and John Wain's early novels are notably close to, and fond of, their fathers and to homely kitchens, football matches, and pubs. (So, even more obviously, are the central characters of Raymond Williams's novels and of Richard Hoggart's writings.) Decadent figures of privilege and perversity, of self-indulgence and overrefinement, are the villains of these novels. It is against their uncles—in the sense we gave to that term before—that these heroes rebelled. They chose the old pieties, maturity, responsibility, work, and marriage and rejected the dandy and the rogue alternatives.

It is interesting to trace the gradual rise to power of this new sensibility through the impresario career of John Lehmann. The last issue of his *Penguin New Writing* in 1950 included an essay by John Wain, which attacked neo-romanticism in the name of moral realism. Lehmann also gave Wain a part on his radio program about new writers, called *New Soundings;* but when, in 1951, he lost control of that program, it was to Wain that the BBC handed it over. And Wain used his control of the program to introduce readings from his friend Amis's *Lucky Jim,* which led to the publication of that novel.

Lehmann felt himself ousted, for the new men had no real use for him. He went on to found *The London Magazine* in 1954, on money advanced by Cecil King, the newspaper tycoon. (*Encounter* had started up the previous year under Stephen Spender; the old guard was still in power.) The first issue had an anti-ideological foreword, and the magazine was designed to be "literary"—in fact it became the preserve of the former dandies. The ideological enthusiasms of Lehmann's early ventures were over, and even the aesthetic taste of *The London Magazine* was conservative. This epitomizes the gradual transfer of the initiative from the old guard to the new. (Evelyn Waugh had crossed swords with Wain over the latter's contempt for P. G. Wodehouse, and was to do so again in 1957, apropos of Nancy Mitford's *Noblesse Oblige.*)

Wain was a great admirer of George Orwell, and in his own fiction, particularly in *Hurry On Down,* he translated some of Orwell's imaginative imperatives into fictional terms—such as the vision of the working-class family in its kitchen, united in physical and emotional warmth, an integral human unit. In his fiction, as well as in his essays, he tried to create that modern, but not modernist, imaginative vision that Orwell himself had aimed at. More creative talent was brought to the same enterprise by Philip Larkin and Kingsley Amis; and the novels of William Cooper and C. P. Snow could be considered to some degree allied. John Braine made a success with *Room at the Top,* which seemed to derive from the same convictions, but these did not develop.

In all these writers' work the language given to the hero, or coming directly from the author (even the language of poems), was anti-dandy and anti-aesthete. It was colloquial, coarse, and in some sense flat. It was the language of the man in the street, the man in the pub. Seen in terms of its values, it was the language of the "decent man," made to suit the occasions of simple comradeship and courtship, aggression and self-assertion, deriving from the situations of being a son, a husband, a father, a wage-earner. Amis was the most skillful verbalizer of these tones in prose, just as he was the most vigorous fabulator of anti-dandy situations in his early novels.

Amis deservedly roused the sharpest hostility in the dandies and aesthetes of the older generation. Somerset Maugham wrote a letter to the *Sunday Times,* which was published on Christmas Day, 1954, about the social significance of *Lucky Jim*—a significance that was ominous because the novel described a new class on the British scene, the white-collared proletariat, trained technicians but not educated gentlemen.

> They do not go to the university to acquire culture, but to get a job, and when they have got one, scamp it. They have no manners, and are woefully unable to deal with any social predicament. Their idea of a celebration is to go to a public house and drink six beers. They are mean, malicious, and envious. . . . They are scum.

Maugham foresaw the futures of the Lucky Jims as the schoolmasters, journalists, and, in a few cases, cabinet ministers of England, and counted himself fortunate that he would not live to see what they would make of his country. A considerable controversy followed, and Amis was supported by older anti-aesthetes like C. P. Snow, but above all by writers of his own generation like Wain and Larkin.

Two other talents that emerged about the same time and added themselves to these "new" voices were John Osborne and Colin Wilson. It became obvious almost immediately that Wilson had nothing in common with the Angry Young Men, despite his proletarian ambiance. He was in fact a purveyor of modernism for England, and was saluted as such by Connolly and Philip Toynbee in reviews of his 1956 book, *The Outsider.* They saw in Wilson just what fresh young talent, coming from outside Eton and Oxford, should look like according to their *Sonnenkind* preconceptions. Osborne, on the other hand, spoke in the accents of the Angry Young Men, in *Look Back in Anger* (published in 1957). But it soon became clear that he was rather the Noel Coward of his generation, and that his heart belonged in the Dionysiac movement of the 1960s rather than with the anti-dandies.

Two voices that *were* raised powerfully on the anti-dandy side were those of Raymond Williams and Richard Hoggart. Hoggart's book, *The Uses of Literacy* (1957), was immensely popular for its account of the old decencies and normalities of working class life, and very influential as an account of what makes up a living culture. It warned explicitly against the value-dissolving effects of modern techniques and practices in the mass media of communication, and implicitly against the metropolitan and modernist glitter of life in the great centers. Indirectly but powerfully it organized many imaginative forces in people's minds against "smartness" and dandyism. Williams's *Culture and Society* (1958) and *The Long Revolution* (1961) worked more powerfully at the theoretical level, and with more of an eye on politics and political action, but they had exactly the same direction of sensibility and temperament. At the audience level of university graduates, these two writers have been perhaps the most influential in the country, and their influence has been quite essentially exerted against dandyism. Their taste in literature and method in literary criticism owed a lot to Leavis, while their political, or semipolitical, stance was Orwell's. Of course, both went far beyond these models, being original minds, but still the influence of those models remained detectable in nearly all their work.

These and other influences created a new national mood among the English intelligentsia, an increase in seriousness and responsibility of intellectual style. Some typical expressions of this national mood are to be found in the collection of essays called *The Establishment,* edited by Hugh Thomas in 1959. Thomas explained that his title had first been used in its current sense in 1955, by Henry Fairlie, who had said that Burgess and Maclean had been protected by "the Establishment" in England. (Thus the genesis of this so symptomatic usage relates quite specifically to the disgrace of the dandy and the rogue—the disgrace of the *Sonnenkind.*) This particular book, however, had been provoked by the Suez incident, and the disgraceful behavior of the British government toward both Egypt and Israel. In this incident, again, that behavior was a godsend to Russia's policy of fostering irritation between Britain and America. The government had intended both to secure British oil interests and to recapture something of the grand old *style* of action of the England of 1914; but what it did redounded again to British discredit and humiliation. These essays speculated about why this happened.

The contributors to the collection all announced their ages, and most were between twenty-nine and thirty-one. They wrote as young men, full of epigrammatic satire against the established figures and institutions they were attacking. Hugh Thomas himself, in "The Establishment and Society," described the Church of England as the senior common room of the public schools. He said that the English Establishment was intellectually and artistically dead as compared with equivalent classes in other countries, and that those who wanted to see England's resources and energies developed must want to see its fusty Establishment destroyed. John Vaizey, in "The Public Schools," quoted Orwell on boys' weeklies, and said that we still find scenes out of the *Boys' Own Paper* offered to us in Anthony Powell's novels. Simon Raven, in "Perish by the Sword," pointed to the dandy character of the crack regiments in the British army. Thomas Balogh, in "The Apotheosis of the Dilettante," said that the civil service system still demanded an attitude of effortless superiority in its recruits, combined with a cultured skepticism, and still found that breeding, character-building, and useless erudition were good guarantees of the qualities they wanted. All this was in the line of culture criticism that derived from Orwell and Leavis.

There were other things in the book, and as a whole it attacked the Establishment less on the moral-traditional grounds of Leavis and Orwell than on administrative-efficient grounds; but that there was so much in it that was anti-dandy was testimony to the powerful influence flowing in that direction at the end of our period. Another such testimony was Anthony Hartley's book, *A State of England* (1963), which cited Orwell and Leavis as the major signs of cultural health in the country. Hartley's interests were not primarily literary, so it was proof of a very special state of cultural consciousness that he should cite a literary critic—and one so insistent on limiting himself to literary criticism—as a force for health in the country as a whole.

Of course, the dandy current was still flowing too, and as a sign of that we can take *Noblesse Oblige,* the book that appeared in 1956 based on Nancy Mitford's articles in *Encounter* on upper-class linguistic usage. Her book included, besides her own work, an essay by Christopher Sykes, illustrations by Osbert Lancaster, a poem by John Betjeman, and above all an open letter to her by Evelyn Waugh. He reproached her with "bamboozling some needy young persons"— the working-class university students of literature—by pretending that England has a class system when she knew as well as he that it had instead a system of precedence. (It is quite an important clue to Waugh, and to all his friends, that he should see everything English as arranged in a long chain of preferability; or rather in many such chains, which intertwine glitteringly. To say that precedence matters more than class means that what differentiates Eton from Lancing is more important than what differentiates Eton and Lancing together, as public schools, from all state schools.) Waugh names these working-class graduates *L'école de Butler,* after the Butler Education Act that gave them the scholarships to go to university. They can, of course, make nothing of the novels of Anthony Powell or L. P. Hartley, or (he implies) of Evelyn Waugh. These sour young people—the "primal man of the classless society"—who come off the university assembly lines in their hundreds every year, really need educating into the English system of precedence. They are now trying to become poets and novelists as well as critics. (Waugh is clearly addressing himself to the Angry Young Men.)

This is the voice of the dandy at its clearest and fullest, and it comes right at the end of our period. No doubt much of Waugh's pleasure in using that voice came from his sense of how much opposition it would arouse. The day of the dandy seemed to be definitely over, but that seemed to be true before and had turned out to be premature news.

Another example of the power of the *Sonnenkind* style in these years relates to Randolph Churchill. He was busy about a number of literary projects, the main one being the biography of his father, on which he employed writers and researchers whom he referred to as his "Young Gentlemen." One of these, Alan Brien, has written an interesting account of the effect on him of working with this most old-fashioned of rogues.

> From the moment I met Randolph Churchill in May, 1953, I was never the same again. Before that I had been hollow-cheeked, resentful-eyed, resembling, I liked to think, Epstein's bust of a Young Communist. . . . When I became employed as Randolph's assistant I was transported in an instant from the underworld of Graham Greene to the magic landscape of Evelyn Waugh. . . . It was with him that I learned to accept oysters, caviar, artichokes, mounds of strawberries and cream, as normal ingredients of the ordinary man's diet.[5]

Champagne and whisky followed food as "normal ingredients," and Brien grew fat physically as well as mentally.

> My working-class, Puritanical instinct that it was indecent to stuff yourself, unless you were sure that there was enough for tomorrow, dissolved then and has never returned

> .... I began to see the ruling class of Britain as he saw it from
> the inside—not as an impregnable, armour-plated citadel but
> as a papier-mache stage-set to be shaken and shivered, and, if
> necessary, to be walked clean through like a mirage.

This must remind us of Guy Burgess and his effect on Goronwy
Rees and Hector McNeil. The effect Churchill had on Brien is also
the effect Oxford had on so many imaginative young middle-class
boys in the 1920s, the effect described in so many dandy novels. But
this was the 1950s, and Churchill was still the anarchic spirit of that
Oxford. He addressed everyone as "my dear" and "dear boy," quoted
Saki, Betjeman, and Chesterton, delayed guests in order to make them
miss their trains and have them stay the night, and demanded special
privileges—asking either "Must I be interrupted in my own home?"
or "Am I not your guest and entitled to courtesy?" He was always the
naughty boy, breaking the rules of life. When his American friend,
Stuart Scheftel, visited Randolph with his new wife, Randolph suggested an assignation to her as soon as they were left alone together;
and when she said she would tell her husband, he said she was quite
right, that Scheftel ought to know that he was married to a woman
whose moral standards were so boringly middle-class. This is exactly
the style of Guy Burgess and Basil Seal. That point is obvious enough;
what is more remarkable is that this style still worked the trick in the
1950s. It could still intoxicate and seduce rebellious young Englishmen who had seen themselves as "Young Communists," inducing
them to see themselves as rogue-rebels instead.

Trouble in Institutions

Meanwhile the repercussions of Burgess and Maclean's flight
continued. In 1952 Cyril Connolly published *The Missing
Diplomats*, three essays that had appeared in *The Observer*, with a foreword by Peter Quennell. The latter took the occasion to write more
about Connolly than about the other two. He describes Connolly's
position of power among his generation, by virtue of a strength of will

that is "positively royal"; where others have scrambled, he has strolled, indolently. He has been both the man of feeling and the center of authority for his generation. And insofar as Connolly's book about Burgess and Maclean sprang from his acknowledgment of his generation's complicity of feeling with that pair, Quennell's reflections are appropriate and relevant.

Page, Leitch, and Knightley's book about Philby was subtitled *The Spy Who Betrayed a Generation,* and the same phrase could have been applied to Burgess and Maclean. The betrayal was their translation into political and tragic terms of what had been gay and amusing in terms of private life and art for the group we have been studying. They had been so typically, and centrally, of that generation that all its members were implicated in their actions and their fates.

Evelyn Waugh had alluded to that complicity of feeling in his wartime novel, *Put Out More Flags.* Alastair Digby-Vane-Trumpington, one of the "bright young people," joins the army when war breaks out and refuses a commission. Although his life-style has been dictated by dandies and rogues like Ambrose Silk and Basil Seal, he has remained a decent Englishman at root, and during the war he not only volunteers for dangerous assignments but becomes a father for the first time—he regains manhood. His Columbine wife, Sonia, later explains that Alastair was "a much odder character than anyone knew"; she likens him to T. E. Lawrence (although characteristically Sonia cannot remember Lawrence's name), and says that he went into the ranks "as a kind of penance."

> You see he'd never done anything for the country and though
> we were always broke we had lots of money really and lots
> of fun. I believe he thought that perhaps if we hadn't had so
> much fun perhaps there wouldn't have been any war.

He felt he had been an unwitting traitor, at least by complicity of feeling. It had taken the war to awaken his manhood, his patriotism, his Englishness. This was written in 1941, and events were to prove Waugh, for once, blandly optimistic. The influence of Basil and Ambrose was not canceled out by the war, as the career of Guy Burgess proves. Moreover, the writers we are studying were more deeply in complicity with Basil and Ambrose than Alastair was, because they were less the normal manly, decent Englishman.

But we must return to the events of this six-year period. Melinda Maclean fled Geneva for Moscow in September 1953, and in April 1954 a Russian defector told the press of the West that Burgess and Maclean had been spying for Russia ever since their days at Cambridge. This succession of revelations and their repercussions forced the British government to issue a White Paper covering the events in 1955. The press had long been saying that the Establishment had covered up the full truth, and now the government could no longer ignore that challenge; but the White Paper was not felt to answer all the questions that had been raised. Then in 1956 Burgess and Maclean appeared before world press representatives in Moscow, and issued statements. Russia was squeezing out of them every drop of usefulness to itself and humiliation for England.

Meanwhile Kim Philby was rehired by the British secret services in 1955, while overtly a journalist in Beirut writing for *The Observer*. He was again a spy for, although really more against, Britain, when our story ends. It was not until January 1963 that he finally had to flee to Russia. There he was finally reunited with Burgess and Maclean. Guy bequeathed his books and clothes to Philby when he died in that year. Among the books were a number of signed first editions of Evelyn Waugh; and among the clothes a number of Eton-made suits—some ordered since he arrived in Moscow—and a large number of the Eton ties that he had always worn. In somewhat parallel fashion, Maclean lost his wife to Philby soon after the latter's arrival in Russia. These cessions of property perhaps indicate the usual style of transaction between Philby and his more flamboyant cohorts—each, in different ways, made submission to him.[6]

Graham Greene, who served under Philby as a secret agent in the war, has remained his loyal friend. He wrote an introduction to Philby's *My Silent War* (1968), written in Moscow, in which he says, "Who has not committed treason to something or someone more important than a country?" Greene adds that now that he knows there was a political motive behind Philby's intrigue against Cowgill (a rival member of the secret service), he likes Philby better, not worse. He compares Philby with a recusant English Catholic living under Elizabeth I, who was necessarily a traitor, politically speaking. In 1955 Waugh, introducing the autobiography of William Weston, just such a recusant, said that England under Elizabeth I had *needed* political betrayal and military defeat. The country needed to be conquered by Philip II of Spain "for the full development of our national genius."

This is in some sense representative of the attitudes of the literary *Sonnenkinder* toward Burgess and Philby and treachery. As we shall see, Auden told Robin Maugham that he himself had become an American citizen for just the same reasons as made Guy Burgess become a Russian citizen—it was the only way completely and finally to rebel against England. These various remarks—by Auden, Waugh, and Greene—surely indicate a kind of complicity in these writers with the traitors. This is not a complicity of action, of course, but of feeling. The writers could not honestly condemn the traitors. For them, and for most English intellectuals, political treachery was not a category of evil, nor patriotism a category of good.

Rebecca West makes this point in *The New Meaning of Treason* (1964). In that book she breaks off her discussion of Burgess, Maclean, and other traitors to tell the story of a British hero of the Korean War, Lieutenant Waters, who died for his country. Then she says,

> For the comprehension of our age and the part treason has played in it, it is necessary to realize that there are many English people who would have felt acutely embarrassed if they had had to read aloud the story of this young man's death. . . . They would have felt more at ease with many of the traitors in this book. . . . [They would also have] felt that Waters' heroism has something dowdy about it, while treason has a certain style, a sort of elegance, or, as the vulgar would say, "sophistication."

They would not have liked William Joyce, "Lord Haw-Haw," the wartime Nazi broadcaster, because he was willing to die for his beliefs (he took patriotism seriously), but they would have accepted Klaus Fuchs, Alan Nunn May, and Burgess and Maclean. "They would have felt that subtlety was on the side of the traitors" and would have quoted Gide in support of their feeling. This feature of modern English feeling is a matter of taste, Miss West says, and so something about which there can be no useful dispute. But I think that the category of temperament, which includes that of taste, does give one something to grasp, to measure, to understand, and so to dispute about in one's study of these times.

The *Sonnenkind* temperament, which Guy Burgess represented so vividly, exercised a powerful attraction over the minds of other Englishmen in positions of power of various kinds. W. H. Auden and Harold Nicolson, for instance, were presumably not in the least drawn to political treachery themselves, but Guy Burgess's "guilt" was too abstract and official, too patriarchal a concept in their minds for them to sincerely condemn. Nicolson was a patron of Robin Maugham, who was himself a good friend of Guy, and Maugham tells the story of a visit to Auden (together with a visit to Norman Douglas) after Guy's flight. Beside his remark about citizenship, Auden recommended Maugham as a novelist to cultivate the acquaintance of Gerald Hamilton, the Mr. Norris of the Berlin stories, a Pulcinello of modern life, saying that Isherwood had not exhausted the possibilities of that fictional theme. Maugham should write more Berlin stories, thirty years after the first, bringing into the '60s that corrosive cynicism about the world of the fathers. Surely the conjunction of these names and ideas suggests a taste and temperament predisposed to defeat and treachery because so hostile to the world of men, the world of the fathers. In any case, the evidence is clear that such a predisposition existed in England then.

In America this was the period of Oppenheimer's disgrace and trial, and of an exaggerated "world of men" normalism in every sphere of life, from politics to sex. Oppenheimer had lost influence with the government, as a result of his opposition to the development of the H-bomb, and in July 1952 he resigned from the chairmanship of the

General Advisory Commission. By the same token, he was a hero again with the intellectual public, and in 1953 he gave the Reith Lectures on the BBC in England. But in December of that year, J. Edgar Hoover sent President Eisenhower a loyalty report on Oppenheimer, which led the President to order that he should no longer be allowed access to secret papers. Admiral Strauss told Oppenheimer the charges against him when he returned from London, and in April 1954 the latter made the charges and his answers to them public. Later that year he was examined by a board, which found him loyal in actual past behavior but not fit to have his security clearance restored for future use—because he had disregarded security arrangements, had opposed the H-bomb, had been uncandid to the board, and had shown himself "susceptible to influence." They were not condemning anything he had done but the kind of man he was, judging his temperament in the name of their own aggressive normality, their heartiness. These were the years of McCarthy and the House Un-American Activities Committee, when all America was in a fever of suspicion of all enemies to the world of men, and especially of all dandies and naïfs.

Ernest Lawrence fully intended to testify against Oppenheimer, but his ill-health prevented him attending the trial. His allies and lieutenants, like Latimer and Teller, did so testify against their former leader and hero. Teller, who was already known to the press as "the father of the H-bomb," became a leper to the scientific community for some time after the trial. But in public affairs Oppenheimer's enemies triumphed. Lewis Strauss was appointed scientific adviser to the president, and he saw to it that Lawrence got the Fermi Award and the Sylvanus Thayer Award. But Lawrence was a very sick man, and he died in 1958.

Of course the problems brought by atomic fission remained and developed. In 1952 there was a minor explosion in a heavy-water reactor in Chalk River, Ontario, which was followed by one much more serious at Windscale in Cumberland, England. The latter ruined the reactor and emitted a radioactive cloud that hung even over South and East England, with an intensity 10 percent of that over Hiroshima.

The scientific community, in America and elsewhere, continued to grapple with the problems of maturity. In 1957 eighteen German scientists, including Max Born, Otto Hahn, and Carl Friedrich von Weizsäcker, who had worked on developing atomic power, declared that they would not work on anything that could be used as an atomic weapon. And in July of that year the first Pugwash Conference was held, on an initiative of Bertrand Russell, to engage representatives of both East and West in discussions of the new problems. Bertrand Russell's role in this can remind us of the other styles of Englishness still extant, besides the one we have been studying.

Aesthetes and Anti-Aesthetes

In the literary world of America, there were still the Southern dandies writing, and there was still Nabokov. In Paris, in 1955, just at the end of our period, he produced the great novel that justified dandyism, *Lolita.* Here all the moral and immoral tendencies in his fiction conflict and combine in brilliant patterns of stress and emphasis, and the reader breathes the heady atmosphere of the dandy's defiance of Reality—including all traditional truth and goodness—without sacrificing his memories and anticipations of other modes of experience. From there Nabokov went on to his translations of *Prince Igor* and *Eugene Onegin,* colossal feats of pedantry, which no English dandy could compete with. (Pedantry is a habitual resource for dandies, because it is an implicit defiance of the humanist scholarship of the mature man. Thus it is natural to find that the author of *A Shropshire Lad,* for instance, was a ferocious pedant.) Nabokov's influence, cooperating with that of Borges and Beckett, was to be felt in America in the work of young novelists like John Barth, Thomas Pyncheon, John Updike, and others. In England it was not acclimatized at any high imaginative level. England's literary critics were still fighting off dandyism.

Scrutiny was defunct, but Leavis went from strength to strength as a cultural force; he published *The Great Tradition, D. H. Lawrence,*

Novelist, and a number of essays, and defeated the influence of dandyism wherever he found it, even within the critical formulas of T. S. Eliot. These were, therefore, also the years of Lawrence's triumph in England, his recognition as the greatest writer of his century. There was, of course, resistance to him; but we might note, as not untypical of the feebleness of such resistance, Edith Sitwell's essay, "The Man with Red Hair." The authorship gave this a certain currency. Miss Sitwell's *Collected Poems* came out in 1957, and she had a kind of "official" reputation as a great poet—she was a Dame of the British Empire, and so on. She said that Lawrence's paintings were of the kind that made one feel "that one had been very severely bumped," and of his novels she described *Lady Chatterley's Lover* as "a very dirty and completely worthless book." She had long before, she reminded us, described Lawrence as the head of the "Jaeger" school of writing, invoking the famous brand of underwear because his books were so hot, so soft, and so woolly.[7] (Similarly Max Beerbohm remarked suavely to Brian Howard that Lawrence had labored under the disadvantage of being mad.) Thus the critical level of the resistance was far from formidable and, for most young people then taking literature seriously, only made the cause of Lawrence and Leavis more worthwhile espousing.

Leavis's students were by this time teaching in most English universities as well as the teachers' colleges, and in the Commonwealth universities, where his influence had long been strong. It seemed that England was now safe for the decent man. Politically and economically it was a second-rate power, obviously, but culturally—as a homeland for an intellectual—it still kept its self-respect. That is the mood that the American sociologist Edward Shils thought he noticed in 1955, when he wrote:

> . . . scarcely anyone in Great Britain seems any longer to feel that there is anything fundamentally wrong. On the contrary, Great Britain on the whole, and especially in comparison with other countries, seems to the British intellectuals of the mid-1950s to be fundamentally all right and even much

more than that. Never has an intellectual class found its society and its culture so much to their satisfaction.

This passage is quoted in Anthony Hartley's *A State of England* (1963). Hartley was not primarily anti-dandy; he was fairly contemptuous of the Angry Young Men's collection of manifestos, *Declaration,* (1957), because of its irascibility of tone and superficiality of analysis. But that made all the more striking his affirmation of Orwell and Leavis as the dominant voices of the period. And he decided, like Shils, that the British intellectual was "far from being a *révolté* or a *déraciné*." He was at peace with his fathers:

> Indeed, since the war his rootedness has markedly increased in that a new generation has reacted against the cosmopolitanism of its predecessors and brought the British provinces into the centre of a cultural picture from which they had been absent since the 19th century.

What is reflected here is not an excited hopefulness nor a complacent contentment.

Between 1945 and 1950 it was all too evident that nothing very ideal was going to happen, but that if a sort of Highest Common Factor of decent behaviour and tolerable living could be established that would be enough to be going on with. How much would be achieved was doubtful (there was not much belief in the efficiency of politics as an instrument of betterment), but the attempt had to be made—primarily for reasons which were moral, however they might be put. Let us say that we were in earnest about doing good but were distrustful of "do-gooders" and their nostrums.

Whether or not one limits the period as Hartley does, this was indeed the mood of the times dominated by Leavis and Orwell, when the dandies seemed to have been defeated—the times in which I grew up.

Chapter Eleven

Confessions and Conclusions

The Critic's Conversation with Himself

THE SUBJECT OF this book has had quite a personal interest for me, since it traces that profile of cultural England, of "England," or rather those two mutually angry profiles, into which I grew up—and between which I had to choose. I chose the decent man, turned my back on the dandies, and never till now asked myself what it felt like to be them. Finding out has been interesting. But finishing the book leaves me with the uneasy feeling that the subject had quietly gone academic on me, that it had ceased to be a living problem, a living part of my past. Why investigate all that in so much detail? I haven't, after all, been finding out that the dandies were a much *larger* phenomenon than I used to think them, intellectually or imaginatively. Have I done anything more than merely understand how Englishmen then could want to be dandies? I could have done that at the time—the time of hating them. I didn't because it was more worthwhile, it made more sense, it served my mind more, to hate them. Is it that now I *have* no first-order intellectual motives, and so spend long gentle years writing a book with only a second-order motive behind it? Or have the robes of academic office swayed me, year after year, procession after swishing procession, into secret sympathy with the dandies?

I could not have been—then—more one of the "école de Butler," as Waugh put it. I won a County Scholarship from my state grammar school to go to university in 1945, the first year the 1944 Butler Education Act made them generally available. If they had not been made generally available that year, I would presumably never have gone to a university, nor met the brightest and best of my generation on such equal terms, nor—perhaps—felt qualified to raise my voice in print on cultural issues. There were in my family no traditional, informal modes of knowledge about power-and-precedence, or art-and-manners, to have replaced those I picked up—or failed to pick up, from Waugh's point of view—at Cambridge. I owed everything, in practical terms, to Butler and Beveridge and socialism. And in intellectual terms I owed everything to Leavis and Lawrence and Orwell.

My generation was the exact equivalent of Waugh's, in the sense that I was eighteen in 1945, when my war ended, as he had been fifteen in 1918, when his war ended. I then, like Waugh and Connolly and Acton and Howard before, looked around an England littered with old and dishonored gods, askew on their pedestals and lighted from the wrong angle, and most apparently on their way to the junkyard. There was a lot of talk about starting new, in 1945 as in 1918, and a confident sense that a lot of old errors and impostures, literary, cultural, and political, had been exploded for us by the war, and would never be able to impose themselves again. The war seemed, as the previous one had seemed, to have been purgative for English society.

But there was a reversal within that equivalence. The young men and the new ideas of 1918 were the old men and the old ideas of 1945. It was Waugh and Connolly and dandyism and aestheticism which seemed to *us* to have been exploded. There *was* a post-1945 dandyism, as I have said, (the ballet, Oscar Wilde revivals, the Sitwells) but it was a recrudescence of the old, and run by the same old people, and it came about because they were now in *power*. The young men turned away, for ideas, toward Leavis and Orwell—toward the idea of decency. I repudiated the dandies as vehemently as they had repudiated Kipling. Waugh's sneers at "uncouth writing" and "State-trained professional critics" were a challenge I joyfully met.

At Cambridge, 1945–48, I read English, and listened only to Leavis, and—very much as Waugh says—formed myself as best I could into the "grim uniformity" of the Leavisite faith. But of course that grim uniformity was also a joyful release, as all true Puritanism is; in this case a release from the painful solicitations, challenges, sneers, of the dandyism all around me. For there it was, not so named, but all its profile's component parts traceable, like a jigsaw-puzzle eye, ear, nose, hidden in here a fanlight, there a silk ascot, there a tone of voice. Cambridge was by its own standards comparatively drab, in 1945, but still by mine it was gaudy. Its architecture was for me decidedly theater architecture, calling for epigrams, outrageousness, brilliance, charm, and elegance of pose and poise. To enter through one of those gateways into one of those courts, to pass under one of those bridges in one of those punts, to drink one of those glasses of sherry in one of those panelled rooms, was to feel every nerve of self-consciousness as unwelcomely stimulated as if I'd walked on to a stage set for *Lady Windermere's Fan*. It was for me the architecture of dandyism, and as for all those other young men who, shabby and homely enough in their native Birminghams, in Cambridge performed (more or less indistinguishably, to my anxiety-blurred vision) as my critical appraisers, they might as well have worn monocles or wielded lorgnettes. From this most unwelcome intensification of adolescence (that too is what dandyism is), from this fever, Leavis's puritanism was a deliverance. It released me from dandyism in the name of manhood—released me from the compulsions to be beautiful and brilliant in the name of a reality which imposed duties—duties which reduced those

other competitive compulsions to insignificance. So did Orwell's preference for Dobbin and George Bowling and the unbeautiful people.
The psychological mechanism was precisely the same as that operating in the early years of Victorianism, and it operated just as effectively on me as it had on those young readers of Thomas Carlyle and
Fraser's Magazine. My place within the cultural dialectic, my role as
soldier against Waugh, could not have been more clearly defined, nor
more satisfactory.

As I gradually found my voice, therefore, it was that of an anti-
dandy; and it so happens that I began to find it, began to write and be
published, around 1957, though in America. (Perhaps if I'd been living
in England then, and more in touch with the currents of English opinion, I would never have found that voice, because I would have known
that its intended audience had already dispersed in different directions.) I had an article in *Partisan Review,* in 1957, critical of England,
and it drew a letter from John Fisher of *Harper's Magazine,* asking
me to write an article on the English Establishment for them. He was
referring, I later discovered, to the idea put forward by Henry Fairlie
apropos of the Burgess and Maclean flight, but I wrote back that I
didn't know enough about the Church of England to undertake such
a commission. However, when he explained that he didn't mean that,
I knew immediately what he did mean, without having to read any of
the essays he mentioned. The line of thought was that of my generation, and we could understand each other with half a phrase or a single word sardonically pronounced. I wrote for John Fisher two of the
articles that later made up my first book, *Mirror for Anglo-Saxons.*

My point of view there was consistently that of "the decent man,"
and the book was legitimately described on the American blurb as
an introduction to the mood of the Angry Young Men. Like them,
I made myself an identity as an "ordinary Englishman," which was of
great importance to my self-respect and my imaginative orientation in
all kinds of ways. Reading Leavis and Lawrence, I found that identity
reinforced; reading Waugh and Connolly—at least while thinking
about or feeling that identity—I saw in them mostly what made them

detestable. Teaching, I taught always "criticism," that activity of the mind which both Leavis and Orwell exemplified in different ways, and which trained men in the temperament of decency.

I took over that image of English culture dear to the dandies—to Osbert Sitwell, for instance—as of a continual war between Cavaliers and Roundheads, and identified myself and my heroes, with glad perversity, as the latter. I remembered that in one of my first tutorials at Cambridge my supervisor had used the image and spoken of the Cavaliers as "our" side—we men of letters, we men of the arts. (He was Hugh Sykes-Davies, a Surrealist poet in the '30s and, among many other things, a friend of Guy Burgess's when they were both Apostles.) Using that rhetoric, I was pleased to say who I was and who my heroes and my enemies were. I returned to England in 1961, to take my place in an honorable battle line.

That is why it was quite a personal shock for me to realize that in fact England was *not* "made safe for decency." Soon after *Mirror for Anglo-Saxons* was published, in 1960, I began to realize that the lines of the cultural conflict were not so clearly drawn as I had thought, that not all the good people were on the same side—or if they were, they wouldn't stay there. I had written enthusiastically about *Lucky Jim* and *That Uncertain Feeling,* and had taken Kingsley Amis to be my prime example of "the decent man" among the new writers. Those novels were comic celebrations of first, normal decency, and then, marriage, and the next one, *I Like It Here,* almost programmatically moved on to attack Mediterraneanism. It seemed clear that Amis was creating a set of icons for the decent man.

It was therefore an important challenge for me to find that Amis did not remain a decent man. Almost immediately after 1960, from the days of *Take a Girl Like You* and *One Fat Englishman,* he offered us representative heroes and points of view that could only be called "anti-decent." Moreover, from the days of *The Anti-Death League* he positively invited us to assimilate him to Evelyn Waugh—his right-wing politics, his blatant polemics, his militarism, his publicity-seeking, his legal suits, his reaction against both left-wing liberalism and the cult of youth. Amis had made himself into a dandy of the English kind—a dandy-gentleman. He had switched his imaginative loyalties from Orwell (a palpable presence in the early books) to Waugh.

In a short article on "My Kind of Comedy" in *The Twentieth Century* for July 1961, he says that the prime targets of his humor are bores and right-wing things, and that his sense of what is funny is limited by his "tender political conscience." But on the other hand he says that he has recently found Evelyn Waugh funny:

> Evelyn Waugh makes fun of things I feel strongly about, but then I made the discovery that we agree about certain basic things. He makes the sort of character I dislike behave in a way I like. . . .

And he says he feels an affinity with Fielding, Powell, and Iris Murdoch. This adds up to a fairly definite turning away from the sensibility of *Lucky Jim*.

In fact, his critical essays had always, from 1957 on, expressed a very irritable consciousness of Leavis, Orwell, and Lawrence. Lawrence seems to have been always a bête noire for Amis, Orwell a former hero whose claque irritated, Leavis something in between. Amis was always keenly aware of the anti-dandy movement and in some sense lived with his mind turned toward it, but his awareness led him as much to a sense that he was different as to any sense of comradeship. What happened in the years after *Lucky Jim* is that he aligned himself with the dandies positively. He made himself known to be a connoisseur of wine and food, clothes, and even snuff. In 1959 he had objected to *Lolita* on moral grounds as sadistic, allied to the charge that it was too "aesthetic." But in 1965 he wrote a James Bond adventure story, and said how much he had always admired Ian Fleming's work, morally and aesthetically. In 1967 he voted Conservative for the first time (having voted Labour for the last time in 1964) and said that experience is a Tory. All these gestures add up to a repudiation of his former position and a going over to the opposition. And since Amis is the most talented, or one of the two or three most talented, writers in England, and since his talent is precisely for *contemporary* truth, for what-then-must-we-now-do?, for the cultural dialectic, this was a considerable challenge to me. It amounted to a demonstration that the dandy tradition was still viable in England and that it offered more freedom and truth to the lively mind than the decent tradition did.*

Moreover, the other brilliantly talented writer among the Angry Young Men, Philip Larkin, has gone through a similar evolution. In his poetry, in his two early novels, in his critical prose, in what he seems to have meant to Amis, Larkin was an anti-dandy force, a plain man as intellectual, and an influence working in the same direction as Orwell, Leavis, and Lawrence. But in the 1960s he began implicitly to ally himself with John Betjeman as a poet, just as Amis allied himself with Waugh. In 1959, in *Listen,* Larkin described Betjeman as "one of those rare figures on whom the aesthetic appetites of an age pivot and swing round to face an entirely new direction." And in 1971, introducing Betjeman's *Collected Poems,* Larkin asks can it be that Betjeman will dominate the second half of the 20th century as T. S. Eliot did the first? He calls Betjeman's the most extraordinary poetic output of our time, praises his advocacy of "the little, the obscure, the disregarded," and lauds his work as a preserver of

---

* Naturally, Amis's dandyism is modern in style, and I am using "style" in one of its more serious meanings. It is modern in the pattern of the accommodations it makes between serious moral principle and defiant amoralism; a pattern marked by cruelty, violence, sexual experiment, and an assertive ugliness of spirit. This modern British dandyism is vividly exemplified in the work of Simon Raven. What distinguishes Simon Raven's sensibility from Anthony Powell's, in other ways so similar, is that which is specifically modern and British; and that is what unites Amis, Raven, and Ian Fleming. (As I pointed out before, James Bond is a figment of an Etonian and *Sonnenkind* imagination, but in a later phase—and of course a cruder mode—than those we have been studying.) Raven is a novelist from whom Amis may perhaps have learned something, as he made his transition from decency to dandyism. Certainly Raven's *The Sabre Squadron*, published in 1966, is very like Amis's *Anti-Death League*, of the same year; and many things in Raven's *Alms for Oblivion* series remind one of Amis's themes. Of course Amis is a much more interesting novelist. Amis, Fleming, and Raven are all three preoccupied with power—with the dominance established by one man over another, with command, self-aggrandizement, humiliation, challenge, revenge—and all three might be accused at times of writing a kind of power-pornography. But in Amis the counterpoint to this preoccupation is always wonderfully vigorous.

the past. In these phrases we glimpse presumably the affinity Larkin feels between his own meanings and Betjeman's. He seems to feel a formal debt to the poet for whom, as he says, "the modern poetic revolution has simply not taken place." Of course, such questions of form bear on the poetry's cultural meaning. Larkin says that in this century English poetry went off on a loop-line that took it away from the general reader; and presumably he feels that Betjeman, who stayed close to that reader, will be a father figure to the English poets yet to come. If so, it will clearly be a patrimony of comic and provincial dandyism that they will receive.

How was I to respond to these challenges? Of course I could say that Amis's and Larkin's changes of side were their own affairs. I could point to weaknesses always present in their work that explained what seemed to me so drastic a mistake. They were, after all, admirable as poets and novelists, not as critics or thinkers. I did, and do, say that— and also that their changes of side only indicate the power of the cultural dialectic we have been studying.

England has remained in many ways the same as it was in 1918. Auden says, in the essay on Beerbohm and dandyism quoted earlier, "In postwar Britain, the clothes, accents, and diction of the siblings may have changed, but, so far as I can judge, the suffocating insular coziness is just the same." And Waugh said, in the 1960 preface to a new edition of *Brideshead Revisited,* that when he wrote the book in 1944 no one could have imagined the revived vogue for English country houses or the self-reviving power of the English aristocracy. Harold Macmillan, for instance, was a very successful prime minister from 1957 to 1963, and seemed able to represent modern England perfectly well—Macmillan, so rooted in Eton and Balliol, the Guards and grouse shooting. All the elegancies of the aristocratic dandy seemed to *work* just as well as ever. The old patterns of alignment have proved amazingly magnetic. When a man ceases to be an anti-dandy in England, he tends to swing right round to become a dandy. Those are his alternatives, either Waugh/Betjeman or Lawrence/Orwell (to choose to be neither—to opt out of the cultural dialectic—carries with it other penalties), and Amis and Larkin have merely demonstrated the power of that dialectic. I still say that, up to a point.

But what I said, primarily, was that after all I too, in a different way, had ceased to be an anti-dandy. To engage in that conflict seemed to me, too, no longer an adventure. When I read pieces that derived from it, I was uneasily aware of, or suspicious of, imaginative repetition or marking time—I mean in the more literary and imaginative, as distinct from the more political and speculative, work of Raymond Williams and his followers.

For that reason, I had long been shifting my own ground. In successive books I had kept expanding the terms of my humanism and somewhat shifting its center, so that in my book on science in 1964 I was in dissent from Leavis and far from any confrontation with dandyism. Even in *Reappraisals,* 1963, one of my enthusiasms had been for Nabokov, with his outrageous aestheticism. I had always been conscious of other countries out there, beyond this dialectic, and had always wanted to include them in the area marked red on my map. The "decent man" had to deal with more than the old authors and ideas, had to become more than the "decent man."

Moreover, beside new things out there to be aware of, there was something *in* me that was *actively* disloyal to decency. I had always indulged that sense of humor I have called hypertrophied—always laughed most at Evelyn Waugh, and at the whole range of humor to which his work belongs, from Noel Coward to Gillie Potter, from the cruelly sardonic to the purely silly. I suffered from, and rejoiced in, the vision of just about everything as preposterous. With the humorous part of my mind, the part that deals with that whole range of experiences that do not "make sense" as they occur, I had always been a dandy—blended with the naïf and other things. At sixteen I wrote a story of which I can remember only one line, but it is enough to indicate a close kinship between my taste even then and that of the comic nonsense that Harold Acton contributed to *The Eton Candle* in 1922. My heroine turns on her stepmother with the riposte, "Man may not live by bread alone, Countess, but little is the spiritual fare that supplements *your* pâté de foie gras." I was soon aware that this sense of humor had radically different value loyalties not only from my father's Mark Twain sense of humor, but also from those of my serious sensibility—from all I was learning to feel from Leavis and Lawrence about experiences that do "make sense." These were two opposing forces in my sensibility, and being a "decent man" *meant* according hegemony to the second. It was a moral *choice* because there was that implied alternative, that insurgent population to be kept down. It seemed to me also that in most of the Englishmen I knew who were committed to decency there was a "sense of humor" (a small name for a large fact) that should be called dandy. The national experience since 1918 has included too much that never "made sense."

So I had been no more single-minded than Amis and Larkin, and was equally unable to keep marching to the drums of decency. Part of me was a dandy too. It was just that my way of dealing with this fact was different. Instead of switching sides in the battle, I had risen above it, transcended it in some balloon of objectivity, impartiality, and reconciliation. I had found a point of view that included both of those below. This ballooning I had often objected to when other critics did it, but now there seemed no point in worrying about anything except whether it was well done, *as* transcendence. To transcend was fairly definitely the fated tactic for an Erasmian or Apollonian temperament. So I claimed—to myself—to be dealing with the same problem as Amis and Larkin, but dealing with it better, explaining the terms of the decent tradition instead of abandoning it. And that was what this book was doing.

The Second Conversation

But Amis and Larkin might protest, it occurred to me, that they had not changed sides in the battle but rather engaged in a new one. They might say that not only had the dandy/anti-dandy debate gone stale and lost its audience, but a new battle had developed, whose issue had the same importance, which occupied the *present* crossroads of English imaginative life, but which demanded a different set of terms and tones, identities, and identifications.

Undeniably, another minor revolution had occurred in England's idea of itself, at just the end of the period we have been considering, just the moment when decency seemed to have triumphed—and it was a revolution in the name of Dionysus rather than Apollo or Adonis.

In 1955, just when talk of "the Establishment" became prevalent, Mary Quant and Alexander Plunket-Greene (son of Waugh's old friend) opened their clothes boutique on the King's Road, Chelsea, the first germ of "swinging London." This was the year of rock and roll in England, the year commercial television began, and the year of Malcolm Muggeridge's scandal-arousing attack on the monarchy in the *New Statesman.* 1956 was the year, in politics, of Suez and Hungary, and in books, of Colin Wilson's *The Outsider* and John Osborne's *Look Back in Anger.* In 1957 John Stephen, only nineteen years old, opened the first boutique in Carnaby Street, Donald Baverstock produced "Tonight," the vanguard of the BBC satire shows, and Jocelyn Stevens bought the magazine, *The Queen,* which he, together with Anthony Armstrong-Jones and Mark Boxer, made into the publicity organ of swinging London. "Satire" and crazy clothes, affluence and political defeat, these were the ingredients of the new ferment, just beginning to be active at the end of Brian Howard's life.

The year 1958 saw the first Aldermaston March for nuclear disarmament. In 1959 there were 60,000 marchers, in 1960, 100,000. This sort of protest against the Establishment was obviously quite different in ideology from the sort that we have been recording, and might seem, at a distance, more likely to ally itself temperamentally with the forces of decency. But in fact—a major fact for the understanding of the period—it was effectively the ally of the Dionysiacs. This is a point that Doris Lessing makes in her description of the march in *The Four-Gated City.*

In 1960 came the trial to decide whether *Lady Chatterley's Lover* was obscene, which assembled in the book's defence all kinds of authorities who were in effect speaking for erotic liberation. These included some notable decent men, for instance Richard Hoggart, but it was appropriate in many ways that F. R. Leavis, who had made Lawrence the great spokesman for mature life-values, not only did not take part but dissented from this apotheosis of Lawrence. The trial (and the book itself, to some degree) made Lawrence a hero of Dionysus as much as of Demeter. The novel was brought out as a Penguin immediately after the trial, and it sold enormously—in 1960 seventeen million Penguin books were sold, as against ten million in 1951. *Lolita* also, which had appeared the preceding year, took its effect as another item in the charter of sexual liberation.

In 1961, *Private Eye,* the satirical magazine, and "The Establishment," the satirical nightclub, began operation. *Beyond the Fringe,* the most successful of the stage satire shows, came to London; the Gaming Act launched a new craze for gambling; there was a mass arrest of the Committee of 100 in Trafalgar Square; and John Osborne sent a letter to *The Times* in which he very emotionally repudiated political England, the England of the fathers.

In 1962 the John Vassall scandal came to light. Vassall was a homosexual civil servant with access to important papers, who for some time had been blackmailed by the Russians into copying documents for them. It seems likely that he was betrayed to the British government by Russia because the resultant scandal would do Britain more harm than the loss of further secrets through his espionage, and thus that this was another move in the sequence that included the Burgess-Maclean scandal, to draw the attention of the outside world, and of Britain itself, to the corruption and enfeeblement of the British Establishment. The same year saw the beginning of the television satire show, "That Was the Week That Was." And in a related line of glossy and amoral worldliness were the first James Bond film, *Doctor No,* and the new *Sunday Times* color supplement. Mark Boxer became the first editor of the latter, and carried into it the spirit of *The Queen,* which had already celebrated the new affluence and its styles in a famous "Boom" issue of 1959. Anthony Armstrong-Jones also worked on the supplement, and it is worth noting that in 1960 he had married Princess Margaret and that David Hicks, an interior decorator, had married Lady Pamela Mountbatten, who was herself practically a member of the royal family. These marriages could be said to symbolize the capitulation to the spirit of the '20s of the last bastion of the old-style Establishment.

And in 1963 came the biggest political and moral scandal of all, the Profumo affair. John Profumo, the minister of war, had an affair with Christine Keeler, a call girl who was also sleeping with a member of the Russian embassy. Although it seems established that no official secrets were in fact betrayed, the investigation uncovered a network of illegal activities, centering on Stephen Ward, osteopath and pimp, which implicated prominent politicians and property millionaires—the fathers of England—in a series of drink, drug, and sex orgies. This case provided a climax to the preceding twelve years of such revelations. And, of course, it immensely strengthened the concurrent demands for a relaxation of old standards and for a general pursuit of anarchic pleasure.

These names and dates are surely enough to evoke the marked eroticization and demoralization of "England" in the years after 1957. Christopher Booker, from whose *The Neophiliacs* I have taken this data, says that in the years 1955 to 1966 the dream of youth, excitement, rebellion, and violence, "grew to fullness and began to fade." He speaks of rebellion and violence because along with the eroticism went rock festivals, fantasy fashions in entertainment and behavior, a spread in the use of drugs, and a steep rise in the rates of crime, illegitimate births, and suicides. This movement toward anarchy was strong enough to draw further strength from other things that could have had quite different and disconnected cultural meanings, like *Waiting for Godot* and the Great Train Robbery, not to mention again the Aldermaston Marches. In fact all these things cooperated in, and contributed to, the same cultural *Gestalt*. This was the Dionysiac or Aphroditean *Gestalt* discernible in Otto Gross's theories, and realized to some degree in Weimar Germany and even, to a lesser degree, in the London of the '20s. But in the London of the '50s and '60s the Dionysiac movement was not so allied to literary dandyism. In Cyril

Connolly's essay, "This Gale-Swept Chip," quoted before, he said he could not connect the England around him in 1963 with the England he grew up in—he could not *imagine* an England without sexual inhibition. And in fact no member of his group welcomed swinging London, any more than the decent men did. Although the entrepreneurs and impresarios of that London have quite often been Eton and Oxbridge types, as they were before, their involvement in the scene seems to have been more purely exploitative, or at least less allied to imaginative work than such involvement was in the '20s.

Or perhaps it is that that imaginative work, for instance the "satire," has not been literary in the way that Waugh's was. I offer alternative interpretations because it is too early to make confident judgments. The serious mind of the times has recoiled away from the anarchy, but so it did also in the '20s at first, and the two may merely be taking time to come together again. Mr. Booker, who was first editor of *Private Eye* and a script writer for "That Was the Week That Was," now describes the movement in which he participated as one of moral decadence. It is not hard to imagine a Waugh of our times, or at least one of his friends, having written *The Neophiliacs*. So perhaps Mr. Booker, or at least one of his friends, may yet turn out to be a later Waugh. As yet, however, the dandies and the decent men have been alike nonplused by the Dionysiac phenomenon.

Now to return to Amis and Larkin, they might legitimately say that all this has been the cultural phenomenon of our times, that the crucial cultural issues all derive from it, and that those issues are all variants on "how do you imaginatively defend older values against these new ones?" For their reactions to it are basically defensive or conservative, even reactionary. Larkin praises Betjeman for these lines, about modern British workmen.

> An eight hour day for all, and more than three
> Of these are occupied with making tea
> And talking over what we all agree—

Larkin says these are a "pertinent summary of a subject no other poet has tried," implying that the others have lacked the necessary courage to seem reactionary. And he says that Betjeman insists on "the little, the forgotten, the unprofitable, the obscure," and that if he were a soldier leaving England, he would want to take the volume of Betjeman's poems with him—"it is what we are fighting for, foremost of all." The terms of the recommendation, as well as the recommendation itself, are defiantly old-fashioned.

Amis also has attacked in essay form the cult of youth and the liberalization of standards—in the Church of England and the educational system, for instance. But he has also taken on these themes in his novels, notably in *Girl, Twenty* and *I Want It Now.* He could fairly claim, I think, to have had more to say about such matters than more accredited moralists, like Raymond Williams and others who remained in the decent man tradition. He has both shown more sympathy with the phenomena of "permissiveness" and spoken more sharply against them. The acuteness of his statements probably derives from his sympathy, so Amis could also claim that he has had something to say only because he has been willing to abandon his decent-man position, willing to participate imaginatively. He long ago complained of Richard Hoggart's treatment of popular culture (among others), saying that the author spoke about things he did not seem to have participated in.

Apart from Amis it is another novelist who seems to have had most to say about this cultural phenomenon, and again her strength has everything to do with her participation in it. I mean Doris Lessing, in *The Four-Gated City* and *The Summer Before the Dark.* In these books her protagonists, who come, like Amis's, from moral-intellectual traditions of responsibility, encounter and experiment with young people who come from anti-moral and anti-responsible traditions, some from the Dionysiac circus. Like Amis, although less explicitly, Doris Lessing has always turned away from her ideological allies on the English scene and has maintained an independent identity as a moral, psychic, and sexual explorer.

This, they might say, is the crucial cultural transaction of our time, and the tradition of the decent man is a positive impediment to taking part in it. With all the Leavisite emphasis on cultural-moral criticism, what Leavisite has found anything to say to this Dionysianism, has found any dialogue with it possible? He cannot do it. And not only because of the decent man's revulsion from moral license. The activity of "criticism," as practiced by both Leavis and Orwell, does not lead naturally into practical action, even of a politically serious and responsible kind. It completes its curve in defeating the irresponsibility of dandyism and aestheticism. Moreover, they might say, *your* way of transcending and expanding the decent man's position is no use either. Soaring upward, you float out of all critical and dialectical contact with the new phenomenon. You may later forgive the Dionysiacs, as you now forgive the dandies, but you could never enter into their experience and help them reinterpret it.

The Third Conversation

My general answer to those voices in my mind must be that they are novelists or poets and I am a critic. If a critic were to attempt to deal directly with the Dionysiac circus, he would have to stop being a critic. That seems to me demonstrated not only by the failure of many who have tried, but by the success of one—Tom Wolfe. He, in some of his pieces, does succeed brilliantly in giving us the feel of experiences that intentionally defy moral and intellectual categories. But he does so by in effect surrendering his own moral and intellectual point of view. There can be no direct dialogue between the spirit of the circus and the spirit of the study. That is why so many academics who have recently tried to bring the two together have only made themselves ridiculous. For the artistic imagination, on the other hand, a dialogue between Apollo and Dionysus is very possible, and perhaps necessary, as Nietzsche showed.

Of course, one job the critic must do is to *follow* the artist. He must follow Amis and Lessing, for instance, into those engagements with Dionysia, to interpret and reinterpret their protagonists' experience. One function of criticism certainly is so to assist and supplement the creative artist, although with somewhat different powers and interests and necessarily in a somewhat secondary way. On the other hand, the critic also has other functions, in which he is quite independent. He interprets the life of ideas in his time, in ways the contemporary artist should follow. In such matters their relationship is reversed.

And what I must most consider is, of course, the relation of this defence to the book I have written. What have I done, by the tactic of transcendence, that could claim to be of the same strength of interest as what the novelists have done by the tactic of engagement? (If I cannot claim the same strength of interest for my subject, I must feel that I should have been writing about them in that subservient role I described before.) What I have implicitly argued is that the tradition of the decent man is still viable but needs revival, and that the decent man must, to renew his vitality, now admit to a much freer and easier relation with the dandy than before. The battle between them is over, and the man of culture needs to shift his terms of allegiance in order to keep alive and alert to everything around him. He needs, to take the most important instance, to let his sense of humor interact with his serious sensibility. His rigid disapproval of dandyism, his self-distancing from it, needs to be relaxed. He needs to work out a vocabulary of feeling that can accommodate the meanings of Waugh as well as those of Lawrence. This does not mean that we should abandon seriousness. The relation the book makes between Waugh and Guy Burgess surely asks us to take Waugh's jokes *more* seriously than we might otherwise do. But it is a good-humored, unaggressive, understanding seriousness that is most useful now.

To proceed to the general case, the critic needs to seek out imaginative life wherever it is to be found and to respond to it generously. And this means he has to look for it without preconceived opinions—or rather, be ready to let go of such opinions, however recently and earnestly arrived at. He must be ready to feel quite blank towards authors and causes and ideas that "ought" to engage him, to drop interests that used to be important to him and with which others identify him. He must be ready to be a bit of a Diaghilev as well as a bit of a Leavis. And this can be a full-time occupation. If and when it conflicts with that other occupation of the critic—standing for something consistently and in full public view, standing for standards, being a standard—then one or the other will no doubt be sacrificed. And a critic may—it is my instinct that in this time and place he should—sacrifice standards to ideas, sacrifice consistency to responsiveness, and sacrifice virtue to fertility. (If he does, it will be a paradox to keep calling him "the decent man," but he might keep thinking of himself as the latter's son and heir.) And transcendence is a tactic for developing ideas, responsiveness, and fertility. But although the spirit of my work is certainly transcendent, conciliatory, and reconciling—I could hardly claim anything else of a book that likes everyone almost equally well—it is also dialectical. For criticism too, a new battle, or cause for battle, has developed since 1957. The enemy against which I am moving is not, like the novelists' enemy, something outside the old dialectic, but inside—something that is to be found in both the dandy and the decent man. I refer to a rigid and exclusive Englishness, a defeatism and provinciality of mind that is demonstrable in the shared and continued prejudice against modernism. Auberon Waugh, for the dandies, recently described modernism as a cul-de-sac of modern literature, and that has long been Leavis's image of it for the anti-dandies. Amis and Larkin have rejected it, in both their critical and their creative work. And as I have said, Nabokov (like Wallace Stevens) has signally failed to find appreciation in England. Besides Amis's remarks, Philip Toynbee has described Nabokov's work as heartless, and Herbert Read has said his talent derives its energy from an obsessive hatred of the civilization it depicts. Julian Moynahan (a critic British in taste though American in nationality), justified his own taste for Nabokov by dismissing the latter's ambitious aestheticism and recommended him to us as a poet of domesticity. (Contrariwise, Frank Kermode, significantly one of the few English appreciators of Wallace Stevens, recommends Lawrence to us as a modernist *rather than* a poet of domesticity. Kermode is the one English critic I can think of who is interested in modernism, but he is not rooted in the decent man tradition, and so the tendency of his work is not to renew that.)

And surely there are signs, in English fiction and poetry as well as criticism, of the limiting and dimming effect of this rejection. When one reads Waugh's war trilogy, and thinks of American war novels, like Mailer's, surely one is struck by the former's limitedness, its predictability, its stolidity. Even Amis as a novelist and Leavis as a critic, much as I admire both, seem deliberately small-scale when measured against the appropriate American criteria. And what is one to say about Larkin's praise of Betjeman, Donald Davie's of Hardy, and the recent repudiation of Eliot and Pound in controversies about modern poetry? The old anti-Americanism is being harnessed to literary nostalgia and negativism, and surely there is a hideous risk of a whole literature of cosy quaintness, a whole landscape peopled by pottery gnomes? There are many signs that England is in the grip of literary Dunkirkism, a dogged, "Dad's Army" retreat from all the big enterprises, which can surely result only in further defeats and defeatism. The dandy and the decent man seem to be settling their differences in an alliance against modernism, and it is against that consolidation that criticism must now direct itself.

One of the starting points of my interest in this subject was a photograph in the Picasso Museum in Barcelona, which showed Picasso with Diaghilev, Cocteau, Stravinsky, and I forget who else, in Venice. I noted that there were Russians, Frenchmen, and Spaniards, but no Englishmen in the group, and then realized that if there had been one, he could not have been one of *my* Englishmen—at best it would have been Sacheverell Sitwell or Lord Berners. I saw on reflection how much of modern art the decent man had cut himself off from; and as I worked on this book I saw how little the dandy too, in England, had made of his opportunities. This, then, is the *dialectical* point of the book—in the dialectic proper to the critic, which is quite different from that proper to the novelist. What the critic can do for the imaginative life of his culture is, as Matthew Arnold said, put into circulation within it the really living ideas of his time.

I should like also to claim to have been dialectical, and not just transcendent, by another token. My attention has been caught, in studying this material, by one group of British intellectuals who avoided dandyism, but also its antithesis, and did so by allying themselves with Christianity and with creative mythopoeia—a strategy with considerable attraction for me, and one that it might seem that my theories led up to. They set themselves to create cultural images for Christ, and for a Christian temperament, that would be meaningful to the age—C. S. Lewis, for instance, allied these concerns with the form of science fiction. Perhaps the major progenitor of all these people was G. K. Chesterton, and he is typical of them all in that he was, as both Waugh and Auden point out, all his life in flight from the sick dandyism of his youth in the 1890s; Father Brown was a complete antithesis of Oscar Wilde, whereas Sherlock Holmes was only a transmutation of the dandy.

Waugh and Auden both learned a lot from Chesterton's imaginative tactics, and Amis has recently shown an interest in him. But Chesterton's most direct descendants were C. S. Lewis, Dorothy Sayers, Charles Williams, and J. R. R. Tolkien—the Oxford "Inklings." These people escaped dandyism and aestheticism—to which they all felt some attraction—but without confronting it. They provided themselves with a handsomer dialectical enemy, the forces of evil as defined by orthodox Christian theology, which they located on the contemporary scene most often in the misuse of science and social science. They invented handsome myths as objective correlatives to their beliefs, and composed poems, plays, and adventure stories about them, all with a good deal of taste and talent. Most aspects of their ideological and imaginative behavior strike me as more generous, intelligent, and dignified than those of either Leavis or Waugh—or Orwell, for that matter—if considered in the abstract. But considered in the concrete, the ideas of the last three have at various times meant everything to me, while the others *mean,* in that sense, nothing. I approve what they did, but theoretically; I read the books it resulted in approvingly, but I am not really at all engaged by them.

And one reason surely is that these writers removed themselves from the cultural dialectic. Undignified as that often was, both personally and intellectually, that was where the action was, between the dandy and the decent man, where it "happened to" Leavis, Waugh, and Orwell—not between the Christian and the anti-Christian, nor between the socialist and the anti-socialist.

Auden's case is the one I find most interesting to consider, because most sympathetic to me, and most clearly the work of a brilliant man who observed all these battles. In his last years, moreover, Auden affiliated himself to that line of taste that I am most concerned to recommend here. He became the friend, admirer, and coworker of Stravinsky, Lincoln Kirstein, and Balanchine; by the time of the Stravinsky Festival of 1972, he was their major ally and propagandist in the world of letters.

His position, as sketched out in *A Certain World,* his book of extracts and definitions of 1970, is that of someone who, like them, has come through dandyism to an Apollonian maturity. His entry under "Baroque" suggests his love of and leaving of dandyism. "Of all architectural styles, Baroque is the most this-worldly, a visible hymn to earthly pomp and power. At the same time, by its excessive theatricality it reveals, perhaps unintentionally, the essential 'camp' of all worldly greatness. It is, therefore, the ideal style for princely palaces. But as ecclesiastical architecture it simply will not do. . . ." His Christianity saved him from serious dandyism. And his theories of Romantic Love (responsible for more human misery and bad poetry than any other notion) and Marriage (much more interesting than love because the creation of Time and Will as well as Feeling), his praise of the English Middle Class (they first practiced financial honesty), and his dispraise of Napoleon (an enemy of civilization)—all these add up to the outlines of a "decent" humanism that I very much like. But it is a *Weltanschauung* almost completely lacking in power. Auden has come round, come through, from dandyism to an Apollonian maturity, but he has not arrived there with imaginative power, and so he does not find the critic waiting for him with the laurel crown outstretched. The artist's job is not to be right in the critic's terms, and the critic's job is not to reward those who agree with him.

My old sense of what the critic's job *is*—to discover and be in the thick of the crucial debate of the time—is as strong in me as ever. So I am no more attracted to Auden and Lewis and Tolkien than I ever was. It is not they but Nabokov who holds the key to the locked door of England's dungeon. I hold on to that sense as some promise that my own development is not leading me up and out into a self-designed empyrean.

Appendix A

A *Dramatis Personae*

THE CENTRAL GROUP of people I am concerned with, and some peripheral figures I refer to, were all born in the decade 1901–1911.

1901 John Strachey, the political theorist (and Robert Boothby, the politician, in 1900).

1902 Christopher Hollis, the author; William Walton, the composer.

1903 Evelyn Waugh, the novelist; "George Orwell," the essayist; Rosamond Lehmann, the novelist; A. L. Rowse, the historian; Cyril Connolly, the critic; Kenneth Clark, the art historian; Malcolm Muggeridge, the journalist; Edward Upward, the Marxist.

1904 Harold Acton (see this book); Nancy Mitford, the novelist; Cecil Beaton, the photographer; Christopher Isherwood, the novelist; Cecil Day-Lewis, the poet; Graham Greene, the novelist; Claud Cockburn, the journalist; Oliver Messel, the stage designer.

1905 Brian Howard (see this book); Robert Byron, the writer; Anthony Powell, the novelist; Peter Quennell, the biographer; "Henry Green," the novelist; Tom Driberg, the journalist; Constant Lambert, the composer; Rex Whistler, the stage-designer.

1906 Alan Pryce-Jones, the editor; John Betjeman, the poet.

1907 W. H. Auden, the poet; John Lehmann, the editor; Louis MacNeice, the poet; Christopher Sykes, the writer; Anthony Blunt, the art historian; T. C. Worsley, the editor.

1908 Osbert Lancaster, the cartoonist; Ian Fleming, the novelist.

1909 Stephen Spender, the poet; Goronwy Rees, the historian.

1911 Randolph Churchill, the journalist; Guy Burgess and "Kim" Philby, the traitors (and Donald Maclean in 1913).

Nearly all of these went to similar prep schools, and often to the same one—for instance, St. Cyprian's, where Orwell, Connolly, and Beaton spent some years together—and then to similar or the same public schools. Beaton and Clark went to Harrow; Waugh and Driberg went to Repton; Betjeman, MacNeice, Worsley, and Blunt went to Marlborough. And to Eton went Strachey, Boothby, Hollis, Orwell, Acton, Howard, Byron, Connolly, Green, Powell, Messel, Pryce-Jones, Lehmann, Fleming, Churchill, and Burgess. From there they mostly went on to either Oxford or Cambridge. To Oxford went Strachey, Boothby, Hollis, Waugh, Rowse, Clark, Connolly, Acton, Day-Lewis, Greene, Cockburn, Howard, Byron, Powell, Quennell, Green, Driberg, Pryce-Jones, Betjeman, Auden, MacNeice, Sykes, Lancaster, Spender, Rees, and Churchill.

They then went on to variously successful and important careers. Most of them England rewarded richly. John Strachey became a minister of the crown, 1946–51; Robert Boothby was made a baron in 1958, Kenneth Clark in 1969. Clark was director of the National Gallery, 1934–45; Alan Pryce-Jones was editor of the *Times Literary Supplement,* 1948–59. Cecil Day-Lewis was Poet Laureate from 1968 until his death, when John Betjeman succeeded him, in 1972. William Walton was made a knight in 1951, Betjeman in 1969, Cecil Beaton in 1972, Harold Acton in 1974. The award of C.B.E. (Commander of the British Empire) was given to Cecil Day-Lewis in 1950,

Osbert Lancaster in 1953, Anthony Powell in 1956, Louis MacNeice and Oliver Messel in 1958, Stephen Spender in 1962, John Lehmann in 1964, Harold Acton in 1965, Nancy Mitford and Cyril Connolly in 1972. Since the Second World War, one may say, they have staffed the Establishment. In literature, for instance, beside the novels, poems, essays, biographies, and travel books they have produced, they have filled between them the key reviewing and editorial jobs on the *Times Literary Supplement,* the *New Statesman, Encounter, New Writing, Horizon, The Observer,* the *Sunday Times.* They have been the central ganglion in the nervous system of "England."

These are the principal actors in the story this book tells. Also present—some of whom played hero parts in other stories—are the non-Englishmen, mostly Americans, Frenchmen, or Russians; and the Englishmen who were born earlier or later, who boarded the national train before or after that great downward-tunneling curve in the national track.

Appendix B

Children of the Sun:
A Short History of the Concept

T HE TERM "CHILDREN of the Sun" was used both by Johann Jakob Bachofen in mid-19th-century Switzerland and his disciples in Munich about 1900, and by Thomas J. Perry and other English exponents of the theory of cultural diffusion in the 1920s.

Perry's use of the term is the simpler to explain because Perry was a more orthodox and academic anthropologist.[1] His theory is that there was a great archaic phase of civilization, preceding ours, that had its origin and center in Egypt and was established in Sumer, India, Mexico, Guatemala, and elsewhere. This culture was diffused by migration, and in the farther-off lands the new king-gods it brought were said to have come "from the sky" because they came from abroad. These kings, and sometimes one section of the ruling class, called themselves Children of the Sun; they claimed the sun as their father, and expected to go up to the sky when they died (it was the normal expectation that one would go underground). In Indonesia these kings were particularly associated with gold, and Polynesia and New

Zealand have similar legends. This class, then, felt themselves to be an elite within their own culture, and felt their culture to be an elite in relation to other cultures. They were distinguished by the possession of gold, turquoise, and pearl and by various skills in polishing and carving precious objects. Theirs was, in a loose sense (it will be seen that I am treating anthropology very cavalierly), a dandy and aesthete phase of culture.

I derive a larger metaphorical meaning from the relation that this phase, according to Perry, held to the one that preceded it. He says this was the culture of the first *food-producers.* They succeeded the earlier *food-gatherers,* who had called themselves children of Demeter, the mother goddess, the personification of Nature. The new culture had—comparatively speaking—mastered the processes of Nature, and did not need to worship it as divine. These men worked metals by means of polished stone tools and made "givers of life," which were charms, objects made of gold, polished turquoise, and quartz, and so on. They moved their settlements often in pursuit of new supplies of these "life-giving" metals, rather than in pursuit of new food supplies. We can think, I presume, of some of the great figures of Egyptian kings, particularly those made of gold.

Their kings were closely related to the sun gods the culture worshiped. In an earlier phase these peoples had worshiped gods of vegetation and fertility, associated with water. But there had been a development in the character ascribed to both gods and kings. In Egypt the king was now identified with Horus (son of Osiris) during his lifetime, and with Osiris himself after death. Isis, the mother of Osiris, had been the great mother goddess of the preceding cultural phase in Egypt. The new phase replaced her with him. In Sumer too the kings were "divine manifestations of the beautiful Thammuz child, beloved of the mother goddess." In both cases the king-god was gradually transformed into a sun god. Perry dates this as happening in Egypt around 2750 BCE, at the beginning of Dynasty V. And he believes that the Children of the Sun gradually disappeared because these sun gods were gradually displaced by war gods. In Mexico, for instance, the newer phase began with the dominance won by the Aztecs, who brought with them the war god Huitzilopochtli, when they defeated the Nahua, worshipers of a sun god.[2] Typically, the *Sonnenkind-worshipers* were overcome by peoples at a lower level of civilization. They had become vulnerable through being overcivilized.

Turning to Bachofen, we find *Sonnenkind* ideas that bear more directly on our subject matter. Let us begin with this passage, in which the translator has rendered *Sonnenkind* as "radiant son."

With the sunrise ancient religion associates the idea of triumph over the maternal darkness, and in the mysteries this idea often appears as the foundation of transcendent hopes. But in this early phase the radiant son is still wholly governed by his mother, the day is a nocturnal day, and as fatherless scion of this great *Eileithyia,* the *mater matuta* (mother of dawn) it still belongs to the matriarchate.[3]

That is, the religion that focuses on, for instance, Osiris, will be inspired by the hope of transcending the "darkness" associated with the religion focused on Isis, a darkness expressed in the dominance of certain cultural images—the recurrence of night and winter, the decay of humus and the death of everything animal, the need for sacrifice and piety to the soil, the reverence before the mysteries of birth and death, the anxiety about hubris and Nemesis, the humility before the Mother in all her forms. The culture of which the Osiris religions are the heart will turn away from all that, toward lightness and brightness, brilliance and individuality; but the change will not complete itself, the independence will not establish itself. Total liberation from the maternal bond occurs only in a culture that worships the sun— the phallic son—when it is at the height of its luminous power, as opposed to when it is in its dawn brightness. This later phase of cultural and religious development Bachofen called the Dionysian. In the *Sonnenkind* phase, the god adored is ultimately dependent on his Isis-mother, even though she is temporarily eclipsed by him, temporarily obscured from public gaze and worship. Dionysus, when he comes, is dependent on no one and responsible for no one. He is neither son nor father, and the culture built around him—perhaps we can get some idea of this from recent rock festivals—must be orgiastic and solipsistic, defiant of all responsibility and all relationship. Osiris is always a son, even though he has no father. Most typically, gods like him were born from an egg, or from a lotus blossom, or from a divine cow—in other words, from the divine mother-earth, without any ordinary impregnation.

The idea of a culture dominated by the *Sonnenkind* was taken up by Bachofen's Munich disciples, Alfred Schuler and Ludwig Klages, who for a time advocated it as the most perfect of all cultural phases.* We might look briefly at Schuler's essay "Die Sonnenkinder," the fifth of his seven lectures "Vom Leben der Ewigen Stadt," given in Munich in 1917, in which he recreated, highly imaginatively, the religious culture of ancient Rome.[4] He described Osiris as passive toward Isis, but as giving light to mankind by virtue of containing the two poles of boyhood within himself. He is both Castor and Pollux, and their love for each other, in him, makes him a radiant god. The cult of Osiris, if reborn, said Schuler, could break the power of Evolution and so save mankind from the self-destruction toward which it was headed. (Evolution was Schuler's category for all the evil Apollonian forces of progress and mechanization, of increase by production and reproduction, of self-justification in one's children rather than in oneself, that he saw ruining his own Germany.) He saw the cult of Osiris in ancient Rome's "houses of life," where boys were brought up in the love of other boys and in isolation from all other forms of life. These houses were shrines, in which the individual beautiful and brilliant boy, worshiped by the others, became divine. This happy state of affairs was ruined by the patriarchal Roman cult of production and reproduction, which made human beings means to some further end.

---

* Bachofen himself declared his faith in the Apollo-centered culture that succeeds to the Dionysian, to which the best "classical" achievements of Western culture belong. At another level of intention, Bachofen may be said to have worshiped Demeter, or Isis, in the enthusiasm with which he investigated and expounded the matriarchal culture. And readers of my *The Von Richthofen Sisters* will remember how I there describe Max Weber's power as deriving from his passionate sacrifices to the male and Apollonian gods, and D. H. Lawrence's as deriving from female and Demetrian powers. This book extends the application of those same ideas.

Schuler also celebrated the ceremonial banquets of Rome, the *caenae*, at which beautiful young boys served the guests as erotic and religious ministers. He described these banquets as the central mysteries of the city's life. And the Caesars he loved were those late decadent figures who rebelled against the patriarchal virtues of the Roman Republic and who presented themselves to the public as hermaphroditic *Sonnenkinder*, wearing female garments on occasion and appearing as all the gods in turn. This late decadent Rome was, of course, a society in which the Roman "citizen" had no more place than the modern bourgeois would have—a society the good citizens called decadent just because it diminished the power of men (patriarchal men), the power on which the early Republic had been founded. But that decadence would have triumphed, had it not been for the malign intrusion of Christianity from outside. Christianity was for Schuler the enemy of all life, being spiritual, ascetic, mental—Apollonian. What he and his disciples loved—what, less ideologically, Oscar Wilde in contemporary England loved—was the culture of the mother goddess in her decadence, when the radiant son was triumphant over her.

Schuler, Bachofen, and Perry do not share the same evolutionary scheme, or the same value scheme, but I am not concerned about their coherence, or their correctness. I am exploiting their ideas, applying them in ways quite remote from their authors' intentions. I inherit no authority from them, and consequently no liability. I am merely using their stimulating conceptual and historical pattern, and picking out of it those elements that suit my purposes. For instance, one such point in Perry's book is the idea that in myths about the discoveries of important skills, discoveries attributed to *Sonnenkinder* heroes, the latter were often represented as twins or as brothers. The Zuñi, we read, worship twin brothers who went down into the bowels of the earth and, after many adventures, released the Zuñi nation and led them up and out into the world, and created a human civilization for them. Similar stories are told by the Hopi and the Hurons. This is significant for us because it associates dandy culture with the fraternal image of two young men, who play and work together, who love and challenge and rival each other—an image that the history of modern dandyism suggests to us as much as the image of Narcissus. For instance, that fraternal image explains the rivalry and cooperation of Brian Howard and Harold Acton, the two principal figures in my main narrative.

Similar twins are, of course, prominent in classical myths. Castor and Pollux, dear to Schuler, were the Dioscuri, sons of Zeus, who did not woo wives but stole them, and their story conveys some rough scorn for the marital bond. They were usually depicted without wives, but on either side of their mother, Magna Mater, or their sister Helen. After death Castor and Pollux, like other *Sonnenkinder,* became stars, orbs of brilliance. Romulus and Remus were also twin brothers of miraculous birth, who had nothing to do with women until they stole the Sabines. They were the heroes of the Lupercal festival, where Roman youths ran about naked and played tricks on each other. Then Amphion and Zethus were the Theban Dioscuri, the first devoted to music and contemplation, the second to warfare and action. And the legend of the Argonauts assembles together a number of *Sonnenkinder* heroes, all on a quest for a fleece of gold. Orpheus, Heracles, Perseus, and Theseus were all heroes who saved mankind from gross materialism. Such figures survive in subordination in the Olympian mythology, which centers on Zeus, a great father god and patron of patriarchal values. The *Sonnenkind* heroes may be regarded as surviving in that mythology although submerged and subdued by gods like Apollo and Ares.

In American Indian culture the Nahua myth of the Popol Vuh— about the gods' efforts to raise humanity to a higher level—is a vivid example of the same fraternal theme. The heavenly twins, Hunapu and Ixbalanque, were born to a maiden who was impregnated by the words spoken by a skull, who was thus all the father they have. It was their task to destroy the gross and primitive giant, Vucub-Caquix, and his misshapen progeny. The twins were playful and skillful boys, always playing tricks, and they were persecuted as children by their clumsier, and earthier, half brothers. After passing certain tests, they went down into the underworld and brought back up the knowledge needed to build civilization. Later they became the Nahua's Sun and Moon.

This story is told by Irene Nicholson in her *Mexican and Central American Mythology*,[5] and she goes on to speculate that something has been omitted from the legend, because the twins' adventures seem "too juvenile"—they do not earn their triumphs by self-sacrifice and hard work, as Quetzalcoatl does in the myths about him. The original Popol Vuh, she suggests, may have expressed a greater sense of compassion and of spiritual transformation. It is, of course, quite likely that the myth has been deformed, but it is also likely that the spirituality of the *Sonnenkind* is originally less serious, less agonized, less effortful, than the spirituality we call mature and responsible.

Within this book these perspectives have the status and function that imagery has in a sentence that is primarily analytical. They give an added scope and dignity to the ideas—the terms, of that sentence, but of a non-discursive kind. They show us how far these ideas could take us—but in a dream vision of journey's end.

Bibliography

THE BIOGRAPHICAL PART of this book is very largely drawn from already published sources. The main source for Harold Acton's life is his two-volumed *Memoirs of an Aesthete*, published by Methuen in 1948 and 1970. (In England they were entitled *Memoirs of an Aesthete* and *More Memoirs of an Aesthete*, respectively; in America they have been brought out as *Memoirs of an Aesthete, Volume I and Volume II*.) For Brian Howard's life the main source is the composite biography edited by Marie-Jacqueline Lancaster, *Brian Howard: Portrait of a Failure*, which Anthony Blond published in 1968. My account of the two men's lives derives almost completely from those sources, and in these notes I have named only those other books and people who gave me, at one point or another, some extra detail.

For the non-biographical parts of the book I have named my source wherever the text left it anonymous or ambiguous, wherever some fact or some phrasing was striking enough for a reader to want to know its context, and wherever I wished to acknowledge how much I owed to the original author.

Notes

Chapter One

Children of the Sun

1. Evelyn Waugh's trilogy of novels about the Second World War were published in England as *Men at Arms* (1952), *Officers and Gentlemen* (1955), and *Unconditional Surrender* (1961). (The last was retitled *The End of the Battle* in America.) Brigadier Ritchie-Hook appears in all three.

2. Ellen Moers' *The Dandy* was published by Seeker and Warburg in 1960.

3. The scene referred to occurs in *Officers and Gentlemen*.

4. Harold Acton's remark about Reggie Temple can be found in *Memoirs of an Aesthete*.

5. The remarks attributed to George Moore can be found in his *Confessions of a Young Man*, published in London in 1888.

6. The quotation from Gautier comes from his *Histoire de l'art dramatique*, Vol. 23.

7. For the account of Deburau and Pierrot I have drawn mainly on the following sources: T. Rémy, *Jean-Gaspard Deburau*, Paris, 1954; Kay Dick, *Pierrot*, London, 1960; Francis Haskell, "The Sad Clown," in *French 19th Century Painting and Literature*, ed. Ulrich Fine, London, 1972; A. G. Lehmann, "Pierrot and Fin de Siècle," in *Romantic Mythologies*, ed. Ian Fletcher, London, 1967; Cyril Beaumont, *The History of Harlequin*, London, 1926. (This last has a preface by Sacheverell Sitwell, to which I refer later.)

8. The fullest account of Jules Laforgue is given in Warren Ramsay's *Jules Laforgue and the Ironic Inheritance,* New York, 1953.

9. My remarks on Proust draw heavily on George Painter's *Proust: The Early Years,* London, 1959, and *Proust: The Later Years,* London, 1965.

10. Connolly says this about Proust in *The Evening Colonnade,* London, 1973.

11. My account of Cocteau derives mainly from the following sources: E. Sprigge and R. Kihm, *Jean Cocteau: The Man and the Mirror,* London, 1968; F. Brown, *An Impersonation of Angels,* London, 1969; F. Steegmuller, *Cocteau,* London, 1970.

12. The two main sources for my account of Diaghilev are Arnold Haskell's *Diaghilev,* London, 1935, and Richard Buckle's *Nijinsky,* New York, 1972.

13. Connolly says this in *Evening Colonnade,* London, 1973.

14. The quotation from Osbert Sitwell comes from his *Great Morning,* London, 1948, and that from Harold Acton from his *Memoirs;* the others in this paragraph are quoted by Buckle in his *Nijinsky.*

15. T. S. Eliot and Malcolm Cowley are quoted on Laforgue in Warren Ramsay's book.

Chapter Two

England in 1918

1. Auden says this in his essay, "A Worcestershire Lad," in *Forewords and Afterwards.* Orwell makes the same point in his essay, "Inside the Whale," included in the *Collection of Essays* published by Doubleday Anchor in 1954.

2. Alec Waugh's remark can be found in his autobiography, *The Early Years of Alec Waugh,* London, 1962.

3. Connolly says this in *The Evening Colonnade.*

4. Philip Toynbee recounts this in *Friends Apart,* London, 1954.

5. Richard Rees, *George Orwell; Fugitive from the Camp of Victory* (Carbondale: S. Illinois Press, 1962); Christopher Isherwood, *Lions and Shadows* (London: Leonard and Virginia Woolf and the Hogarth Press, 1938).

6. Some of these details of social history are taken from Andrew Sinclair's *The Last of the Best,* London, 1969; others come from C. L. Mowat's *England Between the Wars,* London, 1955.

7. My social history of England here and later draws on *The Long Week-end*, by Robert Graves and Alan Hodge, London, 1940; *The Baldwin Age*, by John Raymond, London, 1960; *Life in Britain Between the Wars*, by L.C.B. Seaman, London, 1970; and *The Age of Illusion*, by Ronald Blythe, London, 1963.

8. The Betjeman poem is entitled "Death of King George V" and can be found in his *Collected Poems* of 1959.

9. Buchan says this in *Memory Hold the Door*, London, 1940. Other details about Buchan, including the remarks by G. M. Trevelyan and Catherine Carswell, are to be found in *John Buchan, by His Wife and Friends*, London, 1947.

10. The fullest account of F. E. Smith is to be found in the biography, *F. E.*, by his son, the 2nd earl of Birkenhead, London, 1960.

11. The fullest account of F. A. Lindemann is given by Lord Birkenhead in his biography, *The Professor and the Prime Minister*, London, 1962.

12. My main source on Beaverbrook is A. J. P. Taylor's *Beaverbrook*, London, 1972, although a lively supplement was provided by David Farrer's *G for God Almighty*, London, 1969.

13. The details of social history came mostly from Robert Graves's *The Long Week-end*.

14. Lord Berners says this in *First Childhood*, London, 1934.

15. James Stern's chapter of autobiography appeared in *The London Magazine*, June, 1970.

16. Edith, Osbert, and Sacheverell Sitwell, *Trio*, London, 1938.

17. Moore's letters to Lady Cunard were edited by Rupert Hart-Davis and published in London in 1957. Nancy Cunard wrote *George Moore* in 1951 and *Grand Man*, about Norman Douglas, in 1954.

18. Acton speaks of his luncheon with Norman Douglas in *Memoirs of an Aesthete*.

19. Connolly's remark about *South Wind* can be found in Part I of his *Enemies of Promise*, London, 1938.

20. All Sitwell's remarks about Firbank can be found in his essay on Firbank in Ifan Kyrle-Fletcher's *Ronald Firbank: A Memoir*, London, 1930. The fullest biography of Firbank is by Brigid Brophy.

21. Edith Sitwell's autobiographical remarks can be found in her *Taken Care Of*, London, 1965.

22. "Colonel Fantock" can be found in Edith Sitwell's *Collected Poems,* New York, 1954.

23. One can read about this party not only in David Garnett's autobiography, *The Golden Echo,* but in Nina Hamnett's memoirs and in biographies of D. H. Lawrence.

Chapter Three

The New Dandies Arrive

1. The quotation about Brian and Harold at the Alhambra comes from Marie-Jacqueline Lancaster's book about Brian Howard, referred to above.

2. Both Auden's description and Brian's self-analysis are to be found in Mrs. Lancaster's book.

3. The account of the Actons' life comes from *Memoirs of an Aesthete.*

4. Some details here, not to be found in Mrs. Lancaster's book, were given me by Brian's cousin, Mrs. Carley Dawson.

5. The account of Chicago architecture comes from H. D. Duncan's *Culture and Democracy,* New Jersey, 1965. For a fuller history of Chicago in this period (including extra details on the Mitchells) see Volume III of B. L. Pierce's *History of Chicago,* Chicago, 1957.

6. The story of Stanford White's murder can be read in Rupert Furneaux's *Courtroom US.A.,* Volume I, Penguin Books, 1962; other details about White come from the Dictionary of American Biography.

7. Osbert Sitwell, *The Scarlet Tree,* London, 1946; Alan Pryce-Jones, *Private Opinion,* London, 1936.

8. There is an anonymous preface to Gassaway's *Poems* (New York, 1920), which gives the anecdotes about the recitations of "The Pride of Battery B."

9. Elizabeth Howard's autobiography, *I Myself,* was published in London in 1910.

Chapter Four

1918–1922: Eton

1. This historical account of Eton derives from J. D. R. McConnell's *Eton: How It Works,* London, 1967, and Christopher Hollis's *Eton,* London, 1960.

2. The extract from Cory's diary is quoted by Percy Lubbock in *Shades of Eton,* London, 1929.

3. The Connolly remarks come from his autobiographical *Enemies of Promise,* London, 1938.

4. One can read about Orwell's Election in *The World of George Orwell,* ed. Miriam Gross, London, 1972.

5. Connolly's essay on *Anthony* is reprinted in *The Condemned Playground,* London, 1945.

6. Connolly describes Brian in *Enemies of Promise* and in Mrs. Lancaster's book; he describes Cecil Beaton in *Enemies of Promise.*

7. Connolly talks about Petronius in *Previous Convictions,* London, 1963.

8. The quotation is from *Enemies of Promise.*

9. Connolly's essay about the civilian in wartime is reprinted in *Ideas and Places,* London, 1953.

10. The allusion is to the publication date of *Enemies of Promise,* in which Connolly describes his fears of going to Oxford.

11. Orwell's remarks on "A Georgian Boyhood" were made in the essay "Inside the Whale," reprinted in Volume I of *The Collected Essays, Journalism and Letters of George Orwell,* ed. Sonia Orwell and Ian Angus, London, 1968.

12. The review of *The Rock Pool* is also included in Volume I of Orwell's *Collected Essays. . . ,* as is the letter to Connolly quoted in the next paragraph.

13. Powell's remark about Brian Howard is in Mrs. Lancaster's book.

14. Henry Yorke's remarks about Brian are quoted from Mrs. Lancaster's book.

15. Hollis says this about Eton in his autobiography, *On the Road to Frome,* London, 1958.

16. Edith Sitwell's letter to Brian Howard is printed in Mrs. Lancaster's book.

17. Edith Sitwell's review of *The Candle* is partly reprinted in Mrs. Lancaster's book.

18. The passages from Brian Howard's letter to Harold comes from Mrs. Lancaster's book.

19. Diaghilev's remarks about French and German music are to be found in Arnold Haskell's *Diaghilev.*

20. Gerald Murphy's remark is quoted in Calvin Tomkins' *Living Well Is the Best Revenge*, New York, 1962, from which my account of the Murphys is taken.

21. This letter is quoted in Mrs. Lancaster's book.

Chapter Five

1922–1925: Oxford

1. Brian Howard's letter is quoted in Mrs. Lancaster's book.

2. The account of the Bates College debaters comes from Christopher Hollis's *The Oxford Union*, London, 1965.

3. Connolly's remarks were made in a contribution to *Harper's Magazine*, June 1973. The account of Oxford fashions derives in part from Robert Graves's *The Long Week-end*, in part from Emlyn Williams' autobiography, *George*, London, 1961.

4. Peter Quennell's remark occurs in his contribution to *The World of Evelyn Waugh*, ed. David Pryce-Jones, London, 1973.

5. Alan Pryce-Jones talks about the aesthetes at Oxford in his *Private Opinion*, London, 1936.

6. Harold's letter to Brian and the latter's reply are quoted in Mrs. Lancaster's book.

7. Brian described William's lunches in an article for *The Cherwell*, also reprinted there in Mrs. Lancaster's book.

8. Maurice Richardson's anecdote appears also in Mrs. Lancaster's book.

9. Lord Birkenhead's comments are to be found in the Lancaster book.

10. The story of William Acton's fall is to be found in his brother's *Memoirs*.

11. Louis MacNeice talks about Oxford in his autobiography, *The Strings Are False*, London, 1965.

12. Betjeman's lines are quoted from his verse autobiography, *Summoned by Bells*, London, 1960.

13. Harrod's remarks about Harold Acton are in Mrs. Lancaster's book.

14. The Oxford clubs are described in Acton's *Memoirs,* among other places.

15. The anecdote about Willemowitz-Moellendorf is told by Goronwy Rees in his *Chapter of Accidents,* London, 1972.

16. Waugh and Connolly's rivalry for Richard Pares is mentioned by Connolly in the article for *Harper's* mentioned earlier.

17. The figures of the national income are given in C. L. Mowat's *England between the Wars*.

18. Cecil Beaton discusses the changes in style of feminine beauty in *The Glass of Fashion*, London, 1954.

19. London nightclub life is discussed in Graves's and Hodge's *The Long Week-end* and in J. Montgomery's *The Twenties*, London, 1957.

20. John Reith's autobiography, published 1949, is called *Into the Wind*.

21. Connolly's reflections on the Sitwells are reprinted in *The Evening Colonnade*. Waugh comments on them in his autobiography, *A Little Learning*, London. 1964.

22. This passage quoted comes from Evelyn's autobiography. Some details of the Waugh household are derived from Alec Waugh's book, *My Brother Evelyn*, London, 1967; others from Evelyn's autobiography.

23. Evelyn Waugh's remark about the tailcoat is cited by Alec in *My Brother Evelyn*.

24. Hollis reports these facts about Waugh in his introduction to *To the War with Waugh*, by John St. John, Whittington Press, 1973.

25. Beverley Nichols tells about Cuthbert and his trip to America in *25*, his autobiography of 1926.

26. The facts about Betjeman are taken from Derek Stanford's *John Betjeman*, London, 1961. Those about Basil Ava come from Lord Birkenhead's introduction to Betjeman's *Collected Poems*, 1958, and from his contribution to *Randolph Churchill, The Young Unpretender*, ed. Kay Halle, London, 1971.

27. Jocelyn Brooke's comparison of Betjeman with Firbank comes in his British Council pamphlet of 1962 on the two writers.

28. Tom Driberg's book, *Guy Burgess*, was published in London in 1956.

29. Peter Quennell's Masques and Poems was published by the Golden Cockerel Press in 1924 and his Poems in London in 1926. Both extracts quoted come from the first volume.

30. Claud Cockburn has two volumes of autobiography, *In Time of Trouble*, London, 1956, and *Crossing the Line*, London, 1958.

31. Tom Driberg's remarks about Waugh occur in a contribution to *The Observer,* in London, which concluded the serial publication of Waugh's diaries, in 1973.

32. Connolly's remarks about Oxford occur in his contribution to *Harper's Magazine.*

33. Goronwy Rees's volumes of autobiography are *A Bundle of Sensations,* London, 1960, and *A Chapter of Accidents,* London, 1972.

34. Henry Green's account of Oxford is to be found in his autobiography. Maurice Bowra discusses Connolly and the other Oxford dandies in his autobiography, *Memories, 1889-1939,* published in 1966.

35. The main sources of information about Nabokov's life are his autobiography, *Speak, Memory,* published in 1947 and revised in 1966; Andrew Field, *Nabokov: His Life in Art,* London, 1967; and Alfred Appel and Charles Newman, *Nabokov,* London, 1971.

36. Norman Douglas's pamphlet, "D. H. Lawrence and Maurice Magnus: a Plea for Better Manners," was published privately in 1925.

37. The details of Brian's farewell party can be found in Mrs. Lancaster's book.

Chapter Six

1925–1932: London

1. Beaton's comments are given in his *Glass of Fashion.* The social history is derived from the same books as before.

2. Simon Raven's essay on the English Army, entitled "Perish by the Sword," is printed in *The Establishment,* ed. Hugh Thomas, London, 1959. Osbert Sitwell's account of his years in the Grenadier Guards is given in *Great Morning.* The account of the officers' life also draws on Nigel Nicolson's biography of General Alexander, *Alex,* London, 1973.

3. Beaton talks of the Brummell tradition in London in *Glass of Fashion.*

4. David Herbert's autobiography, *Second Son,* was published in London in 1972.

5. The story of the Nicolsons' marriage is told by their son, Nigel Nicolson, in *Portrait of a Marriage,* London, 1973. He edited Harold Nicolson's *Diaries and Letters,* in three volumes, New York, 1966.

6. Cecil Beaton's comments on Brian Howard come from Mrs. Lancaster's book.

7. Rosa Lewis is described in Daphne Fielding's *The Duchess of Jermyn Street,* London, 1964.

8. The Harold Acton story, entitled "The Machine Breaks Down," is printed in *Tit for Tat,* London, 1972.

9. The Lovers through the Ages party is outlined among Brian Howard's papers, collected by Mrs. Lancaster while writing her book.

10. Cecil Beaton has several autobiographical volumes, of which the ones most used here are *Photobiography,* London, 1951, and *The Wandering Years,* London, 1961.

11. Connolly's remarks come from "A Georgian Boyhood," in *Enemies of Promise.*

12. The fullest account of Tchelitchew is given in Parker Tyler's *Pavel Tchelitchew,* New York, 1967.

13. The Mitford family is described by Jessica Mitford in *Hons and Rebels,* London, 1960.

14. Nancy Mitford talks about herself in *Twentieth Century Authors.*

15. Nancy Mitford's volume of essays, *The Water Beetle,* came out in 1962 in London.

16. This account of Waugh draws on his diaries, to be published in Boston.

17. The fullest account of Randolph Churchill, including the remarks by Betjeman and Harrod quoted here, is given in Kay Halle's book. See also his own *Twenty-one Years,* London, 1965.

18. Guy Burgess is described in Goronwy Rees's *Chapter of Accidents,* and, with Maclean, in *Burgess and Maclean,* by Anthony Purdy and Douglas Sutherland, London, 1963. Kim Philby and his father are described in *The Third Man,* by E. H. Cookridge, London, 1968, and in *Philby,* by Bruce Page, David Leith, and Philip Knightley, London, 1968. The other two are also described in the latter sources.

19. Waugh's remark about the Jesuit house is made in his diaries for 1930.

20. Christopher Sykes has an essay on Byron in *Four Studies in Loyalty.*

21. Waugh's comments here come from John St. John's *To the War with Waugh,* Whittington Press, 1973; Birkenhead's account of his Yugo-

slavian mission can be found in his *The World of Evelyn Waugh,* and the Nancy Mitford quote is from *The Water Beetle.*

22. D. H. Lawrence's review of *The Station* is reprinted in *Phoenix,* London, 1936.

23. This account of Orwell derives from Peter Stansky and William Abraham, *The Unknown Orwell,* New York, 1972, and from *The World of George Orwell.*

24. The account of political events comes from L. C. B. Seaman's *Life in Britain between the Wars;* Julian Symon's *The Thirties,* London, 1960; and S. Samuels' "English Intellectuals and Politics in the 1930s," in *On Intellectuals,* ed. Philip Rieff, New York, 1969.

25. The account of Diaghilev and Balanchine here derives from Bernard Taper's *Balanchine,* New York, 1963, and from Lincoln Kirstein's *New York City Ballet,* New York, 1973.

26. Nancy Cunard is described in Hugh Ford's introduction to her anthology *Negro,* which he reissued, abridged, in 1970, in New York; also in Daphne Fielding's *Emerald and Nancy,* London, 1968.

27. The idea of *Values* is described in Mrs. Lancaster's book. Some of the details come from the Brian Howard papers, which Mrs. Lancaster showed me.

Chapter Seven

1932–1939: Chinese Philosophy and German Politics

1. Many of the historical details that follow come from S. Samuels's contribution to *On Intellectuals.*

2. Julian Symons makes the remark about Auden in *The Thirties.*

3. Hugh Thomas's biography, *John Strachey,* London, 1973, was the principal source for this account.

4. The main account of Esmond Romilly is to be found in Philip Toynbee's *Friends Apart,* London, 1954. The autobiography of the Romilly brothers, entitled *Out of Bounds,* was published in 1935.

5. Jessica Mitford's account of Esmond is to be found in *Hons and Rebels;* some extra details I was given by Philip Toynbee in conversation.

6. This account of Burgess and Maclean continues to draw on the sources mentioned earlier.

7. The analysis of Burgess's feeling for Russia as another Victorian England is suggested by Goronwy Rees.

8. The 1934 quotations from Auden come from *The Old School*. The 1965 essay is reprinted in *Forewords and Afterwords*.

9. The account of the Auden group is derived from Samuels in *On Intellectuals*.

10. The Auden essays on Beerbohm and on *Alice* are to be found in *Forewords and Afterwords*.

11. The verse quotation comes from "Letter to Lord Byron" in *Letters From Iceland*.

12. Details of behavior-change come from *On Intellectuals;* the account of *New Signatures* and *New Country* from Symons's *The Thirties*.

13. Connolly discusses Spender in *The Evening Colonnade*.

14. Spender's autobiography, *World Within World,* London, 1951, is the main source here.

15. John Lehmann's first two volumes of autobiography, *Whispering Gallery,* 1955, and I *Am My Brother,* 1960, are the main sources of my account of him.

16. Louis MacNeice's autobiography, *The Strings Are False,* London, was published in 1965, and Cecil Day Lewis's, *The Buried Day,* London, in 1960.

17. "Where Engels Fear to Tread" can be found reprinted in Mrs. Lancaster's book.

18. Powell speaks of his literary intentions of 1938 in an interview in *The New Yorker,* July 3, 1965.

19. Quennell's essay can be found in *The Singular Preference,* London, 1952.

20. Beaton describes the house in *Ashcombe,* published in 1949 in London.

21. Waugh wrote about Palestine in *The Holy Places,* Queen Anne Press, 1952.

22. The quotation from the *World of Art* can be found in Haskell's book on Diaghilev.

23. The main sources consulted about Balanchine and Tchelitchew were Kirstein and Taper, cited earlier.

24. The account of Julian Symons comes from his biography of his brother, *A. J. A. Symons,* London, 1950, and from his autobiography, *Notes from Another Country,* London, 1972.

25. The *Scrutiny* attack on Cecil can be found in Volume III. The attack on Huxley, Q. D. Leavis's comments on Forster, and F. R. Leavis's on Auden can all be found in Volume V.

26. Waugh's essay on Wodehouse, "An Angelic Doctor," can be found in *The Tablet,* June 17, 1939.

27. Articles of ballet criticism can be found in Volumes III and IV of *Scrutiny.*

Chapter Eight

1939–1945: The War

1. This account of Beveridge draws on his autobiography, *Power and Influence,* London, 1953, and his wife's book, *Beveridge and His Plan,* London, 1954.

2. The anecdote about Byron and Waugh is told by Waugh in his Introduction to Lord Wicklow's *Fireside Fusilier,* Dublin, 1958.

3. This comment from Gerald Hamilton, and the rest of the account of Brian Howard's M.I.5. career, comes from Mrs. Lancaster's book. The anecdote about Randolph Churchill in Athens is told in Kay Halle's book about him.

4. *The Years Between,* London, 1965, is the main source for the account of Beaton's war years.

5. My account of the secret services derives from the books about Burgess, Maclean, and Philby cited before.

6. Hugh Trevor-Roper's "The Philby Affair" was published in *Encounter,* April 1968.

7. James Tuck's remarks about the Mesa are cited in N. P. Davis's *Lawrence and Oppenheimer,* New York, 1968; this book, together with the one by Jungk cited in the text, and Stephane Groueff's *The Manhattan Project,* Boston, 1967, are the main sources for this section.

8. Oppenheimer's and Jordan's comments on 1920s physics are given in Jungk's book.

9. The Groves remark is quoted in Jungk's book.

10. Connolly's "Letter From a Civilian" is reprinted in *Ideas and Places,* London, 1953.

11. The Quennell-Beaton volume is entitled *Time Exposure* and was published in 1941.

12. The anecdote about Orwell, Senhouse, Connolly, and Longden is given in by Connolly in *The Evening Colonnade.*

13. The Symons quotation come from his autobiography.

14. The letter from Strachey to Boothby is quoted in Hugh Thomas's biography of the former.

15. The essays on Jane Austen are in Volume X of *Scrutiny*.

16. Turnell's attack on Bowra in Volume XI of *Scrutiny*.

Chapter Nine

1945–1951: Exile and the Decay of Hope

1. These social history facts come from Harry Hopkins's *The New Look*, London, 1965.

2. Connolly's comparison of New York with London can be found in *Ideas and Places*.

3. *The Age of Austerity*, London, 1963, was edited by Michael Sissons and Philip French.

4. Harold Acton's books on Naples are *The Bourbons of Naples*, London, 1956, and *The Last Bourbons of Naples*, London, 1961.

5. Osbert Sitwell's autobiography, entitled *Left Hand, Right Hand*, appeared in five volumes: *The Cruel Month* in 1945, *The Scarlet Tree* in 1946, *Great Morning* in 1948, *Laughter in the Next Room* in 1949, *Noble Essences* in 1950, while a related volume of reminiscences, *Four Continents*, came out in 1954.

6. Cecil Beaton's volume of autobiography covering the years 1944-1948, entitled *The Happy Years*, was published in 1972.

7. The volumes of Anthony Powell's novel sequence that cover the postwar years are *Books Do Furnish a Room*, 1971, and *Temporary Kings*, 1972.

8. Waugh's review of Connolly's editorial can be found in *The Month* for July 27, 1946.

9. John Lehmann's volume of autobiography, *The Ample Proposition*, London, 1966, tells the story of his publishing career in these years.

10. The "atomic scientists' crusade" is described in Jungk's book.

11. *Scrutiny's* attack on Bowra can be found in Vol. XIV.

Chapter Ten

1951–1957: Aging and Suicide

1. Harold Acton's article on Eduardo de Filippo can be found in *The London Magazine*, June 1962.

2. Waugh's essay on Wodehouse can be found in *The Month,* August 1, 1961.

3. Waugh's review of Betjeman's book of essays can be found in *The Month.*

4. Connolly's essay, "This Gale-Swept Chip," can be found in *Suicide of a Nation?,* edited by Arthur Koestler, London, 1963.

5. In *Randolph Churchill: The Young Unpretender,* edited by Kay Halle, London, 1971.

6. In addition to the sources already cited for Philby, the account of Philby's years in Beirut and Moscow owes something to Eleanor Philby's *Kim Philby: The Spy I Loved,* London, 1968; Auden's remarks to Robin Maugham are reported in the latter's *Escape from the Shadows,* London, 1972.

7. Edith Sitwell's essay on D. H. Lawrence can be found in her *Taken Care Of,* London, 1965.

Appendix B

1. T. J. Perry's *The Children of the Sun,* was published in London in 1923.

2. Irene Nicholson, *Mexican and Central American Mythology,* London, 1967.

3. The passage quoted comes from *Myth, Religion and Mother-Right: The Selected Writings of J. J. Bachofen,* Princeton, 1967.

4. Alfred Schuler's lectures on Rome are published in his *Fragmente und Vorträge aus dem Nachlass,* Leipzig, 1940.

Permissions

Index

E